The Word Made Strange

'In a scintillating sequel to his upsetting *Theology and Social Theory*, John Milbank once again displays his mastery of classical and contemporary sources in both philosophy and theology, to lead us to a radical revisioning of the universe in its source, animated by faith in a triune creator.' **Professor David B. Burrell, C.S.C. University of Notre Dame**

'This is an important work by an influential thinker. Milbank has emerged as a major voice in contemporary theology, and he commands an audience in broader intellectual arenas as well. Here he extends and enriches the theological perspective of *Theology and Social Theory*, and also addresses criticisms of his earlier work. The analysis is richly textured and ranges over diverse intellectual terrain. Regardless of whether one is persuaded by his arguments, they ought not to be ignored.' **Professor L. Gregory Jones, Loyola College in Maryland**

For Arabella and Sebastian

The Word Made Strange
Theology, Language, Culture

John Milbank

The right of John Milbank to be identified as author of this work has been asserted in accordance with the Copyright, Designs and Patents Act 1988.

First published 1997

2 4 6 8 10 9 7 5 3 1
Blackwell Publishers Ltd
108 Cowley Road
Oxford OX4 1JF
UK

Blackwell Publishers Inc.
238 Main Street
Cambridge, Massachusetts 02142
USA

British Library Cataloguing in Publication Data

A CIP catalogue record for this book is available from the
British Library.

Library of Congress Cataloging-in-Publication Data
Milbank, John.
    The word made strange: theology, language, culture/John Milbank.
        p.   cm.
    Includes index.
    ISBN 0-631-20335-4 (alk. paper). – ISBN 0-631-20336-2 (pbk. : alk. paper)
    1. Theology, Doctrinal.   2. Language and languages – Religious aspects –
Christianity.   3. Christianity and culture.   I. Title.
    BT80.M53   1997
    230 – dc20

Typeset in 10 on 12 pt Ehrhardt
by Best-set Typesetter Ltd, Hong Kong
Printed in Great Britain by T.J. Press Ltd, Padstow, Cornwall.

This book is printed on acid-free paper

On ouvre de nouveau les grands livres:
ceux qui parlent de châteaux à enlever, de fleuves
à franchir, d'oiseaux qui serviraient de guides . . .

Leurs paroles,
on les dirait prises dans les plis d'étendards bleus
qu'un vent venu on ne sait d'où exalte
au point qu'on n'y peut lire aucune phrase jusqu'au bout.

Ou l'on croirait qu'elles marchent entre des cimes,
elles-mêmes immenses, à peine ouïes, inaccessibles,
à moins qu'à la chaleur du coeur
elles ne retombent en neige sur nos pieds nus.

                      Philippe Jaccottet (from 'Le Mot Joie')

Contents

Polis

Acknowledgements

My intellectual debts are too numerous fully to mention. But most important has been the conversations I have enjoyed with friends. Over the long term I should like to thank Rowan Williams, Ken Surin, Nicholas Lash, Fergus Kerr, Stanley Hauerwas and Paul Morris. In relation to the more recent essays I should like in addition to thank Regina Schwartz, Graham Ward, Gerard Loughlin, Gillian Rose, Catherine Pickstock, Phillip Blond and Alison Milbank.

The author and publisher would like to thank the following for permission to reproduce material used in this book: Cambridge University Press for an earlier version of chapter 1, originally published as 'A Critique of the Theology of Right', in *Christ, Ethics and Tragedy*, ed. K. Surin (Cambridge, 1989); New Blackfriars for earlier versions of chapters 2, 3 and 11; Oxford University Press for an earlier version of chapter 4, originally published as 'Theology without Substance: Christianity, Signs, Origins', in *Literature and Theology* 2(1):1–18 and 2(2):131–52; the *Downside Review* for an earlier version of chapter 5; to T&T Clark for an earlier version of chapter 9; The Jubilee Group for an earlier version of chapter 10; and the University Press of America for an earlier version of chapter 12. Chapter 6, 'The Name of Jesus', was first published in *Modern Theology* (Blackwell). Chapter 8, 'The Force of Identity', also appears in L. Ayres and G. Jones, eds, *Studies in Christian Origins I: Theology, Rhetoric and Community* (London: Routledge, 1997).

Especial thanks are due first of all to Stanley Hauerwas, who encouraged me to compose this collection. Second, to Alison Mudditt, its editor. And third, to Hazel Dunn, the indefatigable and extremely helpful Fellows' Secretary at Peterhouse.

Introduction

Today, theology is tragically too important. For all the current talk of a theology that would reflect on practice, the truth is that we remain uncertain as to where today to locate true Christian practice. This would be, as it has always been, a repetition differently, but authentically, of what has always been done. In his or her uncertainty as to where to find this, the theologian feels almost that the entire ecclesial task falls on his own head: in the meagre mode of reflective words he must seek to imagine what a true practical repetition would be like. Or at least he must hope that his merely theoretical continuation of the tradition will open up a space for wider transformation.

In the past, practice already 'made strange', already felt again the authentic shock of the divine word by performing it anew, with variation. The theologian could articulate this and add her own further twists that might contribute to renewed vision. Yet today it can feel as if it is the theologian alone (as in another cultural sphere the artist, or the poet) who must perform this task of redeeming estrangement; the theologian alone who must perpetuate that original making strange which was the divine assumption of human flesh, not to confirm it as it was, but to show it again as it surprisingly is.

Thus in all the following essays, I have hoped to be surprising, since otherwise I should have no chance at all of being authentic. And perhaps the most surprise, the most shock, should arise when what is said is really most orthodox and ancient, since the tradition is so rarely re-performed in practice today. Here rehearsal of ancient formulations (although they sustain an inexhaustible resistance), too often contaminate them by a corrupt context, while on the other hand any 'contemporary garb' for Christian truth is of course the most puerile form of betrayal.

No: the only chance lies in the composing of a new theoretical music. Hence my endeavour to make the Christian *logos* sound again afresh, even in its dying fall, and so in a major as well as a minor key: the 'English cadence'. But not only are the following essays concerned with language as an inescapable means, or better, event of truth, they also take language as their subject matter. They seek, first, to develop a specifically theological account of language, and second to show how a theology which takes 'language' as one of its central preoccupations, but language construed in a specifically theological manner, might treat its traditional themes of God and Creation, God the Son, the Incarnation, the Holy Spirit, Christian life and Christian society: *Arche, Logos, Christos, Pneuma, Ethos, Polis*.

In the two essays of the first part, *Arche*, I criticize approaches to theology which seek for it foundations supposedly prior to linguistic mediation: first, that of Kantian transcendentalism, second, that of Phenomenology. In the first essay I seek to reconfigure against Kant a Thomistic account of analogy and participation in terms which acknowledge the reality of linguistic construction of the human world. In the second essay I argue that traditional theology never entertained a 'metaphysics' or 'ontology' in autonomy from a discourse illuminated by God.

In the second part, *Logos*, I seek to show how theology should recognize the primacy of linguistic mediation, but at the same time must develop its own construal of the meaning of this mediation – and so of 'the meaning of meaning' – which in rational terms is as valid as a more sceptical, nihilistic construal. This attempt is seen as in keeping with traditional attempts to elaborate a specifically *theological* ontology, but departs from them in so far as it is only since the Renaissance that we have fully recognized the inescapability of culture: the way we make signs, yet signs make us and we can never step outside the network of sign-making. Hence I seek, after George Berkeley, especially, to elaborate a notion of the real *itself* as linguistic, and as divine language, and, after Robert Lowth and Johann Georg Hamann, to develop a theory of human being as linguistic being which participates in the divine linguistic being. Throughout the book, I do, nonetheless, also gesture towards intimations of the priority of 'temporal event' – of which linguistic priority is an aspect – rather than 'given fact', in some of the church fathers, especially Gregory of Nyssa and Augustine.

In focusing in this section on Lowth and Berkeley, I am also deliberately trying to disinter a spirit within British tradition which runs counter to the myth of British identity to which it has nonetheless surrendered: that it is empiricist, philistine and basely pragmatic. For there is an alternative vatic, 'Platonic' tradition within British culture which construes empiricism as openness to the strange and unclassifiable, and pragmatism as surrender to the surprise of that which is mediated through us in language, from a transcendent source. This tradition has of course many affinities in (plus influences from and back to) the rest of Western culture, and one might mention especially Vico in Italy, Blondel and Péguy in France, Grundtvig and Kierkegaard in Denmark, Peirce and Royce in America, as well as the early romanticism in Germany of Hamann, Herder and Jacobi, so influenced by Britain and so distinct from later German Romanticism and idealism. The latter, together with longer-term European rationalisms, is but the alternative mode (alongside empiricism) of modern secular and metaphysical claims to isolate something 'given' apart from a faithful reception of the divine 'gift'. By comparison it was precisely those eighteenth-century thinkers who first intimated the priority of language who were also, not accidentally, amongst the truest re-thinkers in modern times of the Christian *logos* itself.

In the third part, *Christos*, I seek to elaborate and apply what I have learnt from their endeavours. The first essay seeks to show how language is first and foremost expressive and 'poetic', and how this requires us to re-think our sociality, historicity and ethical constrainedness. It shows how these considerations open up certain *aporias* which either point to a nihilist abyss, or can only be resolved by the *supremely* poetic figure of Jesus, the incarnate *Logos*. In the following essay I elaborate the way in which Jesus is essentially a linguistic and poetic reality.

This approach to Christology also allows me to avoid a reduction of Christ to pre-given, permanent human categories after the fashion of 'liberalism', while at the same time permitting me to avoid a positivistic construal of revelation in terms of God speaking a word what is 'other' to human words. Rather, on the 'poetic' conception, creation itself is, as Hamann put it, God's 'speaking to the creature through the creature' and 'revelation' is the absolute incarnational consummation of this process in order to redeem it. Such a stress has affinities with Hans Urs von Balthasar's 'aesthetic' approach, but I seek much more to emphasize the cultural mediation of 'fictional constructs' which are not facts, but events.

In the same way, throughout the book, while insisting that no human discourse has any 'secular' or 'scientific' autonomy in relation to theology, I seek to recognize equally that theology has no 'proper' subject matter, since God is not an object of our knowledge, and is not immediately accessible. Instead, theology must always speak 'also' about the creation, and therefore always 'also' in the tones of human discourses about being, nature, society, language and so forth. A 'theological' word only overlays these discourses – or can be judged to do so, since the overlay is never unambiguous – in a certain disruptive *difference* that is made to them. Here, also, there is a 'making strange'.

The fourth part, *Pneuma*, is preoccupied with the question of *reception* of language and so of *psyche* or subjectivity in relation to language. In the first essay I treat this problematic as a key to the place of the Holy Spirit in the Trinity. Here I argue first that it is *only* an insistence that the Son is also *logos* in the sense of language, that allows us to make any sense of this place at all; second, that a non-nihilistic construal of the meaning of meaning requires us to allow that language gives rise to a 'subjective' excess within language which also ceaselessly generates language, since only such a subjective power can judge and discriminate beauty and order. The second essay, on Gregory of Nyssa, argues that a Christian view of subjectivity nonetheless sees it as a communicable force in which activity and receptivity are indistinguishably fused, rather than as an active power governing 'subordinate' passions or non-psychic elements. This is shown to be an intrinsically Trinitarian account of subjectivity, and to be lodged also within an ontology of creation that dispenses with a 'substratum' in a fashion that has great affinity with Berkeley's later account, already discussed.

In the fifth part, *Ethos*, I seek to expound explicitly the consequences for ethics of construing humanity in the image of God as fundamentally 'poetic' being. The second essay on Niebuhr shows how this rules out any Christian *rapprochement* with political liberalism, while the first essay, 'Can Morality be Christian?', insists that the Christian paradigm for a virtuous act is a spontaneously creative act, which does not fundamentally assume a prior evil to be contained. In this respect, I argue, it is utterly *unlike* what we usually take to be 'moral'.

Finally, in the sixth part, *Polis*, I argue in the first essay that 'eco-theology' and most environmentalism in general ignores the priority of language, and the indistinguishability of nature from culture. This, I claim, exhibits a secret collusion with the scientism that they claim to oppose. By contrast the Biblical tradition, and a stress on both transcendence and cultural mediation, is more likely to restore and enhance the natural world. In the second and concluding essay, I contend that the traditions of 'Christian Socialism' have at their heart the enterprise of a specific poetic reconfiguration of natural and social space.

These essays have all, with the exception of 'The Force of Identity', been previously published in earlier versions, but have all been considerably revised, and can all be taken to represent 'What I think now'. In the case of the essay on Warburton, Derrida and Lowth, 'Pleonasm, Speech and Writing', I have greatly extended the section on Lowth, and elaborated my critique of Derrida. All the essays can be read on their own, or in any order, but nonetheless the order in which they have been arranged is designed to lead the reader most naturally from one theme to another, and to engender a loosely cumulative effect.

Arche

1
A Critique of the Theology of Right

This opening chapter re-examines the post-Kantian character of modern theology. Its aim is to indicate how pervasive are its transcendentalist presuppositions and to suggest that these be eradicated. At the same time it argues that the possibility of theology 'at the end of epistemology' has to be construed at once as a historicism and as a 'metaphysics'.

In the first part of the chapter I shall examine the way in which Kant is considered to have put a critical block in front of the 'way of eminence' and of what one might call the 'discourse of participated perfections' as discovered, especially, in Thomas Aquinas. Having shown that the basis of critique is here itself dogmatically metaphysical, and in a disguised fashion, political, I shall then proceed in the second section to suggest that theology proceeding in the wake of transcendentalism is partially reducible to a liberal rights ideology. This verdict will be applied both to theologies seeking for themselves epistemological foundations, and to theologies which assume that ethics has some extra-theological and well-grounded autonomy. In the final section I shall ask whether the recent revival of a neo-Aristotelian 'ethics of virtue' and a specifically theological exposition of 'the good' as prior to 'the right', points a way towards the retrieval of the 'discourse of participated perfections'. But the answer given will insist that there can be no relapse towards premodernity; rather, any retrieval must assume a post-modern, metacritical guise.

1 Kant and Aquinas

In his book *God As the Mystery of the World* Eberhard Jüngel seeks to escape not only from Cartesian foundationalism, but also from Kantian transcendentalism. The latter is for him the very consummation of a metaphysical tradition which is culpable, not because it illegitimately extrapolates from the limited to the absolute, but because of its rigorous agnosticism with regard to the content of that absolute. The achievement of metaphysics is 'to refer ourselves to an unknown without which we could not continue to exist', and

> the theological critique to be directed against this metaphysical tradition focuses on the fact that in its obtrusiveness the unknownness of God has become an unbearably sinister riddle. For it is intolerable to live in the awareness of a condition which comes into view only in order to disappear again into unknownness. It is difficult enough for a person, with his earthly conditionedness, to have an unknown father, as a procreator, but not a father.[1]

For Jüngel the *via negativa* in its classic form is a characteristic achievement of metaphysics, and its bad infinitude and projection of emptiness is the subtlest and most insidious form of idolatry.

However, one may well call into question Jüngel's effective conflation of the traditional *via negativa* with transcendentalism. The immediate context for his censure is a discussion of the treatment of analogy in Kant and Aquinas. In Kant's remarks on analogy in the *Prolegomena*, Jüngel discovers a culmination of the use of analogy in a strictly agnostic fashion. It is legitimate, according to Kant, to talk of God as cause of the world if we confine ourselves to true, original analogy (derived from the figure of analogy in rhetoric), namely, analogy of proper proportionality which involves comparison of two similar ratios, rather than two single things, or two things in relation to a third common element.[2] Pure reason demands that we regard the world 'as if' in a relationship of dependence on a highest cause, as a clock depends upon an artisan. This allows us, however, no room to speculate about that cause as it is in itself, and if we are forced to conceive this cause by reference to the schematizations involved in concepts of our experience, then this should involve us in nothing more than a 'symbolic anthropomorphism' which, as Kant says, 'only concerns language and not the object'. Hence for Kant, any apparent positive content in analogy really concerns certain necessities of our finitude with respect to the use of language, and analogy can certainly tell us nothing more about God than that all the conditions of the world that we know must be in a relation of total dependence upon him.

By making Kant's treatment of analogy pivotal, Jüngel associates an agnostic treatment of 'naming God' with proper proportionality. He tries to argue that, even in Aquinas, proportionality is more basic than attribution – the comparison of two things, or of several things in relation to one element, such that in either case the term is more properly applied to the 'primary' instance of this reality (though in theology, the primary instance 'God' is also the entire medium of any comparison, which is Being). Jungel claims that when Aquinas attributes, for example, 'goodness' to God – as the primary pole of comparison – 'in a more eminent sense', this merely means that an unknown goodness belongs to God in proportion to his unknown being, just as we possess goodness in due proportion to our being, Yet this conclusion certainly conflicts with at least the appearance of Aquinas's mature texts, which talk preponderantly about attribution, and it fails to reckon with the way in which, for Aquinas, any predication of goodness or Being to finite things already refers to a dynamic ontological tension in which they are constantly drawn forwards towards the divine perfection. Beings are, ontically, only to the degree that they continuously receive existence from *esse*, which simply of its nature is 'to be'. This ceases to be true only with Duns Scotus, who makes perfection language belong to a pre-theological metaphysical discourse concerned with a 'common being' indifferent to finite and infinite. One can almost say, with hindsight, that this metaphysics has a 'proto-transcendentalist' character.[3]

Still more significantly, however, Jüngel fails to reflect that while, from one point of view, proper proportionality is 'more agnostic' than attribution, from another point of view it is less so, because the common ratio can be univocally specified. In Kant's usage, analogy of proper proportionality tends to posit a specifiable, fixed, precisely known sort of relation of God to the creation; God is only related to creation as efficient cause conceived univocally as like finite efficient causes, and so ontically rather than ontologically. God 'constructs' the world outside himself as an artisan manufactures a clock.

This observation can open the way to our grasp of a hidden contradiction in many recent treatments of analogy. In so far as they characteristically try to combine a preference for analogy of attribution seen as 'more agnostic' with a post-critical confinement of analogy to 'our use of language', detached from questions of participation in Being, they fail to be aware of the alliance of the post-critical perspective with proper proportionality.[4] What emerges to view is that there are really two possible agnosticisms – the metaphysics of Kant, which is totally agnostic as concerns God-in-himself, but in a way dogmatic as concerns his relationship to finite beings, and the metaphysics of Aquinas, which is less agnostic concerning God-in-himself, but also more agnostic concerning the conditions of our relationship to God. It is only Aquinas's agnosticism which really exemplifies the principle that there is no *ratio* between finite and infinite, and upholds the ontological difference.

Let me try to substantiate this, first of all with respect to Kant. Recent Kantian scholarship has tended to stress that, while Kant is giving a critical, agnostic version of the Leibnizian–Wolffian metaphysics, nonetheless he remains within the basic terms of this metaphysics which posits a noumenal substrate to appearances, a world of monads without composition in themselves and without external relations, on which spatial–temporal relationships are yet themselves founded.[5] Metaphysics has, in this world, a specific and 'scientific' object, and while for Kant this sphere of pure reason becomes very restricted of access, it is still, all the same, attainable. That we possess theoretical 'ideas' which we use regulatively with respect to the concepts of the understanding, and that we are able to exercise a practical reason with respect to the self-grounding logic of the rational will itself, means that we are truly able to stand at the *boundary* of reason and understanding, of noumena and phenomena. Unlike a limit, says Kant, which involves merely an asymptotic progress towards an unreachable goal, and is an aspect of pure phenomenality, a boundary has something positive to it – to grasp it one must in some way stand outside it.[6] Nevertheless, this standing outside is for Kant very minimal: one knows absolutely that there is an outside, but not the content of 'things in themselves' in this realm beyond the boundary. In this respect Kant's entire philosophy is in a sense an aesthetic of the sublime in which one is brought up against the margin of organized, formal, 'beautiful' experience, and at this margin becomes over-whelmed by the intimation of the materially formless, and infinitely total. In the *Critique of Judgement* Kant tells us that the sublime in the imagination is the indeterminate form of pure reason, and also that the sublime, unlike the beautiful, more enters into itself when we pass from imagination to the theoretical.[7] Here vague intimation becomes a known relation to other noumena, and fears of the overwhelming and pleas for grace are transformed into awesome respect for the moral law within us.

The minimality of content with respect to the sublime reasonings concerning the noumena can easily cause us to overlook the fact that for Kant the supposition of transcendental relation to unknown things-in-themselves is all important. For it is upon this formality of relationship alone that he constructs the centrepiece of his philosophy, a natural, moral law derived sheerly from the self-establishing of the rational will. Furthermore, the differences between Kant's attitude to finite things-in-themselves – other transcendental egos – and the quasi-intelligences which underlie physical substance on the one hand, and to God the supreme thing-in-itself, the Monad of monads, on the other hand, are not as marked as is sometimes supposed. If one surveys the entire course of Kant's post-critical writings, including the *Opus Postumum*, then it would seem that in relation to both God and things-in-themselves there is an element of an 'as if' attitude, a positing for regulative purposes, which nonetheless does not belie an ultimate requirement for real belief in a realm of inner, noumenal relationships, since the reality of this hidden realm alone accounts for the experienced necessity of this 'as if' attitude, or our naturally given, metaphysically speculative disposition.[8]

Given the above kind of analysis, it is easy to show that Kant's strictures on attribution, and a metaphysics of eminence, are themselves grounded in a meta-physics that may well seem to us more sheerly dogmatic than much of the meta-physics of the Middle Ages – indeed in a metaphysics more *purely* metaphysics, since it no longer subordinates itself to theological faith which surrounded *all* 'known' objects with a certain halo of agnosticism. It is not at all the case that Kant offers us an innocent, descriptive account of our finitude, or the permanent limits of our human being. One can see this in two ways: first of all, Kant's confining of categories like cause and substance to the world of our experience is mainly impelled by the 'scientific' establishment of a metaphysical world as strictly distin-guishable from the phenomenal world in terms of the realities of freedom and a pure reason able to proceed from possibility to actuality. For it is only because one stands metaphysically above phenomena that one is able to determine dogmatically the 'range' of concepts like cause, substance, unity, necessity and so forth.

In the second place, it can be pointed out that the Kantian demand that such categories should not be applied outside the range of their possible schematization is not the simple equivalent of a Thomist reminder of our *modus significandi*, but instead assumes, in 'empiricistic' fashion, that there is a mass of information, a 'sensible manifold' recognizable as separate from its categorization, and that it is this that the categories of the understanding must 'apply' to. One can call into question this dualism of organizing scheme and empirical content by suggesting that it is entirely unwarranted to suppose a mass of information somehow coming 'into' our mind from 'outside' – once one abandons this picture of a mind as a mirror or a receptacle, there is in fact no reason to posit such 'unorganized' material at all.[9] But without this atomistic material base, it no longer appears that categories like cause and substance have a necessarily restricted orientation towards finite, material things, in accordance with what can only be (as clearly emerges in the *Critique of Judgement*) a divinely pre-established harmony.[10] And one will recognize that far from being (like Aquinas) agnostically cautious about the extrapolation of categories from our material, finite, temporal experience, Kant was *metaphysically dogmatic* in affirming that they *do not at all* apply, precisely because he believed (unlike Aquinas) that he had direct cognitive access in practical reason to what the immaterial and atemporal is like. From this vantage he supposedly 'saw' that certain categories like cause and substance, though not derived from sensation, are pre-appointed only to illuminate the deliverances of sensation. Once the notion of a pre-established harmony and a noumenal exceeding of categories of the mere 'understanding' are abandoned, one will realize that such categories simply belong to our linguistic being-in-the-world, and the question, 'Can they be extrapolated?' pertains to the question, 'Is there a "beyond", a transcendent, at all?'

It follows from this, that Kant's refusal of any extrapolation from phenomenally instantiated categories and content depends wholly upon his 'metaphysics of the sublime', according to which one can step up to a boundary where one 'sees' that phenomenal categories no longer apply, and where one grasps, with necessity, that there are things-in-themselves, even if one can give no content to them.

This agnosticism does not simply register a margin outside our empirical and practical knowing; on the contrary, it is the very *mode of being* of our practical and political existence. While physical science is not able to deal with things-in-themselves, the laws of the state – we are told in the *Metaphysics of Morals* – *must* treat things as things-in-themselves in so far as they are not here regarded as a chain of causal appearances but rather are correlated with human freedom, so as to become 'private property'.[11] In the world of human relationships, both 'personal' and political, it is the very vacuity of things and the very lack of specific content in genuine freedom which is made to organize rational behaviour. Hence 'agnostic' emptiness of content with regard to things-in-themselves is so far from being irrelevant to human empirical practice that it actually *defines* genuine, normative human practice. Rational, moral behaviour is universalizable behaviour which treats every rational being as equivalent in his formal freedom and every object as equivalent in its ability to be possessed, together with its standardized exchange-ability. To say that God can be conceived as being in a relation to the whole world which is similar to the relations of freedom between things *within* that world, and to postulate this God as the ultimate harmonizer of the laws of nature with the law of freedom, is to say that God is fully known as the guarantor of the noumenal relations of rational law and so fully known as law-giver. That this is really to know quite a lot about God is indicated by the *Opus Postumum*, where it is suggested that God as rational will remains unknown in his ultimate ground even to himself.[12] In the metaphysics of the sublime the absolutely equal and formally fixed relationship in which we all, as liberal subjects, stand to the unknown absolute, serves to confirm the world (the enlightened, bourgeois world) as it is.

Thus this metaphysics, including *especially* its agnosticism, is reducible to the ultimately political promotion of abstract, negative right as the foundation of human society, as opposed to any positive conception of a common 'good' as a collective goal. It is important to stress – because this is obscured in certain 'benign' readings – that this formalism is affirmed most of all at the metaphysical level. Although it is true that Kant is religiously concerned with more than the pragmatic workings of mutual respect for negative freedom in liberal society, the truly moral will, asymptotically approaching the 'holiness' of the divine will which is moral by nature, simply has a genuine, and not merely self-interested, respect for this freedom.[13] This is not to ignore an intriguing countervailing tendency in Kant's thought, whereby precisely the religious dimension concerns an attempted recon-ciliation of duty with happiness, under the aegis of 'judgement', because this reconciliation, which includes *the duty* to endeavour to coordinate duty with hap-piness, nonetheless maintains a distinction and hierarchy between the two. Even a happiness *intrinsic* to duty is confined by Kant to the aesthetic, and the aesthetic is still subordinated to the ethical, which remains the most noumenal and the most divine.

The noumenal 'genuineness' of the ethical is construable, unlike aesthetic judge-ment, in terms of *virtue* only in so far as human beings are engaged in a struggle with an originally perverse will which subordinates our noumenal to our phenom-enal nature. Otherwise, as regards the *telos* of holiness, the moral will is genuine merely by according with the formal–practical rules governing the relations of purely noumenal beings, and following from the necessities of their being by nature free. This is why, in Kant's version of 'justification by faith', the moral will, abstracting entirely from its real, phenomenal 'character', can be wholly converted all at once as regards 'principle', and 'cast of mind', although only gradually can this grasp of principle be translated into a constant disposition to subordinate phenom-enal interest in our own happiness to noumenal disinterestedness. Hence it is not the case that for Kant human virtue strives to instantiate an unknown plenitude of good belonging to the *telos*. Rather, what is essential to the eschatological goal, namely the formal principle, is already known, and this knowledge takes precedence over any actual virtuous formation. If one is not misled by the very particular manner of Kant's separation of practical from theoretical reasoning, then one will clearly see that Kant in fact perpetuates the post-Suarezian severing of natural law from *Aristotelian* practical reasoning by continuing to ground moral imperatives on theoretically known conditions of rational nature. The ideological supremacy of 'right' over 'good' is correlated, after Suarez, with the notion that one can 'read off' from the given world the permanently divine-willed formal conditions of true human behaviour. 'Agnosticism' in Kant is the reverse face of a great formalist confidence – even as regards metaphysics.

Let us turn in the second place to Aquinas in order to demonstrate that *his* agnostic reserve obeys an entirely different economy, one which is ultimately in harmony with the supremacy of 'good' over 'right'. It is easy to suppose that when Aquinas says that one can know nothing of God save that he is, what he is not, and his relationship to creatures, he is coming close to the critical position of Kant. In a number of ways recent writers have sought to make this connection, but it is possible to argue that it is in fact anachronistic. To take an important example: David Burrell, in his brilliant book, *Aquinas: God and Action*, endeavours to exploit the notion of *modus significandi* in such a way as to make it appear that Aquinas employed speculative grammar to indicate the range of possible meanings available to us in our finitude, and by this operation to show, indirectly, what terms cannot apply beyond our finitude, and what terms might enable us to 'go on talking' with respect to the unknown, though without providing us with any real knowledge.[14] This involves the assumption that Aquinas thought in terms of straddling the boundary of the sublime in a way different from, but not wholly dissimilar to, that of Kant. It is relevant here to point out that such an aesthetic was not culturally available to Aquinas. It is also relevant to ask whether associating Aquinas with 'speculative grammar' of this precise type is not slightly anachronistic in terms of the chronology of mediaeval thought; as I indicated with respect to perfection terms, it is rather Scotus who later uses grammar in a 'quasi-foundationalist' way to delimit the scope of certain meanings prior to their employment in theology (although Burrell alludes specifically to twelfth-century grammar, some elements in his treatment of *modus* seem more consonant with the reflections of the post-1270 *modistae*).[15]

Burrell does not recognize that there is a tension between his notion of a 'grammatical' approach to the unknown beyond the known, which is a conversion of Lonergan's transcendentalism into linguistic terms, and the very different idea that throughout his writings Aquinas is spelling out the specific 'grammar' of creation *ex nihilo* in which the 'unknown' and the 'known' are specified together according to a particular religious assumption about ultimate reality (an assumption that Aquinas may have seen as universally available according to rightly-directed reason, but which, it is hermeneutically important to stress, is actually rooted in the Biblical tradition). Burrell's own exposition seems to veer between these two different notions – grammar as giving the transcendental possibility of a negative specification of the unknown, and grammar as explication of the culturally-specific meaning-presuppositions involved in the logic of creation *ex nihilo*. (In the latter case the term 'grammar' is a heuristically useful term quite apart from arguments about the mediaeval discipline. Where grammar refers in this way to culturally specific assumptions, then linguistic analysis is saved from being a new mutation of transcendentalism.)

It is only when one sticks to the latter notion that one can really make sense of Aquinas's 'discourse of participated perfections'. As Burrell says, the key principle here must be that Being is not a 'mere fact'; rather, Being, even when it concerns our own doings and makings, is sheer 'givenness'. On the other hand, it has to be said that Aquinas is not at all interested in the later Leibnizian question of why there is 'being in general', or in the related quest for sufficient reason, since he takes *ens commune* to be only an abstraction apart from its instance in beings, which always 'are' in a particular restricted way, so disclosing automatically their participation in Being as such. In this conception the transcendent reality of *esse is* the final conclusion of illumined rational apprehension and not something that needs to be provided with a metaphysical foundation in the guise of an adequate 'cause'. Neither is Aquinas precisely interested in the Kantian principle that Being is not a predicate, since he does not regard Being, like Kant, as the mere factual correlate of referentiality, but rather as a kind of super-ordinate trans-essentiality which gives reality to essence (what a thing is) even in terms of its mere 'sense' or comprehensibility.[16] Hence his 'real distinction' of *esse* from *essentia* is concerned firstly to establish a new supremacy of act over form, and thereby to deny that reason and intelligibility have any priority over existential activity, and second to associate the concrete and particular subsistence of things with a constant and unpredictable 'addition to' given essence and species (S.T.I.Q. 1 a 4). From a modern perspective, Aquinas's terminology appears strangely muddled, because the *essentia/esse* contrast mixes comparison of the possible with the actual and that of the categorically general with the contingently particular (*this* particular actualized essence). Yet this 'muddle' is wholly germane to the 'grammar of creation', because it both secures a new connection between substance and particularity and also allows that the actual always 'supersedes' a foregoing determination of possibility, hence denying the ontological rule of either logic *or* grammar, in the sense of conceivablity of meaning. In this way ultimate *differentia*, extending especially to the differences of human persons, are made relevant to the teleological directedness of things. One might say, by making essence to be in 'active potency' to Being for every finite creature, Aquinas effectively 'eschatologizes' the notion of teleology throughout every level of reality, in a way which can then be understood as a preparation for the theology of grace. That which is aimed for, especially as regards human beings, is always, also, that which is 'superadded' (S.T.I.Q. 5 a 1 ad 3, a 4 ad 2). (I do not, however, endorse this explication of the 'grammar of creation' as in any way final. Following Erich Przywara and Hans Urs von Balthasar, I should prefer a more dialectical account in which 'essence' no longer figures as the definitely identifiable principle of finite limitation but marks an active, open – and not predetermined – possibility sometimes transcending given actuality. This makes the dynamic non-identity of being and essence *itself* the mark of finitude.)[17]

There is nothing, in a sense, 'mysterious' about these 'superadditions'. They involve, simply, further acts of intellectual synthesis, further strengthening in virtue, further insight into the truth that virtue, as, especially, charity, is not merely perfection in us but a constant spilling over into the strengthening of others after the pattern of the divine creative perfection itself (S.T.I.Q. 5 a 3 ad 2). But this is not at all to say – following interpreters like Rahner and Metz – that Aquinas builds on an anthropological foundation. On the contrary, there is for Aquinas no grounding of the good in a given, self-transcending rational nature. Instead, to define humanity as located in the increasing imitation of divine goodness and of divine being, is to have a wholly theological anthropology; it is to say that human beings are only properly known within our imitation of God. To start to specify what is humanly common to us is already to enter into theological discourse, and at the same time, according to our *modus significandi*, to keep our attention upon the very particular sorts of goods that are actually realized by human beings in specific kinds of social existence. There is no appeal, as with Kant, to an abstract non-phenomenal source of validation, but by the same token there is no appeal to God as the transcendent guarantee of a world construable as good and finitely existent within its own terms.

For Aquinas the possibility of analogy is grounded in this reality of participation in Being and goodness. Analogy is not, as he conceived it, primarily a linguistic doctrine, even if (as I shall insist later) it must become so for us – though not in a manner which persists in the transcendentalist illusion that a 'semantic' account of analogy can be given before an ontological account of participation. Signs, for Aquinas, reflect ideas, which (more or less perfectly in different instances) reflect existing realities (S.T.I.Q. 13 a 1). It is things themselves which declare to us their relationship to God. Restriction of theology to knowledge of this relationship means for Aquinas something quite different from that indicated by apparently quite similar statements in Kant, because Aquinas thinks of divine causality in terms neither of sufficient reason nor of efficient causality alone, but rather in terms of a complex unity of formal–final–efficient causality which suggests that as all being is from God, then everything in some sense pre-exists within the fullness of the divine simplicity (S.T.I.Q. 13 a 3, a 5, Q. 12 a 11, Q. 6 a 4) (or within the divine *Ars* that is the second person of the Trinity). Hence, to know God as cause is not just to know him as cause of the Good, but also to propose him as the perfection of goodness, and in a certain sense as the exact, perfect reality of one's *own*, human being (S.T.I.Q. 6 a 1 ad 2) which paradoxically we cannot ourselves possess. The degree to which this is not a purely empty attribution is precisely the degree to which one thereby conceives, and personally enters into, the dynamic of created being. Aquinas sums it up in the *Summa Contra Gentiles*: 'God is called wise not only in so far as he produces wisdom, but also because, in so far as we are wise, we imitate to some extent by the power which makes us wise' (S.C.G. 1. 31, 2).

This version of analogy, and Aquinas's metaphysics as a whole, is only comprehensible in terms of the absence of any 'critical', transcendentalist claim to have surmounted finitude, to be able to catalogue its categorical conditions, delimit their relevance and pronounce upon the foundationally formal conditions of the realm beyond finitude. *Because* this is impossible, neither is it possible to know (and one will be likely to assume otherwise) that our knowledge of finitude is not inextricably bound up with partial, but substantive knowledge of infinitude. Yet this 'knowledge of the infinite' may go along with a much greater degree, as compared with Kant, of agnosticism about the conditions of our relation to God. It may be that only an allowance of this imperfect substantive knowledge permits a rigorous adherence to the rule that there is 'no proportion', no 'third measure of comparison', between finite and infinite. This is the case with Aquinas: to say that 'God is eminently good' is for him in effect to make a statement in which the *analogans-analogatum* 'good' can itself be explicated as an entire theory of that participation which makes all analogy possible. 'Good' offers us a semantic depth not because this word already happens to have this character within some sphere of ordinary secular language which Aquinas could never have conceived of, but because actual, given human being is involved in some indefinition in relation to God. Against Burrell one must say that to ascribe real degrees of perfection to being, indeed any use of evaluative perfection-terms, *already* assumes a metaphysics of participation, such that grammar here grounds itself in theology, not theology in grammar. Thus to have some knowledge of virtue, of perfection, is imperfectly to know one's humanity, which is only absolutely comprehended in the divine inclusion – as *esse ipsum* – of all *differentia*. To say 'good' for Aquinas, is not to allow oneself any semantic resting place; instead religious–moral self-dissatisfaction here colours the very conditions of possible meaningfulness. And this indefinition extends to both the content of virtue and the indissociable 'eternal law' of the formal–final terms of our relationship to God.

To sum up this section: knowledge of God for Aquinas is change within the circumstances of a certain formal, 'beautiful' constancy of teleological development; knowledge of God for Kant is confirmation of this world as it is, or else a 'sublime' aspiration which is a contentless bad infinitude, unrelated to actual social behaviour.

2 Kant and Modern Theology

From the foregoing analyses it would seem possible to suggest that the Kantian agnosticism is dominated by a liberal priority of right, while the Thomist agnosticism is grounded in a notion of common and always particular good, conceived both as fact and as value, but imperfectly known and subject to an always revisable practical judgement. One can then perhaps argue that the choice between these two agnosticisms is not really a speculative matter at all, but a matter of different ethics, different politics, different ecclesiologies. However, by posing the matter in this way I do not mean to suggest that the position of Aquinas is retrievable without revision.

In the second part of this essay I shall switch to this level of practical considera- tion. First of all I want to consider the presence of liberal deontology in modern theology. The most extreme form of this occurs in the guise of attempts to provide theology with 'foundations', or to determine *a priori* the precise, scientific subject- matter of theology in terms of a general positioning of all scientific knowledge, just as Kant sought to determine the subject-matter of metaphysics. The most striking and exemplary instance of this occurs in Helmut Peukert's *Science, Action and Fundamental Theology*.[18] More, perhaps, than any previous theologian, Peukert seeks to build his whole theology from the base of Kantian practical reason. Follow- ing Jürgen Habermas and Karl-Otto Apel, he argues that philosophy of science has now led us to see that theoretical knowledge and political authority have precisely the same ground of legitimation – namely the unlimited extension of free commu- nication pursued without coercion or domination. He attempts to show that there is an *aporia* in the restricting of this ideal merely to communication among the living. Resurrection of the dead, of the victims of past injustice, as a new equivalent of the Kantian eschatological harmonizing of nature and freedom (happiness and duty) thus becomes the site of genuinely rationally authorized theological consid- eration. However, this doctrine of 'anamnestic solidarity' really bursts the bounds of the theory of normative communication with which Peukert begins, and reveals that, far from being a uniquely foundational starting-point, the doctrine of resur- rection belongs within the whole wider context of Christian life and teaching. This is because normative communication is only concerned with adjudicating relations of mutually compatible freedom between subjects present in a single space. As it has no concern with the interruptive *difference* of subjects, and the way in which real communities find their direction and their identity in the narrative relating of these differences, it cannot really have any interest in resurrection; where one thinks only in terms of abstract subjective will, then death altogether removes the person, and any problem of justice due to her.

There is also the danger, within this kind of approach, of treating the natural limitation of death as a sort of transcendental limitation, and then deploying death, after the manner of Heidegger, as a categorical organizer of the content of our historical lives such that the 'fundamental' problem of our lives is our own death, or (for Peukert) the death of the other. This will not do as a foundation for ('authentic') knowledge, because the social possibility of knowledge is partly consti- tuted by our collective survival of death, our writing on tombstones. And we always write specific names, which are precisely the *personae* which we ourselves inherit. In fact only identities *unlimited* by death define our humanity, if one remembers that we do not first of all exist as isolated individuals. And resurrection, as its intimate link with the eucharist shows, is *not* the return of a 'present' subject to whom justice can again, or after all be done, but rather the manifestation of remembered and narrated life, of life 'shed' in time as self-giving to the other, as after all 'real' life beyond the possibility of death.

Peukert is important because he gives an extreme example of an attempt to proceed from a liberal deontology, legitimating a secular, pluralist politics, and then to conjoin to this base a Christian theology which is precisely a 'theology of right', or, one might say, of the liberal cemetery, the anonymous tombs. But much more interesting than the case of theologies which seek foundations, is the consideration of how a broadly 'neo-orthodox' theology which refuses foundations may some-times seek to relate itself to the Kantian heritage. Here a reflection on the thought of the influential Anglican theologian Donald MacKinnon proves highly instructive.

MacKinnon's thought straddled the boundary of the sublime, but it did so with more perplexity and more intensity than almost anyone else's. The perplexity is shown in the hesitation MacKinnon exhibited about moving forwards from 'purga-tion', or a strictly 'descriptive', and not speculative, metaphysics, conceived in broadly Kantian terms, towards 'illumination', or some sort of positive affirmation of transcendence. 'The problem of metaphysics' delineated for MacKinnon a certain groping towards a version of an analogy of attribution, and an attempt to build theology in its entirety upon a kenotic and tragic Christology. However, my analysis of Kant would suggest that to conceive of purgation entirely as a *prelude* to illumination, or of 'description' as a task innocent of speculation, may forestall illumination altogether, or else radically determine its instance. Thus it might be possible to argue that MacKinnon did not altogether escape the 'theology of right'.

Let us consider first MacKinnon's thoughts on representations of the absolute. He tends to suggest cautiously that a deontological ethics requires qualification in so far as our conduct may be radically guided by attention to particular facts, or particular persons regarded as embodying particular sets of values. Likewise he suggests that metaphysics may have to become 'constitutive' rather than merely 'regulative' to the degree that our naturally given metaphysical disposition cannot help assigning to this or that representation a better clue to ultimate reality than what is found elsewhere. If at moments MacKinnon seems to endorse a certain positivity of revelation in relation to Christology, at other times he more interest-ingly associates Christology itself with the possibility of metaphysics. And this is an association I would want to uphold.

Nevertheless, the metaphysics cautiously brought forward itself seems to carry a certain freight of positivity, which can be doubly related to MacKinnon's 'Butlerian' inheritance. In the first place, only this specifically Anglican back-ground helps to clarify how MacKinnon understands a critical metaphysics as sitting quite naturally with a belief in revelation. Both in the eighteenth-century theologian Joseph Butler and in the nineteenth-century theologian Henry Mansel there was an absence of the Kantian rationalist notion of access to a non-phenomenal realm of 'pure reason', and this meant that, correspondingly, the grounding of natural law became more vague – appeal was made to universal 'dictates of conscience', as well as (in Butler) to considerations of benevolent utility. Yet it was even more the case for Mansel, following Butler, than for Kant (as he makes clear) that natural law is derived from the total set of the given conditions of finitude (as Mansel put it, it is these and not transcendent speculations which are *regulative*) rather than from the pull towards transcendence.[19] Given the positivity, and at the same time the derivational vagueness, of the principles of natural law in this tradition, it becomes easy to understand revelation as a *supplementary* legal system of essentially practical injunctions regarding both morality and worship (hence 'the analogy of religion to the course and constitution of nature' as a new version of a theology conceived as 'laws of ecclesiastical polity' and within the terms of post-Suarezian natural law). The new 'facts' and ordinances belonging to revelation give us no more knowledge than does natural law about the content of the infinite. Mansel was consequently anti-mystical and clearly stressed that the positive critical determination of the 'limits of religion' and positive finite knowledge of revelation was *opposed* to any *via negativa*.[20]

MacKinnon, by contrast, wrongly supposes that the Kantian–Butlerian critical path and the *via negativa* naturally belong together. And yet one can discern in his theology also a contradiction between the two. Following Scott Holland, MacKinnon effects a sort of Christological reworking of Butlerian analogy, such that the essential content of revelation tends to be reduced to a more intense affirmation of the essential 'natural' limits of human existence as providing sufficient guidance for our lives.[21] We shall return to this shortly.

The second 'Butlerian' element, making for positivity, concerns MacKinnon's 'realist pluralism'. The tendency of this doctrine is to insist that things can be adequately known and distinguished as they are in themselves without believing that their full determination awaits upon the infinity of relations they may have to everything else. Yet it is perhaps possible to hold the latter, essentially Hegelian, view, within an open perspective of infinity, rather than Hegel's own perspective of quasi-finite totality. This should adequately avoid any absolute determinism, because here there can be no 'whole' distinct from the network of relationships, which are always relations of particular, distinguishable things. Certainly, to maintain this distinguishability, one needs to say that entities may be relatively discrete, relatively indifferent to certain relations in which they may fall. And yet even such indifference, such 'resistance', can help negatively to determine what they are and what they become. The antinomy between simpleness and compositeness which Kant located 'at the margins' of the normal processes of the understanding, in fact runs dialectically throughout our reasonings about the composition of the world. Hence while MacKinnon is right to insist on the category of 'substance' as a barrier against any metaphysics of pure 'process' which is necessarily 'totalizing', 'substance' needs to be reconstrued as a linguistic marker for certain patterns of narrative consistency in which, nonetheless, we can never identify any 'underlying' constant element.

But by sticking with an Aristotelian notion of substance which distinguishes within 'primary substance' (the real concrete thing) a degree of 'self-existence' deriving from its essential and non-accidental information by 'secondary substance' (the real, though non-hypostatized universal), MacKinnon pays insufficient attention to the kind of antinomies that can open up here.[22] As things are, in fact, entirely constituted through networks of changing relationships and any distinction of 'substance' from 'accident' can only be pragmatic and temporary, the more one seeks to isolate them in their determinate finitude, the more their concreteness altogether escapes us, and their sheer particularity becomes paradoxically their only remaining property: a particularity about which we can say nothing, with the result that for all practical purposes one particular becomes the same as all other particulars. We are back to the Kantian things-in-themselves which turn out to be the economic and political equivalences of liberal, post-enlightenment society.

MacKinnon's ideas about the representation of transcendence are affected by this kind of antinomy. Thus, while he is concerned with the unique relevance, for ethics, of isolated figures like Socrates, he does not consider how their virtue is located in a particular social practice, a particular *paideia* designed to be formative of character. The same tendency in Christology can lead towards a Christomonism, in which not enough attention is given to Jesus's specific social practice, its rooting in a tradition and its ecclesial viability. Since MacKinnon attempts to establish Jesus's uniqueness in isolation from his practice and social relations, he naturally focuses upon Jesus's invisibility, his aloneness at Gethsemane and his inner perplexity. But foregrounding perplexity as the mark of the specific is but another manifestation of the transmutation of concrete content into absence of content.

A similar thing is true of MacKinnon's analysis of parables. Very significantly he attests affinity for the Romantic notion of the symbolic which contrasts the parabolic with the allegoric (whereas traditionally both are 'chains of metaphor').[23] This notion suggests that the parabolic–symbolic conveys us out of language towards some underlying transcendent essence, rather than that the category 'symbolic' is intended to register a non-arbitrary dimension of essential 'resemblance' within the play of signs itself (even if this can never be abstractly isolated from 'conventionality'). Within the latter conception – which denies that one can reach the sublime 'edge' of language – it can be seen that the associations of a story, which control its interpretation, are never free from the socially and historically instantiated network of connotations which might be said to constitute the 'allegorical' (unlike the Greek tradition, which aimed for mimesis, and sought to contain allegory as a 'device' – so reducing its capacity to indicate the mystery of that which it manifestly represents – the Biblical and post-Biblical tradition actively promotes the allegorical condition of narrative, foregrounding its pre-emptive, 'prophetic', as well as recapitulatory character). The formality and conventionality of the signifying substitutions at work here tend to put limits upon the 'realistic' construal of parabolic characters – for example of the woman seeking after the coin as 'obsessional', or the father of the prodigal as approaching Lear's blindness towards filial loyalty.[24] MacKinnon can contrive such readings, because he takes the parables as woven out of a 'real life' unmediated by emplotment and carrying all the freight of a 'given' human ambiguity which can then become the symbolic vehicle of a gesture towards transcendence. There is half a suggestion in MacKinnon that the element in the parables which indicates the absolute is the pointing up of some finitely irresolvable hesitation. In a series of brilliantly 'deconstructive' readings (but, given the 'realist' fallacy, it is as if deconstruction were being done by A. C. Bradley) MacKinnon appears constantly to suggest that their implications, their bias, might just as well be 'the other way round'. And yet, perhaps, he does not *quite* do this. This 'not quite' I shall return to.

After this consideration of 'representation of the transcendent', let us pass, in the second place, and in continuation of our exposition of his liberal trans- cendentalism, to MacKinnon's understanding of the tragic. Here very similar considerations apply. It can be suggested that besides MacKinnon's intense exis- tential concern with tragedy, there may also be a disguised formalist reason for his concentration on this mode of narrative. In his reflections upon transcendence he is much more preoccupied with the 'Platonic' notion of presence than with the Aristotelian stress on *telos*, and therefore concentrates on tragic indecision which occasions a kind of *exit* from the narrative, instead of remaining in the plot and seeking for resolutions. One's suspicion here is that it is not that MacKinnon simply *discovers* history to be tragic, but that he also *emplots* history within a privileged tragic framework.

Thus MacKinnon appears to convert the categorical imperative itself into some- thing very like the view that it is *only* in tragic perplexity that we know we are free, and at the same time are brought up against the very margins of the humanly responsible world.[25] When we do not any longer know how to act, then we discover ourselves as transcendent subjects standing 'above' our usual narratively instanti- ated characters. But this has to be read as an extremely subtle version of the aesthetics of the sublime, of the liberal discourse of modernity.

To substantiate this: in A *Study in Ethical Theory* MacKinnon pursues an elusive 'Butlerian' balancing of the claims of deontology as against the claims of utilitarianism. The latter he associates with public duty, with refusal of the kind of 'personal' sentimentality often associated with the doers of good works, and also with the concept of *raison d'état*. It is important here to note that this tension, especially when utilitarianism is spelled out in the manner indicated, need not necessarily project one outside the scope of comprehension of deontology. In Kant himself the embodiment of (noumenal) natural right in (phenomenal) legal right involved the intrusion of a certain hypothetical imperative which permitted, in public affairs, an element of merely prudential calculation. Nevertheless the ten- sion becomes for MacKinnon, as not for Kant, the site of tragic conflict. And one should stress that this frequently is *the* site of tragic conflict in MacKinnon. There consequently opens up a suspicion that when he insists on the 'tragic' as virtually a surd element in human affairs, there is unconsciously smuggled into this view an ahistorical assumption about the permanence of the conflict between a public sphere of objective, and strictly equivalent justice, and a private sphere of forgiving cancellation of fault. Yet this is surely a failure to historicize which may mean both a 'taking for granted' the liberal state, and also a failure to reflect that *Antigone* and the Gospels have the place in our culture which they do because they record the extraordinary *institution* of an entirely unprecedented degree of scruple, belonging to a new sort of social imagination.

MacKinnon, of course, is totally right to take seriously the way in which good intentions can have tragic consequences, and the way in which one virtue can in itself inhibit other excellencies. There can be no flippant resolution of this sort of question; nonetheless, it is legitimate to ask whether the ultimate Christian perspective may not be one of tragicomic irony rather than unappeased tragedy – that is to say *in retrospect* it may become possible to determine our failure to attain the Aristotelian mean, or else we may be able to trace these sorts of conflicts, and these sorts of 'perverse upshots' of apparently desirable courses of action, to a lack of integration in our society, or the lack of a sufficiently encompassing social imagination. To say this is also to say that every evil is traceable to some lack, or perhaps rather to some sort of symbolic distortion, or imperfect vision. Such an Augustinian analysis can accommodate the Baroque 'play of mourning' (*trauerspiel*), whose allegoric deciphering of the action in terms of our voluntary fallen submission to sin and death yet must of itself always signify the resurrection hope (drama exemplified in Calderon and the Shakespeare of the 'romances' rather than Racine), if not pure classical tragedy.[26] At the same time it seems also in keeping with a process of constant social self-revision, of historicizing critique.

By contrast one must be suspicious of any suggestion that evil is a surd and tragic element. This seems to suggest that we are irretrievably locked into essentially private, genuine, yet fatally partial intimations of the good, which will never receive any adequate communicative mediation. Our only true community is then in abstract repentance and formal forgiveness (which MacKinnon significantly implies at times is 'fact-defying', compared to legal justice) that can scarcely receive social embodiment. The tragic gap between the political state bound to justice and the finally non-mediable wills of individuals thereby sinks into an ontological abyss, which is nevertheless a sublime opening beyond our perplexity. Evil, in this conception, seems akin to Kant's 'radical evil' – almost a necessary background for the *söllen*, the moral will towards the absolute. Moreover, the absolute for MacKinnon, as for Butler, Mansel, and Scott Holland, is encountered as a confirmation of the conditions of our perplexity. God himself dies in the space opened up by the tragic abyss, and the meaning of the resurrection tends to be limited to a corroboration of the fact that God is the God who is with us in our suffering – the unlimited God who yet enters fully into our (tragic) limits, without mitigating them. One needs, perhaps, in this context, to be reminded of Rousseau's reflections on the way in which sympathy can turn into a kind of displacing or usurping of the experience of

the person sympathized with. Without some notion of evil as ontologically preda-
tory it becomes indeed impossible to grasp that while God may truly have suffered
evil, he can yet, in some important sense have 'left evil behind'. For if evil is not a
surd element outside the world-text which human beings write, then within this
narrative it can be constantly re-enacted, re-presented, shown up as mere subjectivity, and so negated.

Indeed, unless the contingency of evil is privative, such that those caught in its
toils can always go in hoping for total liberation, one can say that kenotic theology
itself (and MacKinnon's thought is self-questioning enough to be alert to this
danger) may become a new mode of consolation or theodicy. For here one tries to
'deal' with evil conceptually, by relocating it within the context of providence as
kenotic suffering, while yet leaving evil as a 'limit' element of the known world.
This remains subtly within the eighteenth-century theological paradigm of design/
theodicy, whereas *traditional* teleology suggests a narrative restriction and redemption of an evil construed as subjective and contingent. Only this latter view avoids
pretending that evil is not really evil: *because* evil is evil it is, in its innermost
experienced subjectivity, not rightly 'to be known', but rather, in this aspect, to be
'forgotten about'.[27]

There are, then, genuine grounds for suspicion of the Scott Holland/Forsyth/
MacKinnon (metaphysically Butlerian–Kantian) tendency to restrict kenosis to the
making known of limits and of evil. MacKinnon rightly follows his predecessors in
eschewing any notion of a temporary 'putting off' of omnipotence – it is rather that
we must re-understand omnipotence as creative love, and therefore as not conceptually opposed to the idea of the 'limit' represented by the assenting (so possibly
not-assenting) will of created persons. Yet it may be that these thinkers stress only
one side of the *communicatio idiomatum*, the God–humanward direction. If we are
'redeemed', and if this is more than 'legal' conformity to ahistorical limits compensated for by a notional faith that God himself has also submitted to these limits,
then 'omnipotence' must be inscribed within the form of Christ's life and the
Christ-formed world (but no one, and not Christ himself, is the simple 'possessor'
or manipulator of this form). In MacKinnon's later writings there was a profound
search for a way to hold together an 'ethical' attention to Christ's actual life and
teachings with an 'objective' doctrine of the Atonement. But this can only be
achieved if the mode of the inescapable 'failure' in Christ's mission can yet be
ecclesiologically integrated into an account of a historical practice which uniquely
provides resources even in and through 'defeat'.

My suspicion, then, is that there is a hiatus in MacKinnon's work. The secular
groundwork in ethics is all designed, following Kant, to safeguard the absolute
disinterestedness of ethics, and the purity of ethical freedom, by stressing agnosticism with regard to transcendence as a counterpart to an existential refusal of any
materialist necessitarianism. It is an insistence on the inescapable significance of a
'modern' biography like that of George Eliot (yet does not the positive content of
virtue here now appear to derive from the religious resources of the past?). The
problem with this is that, by severing ethics from theoretical knowledge, and failing

to observe that terms like 'good' and 'right' are no less caught up in imaginary cultural constructs than the term 'God' (such that the separation of ethical from religious language is itself just another 'convention'), MacKinnon really endorses an empty, abstract notion of the individual subject, from which it is impossible to derive any concrete notion of desirable human goals. This remains true, even though MacKinnon reworks the transcendental subject in terms of categories of performative linguistic action, giving to Butler's 'deliverances of conscience' a slightly existential note in which certain forms of discourse carry the burden of upholding the possibility of freedom. Yet what is still seen as metaphysically significant is just this possibility, a freedom which can go counter to any perceived subjective 'interest'. Where notions of the 'good' are divorced from visions of 'happiness', of what is ultimately desirable, then only negative precepts of 'right' can finally remain in place.

This 'quasi-Kantianism' with regard to the moral subject shows up in MacKinnon's comparison of ethical decision to a creative act – it is, as regards its formal freedom, 'without grounds'.[28] In this respect he is actually *less* realist than the Hegelian tradition which sought to remind us how all our values and any possibility of freedom follows from *sein*, from an always already-realized goodness (in some degree). On the other hand he tends to prescind from the real site of an 'absolute' human creativity, namely the erection of entire cultural formations which represent new 'types', in no essential way imitative of anything naturally given. Thus while MacKinnon acknowledges the importance of Hegel's attention to the historical, he thinks of historical situatedness in semi-Kantian terms as a further categorical restriction on knowledge and behaviour, and not as the positive fact of the culturally constructed character of theoretical and ethical categories. Hence culture is seen too much as the given, too little as the imagined, and 'surd' elements of evil are supposedly brought to view.

The 'agnosticism' of the secular groundwork finally rehearses the thoroughly ideological conditions of secular liberal autonomy. The practical 'contentlessness', which is essential here, is the disguised theoretical source of the insistence on a contentless infinite which goes with an exclusion of constitutive metaphysics. When MacKinnon passes to theology, and the quest, after all, for such a metaphysics, including an analogy of attribution, then an attempt is made to pass beyond epistemological and deontological closure. Yet here arises the hiatus, which can only be overcome in positivist, Butlerian terms. For the Kantian backdrop, however much it may be seen as the setting for 'something else', always dominates the entire later performance.

3 The Retrieval of Participation

In the previous section, I hope that I have shown how modern theology, both 'liberal' and 'neo-orthodox', can have a tendency to be overwhelmed by the ideological character of transcendentalism and deontology and consequently to present something really at variance with the traditional *via negativa* and *via eminentia*.[29] In the final section I want to pose tentative questions about the retrieval of a 'discourse of participated perfections', and at the same time to show where I think MacKinnon's thought still retains some value.

Discontent with both consequentialist and deontological ethics among Christian and non-Christian thinkers has led recently to a revived Aristotelianism, which is characterized by the view that to act ethically is to act out of a steady habit of virtue and to aim for a certain sort of perfection of character.[30] In this conception, aiming for a *telos* is understood as a practice in which the goal sought is internal to the nature of the activity (and hence quite different from an external 'consequence' and yet more 'factual' in character than a deontological law or principle). A society in which such an ethics is instantiated is a society taking seriously *paideia*, or the idea that its purpose is the formation of its members through the assigning to them of certain worthwhile roles. Ethics here depends upon a collective notion of the particular goods, or even the ultimate Good, to be aimed at.

Certain problems, however, arise for all these theorists, that are to do with relativism and 'ultimate grounding'. These no longer concern the descriptive rather than prescriptive character of the word 'good' – once fact/value dualism is abandoned in a 'holistic' theory of language this is seen not to be a problem at all. However, if one admits that this description is always socially mediated, and also allows that societies have the capacity for increasing insight into the nature of the good, then how does one discriminate between these mediations, and how is the immanent capacity for revision possible?

In the wake of MacIntyre's *After Virtue*, recent writers favouring his *sittlich* conception of ethics, like Jeffrey Stout and Sabina Lovibond, have been preoccupied with these problems. However, secular writers (as these are) have an obvious interest in qualifying the scepticism concerning uninflected 'reason' evinced by the French 'post-modernists'. Consequently they tend to present historicism as a sustainable secular option, an adequate context for the development of the virtues. But theology is bound to ask whether this is any more convincing than the ahistorical Kantian attempt to secure a sphere of secular neutrality.

Thus Stout plausibly contends that scepticism is the upshot of a disappointed quest for foundations: if one realizes that practical and theoretical truth are not in need of 'founding', scepticism also dissolves. In essence, this conclusion is perfectly valid, because once foundationalism is abandoned, truth ceases to be a set of 'principles' that we can manipulate; instead we have to conceive of truth as working itself out through our reasonings, taken as participating in something which we intimate, but never fully grasp. Although this is implicitly the case for all our human discourses, this does not normally lead to a sceptical paralysis.

However, this will not solve the problem for theoretical scepticism of drastically divergent intimations, and of radical change within particular traditions of reason.

At times Stout seems content just to say, quite validly, that relativism is not a real practical problem because people are constantly convinced by all sorts of 'good reasons', which lead to conversions. A diachronic, historicist approach will soon reveal that humans do not conceptually occupy tidily discrete and mutually exclusive 'world views'. Yet to cope with *theoretical* scepticism, Stout has to go further to imply that, at given points of time, certain sets of reasons or certain intellectual programmes present themselves irresistibly to those reacting rationally. This, however (as Feyerabend has shown in relation to Lakatos), must still suggest that some 'evidence' disentanglable from the theory-laden terms of the programme is objectively decisive in causing a change of mind. Davidson, Stout and others are quite wrong to suggest that relativism is basically an upshot of scheme-content dualism: on the contrary, it is precisely because thinkers like Feyerabend and Foucault have rejected this dualism that they can contend that there is no accessible 'content' which can ever adjudicate between clearly incommensurable theories.[31] Likewise, when we are engaged in 'radical interpretation', or a situation in which we must simultaneously ascribe beliefs to, and find equivalents for, the words of alien others, then the indissociability of their beliefs from the system of their language must mean that where this language demands that a radical (and even contradictory) 'difference' be made in our language in the process of translation, then there is no way for us to avoid the ascription of alien beliefs. This seems a more basic implication of 'radical interpretation' than that which Stout stresses – namely the possibility that any apparently radical alien meaning may always be an effect of false belief ascription, demanding a revision in our finding of linguistic equivalents. For when, as happens, we cannot carry out such revision, we are left with no further, 'extra-linguistic' recourse.[32] It is true that in any such encounter there is always a large area of negotiable meaning, and true that we can scarcely ever say that an apparently radical incommensurability may not be transformed by a new synthetic development; yet this should not obscure the fact that this circumstance does not render such syntheses self-evidently 'superior', nor that most intellectual revolutions are not straightforward syntheses, but usually contain elements of seemingly 'arbitrary' theoretical change.

It is highly significant that, with the same instrument, Stout seeks to show that scepticism is beside the point, and that secular reason is now non-foundationally secured in a way that also makes theological reason permanently marginal and outdated. This instrument is the 'new probability', deriving from the logic of Port-Royal, which, according to Stout, following Ian Hacking, introduced the notion of 'internal evidence', or the inherent probability of a thing, as distinct from an older meaning of probability, which was confined to 'opinion of trusted authorities'.[33] Stout considers that this new scientific standard both made Cartesian foundationalism redundant because 'well-attested belief' could now become synonymous with 'true knowledge', and meant that any not merely fideist theology must strive to make its beliefs 'well-attested' after a probabilistic fashion, as, for example, in Butler's *Analogy*. Hume then finally showed that theology could not meet this standard: so Hume, not Kant, becomes the pivotal figure in Stout's intellectual history of modernity.

However, this argument can be easily broken down. First of all, Hacking is not quite right about the 'old probability'; appeal to authorities was complexly conjoined with 'probable' arguments from analogy, jurisprudential considerations about testimony and theories of the imprecise knowledge obtainable for the sense of *phronesis* in ethical reasoning. Secondly, the 'new probability' was a strictly formal affair, linked to the discovery of the calculus, and belief in its ontological value had to be correlated with either an empiricistic confidence in sensory evidence or a Stoic–rationalist confidence in ordered chains of rational representation (as in Leibniz) as giving in themselves an adequate ontology. A collapse of these confidences, as Stout advocates, is not compatible with the view that the new theory of probable evidence can shield us from scepticism, and be our basic guide. The 'new probability' will not provide us with the necessary and necessarily conventional *standards* of what is likely, outside a given set of formal rules, nor of what counts as factual, or a good explanation, or catastrophically 'anomalous'. (Stout's claim that a decisive difference, beyond simple concentration on prediction and control, between scientific and pre-scientific thought is a 'refusal to accept the anomalous' is highly tendentious, and involves him in projecting back into the Middle Ages a 'paradoxical' appearance for theological beliefs which clearly did not appear as so sharply paradoxical within the mediaeval rational construal of things. The mediaevals did not need sheer recourse to 'authority' to help them out here.) And probabilism of the recognizably modern sort in fact proved perfectly compatible with a 'calculus' of theological authorities in so-called 'positive theology', where the attempt to argue with this formal instrument alone in fact *encouraged* a more sheerly positivistic view of 'authority'. Hence one can conclude in the third place that theological probabilism did not represent the only remaining way to avoid fideism, but rather was simply an aspect of theology's bondage to empiricism/rationalism. And Stout's over-estimation of what probabilism can achieve suggests that empiricism/rationalism is still at work in any secular attempt to be at ease with historicism.

More convincing is an effort like that of Lovibond, working in a Wittgensteinian mode, to account for the 'semantic deepening' of our increased insight into the good in terms of a gradual unmasking of ideological subterfuges.[34] This supposes that without such subterfuges good reveals itself unreflectively as a given feature of our 'undistorted' interaction with nature, including other human beings. But this ignores the kind of exposure made by thinkers like Baudrillard and Castoriadis of such theories (including aspects of Marxism) as new variants of natural law, because they arbitrarily associate cultural construction more with ideological distortion than with approved, non-ideological values.[35] In these sorts of theories it is implied that 'real' human needs are just 'given', whereas, in fact, all needs are constructed or refracted through complex signifying processes which direct and promote desire. It is in this area of concrete cultural values that one can see the continued *inevitability* of metaphysics, and the continuing significance of Hegel's argument that the enlightenment claim to 'end' constitutive metaphysics is itself the result of ideological manoeuvrings to guarantee the self-sufficiency of a liberal 'civil society'; manoeuvres initially conjoined to the promoting of a private relation to an empty deity.[36] This insight of Hegel's is perfectly separable from the form of his own metaphysics as a rationalist determinism, a form in fact traceable to his failure fully to *emancipate* himself from the Kantian–Fichtean stress on history as the rational coming-to-be of freedom and the consequent formalism of their model of civil society.

The foregoing considerations may lead us to decide that Stout too easily concludes that there is a third way 'after historicism' between some sort of scepticism on the one hand, and a theological and teleological history on the other, even if this be disconnected from Hegel's continuing foundationalism. Without desperate devices like Stout's probabilism, or Lovibond's naturalism, it becomes apparent that the science of the order of our changing reasons and actions is but a branch of aesthetics, a matter of the formation of 'taste'. There is no way out of this aesthetic historicism, and it cannot be epistemologically founded. But an ultimate 'metaphysical' grounding is a different matter; a tradition does not simply maintain itself within a cosy humanistic hermeneutic circle (this can be the last, remote permutation of transcendentalism which is in itself a 'purer' metaphysics, free of faith) because the normative sense of 'where it is going' is indissociable from, is in fact the same thing as, conjecture about how things ultimately *are*, how they exist in such a fashion as to render this tradition valuable and truthful. As the artist is always painting also his aesthetic, so our acts and constructions can only be really moved and shaped by a kind of 'metaphysical faith'.

For this reason, to say that our moral virtues are legitimated within a 'narrative framework' cannot itself be a solution to the post-transcendentalist problem of legitimation, if this be taken to mean that narrative is for us a substitute for a natural human *telos* which is now, after historicism, no longer available. (I am not convinced that the fate of teleological biology is relevant here.) Nevertheless, the narrative mediation of goal, virtue and character, stressed by MacIntyre and Hauerwas, but necessarily invisible to Aristotle and Aquinas, is now inescapable. It marks our historicist sense that we are the authors of the human text, and at the same time the names marked within that text. It is this sense that can itself be regarded as the irreversible 'turn to the subject', a turn which Descartes and Kant attempted to hijack for 'epistemology' in order to neutralize its sceptical implications. The same historicism is able to carry out a 'metacritique' of Kant, but at the same time it places us at a distance from Aquinas's 'discourse of participated perfections'. This can only again be possible if we take account of that other Christian Aristotelian, Hegel, and his reflections on history, ideology and metaphysics as referred to above.

This approach is preferable to a more purely 'Barthian' one which thinks of the Christian moral narrative too schematically as presenting to us plots and goals provided by 'revelation', reflecting a revealed 'story of God'. But Stanley Hauerwas has progressively moved away from any such suggestion, towards an emphasis that the Christian narrative is, first and foremost, the lived narrative of the Church.[37] A development of this perspective would allow one to say that the site of theology is at one with a specifically Christian metaphysics (a 'metaphysics of faith', one might say, or 'theological ontology'). Talk of 'metaphysics' here serves to register the idea that the process of 'revelation' is identical with a particular rational and emotional quest for God. Also that through the encounter with Greek culture this tradition has passed definitely into a more reflective mode, although as Hegel realized, there is no limit, to the possibility of the transformation of specifically Greek metaphysics – i.e. 'philosophy' – through its subsumption into Christian tradition: we can say, into theology. In this conception the *sensus eminentior* is given not just through the dynamic of individual *praxis*, but through the whole practical and 'poetical' activity of constructing the narrative, projecting forwards the divine horizon, and living out this plot – always supposing that it has been formed in a finally exemplary way by Jesus Christ. Ecclesiological mediation might then finally allow the *analogia entis* and the *analogia Christi* to come together.

But in this reconception of analogy one has to say that the imitation of the divine power spoken of by Aquinas (an imitation which in the elusive yet concrete centre of the Christ-*figura* and in the eschatological prospect of the spirit is actually an identity with) must also include the creation of language itself, because language does not stand for ideas, as Aquinas thought, but constitutes ideas and 'expresses' things in their disclosure of truth for us. In this case language itself in its expressive relation to beings belongs to the *analogatum*. Language is also 'like God', and our linguistic expression mirrors the divine creative act which is immanently contained in the *Ars Patris* that is the *Logos*. 'Analogy of being' becomes 'analogy of creation' because our imitative power is a participation in the divine originative–expressive capacity (this also accords with a more dialectical conception of the *esse/essentia* difference). Teleological constraint is here mediated through our sense of the 'rightness' of our emergent linguistic product.[38]

Language, however, is always particular and traditioned. Those suspicious of the strictly ecclesiological character of this new 'discourse of participated perfections' might very well want to ask about how one conceives of the relation of the ecclesial tradition to secular society and secular reason. The minimum, but very significant, 'concession' that can be made here, is that the principle of non-obfuscation of historicity and non-obfuscation of our cultural constitution through language can operate in a way as a 'control' upon our ecclesiology, with the proviso that no secular historicism (not even Marxism) can provide positive content to the *sensus eminentior* – to suppose otherwise would be to lapse back into the formalist foundationalism of the natural law tradition which characterizes modernity. Also it should be stressed that this valuation of history and language is actively promoted by Christian faith; for another tradition these conditions might appear restricting, or something that we need to obscure or forget (but this does make them, in some absolute sense, 'irrational').

However, there might arise another and more serious doubt. Hauerwas is absolutely right to proclaim that to be a Christian must mean to live in the Church, to be formed by the Church. But how far is this *possible* – the tendency of a *sittlich* ethic may be to insist that we can really only be fundamentally formed by the political community, as being the real community of power and interest. The shadows of F. H. Bradley and T. H. Green are not so easily banished. And in this light one can perhaps read more sympathetically MacKinnon's retreat into deontology after the Second World War; somehow it seems to reflect the Church's minimal and very ambiguous social presence. One can also read more sympathetically MacKinnon's account of our tragic sundering between deontology and consequentialism (although this cannot occlude a more sheerly conceptual failure on MacKinnon's part to grasp the difference between deontological and virtue ethics). This could be taken as reflecting a reality *not* dominated by genuine *sittlich* 'practices', by the virtues, but one in which true 'internal goals' were scarcely available. It could be that in such a society there is a tragic sundering of virtue into integrity of motive on the one hand and measurement of consequence on the other. This more 'sympathetic' reading, then, entails an understanding of MacKinnon's ethical writings as implicitly recording, in a finely attuned manner, the objective fragmentation of social processes making 'virtue' possible.

To show more clearly what I mean, let me refer to Hauerwas's more recent endorsement of pacifism. Hauerwas exhibits great originality in showing that the theme of peace has a more natural home in a *sittlich* ethics than in deontology because deontology only considers peace as a contractual limitation of preceding or possible conflict (just as for Kant 'duty' can only be resistance to contrary inclinations), and not as a fundamental way of being with other persons. One may also want to agree with Hauerwas that it is not that nation-states just *happen* to find themselves tragically involved in wars – it is rather that the whole 'narrative plot' of the nation-state presupposes war as the dimension outside law between states and as the ultimate threat which finally conserves the nation's identity and nurtures certain preferred 'heroic' virtues.[39] Given this dark and Clausewitzian, yet irresistible, analysis, it is difficult to disagree with Hauerwas that (at least usually) for Christians to fight is to assign to the nation-state greater ultimacy than the ecclesial community.

Nevertheless, one might ask in relation to many a secular situation – both 'totalitarian' and those dominated by extreme market liberalism – whether it is not the case that the Church here is simply robbed of certain possibilities of realizing certain practices that should define its nature? In such contexts 'peaceableness' may inhibit or prevent the exercising of other Christian virtues such as justice, or even comfort and support of others. So in this sort of situation does one not have to say that our action is in a way alienated from itself, such that we cannot evade tragic choices, none of which seems perfectly to instantiate integrated 'practices'? From such a perspective MacKinnon may be quite right to insist that one cannot legislate in advance the criteria for correct choices, even in the case of Jesus's decision to go up to Jerusalem and not to become a messianic leader. To say that a particular mode of action – here 'non-coercion' – should be persisted in whatever the circumstances must tend to lapse back into deontological schematism, because an ethics of virtue can never escape the problematic of 'moral luck' which reveals that all possibilities of good require a particular social context for their viability. Hauerwas wishes to stress that we need the imagination to realize that a peaceful response always has capacities to transform an apparently fixed, tragic situation: *Christian* virtues of charity and forgiveness are directed towards transforming the very conditions of moral luck themselves. This is important (and a dimension certainly underplayed by MacKinnon) yet one wants to reply that given the stress on *habitus* in the Aristotelian tradition, there must be cases where one knows that a sudden change of heart on the part of the violent and unjust is virtually impossible.[40] One can, however, hold out for a tragic refusal of the pacifist position without denying that it is likely that any implication in violence is likely to prove futile in the long run.

And when we consider the *via crucis* it is true, as I intimated in relation to the parables, that the bias for MacKinnon can never quite go 'either way': in that unique circumstance Jesus judged rightly, although this judgement was its own exemplum. This 'not quite' can then rejoin Hauerwas's insistence that the way of peace, the way of exemplary persuasion and forgiveness, is always the more final way, not on account of a sublime imperative, but because it belongs to a more desirable way of life that we should strive to realize – a way of life no more and no less 'imaginary' than existing social practices which always write violence into their scripts.

What we seem to need, however, is some account of the *sensus eminentior* which takes into account the partial (never complete) alienation of the very possibility of virtuous action. Perhaps in our modern plight, as Walter Benjamin implies, it is the *narrator of* alienated action (the theologian?), of disjointed and so inoperative virtues who is initially the 'just man', the 'just woman'.[41] Only redemptive re-narration or 'recapitulation' may open up a new space for future practice and for a more socially embodied *poesis*. The tragic abyss that is *represented* rather than mutely indicated is *contained* in its historical occasion and final non-necessity, the obscurity of its opening is yet bounded and enabled by the concrete instance of a 'ruin' (which is always an emblem of Golgotha). And in this redemptive movement we have not to do with the empty post-Burkean sublime, but with an earlier sublime of Boileau and others: the represented rupture and 'suspension' of our reaching towards transcendence. As in a Baroque Church, the angels fall half out of the ceiling, because the boundary which they cross is just as much an illusion in so far as we seem to fix and comprehend it, as their seeming to appear three-dimensionally in the space below. A historicist theology knows that the *whole* thing – 'God', 'heavens', and the economy of their relation to *our* finitude (the counterfactual of angelology by imagining 'another finitude' reminds us that we have no transcendental knowledge of finitude 'as such') – is the product of our representation, and it is this whole picture which must be – if anything is to be considered such – an imperfect registration of final reality.

If art as redemption – art purportedly beyond sign, beyond allegory, art as attainment of the immanent oblivion of disorientation – is modernity's own antidote to modernity, then *poesis* may be the key to a retrieval of the *sensus eminentior* and to a post-modern theology.[42] *Poesis*, we now more clearly see, is an integral aspect of Christian practice and redemption. Its work is the ceaseless re-narrating and 'explaining' of human history under the sign of the cross. To act at all is to re-narrate, and to act in the Church is to take this re-narration not as transparent and complete within supposed 'bounds' of our finitude (the Kantian modern), nor yet as ecstatically indeterminate (the sceptical post-modern), but rather as an utterly concrete allegorical outline, which remains, precisely by that token, all the more a mere sign of that mystery into which it must still enter in order to define itself.[43]

Notes

1 Eberhard Jüngel, *God as the Mystery of the World*, trans. D. L. Guder (T. & T. Clark, Edinburgh, 1983), p. 277.

2 Immanuel Kant, *Prolegomena to Any Future Metaphysics That Will Be Able to Present Itself as a Science*, trans. P. G. Lucas (Manchester University Press, Manchester, 1962), pp. 121–8.

3 Duns Scotus, *Philosophical Writings*, trans. A. Wolter (Nelson, London, 1963), pp. 2, 5, 9–12, 24.

4 See Thomas Aquinas, *Summa Theologiae*, vol. 3, ed. Herbert McCabe O. P. (Eyre and Spottiswoode, London, 1964), McCabe's Appendix 4, 'Analogy'.

5 See J. N. Findlay, *Kant and the Transcendental Object* (Oxford University Press, Oxford, 1981), and C. M. Turbayne, 'Kant's Relation to Berkeley', in *Kant Studies Today*, ed. Lewis W. Beck (Open Court, La Salle, Illinois, 1969).

6 *Prolegomena*, pp. 119–20. It should be noted here that, while Hegel views the 'boundary' still more positively than Kant, because the antinomies are not, for him, static, but can be dialectically deployed, he, nonetheless, also refuses the *sensus eminentior* because he sees this as illegitimate extrapolation of concepts of the understanding. But this refusal would collapse if one questioned the dualism of reason and understanding, which for Hegel remains a serious, *ontological* dualism such that there persists a realm of 'mere' externality, mere 'fortuitousness'. This, for Hegel, is the restricted, but legitimate, sphere of the operation of a capitalist economy in 'civil society'. So in Hegel also, refusal of eminence turns out to be connected with liberal politics. See Charles Taylor, *Hegel* (Cambridge University Press, Cambridge, 1975), p. 292 (though Taylor's evaluation here differs from mine).

7 Immanuel Kant, *The Critique of Judgement*, trans. J. C. Meredith (Oxford University Press, Oxford, 1978), pp. 96–128.

8 Findlay, *Kant and the Transcendental Object*, p. 274.

9 See Richard Rorty, *Philosophy and the Mirror of Nature* (Blackwell, Oxford, 1980).

10 Kant, *Critique of Judgement*, pp. 90–1.

11 Immanuel Kant, *The Philosophy of Law*, trans. W. Hastie (Edinburgh University Press, Edinburgh, 1887), p. 67.

12 Findlay, *Kant and the Transcendental Object*, p. 275.

13 Immanuel Kant, *Religion Within the Bounds of Reason Alone*, trans. T. H. Greene and H. H. Hudson (Open Court, La Salle, Illinois, 1960), pp. 27–38, 40–51, 60.

14 David Burrell, *Aquinas: God and Action* (Routledge & Kegan Paul, London, 1979), especially pp. 4–12, 55–68.

15 Duns Scotus, *Philosophical Writings*, pp. 9–12, 15. In the latter place Scotus denies that we know God only as what he is not, because 'every denial is intelligible only in terms of some affirmation'. However, this is not an affirmation of *the via eminentia*, but rather an assertion that one can find a 'simple concept' of God's essence/being (this turns out to be infinity-unity). Already in Scotus, 'foundationalist' moves in relation to meaning and 'transcendentalist' moves in relation to metaphysics, go along with a drawing away from the traditional mystical 'paths'. For the point about speculative grammar I am indebted to Dr Graham White: see Jan Pinborg, *Logik und Semantik im Mittelalter* (Frommann, Stuttgart, 1982) and the article 'Speculative Grammar' in *The Cambridge History of Later Mediaeval Philosophy* (Cambridge University Press, Cambridge, 1982), pp. 254–71. The use by Aquinas of the term *modus significandi* at e.g. S.T. I.Q. 13 a 3 is perhaps different from that of the *modistae* and more in line with Gilbert de la Porrée's Aristotelian 'psychologizing' of philosophic grammar. Aquinas wishes to draw attention to the onto- logical conditions of our knowledge as governing our *intentional* access to the *res*, in this case God. But the *modistae* were interested in dealing with sense in abstraction from reference and for them the *res significata* was primarily a 'general meaning' (of an essentially nominal character) which attaches to a particular *lexeme*. This *lexeme* is then inflected according to various *modi*, including usual parts of speech, which are basic categories of meaning. Although both the general meaning and the *modi* have ontological equivalents, this philosophic grammar tends to a 'Platonic' contrast of focal nominal sense with contingent inflection, such that the *res/modus* contrast is really to do with what is most primary in the realm of meaning, regarded as 'mirroring' the realm of substance. In Thomas this contrast is genuinely to do with our limited and unverifiable access to substance; he is trying to explicate how an intention can direct itself to its object, although its *modus* is not strictly homologous with the object. Although Burrell empha- sizes the connection of *res/modus* with intention (like Gilbert and Aquinas) he makes it sound as if (as for the *modistae*) the ontological and epistemological constraints embodied in the *modi* categorically determine the possibilities of sense and meaning, whereas for Aquinas's 'pre-critical' perspective sense derives mainly from the object of reference, to which the intention has imperfect, indirect access. The contrast is not between sense and reference, but between a mode of being and comprehension of the knower not fully commensurate with the mode of being and sense of the thing known, which, none the less, in the case of God, constitutes the existence of, and meaning available to, the knowing subject. See Burrell, *Aquinas*, p. 62, where he questionably compares the *res/ modus* distinction to that between *Bedeutung* and *Sinn*.

16 See, by contrast, Burrell, *Aquinas*, pp. 42–55.

17 Erich Przywara, *Polarity*, trans. A. C. Bouquet (Oxford University Press, Oxford, 1935), pp. 117–49.

18 Helmut Peukert, *Science, Action and Fundamental Theology* (MIT, Cambridge, Mass., 1986).

19 H. L. Mansel, *The Limits of Religious Thought* (London, 1859), pp. 252–3.

20 Ibid., p. 83. See also pp. 311–12 for Mansel's response to Maurice. Both these thinkers are working within the 'English positivist' tradition of a 'discoverable divine government', and both favour 'literal' and not mystical or allegorical interpretation – quite unlike the Lowth–Coleridge tradition by which Newman, at his best, is influenced. Maurice misreads Mansel as giving a liberal doctrine of divine *historical* accommodation, whereas Mansel teaches a once-for-all accommodation, and Maurice insists that the revealed 'system' more 'Platonically' reflects God as he is in himself. Neither thinker provides in these respects a good example for today, but at least Maurice, unlike Mansel, conjoins to the tradition of 'revealed government' a reflection on the social character of knowledge – here reflecting the path that leads in France from theology to sociology (Bonald to Comte).

21 See Henry Scott Holland, On *Behalf of Belief* (Longmans, London, 1892), pp. 187, 238.

22 See D. M. MacKinnon, 'Aristotle's Conception of Substance', in *New Essays on Plato and Aristotle*, ed. Renford Bambrough (Routledge & Kegan Paul, London, 1965), pp. 97–119.

23 On allegory see especially Walter Benjamin, *The Origin of German Tragic Drama*, trans. J. Osborne (New Left Books, London, 1977), pp. 159ff.

24 D. M. MacKinnon, *The Problem of Metaphysics* (Cambridge University Press, Cambridge, 1974), pp. 84–93.

25 Ibid., p. 145.

26 See Benjamin, *The Origin*, p. 129: 'Fate is the entelechy of events within the field of guilt' (this describes the Augustinianism of baroque drama). Compare MacKinnon, *Borderlands of Theology* (A. & C. Black, London, 1986), pp. 100–1: tragedians are 'true to the facts', 'an irresistible element in the scheme of things that brings even the most steadfast moral fidelity to nought'.

27 It is possible to have a genuine Christian reworking of Nietzschean 'forgetting', as an antidote to the secular, 'scientific' delusion that curiosity is always justified, self-apparent and innocent in its motivation. See Friedrich Nietzsche, 'On the Uses and Disadvantages of History for Life', in *Untimely Meditations*, trans. R. J. Hollingdale (Cambridge University Press, Cambridge, 1983), pp. 57–125.

28 D. M. MacKinnon, A *Study in Ethical Theory* (A. & C. Black, London, 1957), p. 97.

29 These two ways are not 'stages', but presuppose each other.

30 For example, Alastair MacIntyre, *After Virtue* (Duckworth, London, 1981); Stanley Hauerwas, *Character and the Christian Life* (Trinity University Press, San Antonio, 1985); Michael Sandel, *Liberalism and the Limits of Justice* (Cambridge University Press, Cambridge, 1983).

31 Paul Feyerabend, *Against Method* (New Left Books, London, 1975), pp. 181ff.

32 Donald Davidson, 'On the Very Idea of a Conceptual Scheme', in *Inquiries into Truth and Interpretation* (Oxford University Press, Oxford, 1984), pp. 183–99.

33 Ian Hacking, *The Emergence of Probability* (Cambridge University Press, Cambridge, 1975); Jeffrey Stout, *The Flight from Authority* (Notre Dame University Press, Notre Dame, 1981), especially pp. 95–179.

34 Sabina Lovibond, *Realism and Imagination in Ethics* (Blackwell, Oxford, 1983).

35 See Jean Baudrillard, *For a Critique of the Political Economy of the Sign*, trans. Charles Levin (Telos, St Louis, 1981) and *The Mirror of Production*, trans. M. Poster (Telos, St Louis, 1975); Cornelius Castoriadis, *The Imaginary Institution of Society*, trans. Kathleen Blamey (Polity, Cambridge, 1987), especially pp. 457–98. Castoriadis argues that, even in a socialist society, just distribution would be a matter of convention in which different things and activities would be accorded roughly equal value depending on their considered worth, without this necessitating the capitalist 'imaginary institution' of abstract equivalence. Likewise, Baudrillard shows that a 'pure use value', thought of naturalistically outside linguistic exchange, is a myth.

36 See Gillian Rose, *Hegel Contra Sociology* (Athlone, London, 1981). This essay is much indebted to Rose's arguments.

37 Stanley Hauerwas, 'The Church as God's New Language', in *Scriptural Authority and Narrative Interpretation*, ed. Garrett Green (Fortress, Philadelphia, 1987), pp. 179–98.

38 It is in fact with Thomas Aquinas, in relation to both the Trinity and the *verbum mentis*, that a certain conflation of the *forma exemplaris* with the *imago expressa* begins, so transforming the notion of an exemplary idea, such that the idea now only *is* in its constant 'being imaged'. Taken further by Eckhart and Nicholas of Cusa, this development dynamizes our participation in the divine ideas and finally makes our creativity the reflection of the divine rationality. Yet at the same time, teleology remains fully in place, because our 'art' is always a 'conjecture' concerning the completion of the divine 'art'. It is not far-fetched to see here one major and original version of the 'turn to the subject', which later – in thinkers like Vico, Hamann and Herder – becomes an 'alternative version' of this turn, in opposition to the obscuring ambiguity of its foundationalist versions in Descartes and Kant. See, for example, on Eckhart, Umberto Eco, *Art and Beauty in the Middle Ages*, trans. H. Bredin (Yale University Press, Yale, 1986), p. 113.

39 Stanley Hauerwas, *Against the Nations* (Winston, Minneapolis, 1985), pp.132–98.

40 Stanley Hauerwas, *The Peaceable Kingdom* (SCM, London, 1983), pp. 135–51. There may also be a slight tendency, at this stage of Hauerwas's work, to turn the narrative into a *schema* by stressing to an extreme, though necessarily corrective, degree the idea that given virtue pre-empts the 'moment of decision' (this is confusing in relation to my point in the main text, because it means that Hauerwas himself has tended to put all the emphasis on *habitus*). A balanced narrativist re-working of Aristotelianism would have to find a place for the idea that our decisions informed *by phronesis* constantly give slight new inflections to the narrative and develop the form of our virtues.

41 Walter Benjamin, 'The Story-Teller', in *One-Way Street* (New Left Books, London, 1977), and *The Origin*.

42 'Post-modern theology', in my usage, goes further than 'neo-orthodoxy', because it does not, like the latter, tend to leave unquestioned the 'godless' and autonomous self-enclosure of secular modernity, which then for this theology forms a 'background' for the unprecedented workings of faith. In this last section, I am indebted in several ways to past discussions with Kenneth Surin.

43 These concluding remarks may be linked by the reader with discussions of allegory in the section *Logos*, below.

2
Only Theology Overcomes Metaphysics

Jean-Luc Marion, along with several other contemporary French pheno-menologists-cum-theologians, represents a curious final shift in the course of twentieth-century theology.[1] In the traditions of neo-orthodoxy and the *nouvelle théologie*, they seek to think God through the pure reception of his word, which alone gives to us God himself. This strictly theological talk requires no philosophical foundations, and presupposes no metaphysical categories, not even that of Being, which is thought most of all to insinuate a false necessity. And yet, such a thinking out of the resources of revelation alone is specifically seen by Marion and many others as according precisely with the demand of modern philosophy in its 'phenomenological' variant that we should accept nothing as true except according to the conditions in which a phenomenon presents itself to us in excess of any preceding categorical assumptions. One can even go a stage further: not only does the God known from himself alone fall within the phenomenological understanding of 'donation' as the one transcendental condition for simultaneous existing and knowing; this God *most of all fulfils* the demand for pure phenomenality, for reduction to 'the thing itself', since in this instance solely it is impossible for anything in my experience, including my own subjectivity, to persist outside of the donating gift as the independent site of my reception of it. Hence God, whether announced through an ultimate 'natural' appearance, or else revealed through historical events, retains, against all conceptual idolatry, his absolute initiative, and *yet* operates as the phenomenon of all phenomena, the absolutely preceding call which 'interlocutes' us as subjects and provides transcendental permission for all other awareness. If, therefore, Marion continues to develop the characteristic twentieth-century theology of divine word as gift and event, he also effects the most massive *correlation* of this theology with contemporary philosophy, but in such a fashion that at times it appears that he usurps and radicalizes philosophy's own categories in favour of theological ones: donation intricately slides into charity. Compared with Marion, the ambition of a Barth is as nothing, for it is as if, so to speak (albeit in a mode already inscribed by Levinas) Marion seeks to be both Barth and Heidegger at once.

In what follows I wish to explore the coherence of Marion's abandonment (or partial abandonment) of theological correlation with philosophy round 'Being', in favour of a correlation round 'donation' or 'gift'.

The contrast between 'Being' and 'donation' arises, for Marion, out of the history of phenomenology. In the beginning stood Husserl, who erected the principle that one should accept nothing that could not be made explicit for a fundamental intuition.[2] A speculative ontology regarding 'beings' is replaced in its task by a transcendental phenomenology which identifies irreducible appearances which operate a, nonetheless, categorical universality. Even the transcendental 'I' itself is first 'given' in this fashion, but Heidegger later complained against his master that he had not truly grasped just how the 'I' is given to us: not as an object, nor even as the site for representation of objective 'beings', but rather as the site in which the contingency of beings, and hence the Being which is shown in them, but not exhausted by them, is manifest.[3] A site where this Being is *in question*, and hence the issue of what-to-do with beings, how to live amongst beings (as the being whose specific difference is to disclose Being) has priority over the intentional representation of beings. With this shift, the transcendentally eidetic philosophy of Husserl, which performed the ontological task, was transformed into a philosophy for which an unfathomable encounter with Being, and recognition that we are first *in* Being before we know, assumes priority. And yet, as Marion insists, Heidegger did not thereby abandon the priority of donation in favour of that of Being; on the contrary he allowed, following many openings in Husserl himself, for a donation which exceeds both our intentional grasp and even intuitive manifestation, since Being is not one more category which the ego 'intuits', but is the transcendental condition for the categorical itself, and for the ego itself as *Dasein*.[4] Through its exceeding of both intention and intuition Being is manifest *as* that which hides itself in its manifestation. And since, once grasped, it disappears, it is all the more radically maintained as 'given', and inappropriable.

Despite acknowledging that this is the case, Marion, nonetheless, argues that 'Being' in Heidegger obscures the priority of Husserl's 'donation'. This is first of all because *Dasein remains* in a fashion both a Cartesian *cogito* and a Husserlian transcendental ego. For if Being is only apparent in *Dasein*, and even only *is* in *Dasein* (since otherwise it 'nihilates' itself in beings) then it requires *Dasein*'s thinking of itself as a site of exposure, reflection and decision.[5] *With* the ontological difference, *Dasein* must think also its own difference from objects. And however much certain 'existential' features of the analytic of *Dasein* may drop away in the later Heidegger – access to Being via anxiety and (at times) being-towards-death – nonetheless, as Marion rightly stresses, the direct prior 'call' of Being in the later works is still addressed to a *Dasein* presupposed as such. But Marion goes further: for the ego to be able to identify the 'saturated phenomenon' which reveals/hides itself as 'Being', it must make an intentional projection of a universal that we can abstract from beings upon the identity of that which calls us; the call is reduced to Being as a 'screen' for beings. Here, however, Marion knows that he runs the risk of only appearing to say more, since for Heidegger also, Being is not 'in itself' Being, as outside beings it is nothing, and only becomes Being *in* beings, when it ceases to be absolute 'Being as such'. Therefore, for Heidegger, one must speak of Being as also nothing, and as the non-identifiable 'it gives'.[6] Marion's demand, however, is that we be more absolutely agnostic concerning this source in which Being/beings is given. Simply, *it arrives*, but how can we know that it does not arrive from a more absolute distance, from a giving source bestowing Being/beings? This is no abstract issue: on the contrary, it is here that the highest stakes of ethics, politics and nihilism are at issue. For if there is a gift before, beyond and without Being, a donation that we cannot even name Being/Nothing, then the *appropriation* of beings and of *Dasein* in its finitude by Being – whereby every finite 'presence' (of being) in its claim to a share of ultimate reality and of value is folded back into the flux of Being as time or non-present 'nothing' – is no longer the final word.[7] Instead, beings are put back into play, diverted from their absorption into an impersonal Being, and accorded a new status compatible with that of 'creatures'.

Marion's critique of the appropriating *ereignis* of Being in terms of a call from 'before' Being, as a pure possibility not even determined as 'to be' or potential 'act', is correlated with a certain return to a Husserlian priority of the knowing subject over Being, since the ego in its self-presence is no longer fundamentally *Dasein*, but the recipient of a call other than the call of Being.[8] However, the radicality of a non-apparent phenomenon equivalent to an irreducible excess of intuition over intention is maintained, because the 'I' itself first *is* as called, or is subject only as 'interlocuted', as given 'me' before it is an I.[9] The problem here, indicated by Phillip Blond, is that, as with the late 'theological' Husserl of the unpublished archives, and with Levinas, the calling 'other' can after all only be identified as a subjective caller, or as a giver, *by way of* a projection of one's own ego upon the other, an ego that would be once again an initial 'I', constituted first as the ground of intentional representation of objects.[10] In one passage Marion concedes that in order to recognize the caller *as* another subject with *haeccitas* and not just as another ego formally identical to oneself, one must permit him to have intentional projects – to have a *proprieté*, or a *propre* – while renouncing equivalent projects oneself in order that one may be radically interrogated and displaced from one's unethical stance of egotistical dominance.[11] Yet surely such a sacrificial logic is incoherent, since one's own renounced intentionality and particularity is the ground on which one is recognizing the particularity of the other as that of a subject, but in consequence one cannot ascribe any need for him, in turn, to renounce himself and to be interlocuted. The *aporia* of 'reverse intentionality' therefore persists, even if, as Marion stresses, the other has no intentional knowledge of his 'regard' in me. Whereas it can only be avoided if the 'I' is first and foremost not defined over-against objects, but constitutes a specific 'character', or a certain not completed, and not entirely predictable, but recognizable pattern of objectivity or 'embodiment' in the widest sense, including embodiment in language as specific 'idiolect'. In *that* case 'I' am always as external to myself as others are to me, and the specific network of intersubjective connections in which I am interpellated is indeed prior to my abstracted egoity, without this requiring any projection by an initial, autistic ego. With Marion, as with Levinas, the otherness of a first, non-objectivizable other, would seem to be a specifically Cartesian alterity, whereas the only 'other' not subject to 'reverse intentionality' is a specific, embodied, actual subject, a subject who after all always already 'is', even in his giving. *Not* invisibility, but visibility – which as beauty is *not* reducible to 'my aim', guarantees the otherness of the other. By maintaining the opposite, the only ground which Marion can find for the identification of the call as that of 'a caller' (rather than the impersonal *es gibt* of the *nihil*, which seems equally phenomenologically viable) is the act of ethical or even religious faith which 'wills' to respect the free-will of the other, even though every such willing is subject to the suspicion of a disguised self-interest and objectification.[12] Only the will itself *of* our freedom to acknowledge the freedom of the other gaze is inviolable in the face of such suspicion, and from this will alone, from the fact that we *do* love, are we able, says Marion, *univocally* to identify the love of the other, including the love of the ultimate caller.[13] Hence there is a projection of my love, love as I experience it as a pure 'good will' unconnected with purpose or representation, onto the other, who is therefore, despite Marion's claim, no longer the other. Marion implies that the fundamental, overwhelming call, which is that of a transcendental 'being given'[14] identical with a universal 'giver', is mediated through our experience of the gaze of the human person as a pre-ontological ethical demand. However, it is clear that the first is entirely modelled upon the second, and that the second still conceals a 'representing', punctiliar subject whose admittedly irreducible self-consciousness (or *cogito*) is abstracted from his specific and contingent mode of self-embodiment and physical capacity. This being the case, a priority of ethical intersubjectivity conceived as a crossing of invisible gazes, cannot really be made phenomenologically evident, and still less manifest is the identity of the call as that of a caller. For if Being/beings is itself given, then so also is our situation of ethical intersubjectivity, and why should one assume that the latter is itself given by an ethical caller? In just what *sense* is the crossing of regards more apparent than ontological difference? Unsurprisingly, Marion oscillates between (1) the absolute anonymity of the gift; (2) the gift as a 'natural' manifestation of a giver = God; (3) recognition of this manifestation only through an act of will.[15] The latter option appears to (1) deny that God is manifest as a phenomenon objectively apparent (as phenomenological reduction requires) and (2) reduces God after all to a projection of our ego, albeit in the shape of our loving will.

The upshot, therefore, of this reading of Marion's receiving of the phenomenological tradition, is to conclude that his noble ambition to undo the nihilistic 'enfolding' of Heidegger's *ereignis*, cannot be accomplished in the mode which he attempts. This is because the 'distance' between gift and Being/beings collapses back into a subject/object duality on the model of 'representation', which obscures both the 'subjectivity' of objects which only 'are' in their affecting, and the 'objectivity' of a subject which is a receptive site for complex occurrences, since representations represent in a specifically receiving and so creatively transforming mode.

If the gift/Being contrast is still inscribed within the modern turn to the subject, which Marion would purport to see as the fulfilment or 'redoubling' of metaphysical *theoria* as a representing gaze,[16] and therefore to be overcome through radical donation, then one might have hesitations at the outset concerning his attempt to use this contrast to read the history of the interaction between theology and metaphysics (identified with philosophy as such). The great merit of Marion's approach to history is that he takes seriously Heidegger's diagnosis of modernity as the consummation of metaphysics which fulfils the will-to-know objects as the will-to-power over nature, including human beings. Since metaphysics has a fundamentally *onto-theological* constitution, such that the highest being, or first cause, is identified as a perfect instance of what is fundamentally knowable, namely a 'being', while beings themselves are accounted for through the causal efficiency of the highest being, modernity is not at all, in its essence, atheistic.[17] To the contrary, as Marion argues, atheism is a secondary rejection of the conceptual idols which modern metaphysics erects, as, for example, with Descartes' *causa sui*, while atheism itself submits new idols, best exemplified by Nietzsche's Will-to-Power, as the ultimate foundation for our infinite capacity to relegislate and overturn every previous legal foundation.[18] However, it is arguable that recent researches suggest that Heidegger's thesis that 'modernity fulfils metaphysics' should be radicalized as 'modernity invented metaphysics'. This would have to be considered an exaggeration to the degree that onto-theology is clearly inscribed in Aristotle's (after-named) *Metaphysics* itself, but one could point out that first of all, Platonism before Aristotle never sought a categorical inventory of what 'is' in the world, nor explained what is in becoming through an ultimate efficient or final causality, but rather referred what becomes to a partial manifestation (donation?) of a transcendent source or sources which brings about through intrinsic excellence – the Good.[19] This philosophical figure is not onto-theological. Second, one could mention that Aristotle preserves an aporetic oscillation between 'every' being and 'first' being as the subject of metaphysics, in accord with his equal hesitation between substance as the composite and substance as the abstractable form.[20] This circularity, whereby the stability of material *ousia* seems already to require the unmoved mover as a model by which to conceive it, despite the invocation of the first *ousia* ostensibly to account for merely the actuation of material substance, at least exposes its own contradiction. By contrast, the new science of *ontology* which emerged in the seventeenth century, and which coincided with Suarez's use for the first time of 'metaphysics' to name a systematic discipline, finally occluded this contradiction by regarding ontology/metaphysics as first and foremost a science of what constitutes 'being' taken as a possible object of knowledge which is *unproblematically comprehensible* without reference to any non-material or absolute beings.[21] *Metaphysica specialis*, dealing with the latter, is now firmly located as a sub-discipline of *metaphysica generalis* dealing with the former. No longer is there any question of God as 'most being'; rather God is simply a different type of being, infinite as opposed to finite, invoked simply to 'complete' causal explanation, such that as 'first cause' or even *causa sui*, he is univocally conceived as of the same type as a finite cause, and effectively becomes the first in a chain of causes.

In the third place, it could be pointed out that neoplatonism, followed at least by Boethius, Aquinas and Eckhart, sought to resolve the Aristotelian *aporia* in the opposite direction – namely 'upwards' rather than 'downwards', by deriving the 'is' of temporal/spatial beings *entirely* from the first principle, but a principle no longer conceived as itself a representable object or being, which would depend for its foundation upon what it is supposed to found, in line with the characteristic contradiction of onto-theology. This unrepresentable source which one can only 'know' through a negative *élan*, and a flight of *eros*, yet which is implied in all knowledge, was named by Plotinus 'the One', and then by an unknown neoplatonist (perhaps Porphyry) who probably inspired Boethius, as 'to be', since it was argued that the infinitive form of the verb avoided any suggestion of subject/object composition inappropriate to the absolute.[22] Hence in Christian tradition the thought of God himself allowed access to 'the ontological difference' between *esse* on the one hand and contingently being this or that subject or object with a definable *essentia* on the other.

Whereas Heidegger read the entire philosophical tradition and the Christian appropriation of philosophy as the history of metaphysics or onto-theology (which amounted often to reading it through neo-scholastic spectacles), it now seems at the least unclear as to whether this accurately describes Platonism, neoplatonism and Christian theology before Henry of Ghent and Duns Scotus.

However, between the Heideggerean thesis about the history of metaphysics, and the more radical, emerging one, Marion noticeably hesitates, although he is manifestly moving in the second direction. Hence he acknowledges that God only becomes substance (Goclenius), individual being (Cajetan) and cause of himself (Descartes) in the early modern period, and (increasingly) that Aquinas's *esse* is not a conceptual idol, since Thomas speaks of God creating Being as such and not just beings, and conceives the divine *esse* as incomprehensibly other to the *ens commune* of creatures, because it uniquely coincides with his essence, or his infinite 'whatever he is'.[23] This characteristic renders it supremely concrete, and in no sense like the object of a bare existential affirmation. Nevertheless, Marion appears to draw back from the obvious inference: if Christian theology prior to Scotus avoided onto-theology (metaphysics), then this was because it was able to elucidate the hidden manifestness of God in terms of the hidden manifestness of Being in beings. It was possible, in identifying God with Being, to think the ontological difference in a manner that Heidegger denied was accessible for theology. But theology *read* this difference differently, *not* as the 'appropriation' of beings by Being which is also Nothing (even though Gregory of Nyssa and Augustine were able, as much as Heidegger, to relate the *aporias* of time to the non-possession of Being by beings),[24] but rather as the fulfilment and preservation of beings in Being as an infinitely actual source and realization of all essential possibility. Here the temporally becoming 'shape' of an essence does not betray Being through its contingency (in which case Being also univocally *is* this contingency which it immediately cancels) but instead is through and through 'like' Being, in so far as all that in it 'is', entirely derives from Being as a donating source.

This 'reading' of the ontological difference in terms of analogy and participation was never seriously considered by Heidegger, perhaps in part because his neo-scholastic background prevented him from grasping the priority of 'analogy of attribution' in the tradition, which inscribes a doctrine of mystical return to God as unknown source, rather than a logical or grammatical thesis related to predications in the ontic realm. But also, and for certain, it was because Heidegger believed that he had considered Being not 'speculatively' (metaphysically), but according to Being's own giving of itself as a phenomenon. This meant that what was sheerly 'apparent', namely the self-occlusion of Being in beings, was taken as identifying Being as such. But one may ask, is there not a 'transgression of the bounds of pure reason' involved here, since it does not appear valid to identify the concealment of Being from us with the very 'nature' of Being, such that it is seen 'as' that which nihilates itself in beings, while in turn nihilating beings themselves. For if the ontological difference as such is 'seen', the 'event of appropriation' is surely *not* seen, but remains *after all* a mode of 'speculation' in rivalry with that mode of conjecture which is analogy of attribution. Thus while phenomenology was correct to lift the Kantian ban on ontology, since things only 'are' in their mode of appearing, and Heidegger was right against Kant to see that an antinomous relation between being and Beings (as between the 'present' and past/future) invades even the 'valid' finite sphere of pure reason's operation, requiring that we *live* (as *Dasein*) transgressively or metaphysically,[25] phenomenology has perhaps failed to acknowledge that it is *apparent* that Being is not fully apparent, not even in the mode of the appearance of the inapparent, for this *may* be sublime 'appropriation', or it *may* be analogical elevation. Instead, Being calls for a Cusan 'conjecture' as to its nature, and the character of the ontological difference. This is not, however, to re-open the way to a metaphysical deduction from preceding 'causes', since such deductions are without grounds. On the contrary, the conjecture which judges, considers that it 'sees' something or 'receives' something. One has not necessarily departed here from phenomenology, but one is nonetheless insisting on the 'subjectivity', in a Kierkegaardian sense, of reception: to receive one must be rightly attuned, one must judge aright, desire aright, as Platonic, neoplatonic and Christian philosophy have always insisted. Marion's own writings display the difficulty of this issue for phenomenology, since at times he speaks as if the transcendental gift is objectively manifest, arguing that while we must receive, or give back through gratitude the gift, for it to be there for us, this giving back is, nonetheless, a pre-ontological precondition for our very subjective existence.[26] Here he accords with Levinas's strange converting of the categorical ought into something which precedes our willing. And yet at other times, Marion speaks of not merely the stance of faith, but even the *ethical* stance, as depending on a kind of Pascalian wager as to the reality of free will. In this case, it would seem, the free giving of the other manifest through our free response (the 'crossing of regards') does *not* unambiguously appear, but appears only for 'faith' understood as an act of will. To this extent, Marion concedes the apparent need for 'conjecture', but restricts it to a willing which entirely precedes 'reasons' even of an aesthetically judging or ecstatically desiring sort.[27] This is in keeping with his strict dualism of the invisible and visible which correlates the latter – 'Being' – entirely with conceptual mastery, omitting from consideration the aesthetic and erotic cases where one is 'compelled' by a manifestation, yet can never exhaustively or incontrovertibly provide the reasons for this compulsion. (Thus, without historical warrant, he reduces the hypostatic presence of Christ in the icon to the gaze of the eyes alone, whereas its greatest theologians clearly considered the icon to be possible because the divine hypostasis was manifest through *singular* human identity, something like 'character', which is shown through our entire bodily objectivity).[28] This duality preserves, to a large degree, the Heideggerean refusal of analogy, and keeps conjecture to a minimum by taking what is invisibly manifest as a 'will' which precedes what is. However, a pure good will, utterly abandoned to the good of another will, yet not committed to any mode in which I or the other should *be*, is, as Marion says, a giving which does not necessarily require (and, indeed, requires there initially *not* to be) a giver who *is*, nor any actual reception by a donee.[29] It is a pure flux, which washes over every boundary, and as such, it is difficult to know how it is 'the Good', nor how it truly differs from the impersonal Heideggerean flux of the *es gibt*. Without either desire or judgement, Marion's wager that the sublime phenomenon is 'will of the good' appears to reduce after all to a simple reception of the manifestation of the sheerly indifferent; indifferent not merely, as Marion requires, to Being, but also to beings as this or that.

Marion's non-questioning of phenomenology at its most vulnerable point, concerning the manifest non-avoidability of conjecture, means that, first of all, he does not question Heidegger's claim to have made the ontological difference phenomenologically apparent; second, he is in consequence *forced* to speak of God and of human subjectivity in terms of the gift which exceeds ontological difference; third, the manifest non-manifestness of the gift itself appears all too similar to that of Heidegger's *Sein*.

Given this triple stance, Marion has problems in acknowledging that neoplatonic philosophy and Christian theology interpreted the ontological difference in a viable mode other than that of Heidegger. And yet he recognizes that Aquinas's *esse* is a valid theological category and not a metaphysical projection. He is only able to do so because he effectively equates Heidegger's *Sein* with Aquinas's *ens commune*, the created Being of created beings, which Aquinas spoke of as the true subject-matter (not God) of metaphysics. This equation, however, suggests that, for Aquinas, there is an immanent, purely created site of the ontological difference,[30] and that philosophy concerned with 'Being' has an autonomous field of operation (and one should note here that Marion implies that the fold of Being/beings can be left unperturbed within its own 'sphere'). But neither is the case. On the contrary, for Aquinas the difference of *esse* from essence in the *ens commune* of creatures, and yet its real finite occurrence only in essences, is 'read' in *entirely* theological terms as the site of the internal fracture of creatures between their own nothingness and their alien actuality which is all received from God. This means that the domain of metaphysics is not simply subordinate to, but completely *evacuated* by theology, for metaphysics refers its subject matter – 'Being' – wholesale to a first principle, God, which is the subject of another, higher science, namely God's own, only accessible to us via revelation.[31] This is *not* a matter of mere causal referral, but of the entire being of *ens commune* and its comprehensibility. And here we have reached the absolute crux of this matter, and the turning point in the destiny of the West. For insofar as Aquinas appeared to leave some ambiguity regarding how it was possible to speak of God by first speaking of finite beings, Duns Scotus resolved it in an untraditional direction by affirming that this is because one can first understand Being in an unambiguous, sheerly 'existential' sense, as the object of a proposition, without reference to God, who is later claimed 'to be' in the same univocal manner. Here (following Henry of Ghent, who claimed that the essence of God as Being was the first object of understanding, directly and positively present to the intellect)[32] arises for the first time ontotheological idolatry regarding God, and the placing of God within a predefined arena of being, which, as Marion rightly says, persists even in Heidegger's *Letter on Humanism*.[33] Marion sees this, yet it is not clear that he also acknowledges Scotus's *idolatry towards creatures*, or in other words the invalidity of a now autonomous 'metaphysics', later to become 'ontology', which claims to be able fully to define the conditions of finite knowability, or to arrive at possible being as something 'in itself', despite the fact that nothing manifestly is in itself and every 'present' reality is riddled with *aporias* (of time, of space, of particularity and universality). Just where we assume to glimpse the late mediaeval commencement of the decline of metaphysics, in the opening to an autonomous, secular sphere of knowledge, one must on the contrary recognize its inception. Modernity is metaphysical, for since it cannot refer the flux of time to the ungraspable infinite, it is forced to seek a graspable, *immanent* security; hence, as Catherine Pickstock has pointed out, its characteristic project is one of 'spatialization', a *mathesis* or measurement of what is, which can master that which merely occurs.[34] By contrast, the Christian thought which flowed from Gregory of Nyssa and Augustine was able fully to concede the utter unknowability of creatures which continually alter and have no ground within themselves, for it derived them from the infinity of God which is unchanging and yet uncircumscribable, even in itself. Between one unknown and the other there is here no representational knowledge, no 'metaphysics', but only a mode of ascent which receives something of the infinite source so long as it goes on receiving it, so constituting, not a once and for all theory (or account of the ontological difference) but an endlessly repeated-as-always-different theoretical claim which is nothing other than all the biographies of every ascent, and the history of human ascent as such.

The great defender of this tradition, it is now emerging, thanks to the work of Alain de Libera and others, was none other than Eckhart. Against the Franciscans, Eckhart refused the identifying of God with univocal being regarded as object of, and essentially external to, intellection. Instead, he closed the window of ambiguity left slightly ajar by Aquinas and insisted that analogical attribution means that no transcendental predication – of Being, Intellect, Unity and Goodness – belongs positively to any creature, but that all in them that 'is', or is united, 'or thinks', or wills the good, reverts ecstatically back to its uncreated source.[35] Against Scotist idolatry, Eckhart could insist that God is above even *esse* in so far as he is intellect, which as Word 'is' not this or that but only indicates it (although God's Word *causes* to be whereas ours follows being). Nevertheless, the capacity of intellect to 'be' all things also shows for Eckhart (as for Aquinas) that it is itself unlimited Being and precisely the site of the coincidence of *esse* with *essentia*.[36] Hence while, in certain writings, Eckhart goes beyond Aquinas in showing how one can derive *all* the transcendentals from each other (where Aquinas tended to derive unity, intellect and goodness from *actus purus*),[37] he, nonetheless, states yet more emphatically than Aquinas that *esse est Deus*.[38] The point here is not, as von Balthasar claims, that Eckhart is departing from Thomas and inaugurating modern idolatry by identifying God as *esse*[39] – for he is frequently more reserved about this than Aquinas – but that, to the contrary, he is resisting any 'grasp' of *esse* as a univocal term which can genuinely be predicated of a creature.[40] Where Scotus inaugurated a metaphysics independent of theology, Echkart absolutely evacuated the metaphysical site in favour of theology. Everything now for Echkart derives from a distant, inaccessible source: parts only have their being through wholes, accidents through substance, the *homo* assumed in Christ through the hypostatic Word, and substantial beings through Being, rendering all finite beings *entirely accidental*, and thereby more contingent, as more aporetic, than the voluntarists, despite everything, could ever have imagined.[41]

Marion perhaps does not demonstrate a sufficient awareness of the collapse of such 'evacuation' in Scotus, and thereby of the collapse of the discourse concerning analogy and participation as the event of the obliteration of ontological difference and the emergence of conceptual idolatry. In this history, the question of a stress on one or other of the transcendental terms is relatively unimportant, since what is at issue is rather whether any one of them can be mastered by a finite gaze. Respecting the transcendental category of 'truth', this non-mastery is summed up in Eckhart's citation of Augustine, with its highly 'phenomenological' anticipations: ' "When you hear that he is truth, do not ask, what is truth? Remain, therefore, if you can, in that first flash, when you were dazzled as it were by its brightness, when it was said to you 'truth'." Augustine means that this is God.'[42] Indeed, Marion himself claims that the convertibility of the transcendentals, whereby every transcendental path absolutely overlaps with every other and yet none is dispensable or reducible to any other, is a mark of a 'saturated phenomenon'. In that case, one might ask, does not the idea that one transcendental, namely the Good, 'precedes' all the others, threaten do drain this saturation, such that the Good becomes identified with the mere gaze of a subject, his mere good will, quite apart from questions of what it is to be good in act, how we are to live in harmony, unity and in accord with our nature? And if the ultimate phenomenon is exactly describable as the gaze of a subject, it would appear that it is after all merely ontic, and that in seeking to trump ontological difference, one has instead connived again at its obliteration.[43]

These suspicions are confirmed when one considers Marion's applications of the Gift/Being duality to the history of metaphysics and theology. Since he still thinks that Heidegger fully exposed to view the ontological difference, and must in consequence believe that to think God in terms of this difference is idolatrous, he is obliged to view the admittedly non-idolatrous character of pre-modern theology in terms of its supposed privileging of Gift over Being. And yet, for all that Good is the 'first name of God' in Dionysius, one finds (as Marion indeed recognizes) that in Gregory of Nyssa 'Being' is allowed to define the common divinity of the Trinity precisely because it is an entirely apophatic term indicating nothing of 'how' God is.[44] In the case of Bonaventure, Marion does not give the full picture: for the Franciscan, 'Being' is the highest name for God's essence, revealed in the Old Testament, while 'Good' is the yet higher, New Testament name, since it discloses the emanation of the Trinitarian persons (something which for the fathers, as for the early scholastics, was even *foreshadowed* by the 'I am who I am', since this speaking also discloses God as a word, and in the gospels the Word identified himself as 'I am' – the 'before Abraham' which follows, seeming *to legitimate* an ontological misreading of Exodus 3:14, *for all Christians for all times*).[45] Yet within the perfection of Good is included, for Bonaventure, also the perfection of 'to be'.[46] Indeed Marion persists in speaking as if 'Being' has always been used in a primarily existential post-Scotist sense, whereas for the previous tradition it was also regarded from the practical perspective of 'more fully becoming Being', such that while 'to be good' or 'to be true' (for Augustine, for example) is precisely 'to be' *per se*, this suggests inversely that Being is the plenitude of what is genuinely desirable.[47] Marion entirely misreads the Augustinian/Thomist (*not* exactly Aristotelian) priority of act over possibility in terms of the tyranny of a 'given' order, whereas if act is infinite it is on the contrary on the side of 'the surprise of what arrives'. By contrast, a possibility which is not the active potency of an act, but prior to the act, can only be *either* pure logical possibility or *else* an entirely empty freedom of choice, not free in terms of any submission to an objectively life-giving order, nor even the reciprocal interplay of the gift – since the purely 'free gift' fantasized by Marion, outside and before reciprocal relation, presupposes a freedom independent of the gift, a 'pure flux'. In both cases, it is possibility which constitutes a mere transcendental 'given', whereas only infinite act can give transcendent gift.

It is in terms of Being as a plenitude, and as the site of conversion with all the other transcendentals, that one should read Aquinas's relating of Being as the first name of God to *ens* as first object of our comprehension. For Marion, this opens the way to Scotus's idolization of God as univocal *ens*, although he does not mention that in that case it may equally be taken as opening the way to Scotus's claim that there can be an independent science of finite being.[48] But since it does not really do the latter, neither does it do the former: on the contrary, Aquinas says that something is comprehended as *ens* before it is comprehended as *unum*, *vivens* and *sapiens*, precisely because things are the latter of themselves, whereas they only *are* by participation.[49] In other words, *ens* is not the first *thing* that we grasp, but the ungraspable horizon which opens out the possibility of all other knowing. It is not that God is 'placed' in a metaphysical (and epistemological) category, but that this category is evacuated in favour of God from the outset. If there is a weakness here, then it concerns Aquinas's failure to see that one might reverse this proposition in favour of the other transcendentals, making 'Unity' that which does not properly belong and Being that which is proper to us and so forth. Precisely such teasing ruses were played out by Eckhart, although it is notable that he does not appear to have been so often willing to derive the other transcendentals from that of *Goodness*. For while Aquinas only makes *ens* first in the order of intellection, whereas in the always accompanying mode of willing goodness takes the lead[50] (again Marion fails to point this out) it is nonetheless the case that the Dominicans somewhat reduced will to bare 'assent' to the exigencies of the intellect, omitting the Augustinian (and thoroughly Trinitarian) sense that judgement itself depends upon a right desire, even though we inversely desire what we judge to be true.[51] Here Marion supplies a corrective, and his reflections on the gift might be recast in the mode of *one* transcendental path of derivation of the other transcendentals from the Good, in a fashion that does not displace the equal priority of actualized Being and gnoseological/aesthetic judgement. This would surely give a more Trinitarian form to his reflections, for in that case the gift would have a mode and a shape, the shape of giving *as* an intrinsic excellence or harmony, and equally the gift would no longer solipsistically precede relation (so collapsing into a preceding validity of a given, not giving will) but occur only as equally presupposed with reciprocity. However, the same Trinitarian shape would *preserve* Marion's phenomenological stress on a transcendental 'appearing', equiprimordial with Being.

My suspicion, therefore, is that in failing to see that the crux of a 'non-metaphysical' theology regards not gift versus Being, but rather the referring or not of the transcendentals to God via analogical participation, Marion is still somehow the legatee of such a non-referral, still within a self-sufficient metaphysics, which is identical with secular modernity. For the enterprise of phenomenology itself is hitherto 'Scotist' in that, independently of any spiritual discipline, it aspires to 'see' the essences of things, albeit in a highly singular and *a posteriori* fashion. Because he adheres to the phenomenological notion of an unproblematic 'presence', even if of that which cannot be made present (and Derrida himself likewise still adheres to this), Marion regards the Heideggerean fold of Being/beings as valid within its own *temporal* sphere,[52] although it is difficult to see how this is compatible with his brilliant theological reading of the temporal 'present' not as the site of appropriation, but as incorporated into the eucharistic gift of the body and blood of Christ, all the more bodily and all the more 'transubstantiated' because only available in the mode of present as 'gift', not as present objectification. For this renders the passage of time through all its *present* moments as gift, so that here temporal being 'is' a gift, in its very being, not just as a result of a pre-ontological regard.

The same containment and yet endorsement of metaphysics is borne out also by Marion and his pupil Vincent Carraud's (perhaps accurate) reading of the Pascalian 'orders' of political power and secular science as transcended by the logic of charity, and yet left undisturbed within their own spheres.[53] Whereas an Augustinian, Trinitarian, perspective suggests instead 'another' power and 'another' knowledge, albeit realized in and through that other love which is charity, Marion appears to despair altogether of both politics and science, while being resigned to their perpetuation. This is borne out by his analysis of *ennui* as an indifference to being overcome only by the light of love for being, which is itself indifferent to what being is. One might ask, here, is not true being intrinsically loveable *as* what it is, for otherwise it is exhaustively defined as bare, univocal existence, as brute (political) power and sheer (scientific) objectivity. And is it true that love is unconcerned to attend to how things are, or to how they should be, because being is properly the object of a pure objective, metaphysical science? Finally, one might reflect, while boredom with being is possible, is not boredom with the gift also possible? In fact *this* defines *accidie* for Aquinas.[54]

Again with respect to his relation to the metaphysical legacy, one can also note that the correlation in Marion of voluntarism with a refusal to engage in (or at least make discursively basic) the eminent attribution of being and intellect to God, seems to repeat precisely late scholasticism, while ignoring that in the latter case it is admitted that the notion of God as pure will and gift assumes that God is bare existential being in his essence prior to his intelligence, which now merely 'represents' this being, and no longer coincides with it as the *verbum* whose production ecstatically refuses identification with this or that.

However, Marion's lingering 'Scotism', or entrapment within 'metaphysics' which is modernity, is most of all evident in the very heart of his theology, where he demands 'What if God did not first have to be, since he loved us first, when we were not?'[55] For here the question can only hold if (1) the contingency of our being and (2) its referral to the transcendental Good (love) as what does not belong to us over against Being which does (and there is no reason why Marion should not, in the fashion of Eckhart, reverse Aquinas's play with the predication of transcendentals in this manner), is *univocally* transferable to God. Hence, as

Balthasar pointed out, Marion makes the division between creation and creator, understood as that between Being and the Gift, idolatrously recur in God himself, such that God, who also is, is turned into a God beyond God, distant from himself or free in relation to his own being, as Schelling put it, just as we are distant from him.[56] If this distance of God from God is, for Marion, as he indicates, that of Father from Son, then not surprisingly this distance is regarded as identical with that of God as gift, from God in Christ as dead on Holy Saturday (although since Paternal giving *is not*, Marion, unlike Balthasar, allows that the Father is dead with the Son). Since God's Being like ours can also 'not be', Christ in his divinity is dead upon the cross, and here, first and foremost, according to the *logos tou staurou*, God as giving love is disclosed. But then, one might ask, is not the process of life and death in time divinized? Is not the saving action of God reduced to a manifestation of *what God is*? (paradoxically). And is not God's love defined reactively and sacrificially, as that which gives on the occasion of evil as much as out of its spontaneous living plenitude, whereas the cross reveals the life of love *despite* death? And is not this love defined gesturally as a good will, rather than as the event of grace which repeats creation, despite the annihilation that is the fact of Evil, as a new gift of non-violent, harmonious life?[57] Surely it is not true, as Marion claims, that whereas we first are, and *may* love, God loves and *may* also be, for to the contrary, on a non-'Scotist' understanding of *esse*, we only are as we love and remain in love, whereas God who is love cannot not be. God loves-to-be, and not in indifference to being, else death is celebrated as a sacrificial opportunity.

Hence it would seen that, in contrast with my initial suggestion that Marion 'usurps' phenomenological donation to re-think it as Christian charity, this usurpation simply does not go far enough. The phenomenological notion of an objective, isolatable manifestation subverts Marion's thinking of transcendence into the terms of modern 'sublimity' which is dualistically separated from the beautiful, so *disallowing* the 'visible appearance of the invisible' which he seeks.[58] Such sublimity is the extreme instance of the treatment of the world as a series of 'givens' to be known, rather than gifts to be received and returned. And modernity can only reckon with the given, it *must* be metaphysical, as Heidegger half saw, even in its nihilist mode, where the 'spatial' becomes the interminable and unsurprisable flux of *différance*. Whereas, to convert the given into the gift, to receive love, one must admit the mediation of appearing and revelation via the judgement and right desire of 'the inspired man' (as revelation prior to early modernity, when it became distorted into a positive, actual content, was always understood) even if it be equally the case that judgement and right desire are themselves entirely given. When this is done, to receive the gift as love one must further *evacuate* all philosophy, leaving it merely as the empty science of formally possible perspectives and barren *aporias*. An independent phenomenology must be given up, along with the claim, which would have seemed so bizarre to the fathers, to be doing philosophy *as well as* theology. Philosophy as spiritual discipline, orientated to (an always in any case implicit) abstract reflection on the 'context' of our ascent, can indeed be embraced and consummated in a Christian version by theology. In this sense theology can still have recourse to *theoria* and *logos*, and if the latter constitute 'metaphysics', then talk of its overcoming is absurd. But philosophy as autonomous, as 'about' anything independently of its creaturely status *is* metaphysics or ontology in the most precisely technical sense. Philosophy in fact *began* as a secularizing immanentism, an attempt to regard a *cosmos* independently of a performed reception of the poetic word.[59] The pre-Socratics forgot both Being and the gift, while (*contra* Heidegger) the later Plato made some attempt to recover the extra-cosmic vatic *logos*.[60] Theology has always resumed this inheritance, along with that of the Bible, and if it wishes to think again God's love, and think creation as the manifestation of that love, then it must entirely evacuate philosophy, which is metaphysics, leaving it nothing (outside imaginary worlds, logical implications or the isolation of *aporias*) to either do or see, which is not – manifestly, I judge – malicious.

Notes

1 For others, see J.-F. Courtine, ed., *Phénoménologie et Théologie* (Criterion, Paris, 1993); H.-B. Vergôte et al., *L'Etre et Dieu* (Cerf, Paris, 1986); J.-Y. Lacoste, *Expérience et Absolu* (P.U.F., Paris, 1994); J.-L. Chrétien, *L'Inoubliable et L'Inespéré* (P.U.F., Paris, 1991).

2 See Jean-Luc Marion, *Réduction et Donation* (P.U.F., Paris, 1989), pp. 79ff and Edmund Husserl, *Ideen*, § 24.

3 Marion, *Réduction et Donation*, pp. 1–13, 130ff.

4 Ibid., pp. 1–63, 163–210.

5 Ibid., pp. 183–4.

6 See Martin Heidegger, 'What is Metaphysics' and 'Letter on Humanism', in *Basic Writings*, ed. David Farrell Krell (Routledge, London, 1977), pp. 93–110, 213–67; *On Time and Being*, trans. Joan Stambaugh (Harper & Row, New York, 1972).

7 Marion, *Réduction et Donation*, 249–305; Jean-Luc Marion, *God Without Being*, trans. Thomas A. Carlson (Chicago University Press, Chicago, 1991), pp. 25–52, 83ff; Marion, *L'Idole et La Distance* (Grasset et Pasquelle, Paris, 1977), pp. 264–9.

8 Marion, *Réduction et Donation*, pp. 119–61, 211–47.

9 Jean-Luc Marion, 'L'Interloqué', in *Who Comes after the Subject*, ed. Eduardo Cadava et al. (Routledge, London, 1991), pp. 236–46.

10 Phillip Blond has maintained this point in several unpublished lectures and private conversations. See also Jocelyn Benoist, 'Husserl: au-dela de l'Onthologie?', *Les Études Philosophiques*, 4 (1991), pp. 433–58.

11 Jean-Luc Marion, 'L'Intentionalité de l'Amour' in *Prolégomènes à la Charité* (La Différance, Paris, 1987), pp. 91–120, 117.

12 Jean-Luc Marion, 'La Liberté d'être Libre' and 'L'Evidence et Éblouissement', in *Prolégomènes*, pp. 45–67 and 71–88.

13 Marion, *God Without Being*, p. 48 and Jean-Luc Marion, 'De "La Mort de Dieu" aux Noms Divins: L'Itinéraire Théologique de la Métaphysique', in Vergôte et al. *L'Etre et Dieu*, pp. 103–30, 130.

14 Jean-Luc Marion, 'Metaphysics and Phenomenology: A *Relève* for Theology', unpublished paper delivered in the Cambridge Divinity Faculty, June 1993.

15 Ibid.; and see Marion, *Prolégomènes*, pp. 45–67, 71–8; Marion, *Réduction et Donation*, pp. 249–302.

16 Jean-Luc Marion, *Sur le Prisme Métaphysique de Descartes* (P.U.F., Paris, 1986), pp. 14–43. But see also Jean-François Courtine, *Suarez et le Système de la Métaphysique* (P.U.F., Paris, 1990), pp. 484–95 who argues against Marion that the *Regulae*, not the *Meditations*, give Descartes' ontology, such that the determiniation of the *ens* as the transparently knowable has priority over the *cogito*. If Marion's diagnosis here is incorrect, this would accord with his giving too little weight to how modern ontology based on univocity of Being transforms our notions of *finite* being, not just divine being, as I argue later in this article.

17 See Marion, *L'Idole et la Distance*, pp. 15–45.

18 Ibid., pp. 45–106.

19 Plato, *Phaedo*, 968–90.

20 See Edward Booth, *Aristotelian Aporetic Ontology in Islamic and Christian thinkers* (Cambridge University Press, Cambridge, 1983).

21 Courtine, *Suarez et le Système de Métaphysique*, pp. 436–57, 521–38.

22 Pierre Hadot, 'Dieu comme Acte d'Être dans le Néoplatonisme. A propos des Théories d'E. Gilson sur la Métaphysique de l'Exode', in *Dieu et L'Etre: Exégèses d'Exode 3.14 et de Coran 20.11–24* (Études Augustiniennes, Paris, 1978).

23 Marion, *God Without Being*, 'Preface to the English Edition', pp. xix–xxv; and Jean-Luc Marion, 'The Essential Incoherence of Descartes' Definition of Divinity', in *Essays on Descartes' Meditations*, ed. A. O. Rorty (California University Press, Berkeley, 1986), pp. 297–338.

24 See John Milbank, 'Can a Gift be Given?', in *Modern Theology*, 2:1 (January 1995), 119–61.

25 Heidegger, 'What is Metaphysics', in *Basic Writings*, pp. 109–10.

26 Marion, *Réduction et Donation*, p. 297; Marion, *God Without Being*, pp. 104–7.

27 Marion, *Prolégomènes*, pp. 45–67, 71–88.

28 Christoph Schönborn, *L'Icône du Christ* (Cerf, Paris, 1986), pp. 127, 217–74.

29 'De "La Mort de Dieu" aux Noms Divins', in Vergôte et al., *L'Etre et Dieu*, pp. 125–6.

30 Marion, *God Without Being*, 'Preface', p. xxiii.

31 Thomas Aquinas, *In Metaphysica*, Prologue.

32 See Edouard Weber, 'Eckhart et L' 'Ontothéologisme': Histoire et Conditions d'une Rupture', in Emilie zum Brunn et al., *Maître Eckhart à Paris: Une Critique Médiévale de l'Ontothéologie* (P.U.F., Paris, 1984) 79–83.

33 Marion, *God Without Being*, pp. 39–42.

34 See Catherine Pickstock, 'Asyndeton: Syntax and Insanity: A Study of the Revision of the Nicene Creed', *Modern Theology*, 10 (4 October 1994) and *Seraphic Voices* (manuscript in preparation), chapter 2. This is a book version of her Cambridge Ph.D. thesis, *The Sacred Polis*.

35 Alain de Libera, *Le Problème de L'Etre chez Maître Eckhart: Logique et Métaphysique de L'Analogie* (Cahiers de la Revue de Théologie et de Philosophie 4, Geneva, 1980); zum Brunn et al., *Maître Eckhart à Paris*.

36 See Eckhart, Parisian Question number 1: *Utrum in Deo sit idem esse et intelligere*, trans. A. A. Maurer *Parisian Questions and Prologues* (Pontifical Institute of Mediaeval Studies, Toronto, 1974), pp. 43–50. Or see zum Brunn et al., *Maître Eckhart à Paris*, pp. 176–87 for the Latin original plus French translation and notes.

37 Parisian Question number 3: *Rationes Equardi*, Maurer, pp. 55–67; or see zum Brunn et al., *Maître Eckhart à Paris*, pp. 200–23.

38 Eckhart, 'Prologues to the *Opus Tripartitum*', General Prologue, Maurer, pp. 85–6.

39 Hans Urs von Balthasar, *The Glory of the Lord*, vol. V, trans. Oliver Davies et al. (T. & T. Clark, Edinburgh, 1989), pp. 29–31.

40 Eckhart, *Prologues*, General Prologue, Maurer, p. 79; A. de Libera, *Le Problème de l'Etre*.

41 Eckhart, *Prologues*, Prologue to the Book of Propositions, Maurer, pp. 100–4; Parisian Question No. I, Maurer, pp. 49–50; zum Brunn et al., *Maître Eckhart à Paris*, pp. 165–6.

42 Eckhart, *Commentary on the Book of Exodus*, Maurer, p. 110; Augustine, *De Trinitate*, VIII, 2.

43 This was precisely Marion's *own* earlier argument against Levinas. See Marion, *L'Idole et la Distance*, pp. 264–9.

44 Gregory of Nyssa, 'Against Eunomius', in *The Library of the Nicene and Post-Nicene Fathers*, 2nd series, vol. V. *Gregory of Nyssa*, eds Henry Ware and Phillip Schaff (Parker, Oxford, 1893), Book I, section 8.

45 See *Dieu et L'Etre*: essays by Harl, Nautin, Madec and zum Brunn, pp. 87–167; Vergôte et al., *L'Etre et Dieu*, 'Epilogue' by Dominique Bourg, pp. 215–44; Dominique Dubarle, 'Essai sur l'Ontologie Théologale de St Augustin' in *Dieu Avec l'Etre* (Beauchesne, Paris, 1986), pp. 167–258.

46 Bonaventure, *Itinerarium Mentis in Deum*, 5 and 6.

47 See Emilie zum Brunn, St *Augustine: Being and Nothingness* (Paragon, New York, 1988).

48 Marion, *God Without Being*, pp. 80–2ff.

49 Aquinas, *In Librum de Divinis Nominibus Expositio* 635 (Caramello, p. 235).

50 Aquinas, S.T. 1 a Q. 5 a 2.

51 See Paul Vignaux, 'Pour situer dans l'école une question de Maître Eckhart', in zum Brunn et al., *Maître Eckhart à Paris*, pp. 141–54. And see Balthasar, *The Glory*, p. 50.

52 Marion, *Réduction et Donation*, p. 304.

53 Marion, *Sur le Prisme Métaphysique de Descartes*, pp. 338–69; Vincent Carraud 'La Généalogie de la Politique: Pascal', *in Communio*, no. IX. 3 (May–June 1984), pp. 26–37.

54. S.T.II.II.Q. 35 a 3 resp. Marion cites this passage (*God Without Being*, p. 135) yet does not reflect that if, for Aquinas, *accidie* is essentially boredom about Charity (the gift) as much or more than it is boredom about being, then the sensation of melancholy or awareness of vanity is not neutrally 'transitional' in Christian thought as it could be for paganism. It is rather the intrusion of sin under the mask of reflectiveness and profundity, even if its admitted negativity *can be* the occasion for repentance.

55 Marion, *God Without Being*, p. 3.

56 F. W. J. Schelling, *On the History of Modern Philosophy*, trans. Andrew Bowie (Cambridge University Press, Cambridge, 1994), pp. 54–6.

57 See Antoine Delzant, 'Rédemption et Ontologie', in Vergôte et al., *L'Etre et Dieu*, pp. 81–103.

58 See Jean-Luc Marion, 'Le Phénomène saturé', in Courtine, *Phénoménologie et Théologie*, pp. 79–128. See also John Milbank, 'Sublimity: The Modern Transcendent', in Paul Morris and Paul Heelas, eds., *Religion After Modernity* (Blackwell, Oxford, 1997).

59 See Marcel Detienne, *Les Maîtres de la Verité dans la Grèce Archaique* (Maspero, Paris, 1967); Gilles Deleuze and Felix Guattari, *Qu'est-ce que la Philosophie* (Editions de Minuit, Paris, 1991), pp. 38–60. See also Catherine Pickstock, *Seraphic Voices*, chapter 1.

60 See Pickstock, *ibid*.

Logos

3

Pleonasm, Speech and Writing

1 Warburton

It is hard to imagine a professor at the École Normale Supérieure reading, with mounting excitement, the latest work by one of the present episcopal bench of the Church of England. One should of course be less surprised to discover that a book by one of their eighteenth-century forebears has been a stimulus on the recent French philosophical scene. The work in question is *The Divine Legation of Moses*, written by William Warburton, Bishop of Gloucester and literary controversialist, in 1738. It was first set upon by Frenchmen in 1744, when the section of the work dealing with the origin of language was removed from its original theological context and translated by Leonard des Malpeines as the *Essai sur les Hieroglyphes des Egyptiens*. Warburton's subsequent influence on thought concerning language has been compared with that of Saussure in our own day; it is felt at many places in the *Encyclopédie*, and in the writings of Condillac and Rousseau. With the revival of interest in the problematic of the origin of language in the climate of post-structuralism, Malpeines' edition was republished in Paris in 1977, smothered with critical commentary by Patrick Tort and Jacques Derrida.[1] For the latter Warburton has proved a significant influence.

In what follows I am going to give an outline of Warburton's thoughts concerning the origin of language in the original context of his concern with biblical exegesis. Then I shall describe what is made of his reflections by the post-structuralists. Finally, I will call in not one but three samaritans, intellectually alien for Warburton in his own century, whose insights may yet rescue him from his twentieth-century predicament.

My research students Catherine Pickstock and Phillip Blond have influenced the revision of this essay in the direction of more emphasis upon, respectively, orality and embodiment. I am also grateful to Alison Milbank for discussions concerning the sublime and 'graveyard meditation' in English tradition.

Warburton was a Christian apologist described by John Henry Newman as a prime example of a thinker who is highly ingenious without possessing true creative inspiration. But the ingenuity is real: though most of Warburton's speculations are ultimately crass, just a few of them are epoch-making. The general outline of the *Divine Legation* comes under the first category. The deists had proposed that the paucity of reference to human immortality in the Old Testament was an argument against Divine revelation; Warburton sets out to prove that, on the contrary, the lack of a 'natural' sanction for law and morality in the shape of rewards and punishments in the after-life confirms the extraordinary character of the Hebrew religion and polity. Of course there is real historical insight here, but it is ruined by Warburton's crudely positivistic contention that the Hebrew theocracy had its sanctions through a direct providential administration of rewards and punishments in this present life on earth.

Warburton shares with the deists an absolute distinction between eternal truths and contingent facts or historical dispensations. Revelation, because it is more than a 'republication of the religion of nature' has to be considered under the second category. The theologian must *demonstrate* revelation by isolating an absolutely determinate content occurring outside the 'course of nature'. But such a demonstration will only work if it is exhaustive, and thus *The Divine Legation* becomes a 'perfect encyclopaedia'[2] comprising an account of antique culture in its entirety, a theory of knowledge, and a political philosophy. Furthermore, Warburton's procedure is that of the legal advocate who constantly concedes his opponent's point (as for example that the Old Testament contains no doctrine of an after-life) only to show that it leads to an opposite conclusion from the one supposed. This often requires revision of received opinion in the form of lengthy digressions whose intrinsic significance constantly rival that of the book's ostensible theme.

It is with the most important of these digressions that we are here concerned. Warburton concedes the antiquity and independence of Egyptian religion and culture as a prelude to arguing for the independence and integrity of that of the Hebrews. But as this concession is to be now a necessary part of his 'proof', he must establish the integral development of the Egyptians and their isolation from 'Mosaic' influence *more strongly* than his opponents had done, while equally stressing the freedom of Mosaic religion – which Warburton characterizes supremely in terms of its lack of a cult of an after-life – from Egyptian aspirations. At this time Egyptology meant primarily interpretation of the hieroglyphs; and once the hieroglyphic question was mooted, the same current *episteme* demanded a consideration of the origin and nature of language in general.

The dominant, received view of hieroglyphics was still the hermetic and neoplatonic one represented by Athanasius Kircher: namely that they were depositories of a hidden wisdom known only to priests and initiates, the same wisdom that is represented by Mosaic revelation. Warburton rejected this view, because it smacked of an anti-rationalist 'enthusiasm' and also because it was usually linked with a syncretistic legitimation of the pagan mysteries. He proposed instead a highly complex account of the evolution of Egyptian script, which I present here in its barest outlines.

Warburton suggests that there was for all men an original 'language of action' consisting of gestures, pointing and mimicry. This language is a kind of 'pictography', closer to *writing* than to speech. Along with Vico, Warburton thus becomes the first thinker to question the commonsensical view that writing is a secondary, conventional affair compared to speaking. Furthermore he considers that at every consequent stage of evolution, there is a strict parallelism between forms of writing and forms of speaking, with the *former* playing the leading role. After the pictographic stage comes the *hieroglyphic*, in which a conventional abridgement of a natural event is used to stand for that event; the equivalent mode of discourse is the *fable* or myth. With astonishing perspicuity Warburton suggests that what we should now call the 'mytheme', or fictional unit, historically precedes the 'phoneme' or alphabetic unit.

At the next stages further economies intervene. First, the 'Egyptian' hieroglyph becomes the 'Chinese' *ideograph*, and during this transition (which Warburton marks by a further subdivision between the earlier *curiological*, and the later *symbolic* hieroglyph) the characteristic mode of discourse is now the direct conscious comparison or *similitude*. Finally, the ideographical marks become so remote from their mimetic roots that it becomes natural to relate them to speech, which is more commonly in use, rather than the other way around. At the ideographical and the last *alphabetic* stage speech is dominated by *metaphors*, which Warburton decadently regards as abbreviated similitudes.

However, he has a far more dynamic view of this evolution than would appear from the formal account given above. The tropes of rhetoric are invoked to describe the historical transitions. The pictographs, Warburton naively regards as literal description; figurative elements only intrude at the subsequent stages. First of all, the hieroglyphs substitute part for whole through *synecdoche*, and then effect for cause through *metonymy*. At a third stage one thing is substituted for another across a synchronic space by *metaphor*, which here has a specific rather than generic meaning. These three figures mediate the transformations of writing and discourse. But the connections made by metaphor become more and more remote until finally *catachresis*, or forgetting of the original connection occurs, and this is commonplace in both the ideographic and alphabetic phases.

The intrusion of metaphor, whose role is less easily understood in terms of economic convenience than either synecdoche or metonymy, is rightly identified by Patrick Tort as the key moment in Warburton's entire scheme. For at this point the Egyptians and indeed all pagan races start to obscure their own history in the very process of *enacting* and *thereby* recording it through writing. The more gratuitous character of metaphor is, Warburton considers, in refined societies merely an occasion for agreeable ornament, but in its primitive inception it risked subversion of the 'natural', instrumental, character of the first tropes. At first the primitive passion for comparative classification is on the side of discovery and communication: 'For this method of contriving tropical hieroglyphics would of itself produce refinement and nice enquiry into the more hidden and abstruse properties of things.'[3] And a characteristic curiological hieroglyph would be the *Diana multimammia* for the world, which exposes a clear chain of inference. But when we are faced with a symbolic hieroglyph, such as a winged globe with a serpent issuing from it for 'nature', genesis is more a matter for conjecture. As metaphor became more remote, catachresis set in, and the signs started to take on a mysterious, occult, quality which suggested a new function for writing: concealment.

Although this obscuration originates in the hieroglyphic phase, it is *worsened* in the ideographic and alphabetic ones. Its consequence is the mystification of the entire culture. For in addition to the 'natural' reason for the primacy of writing already described, Warburton averts to its social and political function as recording the succession of generations, preserving law and establishing geographical and social boundaries – a culture-engendering role which is less easily fulfilled by spoken words which expire as soon as they are uttered. As the innocent function of the tropes is subverted by metaphor, and the genesis of written signs forgotten, so the entire range of cultural manifestations which they constitute is alienated from its human origins and ascribed to the obscure work of the gods. And Warburton, following Sanchuniathon the 'Phoenecian historian' recorded by Eusebius and Philo of Byblos, regards this alienation of human inventions and supremely of writing, as the real conceptual origin of the pagan deities.

In this enterprise Warburton is clearly following in the patristic tradition of exposing the pagan gods as the product of lies and self-deceit. But his manner of doing so is peculiarly critical and subtle, especially in that he also identifies this process of mystification as the source of political power. Following the clues provided by the myth of Thoth or Hermes as reported in Plato's *Phaedrus*, Warburton relates the occult character of written or *epistolary* language to its political purpose in allowing secret messages to be sent by kings, and in surrounding laws with a terrifying aura which ensures obedience. None of these subterfuges, Warburton notes, are carried out deliberately: for a reified sign to become a source of power, the powerful must be half-deceived themselves.

Nonetheless, the effect of mystification wears off in time. Abbreviations of the original pictographs calls attention to the signifier as separate from the signified and this encourages idolatry; but at the same time the increasingly *conventional* character of the signifier betrays it as a mere instrument in the service of the signified. In the course of time the populace comes to see that the mysterious written marks depend entirely on an arbitrary pattern of usage established by the priest-kings. But just when the politico-religious spell was about to be broken, the Egyptian rulers, *uniquely*, developed a new ruse: this was the translation of their language of power *back* into the script of the once innocent hieroglyphs, now all indecipherable relics (thanks to the forgetting of the 'natural' purpose of the tropes). Warburton dubs this extra language *hierogrammatical* and points out the irony that when Kircher claimed to interpret the hieroglyphs at a historical distance, he was in fact merely repeating the final self-deception of the Egyptians themselves.

With the hierogrammatical system the Egyptian priests practised the art of divination, especially of the images of dreams, whose obscurity relates to the lost order of the original, 'natural', script. In place of the 'natural' meaning of the figurative pictures in dreams the priests deployed an *oneirocritic* which determined their significance according to the new arbitrary rules for manipulating the hieroglyphs. They become thereby virtually self-fulfilling prophets, because the grammar in which they read the future was the very same grammar in which they wrote and thereby determined their future symbolic actions. In consequence mastery of script meant ability simultaneously to predict and control the future: the source Warburton holds of both pagan law and pagan technology.

In this entire scheme it is possible to see the whole modern critique of culture *in nuce*. By examining a remote primitive society whose religion he is bound to regard with suspicion, Warburton suggests in outline all the analyses of Feuerbach, Marx and Freud concerning such phenomena as projection, displacement, alienation, reification and class conflict. Moreover he integrates them around the central phenomenon of language in a manner that anticipates the twentieth rather than the nineteenth century.

However, Warburton exhibits an apologetic dilemma: his critique of pagan religion and culture can and will be used as a critique of Christian religion also. In general he safeguards himself against this only by taking a quite monstrously fideist view of revelation. Nonetheless, he applies his theory of language to the Bible also. He takes another stand against a Hermetic or Kabbalist position by denying along with Locke, Dante in the *Commedia* and Gregory of Nyssa in *Contra Eunomius*[4] (which he cites, as had earlier authors to the same purpose) that Adam spoke the real divine creative language mystically related to the hidden nature of things. (In his fine polemic against the *Divine Legation*,[5] William Law sought to restore this thesis, though he modified it through a stress that the divine language was graciously *added* to Adam, constituting the *Imago Dei* as participatory growth towards the divine life conceived qualitatively and metaphysically; whereas for Warburton the *Imago* was a fixed rational–linguistic capacity, possessing a mere abstract and semi-utilitarian certainty of a future immortality). The statement 'and whatever the man called every living creature that was its name', is taken by Warburton, after Locke, as meaning merely that Adam developed his language according to a rational sequence, in response to clear sense perception. At first this language was 'extremely narrow' and had to be progressively developed by means of the 'natural' tropes. But Warburton combines this naturalism with the crudest interventionism by allowing that the first elements of language must have been directly revealed to Adam simply to speed things up, and thereby ensure that the first man did not begin his life as a semi-beast.

However, the real question is: how do the Hebrews escape the mystifications of the pagans? Warburton has no real answer. He does indeed make legitimate apologetic usage of the 'language of action' by asserting that when the prophets use extravagant symbolic gestures – so dangerously reminiscent of the 'enthusiasts' of his own day – they are simply speaking the language of the times. All the same, he finds it impossible to reduce all the obscure symbolism of the Bible to a series of purely instrumental tropes, and notes that the Hebrews are peculiarly addicted to 'historical allegory' – a diachronic chain of allusion and reference. But this he accounts for in terms of a positivistic view of prophecy and in doing so makes God sound like the most monstrous Egyptian tyrant of all: uttering obscure forecasts in order to keep the Hebrews in further subjugation to his law and to ensure that the Christian revelation be later supported by reliable proofs.

If then, it is Warburton's destiny to have his thoughts described on the back of a French paperback in the late twentieth century as *une étonnante ouverture logique au materialisme*, he really had only himself to blame. Derrida and Tort press home the implications remorselessly. First of all, however, Tort points out Warburton's mistake in not realizing that the very *first* writing must have been *metaphoric* (in both generic and specific senses), because the very possibility of a system of signs is the evocation of one thing signified only through another thing signifying. Once this revision is allowed, Warburton's writings may be read as not merely materialist, but also drastically subversive, as tending to suggest that all language, all culture, inevitably involves those concealments, subterfuges and acts of political violence which emerge through specific metaphor as the very matrices of human meaning. Warburton is thereby recruited to the anti-humanist fashion which denies that 'Man' as a cultural product can ever be free of metaphysical mystification.

This view, as expounded by Jacques Derrida,[6] centres upon the origin of language. Derrida regards writing as the primary force in the origin and development of language for the kinds of reason that we have encountered in Warburton, though it must be stressed he defines writing as any sort of signifying 'trace' whatsoever. Speech, according to Derrida, tends to make us imagine that all meaning is fully 'present', in the manner that the speaking self and her or his interlocutor appears to be. It is *this* phenomenon which encourages the further delusion that there are ideas or things present to us before and outside the signifying system. Even in the case of alphabetic writing, but supremely with pictography, we do not so easily forget the dialectic of presence and *absence*, in which the present signifier relates to an absent signified, which may be past, future, or spatially remote. In particular, written signs (a category which here *includes* oral poetry, which is very pictorial and remains with us like a script through its memorable rhythm) are given the task of preserving temporal continuity. The inscribed signifier carries the signified as both the re-tension of the past and the pro-tension or projection of the future. This is the grammatical context for possible human action. But however far back we look into the human past we must always posit such a signifying trace. Derrida refers to C. S. Peirce's contention that a sign, being a categorical relation, can only be clarified by another sign and so on *ad infinitum*. We can never isolate an original meaning before the rule of signs, and therefore if any cultural element is mooted as the *first* or *basic* element which mediates the transition from nature to culture – as for example, Hobbes nominates 'self-interest' – then this is an entirely arbitrary preference, ignoring the fact that such an element only has *sense* within the play of signification. There is no such natural origin of language or culture, but only a paradoxical 'cultural origin of culture' (as much transcendental as historical) in the original metaphor, or the original relation of present signifier to absent signified. Any 'first' thing for Derrida has consequently already manifested itself through something else, and this is the 'supplement at the origin' or the original *difference*. Difference, he believes or *différance* (to suggest the power of writing to 'store up' and thereby *defer* what it signifies) is the only real transcendental category in *either* the Kantian or the scholastic sense, although this very insight undermines both notions.

For Derrida, difference dissolves language into total equivocation, and this is the prime source of his philosophical scepticism. But there is another source also. Derrida believes that difference ends the Platonic domination of Western culture in which the illusion of the fully present idea encourages the belief that we can grasp reality in its *totality*. In this tradition any realization of the idea in the concrete sign is taken as a lapse from an original completeness. Derrida is anti-Platonic in the sense that he takes the signifying trace to be an absolutely original moment – an emanation *in arche* as it were – but he secretly *remains* Platonic in holding that this imaging is a 'lapse', involving violent deception and concealment: *'Différance* produces what it forbids, makes possible the very thing that it makes impossible'.[7] This further dimension to his scepticism might be described as a kind of Valentinian gnosis, in that it identifies creation with fall and makes both inevitable, though resignation to aesthetic *jouissance* is the nearest that he gets to a motif of redemptive 'return'. Alternatively it might be called unregenerate Hegelianism in that the moment of cultural illusion is not only a fact, but a *necessary* fact: 'the movement of the trace is necessarily occulted, it produces itself as self-occultation'.[8]

It seems that Derrida is not fully aware that the primordiality of metaphor is a separate thesis from the primordiality of mystification. Despite the posited *hiatus* between nature and culture, Derrida only concedes a cultural space in an ambiguous sense, because it is always established by the trace as the illusion of a present, *natural*, plenitude of meaning. No doubt this 'gnosticism' is linked with Derrida's primary scepticism in taking the inescapability of the sign to imply unrestrained equivocation, but *neither* of these positions – the one ethical, the other gnoseological – can really be maintained on the basis of theory alone, but must appeal to 'experience', or purely subjective judgement. Derrida is still, perhaps, too dependent on the judgements of Freudian psychoanalysis (regarding the necessity of mechanisms of concealment) but as he is far from a naturalist view that there is a 'real' unalterable content of the unconscious or real, essential cause of suppression, he would presumably concede that psychoanalysis alone cannot be decisive. The question is whether the human signifying process really *is* or can apodictically be shown to be irrevocably governed by violence and deception in its innermost grammar. Does the uncertainty of meaning involved in reference to an indeterminate absent demand that we suppress that absence in order to have a meaning at all? Or can we elaborate a grammar which is at least plausibly presentable as a metaphorical but also analogical and essentially non-mystifying process?

At this point we return to Warburton. Derrida's gnostic identification of creation with fall leads him to suppose that Warburton's Christian belief in an original innocence before the fall is the essential cause of his affirmation of an original linguistic literalism as well as a state of political non-deception. He cites Malebranche's view that the pre-lapsarian language was non-imagistic, but Malebranche's metaphysics suffer grave 'Platonic' distortions from the Christian point of view, and in fact Platonism was entirely responsible for this tradition concerning the language of Adam. In the eighteenth century itself, some thinkers, notably Vico and Hamann, affirmed the metaphoricity of *paradisal* (Adamic) speech on the basis of a better grasp of the theology of creation. And even in the case of Warburton, the fact of created difference, with its tie to the use of material *means*, is firmly distinguished from the post-fall possibility of moral discord. The literalism which Warburton accords to Adam's first utterances needs only to be ascribed to his Lockean philosophy, not at all to a doctrine of pre-lapse from perfection.

Through this error Derrida and Tort manage subtly to read into Warburton an implicit but unadmitted tendency to see the linguistic process itself as the extra-human source of error and violence. For Derrida it is ultimately inexplicable that the 'powerless' trace yet 'forces force' but fruitless to enquire any further. It is true that the *content* of error for Warburton is linguistic; reification of signs leading to idolatry. It is true also that error is accorded a certain positive historical role in that superstition keeps the masses in subjection. But this for Warburton is only necessary in consequence of the fall; a disease of the human will responsible for the tendency to metaphysical obscuration. Moreover, the comprehensiveness of Warburton's cultural suspicion has a different, but very explicit cause, overlooked by Tort and Derrida: the critique of pagan idolatry.

Idolatry is the consequence of the fall, and therefore Warburton's critique of metaphysics shows no tendency to extend itself to Lockean 'simple ideas' of abstractions, which are there right from the beginnings of language, and are represented univocally by arbitrary marks. And to have achieved such a critique, the Bishop would not have needed to abandon the imagining of paradise, but rather would have needed to reconceive original speech as metaphorical. However, the true source of Warburton's originality is not his incipient materialist reductionism, but rather his perception of the degree to which, *via* language, a religion might dominate a culture, and so illusory gods involve also something approaching an illusory humanity. Yet herein he remains essentially in line with Jewish and Christian tradition; the critique of idolatry always involved something more than the natural suspicion of one religion concerning others, but implied that the true God was most neglected by the 'religious' tendency to make absolute and alien some valued object within culture which is always humanly engendered. Warburton wished to contrast the esoteric politically deceptive 'religion of names' (DL, VI, 300) with the exoteric politically just and open religion of a God who is ultimately nameless.

So perhaps Warburton deserves rescue after all. What is required is a non-fideistic presentation of the ancient Hebrew and Christian religions as a *metaphoric but non-equivocal, non-deceptive grammar* which can legitimately criticize and partially redeem the pagan grammar also. To take non-deception first; can we connect opposition to idolatry with a historical writing that does not necessarily obscure the events it both constitutes and records in law, narrative and prophecy?

2 Lowth

Warburton's theological opponent, Robert Lowth, Bishop of Oxford and then of London, published (in Latin) in 1758, his seminal *Lectures on the Sacred Poetry of the Hebrews*.[9] It is evidence of the lack of interest of English theology today in its own tradition that there exists no major study of this work, described by Meinecke as one of the prime sources for later historicism, and by E. S. Shaffer as vital for the development of Biblical criticism.[10] After its reprinting a few years later at Gottingen it exercised a great influence in Germany, but it is interesting to note that while Herder praised Lowth for attempting to isolate the cultural peculiarities of the Hebrews, he thought that his enquiry was too *technical*, failing to penetrate the *spirit* of an age. It is, however, Lowth's strictly *formal* attempt to position Hebrew poetry *vis-à-vis* the categories of classical rhetoric and poetics rather than simply a proto-Romantic trust in empathy or pure subjectivity which leads him to a new depth of cultural analysis. In the later period, such formalism came to be gradually eclipsed, and consequently the true character of Lowth's contribution was quickly lost from sight.

For another reason also, it is hard to categorize Lowth. His formal, aesthetic treatment of the Old Testament opened up the possibility of accounting for it (without recourse to the wilder absurdities of deist slander) in purely human terms. However Hans Frei was wrong to conclude that because Lowth is not concerned to expound the *truth* of the scriptures, nor to establish their factual veracity, the work is theologically neutral.[11] Rather it is clear that Lowth regards the formal, cultural aspects as in some measure *internal* to theology because so often he relates them to doctrinal points (particularly concerning the after-life, allegory and prophecy: see below). In the introduction the purpose of poetry is defined quite conventionally as *prodesse delectando*, socially useful because of its ability to move emotions. However, in the body of the text, a much more original view is expounded: here we are told that the entire realm of nature supplies the raw material of poetry. The 'poet' is responsible for man's first cognitive move: 'the mind of man is that mirror of Plato, which as he turns about at pleasure, and directs to a different point of view, he creates another sun, other stars, planets, animals and even another self'.[12] Because man is himself structured in structuring his world, and because therefore his relationship to the contents of his own consciousness is in some measure comparative, reflective and creative, it is a natural extension of the primary operations of understanding that we form 'conjectures . . . concerning the manners, affections, conceptions of others'. In this manner poetics includes a hermeneutics, but the objects of nature continue to furnish the prime stock of what we take to be common to all men; poetry, therefore, must convey through images its conjectures about men's ideas and emotions.

This poetics reveals a characteristically 'Baroque' conception in which a Renaissance account of man's participation in the Divine creative power is continued in more cautious and orthodox form. Ideas that man occupies a demiurgic position in the cosmos are forgotten, and instead there is some return to the Horatian, humanist themes of the fourteenth and fifteenth centuries of the poet as the founder of the city and of culture. However, Christian metaphysics tended to turn this into a more absolute origination, assuming less of a 'Platonic' obedience to a fixed set of preceding ideas, and so a relatively autonomous space for culture and history was opened to view. Lowth inherits a tradition of regarding the grammar and rhetoric of the Bible as unique which stretches far back into the Middle Ages; but now this is ascribed to the peculiar *poeticality* of the Hebrews, and it is his *metaphysical* conception of the Hebrews as co-creators which opens up for the Germans the 'critical' space in which the Bible could be viewed as a human work. (The idea that 'modern biblical scholarship' began when an already established 'historical science' was applied to the Bible, is therefore an illusion.)

Why should the Hebrews have been considered the supreme poets? According to Lowth, the original 'poetic' speech of human beings was characterized, in addition to its inventive and conjectural powers, by an extraordinary mnemonic capacity, whereby the 'minutest circumstances' could be retained in the memory and what deserved to be preserved was 'adorned with a jocund and captivating style'.[13] Where Warburton emphasized the positioning and preserving capacity of *literal* written marks, Lowth insisted rather on the power of oral anaphora, involving a *repetition with variety*, as opposed to written literalness. Hence primitive laws, he notes, were originally sung, and many poems were denominated *nomoi*. Alongside this facility of recollection, early poetic speech combined 'a style and expression directly prompted by nature itself', which was 'the true and express image of a mind violently agitated'. The wildness of nature and the spontaneity of spirit were co-expressed:

> the most inmost conceptions are displayed, rushing together in one turbid stream, without order or connection. Hence sudden exclamations, frequent interrogations, apostrophes even to inanimate objects; for to those who are violently agitated them-

selves, the universal nature of things seems under a necessity of being affected with similar emotions.[14]

Here that which is 'inward' was directly manifest as outward appearance, motions of the body in dancing and song accompanying the poetic, metaphoric invocation of the motions of nature.

Now in both these respects, first, mimetic capacity (internally reflected in poetic form as 'pleonasm') and, second, spontaneous merging of expressive spirit with nature ('apostrophe'), Lowth considers the Hebrews to be the most exemplary, the most purely primitive, and in a sense, materialist. First of all, as is well known, Lowth discovered that it was repetition-with-variety or *pleonasm* (often manifested in 'parallelism' or a succession of paired double-utterances) which rendered Hebrew poetry poetry (rather than rhyme, metre, etc.); yet what is more interesting than this, is his claim that such a principle rendered it also *supremely* poetic. Its loyalty to the principle of repetition ensured that it preserved, more than Greek poetry, a *culturally central* function; hence the poet remained, in Israel, 'the recorder of events, the praeceptor of morals, the historian of the past and the prophet of the future'.[15] And as a result, the Hebrews achieved *constancy* (yet not a literal, identical one): they 'maintained the same opinion throughout all the ages'.[16] Second, Lowth identifies a purer poetic spontaneity or 'apostrophic' capacity in the Old Testament than with the Greeks. In a word, its poetry was more 'sublime', it more manifested a singular subjectivity, more permitted the eruption to the surface of naked emotions, and adopted more direct expressive means, using the most natural, universal images, which, nonetheless, remained entirely *figurative*, and not simply literal in character. (The entire thematic of 'sublime' rhetoric, from Boileau onwards, insists that simpler ornaments are more successful and in fact *more* metaphorically transporting.)[17] Hence Lowth emphasizes what he calls (borrowing from Cicero) the *sententious* style of Hebrew poetry: exemplified most of all in its 'brevity', supplying 'a more energetic and pointed effect', which is simple and direct and yet just for that reason results in fascinating 'obscurity' – that is to say invocation of a concrete, yet general, picture which might accommodate many different readings.

The two aspects of 'heightened poeticality', namely oral repetition and 'redundancy' (pleonasm) and oral brevity (apostrophe and sententiousness) – are, for Lowth, fused in the Hebrews' preference for imagery taken from common life, from the most general and habitual circumstances of a primitive *agricultural* existence. And here not only do the same images recur, but also the same metaphorical applications of them were used again and again: the Hebrews 'preserved one constant track and manner in the use and accommodation of them to the subject'.[18] This permitted an equivalence 'in the parabolic style' of the constant use of certain words for 'abstruse and refined ideas' in later, more prosaic language. However, poetic constancy was supremely sublime in allowing an 'apostrophic' fusion of the human and the natural; and here again Hebrew poetry was more poetic, for Lowth, than that of the Greeks: he contrasts Isaiah's direct comparison of armies of men to a corn-drag (Isaiah 12:15–16) with Homer's much less unnerving comparison of horses trampling men, with horses trampling down the corn.[19]

The constancy and naturalness of the Hebrew poetic *topoi* is seen by Lowth to have direct relevance to the main theme of Warburton's *Divine Legation*: namely the Hebrews and the after-life. From the evidence of their poetry he concludes that the Hebrews *did* have some imagination of a future world, but that it tended to be more limited and gloomy (though also more 'sublime') than that of the pagans. Lowth then beats Warburton at his own game by tying this observation to the philosophy of language. At a very primitive stage, he says, only the physical geography of the burial grounds would provide images in which the possibility of an after-life could be mooted. The Hebrews keep up this bleak view (Ezekiel 31:22–32) because more than the pagans they tended to preserve the first 'pictorial' character of language in memory at every stage, however alphabetic the dominant cultural means, and it is this very *poetic* dominance which ensures a *certain ontological faithfulness*:

> The poets of other nations amidst all their fictions, have yet returned a congenial picture of the habitations of the dead . . . But how grand and magnificent a scene is depicted by the Hebrew poets from the same materials, in which their deceased heroes and kings are seen to advance from the earth! Figure to yourself a vast, dreary, dark, sepulchral cavern, where the kings of the nation lie, each upon his bed of dust, the arms of each beside him, his sword under his head, and the graves of their numerous hosts round about them. Behold! the king of Babylon introduced, they all rise and go forth to meet him; and receive him as he approaches! 'Art thou also come down to us? Art thou become like unto us? Art thou cut down and withered in thy strength, O thou destroyer of the nations?'[20]

Here Lowth, for all that he is less rationalist, and more orthodox than Warburton, reveals himself as, nonetheless, more naturalist and less fideist. For, in the case of the Bishop of London, unlike the Bishop of Gloucester, there is no providential mystery concerning the lack of speculation about an after-life in ancient Israel. On the contrary, there *was* such a speculation, but it remained minimal, and 'poetic'. Far from it being 'natural', as *both* the Deists and Warburton imagined, to have a developed view of the immortality of the soul, Lowth realizes that such conjectures in non-Hebrew culture were a result of their greater rational reflexivity. Although he considers (against Warburton) that the Hebrews did, indeed, possess such a belief,

> they had no clear idea or perception by which they might explain where or in what manner it [the immortal soul] existed; and they were not possessed of that subtlety of language which enables men to speak with plausibility of subjects abstruse, and remote from the apprehension of the senses.[21]

As yet, their cultural resources permitted the Hebrews only a sensuous picture of the after-life, and there is no question, for Lowth, as for Warburton, of divine revelation speeding the cultural process up: instead, in a long tradition of thought *stretching back to the Middle Ages*, Lowth stresses that God does not transgress the natural order of human progress, but adapts economically to it.[22]

Also in keeping with his naturalism, Lowth did not need to invoke Warburton's notion that a direct divine governance was required to substitute for the lack of the sanctions of hell. In this episcopal debate, terror plays a lesser role for Lowth, since the Hebrews for him maintained their social and cultural unity in simple pastoral terms by maintaining 'an equality of lineage' which recalled always 'the same ancient stock'. Lack of rivalry served for order in this 'nation of husbandmen and shepherds', for which 'we read of eminent persons called to the highest and most sacred offices; heroes, kings and prophets from the plough and from the stalls.'[23] Here is should be noted that unlike Warburton, Lowth considered that the oral, patriarchal order was, nonetheless, a full *polity*, exercising a form of sovereign sway.[24] Hence he is brought to task by the Bishop of Gloucester for allowing that the patriarchs already punished for the sin of idolatry, something which Warburton is only prepared to attach to the state with its written decrees under the imperative of Jehovah as a *deus ex machina*. Again, for Warburton, this is merely part of an extraordinary economy in the absence of the sanctions of an after-life, destined to disappear with the coming of Christianity. In consequence, he considers that to attach punishment for idolatry to a natural, patriarchal order, is to misconceive the extraordinary as the ordinary, and permit a general civil intolerance of religious deviance. Compared with Lowth, he is the more extreme Lockean, restricting political governance strictly to protection of life and property, whereas Lowth points out in response that even Locke placed some religious views and practices beyond the pale, despite the fact that Lowth himself most strenuously insists on the need for 'free debate', and the original and now revived co-belonging of Christianity with enlightenment.[25] For the Bishop of London, the banning of idolatry was a civic matter, since idolatry invoked of necessity certain moral evils and obnoxious rituals. In this obscure corner of their controversy one can see again how Warburton's rationalism, manifest here in a contractarian approach to political order as being beyond a state of nature, *correlates* with his willingness to entertain the notion of a similarly interruptive direct divine rule, whereas for Lowth *both* the political *and* worship are equally 'natural', and both develop equally from a patriarchal, pastoral condition. And for this relative Toryism of Lowth's, a grounding of politics in worship, state in Church, is no extraordinary arrangement, but something perpetual to human being itself.

How does Lowth's linguistic and political naturalism together with his 'ontological faithfulness' fully contrast with Warburton's theory of the primacy of writing? Supremely with respect to the Bishop of Gloucester's view that pictographs precede speech because of their gestural literalness, their link to *pointing*, and evasion of the moment of the oral cry of feeling which *manifests* nature rather than merely indicating it. Here it is writing that instils a 'metaphysics of presence', *speech* that enjoins a supplementary detour of reaction, or metaphoric 'taking as'. Hence Warburton posits as primitive and original (in contrast to Hebraic miraculous otherness, his fideist and *yet* rationalist thesis) the Egyptian pyramidal order of death, in which there is a direct, literal, written pointing towards and recording of a full life beyond, a spiritual elsewhere, which is yet a mere augmentation of what we know. Lowth, by contrast, as a true heir to the Miltonic tradition of 'sublime' graveyard meditation, posits as primitive and original the Hebrew poetic imaginative remaining with the stark subterranean reality of death, which is yet *less* literal in its metaphoric transposing of burial into an after-life darkly other to anything that we know. No marks point to this domain: its traces are rather in the rhythms of prophetic song, replete with apprehension, yet able also to effect the transformation of inert grave into figure of living divine promise.

The contrast between the two Bishops' views of language – as writing or as orality – can be generalized beyond the graveyard towards the whole of cultural life. For Warburton, pictographs were mere copies of physical things, and mental notions or modes, possessing a Cartesian or Lockean self-evidence, were from the first represented by arbitrary marks. For Lowth, to the contrary, as implied by his poetics, perception of the environment and projection of value spring up together. This idea was later well expressed by the German who inherited it from Lowth, Johann Georg Hamann, when he declared against Kant that space and time can be neither *a priori* forms of intuition, nor just empirically given to our understanding, because time was first grasped through music, and space through the first written, pictographic, poetry.

So for Lowth the common 'stock' of natural phenomena already referred to, in fact consists of culturally mediated phenomena, both usual like growth and decay, or extraordinary like the flood and the events of the Exodus. These together constituted a store of rhetorical *topoi*, or commonplaces, to which the Hebrews referred all that had or might happen to them.[26] He believed that the Hebrews were unique in always holding to such a *concrete* classification and in maintaining a daring but *consistent* pattern of reference to the *topoi* whereby they acquired in *cultural usage*, an enormous potential of meaning:

> There is indeed this difference between the sacred and profane writers, that among the latter we find frequent examples of metaphors taken from some remarkable person and event applied to some other event of character; but we never find from such facts a general or common image derived, which as an established mode of expression, is regularly applied to the illustration of similar objects, even to the designation of a universal or *unlimited* idea.[27]

The concrete *topos* supplies a universal which is open-ended, *and yet* manifestly tied to a particular history. It is this conception which supports Lowth's idea of the *mystical allegory*. Like Warburton he notes the Hebrew predilection for diachronic figuration, but elucidates this non-fideistically. In the 'mystical allegory', unlike any figure known to pagan antiquity, *both* the temporally separated poles of comparison are real natural–cultural events, and both poles cast light on each other, increasing the topical potential, without one being essentially a 'fictional' shell and the other the 'real' content:

> Sometimes the principal or figurative idea is exhibited to the attentive eye with a constant and equal light, and sometimes it unexpectedly glares upon us, and breaks forth with sudden and astonishing coruscations, like a flash of lightning bursting from the clouds. But the mode or form of this figure which possesses the most beauty and elegance is, when the two images equally conspicuous run, as it were, parallel through the whole poem, mutually illustrating and correspondent to each other. We may then perceive the vast disparity of the two images, and yet the continued harmony and agreement that subsists between them, the amazing resemblance as between near relations, in every feature and lineament, and the accurate analogy which is preserved, so that either may pass for the original whence the other was copied. New light is reflected upon the diction, and a degree of dignity and importance is added to the sentiments, whilst they gradually rise from humble to more elevated objects; from human to divine, till at length the great subject of the poem is placed in the most conspicuous light, and the composition attains the highest point of sublimity.[28]

For Lowth, this double play between two poles, in which *neither* pole is more literal (here his conception of Biblical allegory is more radical than that of the Middle Ages) rises finally to the tension between divine and human. What enables this most 'sublime' of oscillations is again precisely the Hebrew predilection for 'the imagery of nature', for natural powers and works, invoked by personifying apostrophe, which can stand equally for the divine or human spirit: 'a certain analogy being preserved in each'.[29] Much the same applies to imagery drawn from Hebrew rites, which remained close to a pastoral existence, and which formed 'one great and complicated allegory, to the study and observance of which, all possible diligence and attention were incessantly dedicated by those who were employed in the sacred offices'.[30] In both cases a 'natural' image 'easily admits that degree of ambiguity which appears essential to this figure', rendering it 'diversified and perspicuous, applicable to both senses'.[31] The 'degree of obscurity' resulting from the ungrounded meaning of reciprocal echo is then stretched out in a diachronic fashion, turning poetry into prophecy. Thus the mystical allegory 'described events in a manner exactly conformable to the intentions of prophecy; that is, in a dark, disguised and intricate manner, sketching out in a general way their form and outline, and seldom descending to minuteness of description, and exactness of detail'.[32]

Again, unlike Warburton, Lowth eschews an extrinsicist, positivist view of prophecy: prophetic fulfilment is no proof of extraneous divine intervention, but is rather in line with the 'natural' genesis of new meanings from topical founts through time. Here what is unique to the Hebrew mystical allegory, and what renders it 'prophetic', is the priority given to *future* exemplification of meaning opened out by the principle of reciprocal echo between two non-literal poles. Thus Lowth declares that whereas most figures are *obscured* by time, the prophetic receives thereby clarification: 'time, which darkens every other composition, elucidates it.'[33]

Lowth's account of orality as 'prophetic' is, therefore, in Derridean terms, 'supplementary', and indeed one can go further: by blending the principle of pleonasm with that of reciprocal diachronic echo, it is precisely Lowth (though he was no developed metaphysician) who *first intimated* supplementarity or non-identical repetition. From Lowth the thought is bequeathed via Hamann down to Kierkegaard himself, and thence to its post-structuralist retrieval. However, this retrieval so far refuses to reflect on the original insistence, up to and including Kierkegaard, that a pleonastic rhetoric (which to be valid must involve an 'amplifying', non-identical repetition) is peculiar to a Biblical construal of reality (and so implicitly, its 'ontology'). Moreover, the same tradition also recognized that this pleonastic practice was primarily an *oral* and *not* a written one, which precisely for that reason linked the necessary repetition of ideas in words to the 'prophetic' unfolding of always incompletely grasped *topoi* in time, through a series of performed human utterances. Far from the breath of speech fading here to the benefit of a spiritual, solipsistic intentional presence (which, Derrida intimates, speech *as a phenomenon* must necessarily do), it rather fades to make way for the arrival *both* of a new sign and a new speaker, or new speaking-event. This arrival grants to 'difference' *a known content* (though not a totalized one) whereas Derrida's written difference, defined by its possibility of surviving the death of every speaker, is necessarily a deferred difference, a difference that never arrives, that is therefore nothing, no-difference. For a regime of the primacy of writing is perforce a disembodied, ahistorical regime, in which *sign* does not finally decay along with its speaker; in which, therefore, sign is falsely hypostasized in abstraction from figured event, and construed as a 'pure value' which never can be, and is in consequence 'nothing'. Writing, as a practice, tends to abstract from occasion and context and to insinuate the illusion of ideality and identical repetition in apparent textual completeness and 'exact' reprintability, iterability. It is therefore more 'the text' and not as Derrida claims 'the voice' which appears (or has tended to appear in the Western construal of the text) to us as at once ideal and empirical.[34] Moreover, Derrida simply pursues (for deconstruction only reveals the essence of what it deconstructs) this idealism of the text to its logical conclusion: if the sign if not oral, if it is not also an embodied event with a certain concrete 'expression' of what it conveys, if it is not also something which dies, can be wiped out, forgotten, but is *defined* (as Derrida explicitly defines it)[35] by its survival of the death of the speaker, or of any empirical existence, then, as Catherine Pickstock has argued, it *is* death, *is* 'the impossible', is absolute deferral, is no-thing: the ideal. The absolute stasis, formalism, obscurity and fetishized capacity for *manipulative tyranny* of the regime of 'pure writing' (as identified by Socrates in the *Phaedrus*), is *preserved* by Derrida, and simply more precisely defined – as nihilism. And is this not indeed 'Egyptian' rather than 'Hebraic'? Not at all the logic of a purely consonantal writing awaiting the incidence of breath, but rather of a hieroglyphic tyranny whose possibility Warburton well realized.

And, after all, Warburton was simpler and more percipient than Derrida in associating writing with the 'literal' (though wrong in ascribing this literalness to human origins), and equally with 'the arbitrary'. For the Bishop of Gloucester, the recourse of the Hebrews to pleonasm had to do with the terrible paucity of their linguistic resources, which meant that they were forced to use the same words in different combinations to express different ideas. This was, for him, in turn allied to their poverty of alphabetic means, which lacked or had lost the pictographic, Lockean literalism of one written symbol for one idea. Instead, he argued, the earliest Hebrew manuscripts showed a mere succession of consonants without vowels, run together without breaks for words, so rendering the Hebrew scriptures impossibly obscure, a lure for Kabbalists. In Hebrew writing, a lack of distinct terms made every word run into every other.[36] This analysis construes repetition primarily in terms of 'writing', in the sense that it is the result of a paucity of signs or marks, leading to 'obscurity'. And every such analysis *must* point to this conclusion: even in the case of Derrida, since the repeated sign is a 'written' sign it modulates a repertoire of signs or words which *are never adequate* to an always insisting pressure of differentiation (or original absence) so ever-repeated (always with difference) and never – even to any degree – clear; rather indicating a final, real, lack of clarity.

But Lowth construed repetition in an opposite fashion to Warburton – and to Derrida. Pleonasm was not, for the Bishop of London, evidence of paucity of words, but of copiousness, since it did not struggle to utter different ideas with the same linguistic means, but to say the same idea in complicatory fashion: thus Psalm CXIX finds twelve or fourteen expressions for the law and 'four times as many parallel phrases to express the keeping of the Law'.[37] In consequence repetition does not result in confused obscurity, but in clarification, yet a process of clarification that is never foreclosed, just as there were after all intervals between written Hebrew words, rendering Kabbalistic exploitation improper. Such a notion of repetition is an inherently 'oral' one, since it relates it *not* to a repertoire of signs or marks, but on the contrary to the vast *number* of synonymous signs in spoken inflection available, thereby allying words in their 'copiousness' *as far as possible* (and new words can be minted, just as words can die) to the variety and change of life itself, to history, and the 'spoken' performance or sign which is necessary for there to be a sign at all (even if the subject can *only* speak, be a subject, through signs). Here, as for Derrida, there is an infinite sequence of mutually clarifying signs, and never foreclosure; yet still the 'next sign' as subjective performance clarifies, to a degree, and therefore *actually* differentiates (within 'the identical') instead of delivering us to a postponed, ideal, self-identical, non-differentiated *nihil*. (Although this is *not* to say that reason may 'disprove' the ontological tyranny of 'writing'.)

From the preceding account of Lowth's 'mystical allegory' which fuses pleonasm and 'reciprocal echo', we may legitimately extrapolate two further points
relevant to our quest. First, that the consistency of Lowth's figurative usage
through pleonastic variation, stretching right back to the first necessarily concrete
language, would tend to guard against the possibility of Warburton's *catachresis*.
Certain things are of course *forgotten*, but they are not thereby betrayed, distorted,
or suppressed, as among Warburton's pagans. One is still left with the question of
what, if anything, this 'usage' is responding to, but if one wishes to argue that it is
some objective standard of what it is to be human, then it seems legitimate to be
able to cite in *support*, though certainly not more, that this 'usage' is relatively free
from an alienation of the original 'poetic' proceedings of language, resulting in
historical falsification and cultural mystification.

Secondly, we may follow Hamann's interpretation of Lowth's mystical allegory
as permitting an exact distinction between Hebrew prophecy and pagan divination.
Although diachronic figuration based upon reciprocal echo does not betray the
original *topos*, it ensures that it is never reduced to a 'total system' whereby
everything future must be allocated to the original space, and the way is made
open for magical manipulation. This is the other aspect to the prevention of
catachresis; *new* insights may illuminate rather than obscure the topical heritage.
Their intrusion is non-violent: Lowth, as we have seen, stresses the egalitarian
nature of Hebrew society, and he links the preservation of a pastoral political
innocence (at least as the normative standard) with the continuity of the first
pastoral speech.

3 Vico

The tradition of figurative usage purports to be a reference to the one true God and
an avoidance of idolatry. It was the Neapolitan, Giambattista Vico, who explained
in more detail, how the grammar of monotheism might also be a grammar of
historical verisimilitude and social justice of the kind indicated by Lowth. Vico,
however, held somewhat similar, though more sophisticated views to those of
Warburton concerning language and writing, though there is no evidence of Vichian
influence on the English bishop. His views on the Hebrews (which I controversially
consider vital for his overall outlook) are to be found in scattered references
throughout the *Diritto Universale* and the three versions of the *Scienza Nuova*.[38]

Vico believed Hebrew history to be particularly reliable not because he necessarily thought that it recorded all important events with exactitude, but because it
preserved a better record of a patriarchal kinship society than do the pagan myths.
Precisely because Hebrew culture and social order aspired to be, and partly was,
more exoteric and equitable in its written, legal usages, it also possessed a better
memory (though of course it was still a selective one – a memory for essentials) or

written record. This of course entails a hermeneutic circle: to make the latter judgment concerning the truth of cultural facts, the historian must first make a judgment concerning the worth of cultural values which those facts convey.

However, Vico does not judge the Hebrews to be less *fictionally minded* than the pagans. He considers that all culture and all humanity begins with an original metaphoric tension – manifest through ecstatic bodily gesture – in which the world is symbolically grasped as the story of a divine power whose presence constitutes a teleological imperative for human beings. This is the first *written* narrative or fictional space – suspended between trace and deferral – which is then *inhabited* by men and women to produce history. In paganism, Vico believes, this metaphoric tension is immediately collapsed; the absent God is *reduced* to his presence in the inscribed sign, and from thenceforwards he is manipulated by divination through a series of *metonymic* and *synecdochic* reductions. The Hebrews, by contrast, in maintaining the original metaphoric tension, preserved both the divine transcendence and awareness of an integrally human activity in the formation of human culture, which Vico in 'Baroque' fashion considers to be an image of the divine creative *Logos* or *Ars* (though this same view also affirms God as the ultimate, creative, cause of culture). The Hebrews, like the pagans, continued to inhabit their enabling fictional projections, but they did not so much mystify the *fictional process* or *making*, which is also a real process, so that history remained for them the work of men, and Genesis records the work of founding fathers and not the intervention of demi-gods like Orpheus and Hercules.

It will be noted that Vico's attribution of metaphor to the Hebrew historical narratives, metonymy to the pagan myths, runs directly counter to the classification made by Roman Jakobson in our own day. Jakobson was making a structuralist contrast between metaphor as synchronic, metonymy as diachronic; Vico, however, was making a 'phenomenological' contrast between metaphor as the entire interaction of the human subject with the world in the genesis of meaning, and classifiable tropes, which in certain cases like metonymy and synecdoche, are readily reducible to merely ornamental or instrumental displacements among previously constituted meaning.[39] Pagan metonymy for Vico was a reduced figure in the sense that the representative relation has become fixed and predictable, allowing a 'poetic logic' which is a sort of calculus of cultural facts and values. Generic metaphor, on the other hand, is as much diachronic as synchronic, and only realizes its logic with the series of temporal responses to the tension it originally disclosed.

Lowth and Vico give us clues about how a non-idolatrous might also be a non-deceptive, non-violent culture. But can we, in the second place, save Warburton from the prospect of total equivocation implied in the dialectic of presence and absence opened up by writing? Lowth has already provided clues, but now we must call in the assistance of Hamann, influenced by Warburton as well as Lowth,[40] who developed a philosophical–theological view of language in which an equilibrium is maintained between writing and speech.

4 Hamann

For Hamann, following, like Vico, in the tradition that human beings participate in the creative activity of the divine *Logos*, there is for Adam as for God a primordial word, an original sign, a paradoxically necessary grace-given 'extra' which constitutes humanity. Warburton's 'pictography' has become for Hamann a transcendental and theological category; it is the total metaphoric process of history as most *concretely* present in and for the second person of the Trinity. Humanity, by comparison, writes always in the 'abbreviation' of *hieroglyphs* as if weaving 'on the underside of the carpet' and not seeing the full pattern that he makes above.[41] Because of this mystical harmony between divine and human creation, Adam gives things in some measure their 'real' names, but this is by virtue of his obedience to the metaphoric condition of human language, not some direct inner illumination of a neoplatonic, hermetic kind, which Hamann explicitly rejects. For Hamann, the 'naturalness' of the origin of language in fact implies that it is simultaneously humanly produced *and* divinely revealed. The latter indeed (more than for Herder) has priority in so far as the world itself already constitutes language – a divine speaking. (The absence of this notion in the earlier Herder actually renders his notion of revelation sometimes more 'fideistic' than that of Hamann.) Yet for all this, nature only constitutes for Hamann a series of *disiecta membra poetae* which 'the poet' must 'bring into order'.[42] In the conscious co-creative work of human beings which 'gives to all creatures their content and their character',[43] the divine creation is most fully realized, for it is always 'a speaking to the creature through the creature'.[44] The latter phrase conveys precisely how for Hamann 'revelation' *adds nothing* to 'creation', for the latter is precisely revelatory. Since God is genuinely transcendent and *not* a mere higher transcendental reality within the same order as us, he never confronts the creature in an 'I–Thou' relation but always addresses the creature (from the beginning and always) *as* the expressive self of this and other creatures.[45]

Creation, therefore, through man and by the power of God, writes an abbreviated, hieroglyphic version of the divine pictograph. 'Nature and writing are the materials of beautiful, shaping, imitating spirit'.[46] By writing this hieroglyph humanity is constituted *as* Human. In this way, Hamann, in line with the tradition of theological speculation on *logos* or *verbum*, stretching back to Cusanus, Eckhart and Aquinas and also received by Vico, understands as well as Derrida that *logos* is a 'supplement at the origin', or original emanation. Like Derrida also, and Vico, he realizes that the actual-transcendental written difference includes reference to an indeterminate and deferred absence in its signifying presence. Any human meaning, Hamann says, requires the 'spirit of prophecy' as well as the 'spirit of observation':

> what would the most exact and careful knowledge of the present be without a divine renewing (remembering) of the past, without a presentiment of the future, for which Socrates was indebted to his *daimon*. What kind of labyrinth would the present be for

the spirit of observation without the spirit of prophecy and its guidelines into the present and the future.

As 'the sum of the present is infinitely small over against the manifold aggregate of the absent, and the spirit of prophecy is infinitely superior to the simple spirit of observation' it follows that 'our power of cognition depends upon the many-headed modifications of the inmost obscurest and deepest instincts of approval (of what is there) and desire (of the *possible*) to which it must be subject'.[47] Hence it turns out that 'the firm prophetic word'[48] is after all more rational than reason, which is actually a mode of pagan *divination*,[49] since it treats written signs as if they could be fixed in terms of an absolute corresponding equivalence of 'empirical concept' in abstraction from 'their appointment and meaning in use.'[50] We have to remember instead that every sign – written or spoken – is 'an impression' and 'an inscription' which 'has a similarity to the pattern of our race',[51] since thought depends upon traces, and traces trace desires and vague expectations for the future.

Thus the original hieroglyph, through its primary metaphoric reference, simultaneously retains the human past and projects the human future as a horizon of desirable action: 'the hieroglyphical Adam is the history of the entire human race in the symbolical figure'.[52] Because all human existence is inscribed in this written narrative, it is impossible ever to arrive at total comprehension, or an absolute starting point. One's certainty is always given in the dynamic of an absent fact evoked through a present sign, together projecting the future of what is truthfully and morally possible. Geometricians, Hamann avers (unknowingly looking back to Cusanus and forward to Wittgenstein and the Husserl of the *Origin of Geometry*) implicitly recognize that ideal space only emerges with the first written construction of dot and line which projects all future possible geometric space, but philosophers like Kant, with their dualism of scheme and content, fail to realize that *all* abstract concepts arise in the linguistic mediation between man and the world in which ideal meaning cannot be reflectively isolated from material content by rational analysis.[53] This, thinks Hamann, is no more possible than prising away the letters from a page to get at a remaining content underneath. When we seek to clarify the conceptual import of a word, we must use another word and so invoke a further network of material references. And inversely, when we seek to isolate a material content for a word we must use other words, with their pre-established associations of ideal value. As with language, so with thought, we must write and think through the opaque natural world which we reactivate through metaphor.

But if there is no bedrock, no absolute *presence*, either of ideas or of empirical objects, then how can there be any objective truth? Hamann is only a step away from Hume, from Derrida. However, that further step, he claims, completes the distance which the philosophical sceptics have half-travelled between the idolatries of both pagan and rationalist on the one hand, and Christianity on the other. Hamann recognizes that writing *also* carries a totalizing danger. Derrida is of course aware of this, but he deals with it through a rather questionable distinction between writing and 'the book', as if the latter were the outcome of writing's seduction by speech. In her book about ancient Babylon,[54] in which like a twentieth-century Warburton she described a society dominated by writing, M. V. David judiciously remarked that while writing may encourage the 'active memory' in the need to invoke the past by making constantly new connections, it can also stifle the spirit through its false encyclopaedic, divinatory, pretensions. Walter J. Ong further explored this negative potential when he described how medieval obsession with texts and the invention of printing led to a tendency to view all knowledge in terms of a spatial calculus and a consequent 'decay of dialogue'.[55]

Hamann makes a similar point when he objects to Moses Mendelssohn's Leibnizian view (which Hamann teasingly dubs 'cabbalist') that writing is or can be 'the direct description of the thing' in contrast to the vagaries of speech'.[56] Like Warburton, Mendelssohn has forgotten that a pictorial convention is still figuratively mediated. And writing can encourage rationalist as well as empiricist prejudice: philosophers may be tricked by the sheer repeatability and manipulability of alphabetic 'abbreviations' into imagining that they correspond to eternal, rational, entities.

If we are to understand how there can be real, but non-totalizing constraints on language, then speech, or dialogue between persons, must be brought back into consideration, though it alone does not provide the answer. Hamann considers that the deepest dimension to Israel's unique linguistic integrity and profound metaphoricity lies in the prevalence of that variant of Lowthian apostrophe which is *paranomasia*, or change of persons.[57] This 'metaschematicism' has a subjective as well as objective aspect: it involves sudden change in the *intentional reference*, as when a parable is suddenly applied to its audience. Often the play of diachronic figuration has such a dialogue for its context and one may say that it is the (non-totalizable and asymmetric) *presence* of subject to subject which helps to sustain so acute a dialectic of presence and absence in writing. But this might mislead: for Hamann the biblical narrative may equally wish to turn us towards an absent, past, or future, subject, traceable only in the written text.

Yet such an encounter only has meaning for us if it is a dialogue at a distance, just as, inversely, a conversation is secretly situated within the 'written' text. Meanings in both moments are not finally determinable, yet they impose some immanent limitations upon interpretation. This is because they emerge within the horizon of spiritual intentionality which is infinite and 'complete', although not separate and distinct from that very horizon of historical possibility which only emerges through the *actual* performance of human history. This performance, for Hamann, is certainly 'written' in so far as we are always dealing with remembered 'inscriptions' or traces. However, this written aspect does not exhaust his understanding of the 'prophetic', or present-eluding character of language. There is also an oral aspect, as emerges in the following passages:

consequently, in accordance with the old tune of antithetic parallelism, words as indeterminate objects of empirical concepts are critical appearances, ghosts, non-words, and only become, by their appointment and meaning in use, determinate objects for the understanding.

He goes on to clarify the reference to pleonasm by saying 'it is by means of the repeated bond of the word-sign and the intention itself, that the concept . . . is incorporated in the understanding'.[58]

In other words Hamann here refuses to allow, like Kant, any *a priori* 'presence' of the concept, but instead insists that a *necessary* moment of conceptual indifference (belonging to language) only becomes determinate and thereby fully conceptual through the *repeated* use of the sign in different contexts in which it cannot be (even abstractly) prised apart from particular intuitions or embodied *perceptions*. These extracts show that for Hamann supplementation or pleonasm is 'oral' (hence the invocation of Hebrew poetry as discovered by Lowth) as well as 'written', since without 'use' and 'appointment', or in other words without the formation of a sign by a living body in a specific content, there would be no limit whatsoever on indeterminacy. The latter, for Hamann, is not, as with Derrida, *opposed* to metaphysical presence, rather it is *of the essence* of metaphysical presence, since the trick of metaphysics is always that of a naive realism (in the sense of 'opposite to nominalism'), that is to say of treating the signified of a sign as if it were a 'something'. To do this for Hamann is always to engender something 'indeterminate' that then becomes an utterly manipulable encounter in a futile game. From this point of view 'deconstruction' does not end the game, but rather takes it to its logical (*sic*) conclusion. And against this Hamann reinvokes an 'oral' non-identical repetition – including a 'written' moment – which is *not* pure postponement (and hence again the sheerly indeterminable) but rather a particular *tradition*, a repetition with a particular concrete shape according to the series of specifically embodied speakers and the spatial (but not closed) circles of circumstance which embrace them along with their listeners. However, this is not to invoke 'a real' which constrains language from without, and to which there could be an appeal outside a specific faith, reason, or desire. On the contrary, Hamann's entire philosophy of language disallows this contrast, since the creature is in itself 'a speaking', and nature always manifests itself in the conventionality and bewilderment of cultural sign-systems. The 'constraint' and the ground of possibility for taking there to be (on faith) a somewhat determinate meaning through usage and application ('Wittgenstein' modifying 'Derrida') is rather that (reverting the previous insistence) a cultural sign-system remains throughout a new and unpredictable, unmasterable re-manifestation of nature in all its embodiment and 'actual' spatial linkages and exchanges.

Hamann's category of 'the prophetic' therefore fuses 'the oral' and 'the written' (or the relative stresses of Lowth and Vico). The former secures an element

of 'presence' in the sense of the embodied, spatial and mutually dialogic. Yet
not in Derrida's sense of spoken word fading to make way for the ideal 'breath'
of pure conception, which for Hamann, equally, is pure phantasm. To the
contrary, it is clear for Hamann as it was for Lowth that the presence of body
is a *temporally* fading present, whose energetic longings make way for necessary
supplementation by the next oral prophet.[59] By contrast he considers that it is the
retaining of the word as a written inscription, which appears to remain the same,
that encourages an idolatry of observation or the idea that there can be 'a direct
description of the thing':

> metaphysics misuses all word-signs and figures of speech drawn from our empirical
> knowledge, and turns them into sheer hieroglyphs and types of ideal relations; by this
> learned mischief it works up straightforward language into such a senseless . . . some-
> thing, that nothing is left but a rushing wind.[60]

However, if observation is returned to its oral, prophetic content, Hamann nonetheless realizes that this also reveals an inescapable, and non-metaphysical dimension of 'writing' in all language. Every speaking appeals in memory to the already
'inscribed'. An allowing, by faith, of equal weight to both dimensions, which means
that a lust for 'present' knowledge does not refuse the guidance of desire (whereas
a Derridean discovery that presence is absence still refuses this guidance) will
render, precisely, faith possible: that is to say a trust that all the words we now use
with a particular range of relative determination will be able to carry an endless
succession of significations as yet undreamt of, and yet remain recognizably 'cir-
cumscribed' by previous usage.

Hence, in faith we trust our written narratives as *circumscriptions* (my term) and
if they are wrong then this can only be realized through a linguistic correction of
language, or a retracing and resuming of the first narrative through later ones. Any
explication of this mysterious situation can only, for Hamann, it will be realized, be
a *transcendental* one. But as we have seen, this is no pure *a priori*, but rather a
metahistorical foundation which invokes (via encounter with the historical Jesus)
acknowledgment of the writing, speaking God of Israel. This God, says Hamann,
like Jesus in St John's Gospel 'stoops to scrawl on the ground',[61] and by this *kenotic*
act of writing, creates the world and human history as a present sign whose
concealment–revealment of the absent God is the possibility of man's free creative
response which unravels gradually through time. At the same time God *speaks* the
entire human text in the eternal Word and interprets it in the Holy Spirit. However, this plenitude of speech does not cancel out all written or oral difference, it is
rather the *infinite* real difference, since 'infinity' posits a plenitude that does not
lapse into a tyrannizing totality.

It must be added that Hamann considered all human grammar, even the
Hebrew, to be irrevocably disfigured, and that this had necessitated what must
for sinners appear to be the divine counter-deception, whereby God the Son, the

utterly reliable Word, was himself substituted for the human signifying process, so providing a final, though still prophetic, language of humanity.

5 Conclusion

Warburton's 'hermeneutic of suspicion' has then been rescued from the hands of the post-structuralists, in so far as I have been able to indicate how other eighteenth-century writers, grappling with some of the same issues as the Anglican Bishop, suggest the possibility of a non-violent, non-deceptive grammar in the case of Israel, and also the possibility of a metaphoricity within analogous bounds, albeit only in terms of a metahistorical scheme which passes over into an affirmation of faith.

Can these insights be taken further? They suggest the need both for a hermeneutic and a metaphysic or metahistory. First, if Derrida can give a gnostic hermeneutic of the human text in the light of the gnostic logos, then we should have the confidence to give a Christian hermeneutic in the light of the real one. It may be that all mere humanisms tend to mystify human values as perpetual presences, thereby deifying humanity, and that in the future thought will be faced with the stark choice: either this gnostic, anti-humanist reading in which culture which constitutes man is criticized and destroyed, or else an implicit or explicit commitment to Hamann's *philologia crucis* in which it is more deeply rent apart, yet finally preserved through the divine trans-figuration, or *paranomasia*.

Second, we need a Christian ontology which does justice to culture and history as an *integral* element of Christian being alongside contemplation and ethical behaviour, rather than as a 'problem', external to faith. I have indicated my belief that specifically cultural and historical awareness among philosophers emerged out of the theological space opened up by the idea that man as an *original* creator participates in some measure in creation *ex nihilo*, expressed in orthodox form especially by Cusanus, Vico and Hamann, as well as in many heterodox versions. It is a lack of consideration of man as maker (in any detail) and a *consequent* neglect of culture and history rather than any alleged 'neglect of the subjective contribution to knowledge' which renders Thomism (but less so, Augustinianism),[62] an incomplete theology for today. Medieval philosophy centred around Being, modern philosophy (of which linguistic analysis, structuralism and phenomenology are all forms) has centred round Unity, or the *possibility* of ideas and things. But a philosophy apprised of the problematic of culture can accord no priority either to actuality or possibility in the case of the linguistic, cultural objects which we make (and which mediate to us ethical goals, natural realities and God as the permanent object of understanding). We are never in the situation of the pure possibility of culture, but no cultural actuality would be registered *before* one's sense of its possibility, albeit this is only *fully* determined with the actuality itself.

If then we are to find a transcendental constraint for cultural activity, then this cannot be purely *a priori*, nor consist in the 'nature' of things, but must somehow emerge from the cultural objects themselves. This seems to be what Vico was trying to say with his axiom *verum et factum convertuntur*. *Factum* for Vico is *Verbum* in God, and so the made, cultural object is promoted to the status of a divine transcendental (in the scholastic sense), and this is equivalent to saying that God in his creation *ad intra* in the *Logos* 'incorporates' within himself the creation *ad extra*, including human history. As we saw, a nearly identical position is held by Hamann, and both thinkers are ultimately preceded by Nicholas of Cusa. For all these three the key transcendental is neither Being, nor Unity, but the *Verbum* itself, just as for Derrida, in a less serious sense, it is written *difference*. Because *Verbum* marks a primordial difference in the Godhead, it realizes a perfect tension between Unity and Being (for it is an actual difference over against the 'indifference' of Unity and a possible difference over against the realized 'presence' of Being – as we might tend finitely to conceive these two terms) and allows no lapse into either a henological totality of system or structure, nor an ontological totality of the isolated subject. (I am not of course insinuating that Aquinas falls into this – but this is precisely because he does not reduce *esse* to 'a supreme being' and so allows it to be integrated with *Verbum* and *potentia activa*). When *Verbum* is included as a transcendental, all the transcendentals are transformed into personal, intersubjective, trinitarian categories: but this leaves us with more than a 'social God' which might be open to appropriation by an ahistorical theology, it leaves us also with a *cultural* God.

A Christian ontology that takes account of language and culture, will then be, more fully than before, a *Trinitarian* ontology.

Notes

1 William Warburton, *Essai sur les Hiéroglyphes des Egyptiens* (Maspero, Paris, 1977).
2 Robert Lowth, *A Letter to the Right Reverend Author of the divine Legation of Moses . . .* (Oxford, 1765).
3 William Warburton, *The Divine Legation of Moses* (London, 1846), Book IV, p. 197.
4 See Hans Aarsleff, *From Locke to Saussure* (Athlone, London, 1982), pp. 42–84; K. O. Apel, *Die Idee der Sprache* (Kluwer, Bonn, 1980), pp. 109–10.
5 William Law, *A Short but Sufficient Confutation* (London, 1750), pp. 99, 107.
6 See especially, Jacques Derrida, *Of Grammatology* (Johns Hopkins, Baltimore, 1976).
7 Ibid., p. 143.
8 Ibid., p. 47.
9 Robert Lowth, *Lectures on the Sacred Poetry of the Hebrews* (London, 1787).
10 Friedrich Meinecke, *Historism* (Herder and Herder, New York, 1972), p. 54; E. S. Shaffer, *Kubla Khan and the Fall of Jerusalem* (Cambridge University Press, Cambridge, 1975), pp. 20–6.
11 Hans W. Frei, *The Eclipse of Biblical Narrative* (Yale University Press, New Haven, 1974), pp. 141–2.
12 Lowth, *Lectures*, I, pp. 116–17. A fuller quotation runs: 'The whole course of nature, this immense universe of things, offers itself to human contemplation, and affords an infinite

variety, a confused assemblage, a wilderness as it were of images which being collected as the materials of poetry, are selected and produced as occasion dictates. The mind of man is that mirror of Plato, which as he turns about at pleasure, and directs to different points of view, he creates another sun, other stars, planets, animals, and even another self. In this shadow or image of himself which man beholds when the mirror is turned towards himself, he is enabled in some degree to contemplate the souls of other men; for from what he feels and perceives in himself, he forms conjectures concerning others, and apprehends and describes the manners, affections, conceptions of others from his own. Of this assemblage of images, which the human mind collects from all nature, and even from itself, that is, from its own emotions and operations, the least clear and evident are those which are explored by reason and argument; the more evident and distinct are those which are formed from the impressions made by external objects on the senses, and of these the clearest and most vivid are those which are perceived by the eye. Hence poetry abounds most in those images which are furnished by the senses, and chiefly those of the sight; in order to depict the obscure by the more manifest, the subtle by the substantial, and as far as simplicity is its object, it pursues those ideas which are the most familiar and most evident, of which there is such an abundance, that they serve as well the purpose of ornament and variety as that of illustration.' See also *Lectures*, I, pp. 13–14.

13 Lowth, *Lectures*, I, p. 82.
14 Ibid., p. 79.
15 Ibid., p. 97.
16 Ibid., p. 97.
17 See M. Boileau, Preface to Longinus, *A Treatise of the Sublime* (London, 1712) and 'Three New Reflections on Longinus', in Boileau, *Works*, vol. III (London, 1713), pp. 51–70.
18 Lowth, *Lectures*, I, p. 124.
19 Ibid., pp. 149–51.
20 Ibid., p. 165.
21 Ibid., pp. 162–3.
22 See Amos Funkenstein, *Theology and the Scientific Imagination* (Princeton University Press, Princeton NJ, 1986), pp. 213–71.
23 Lowth, *Lectures*, I, p. 145.
24 For this aspect of the Lowth–Warburton controversy, see Warburton's *Appendix* to the fifth volume of *The Divine Legation*, reprinted together with the ensuing exchange of letters in *Remarks on Dr Lowth's Letter to the Bishop of Gloucester with the Bishop's Appendix and the Second Epistolary Correspondence Attached* (London, 1766) and see also *A Letter to the Right Reverend Author of the Divine Legation of Moses* (as cited, note 2, above) by Lowth, which sparked off this dispute. Its ensuing virulence may appear unsurprising in the light of the following sample, wherein Lowth denies Warburton's contention that Abraham's plea for mercy for Sodom is evidence that the patriarch did not punish idolatry: 'for if in this case he [Abraham] was an advocate for toleration, it must have been for a toleration of the crime of Sodom, whatever that may be: now what that crime was, is a matter in all hands supposed to be very well known, and your [Warburton's] putting us off with idolatry is only an artful disguise, they (suppositious readers) will say, thrown over your real design' (*A Letter*, pp. 16–19).
25 Lowth, *A Letter*, pp. 47–8. For Lowth's own advocacy of religious toleration, see *Memoirs of the Life and Writings of the Late Rt. Revd. Robert Lowth* (London, 1787) (by

82 Logos

Lowth's son, also Robert Lowth, Vicar of Halstead), pp. 14–15, citing Lowth's Visitation Sermon at Durham (Sermon II in Lowth's *Remains*).

26 Lowth, *Lectures*, I, pp. 167–203.
27 Ibid., p. 202.
28 Ibid., p. 242.
29 Ibid., p. 245.
30 Ibid., p. 170.
31 Ibid., p. 245.
32 Ibid., p. 246.
33 Ibid., p. 247.
34 See Jacques Derrida, *Speech and Phenomena*, trans. David B. Allison (Northwestern University Press, Evanston, 1973), p. 78 'the phoneme is given as the dominated ideality of the phenomenon', p. 19; 'as pure auto-affection, the operation of hearing oneself speak seems to reduce even the inward surface of one's own body; in its phenomenal being it seems capable of dispensing with this exteriority within interiority, this interior space in which our experience or image of our body is spread forth'. Derrida's primary thesis is that 'the trace' (of a never-present past) is more original than the phenomenological originality of pure presence-to-self. However his *additional* thesis, that the trace is inherently ideal and abstract, outlasting the death of every body, every possible 'being' – a thesis which *runs with* a neo-Kantian/Husserlian idealism of non-ontological meaning, albeit to deconstruct it as also unmeaning – is only established by affirming the trace to be more 'written' than 'spoken'. And the characterization of both writing and speech which this involves, which in particular claims that the experience of speech is tied to the illusion of spiritual presence, depends entirely, as this quotation shows, on a *phenomenology* of speech in contrast with writing, which inherently claims apodictic originary self-evidence before the intervention of the trace. Similarly, it is secretly a phenomenology of writing which assists Derrida in claiming, in effect, that the trace as a category can be intuited as (in a certain fashion 'appear as') self-obfuscatory, self-obliterating, even though other *judgements* concerning the trace as such – especially theological ones – remain from the point of view of reason possible.

The reflections on *Speech and Phenomena*, here and below, owe a great deal to conversations with Catherine Pickstock concerning this text.
35 Derrida, *Speech and Phenomena*, pp. 54, 77, 93, 102.
36 Warburton, *The Divine Legation*, Book III, p. 174; 'The Pleonasm Arose from the Want of Words'; see Lowth, *A Letter*, p. 91, for Warburton's agreement with the kabbalists concerning the lack of breaks between words in the earliest manuscript of Genesis.
37 Lowth, *A Letter*, pp. 85 and 86: 'the Pleonastic character in particular must arise from the abundance of parallel terms and phrases in the language'.
38 G. B. Vico, *Opere*, vols 2, 3, 4 (Laterza, Bari, 1936–1942). Vico, *Selected Writings*, trans. Pompa (Cambridge, 1982), especially p. 91. See also John Milbank, *The Religious Dimension in the Thought of Giambattista Vico*, Part 2: *Language, Law and History* (E. Mellen, New York, 1992), pp. 9–119.
39 Paul Ricoeur, *The Rule of Metaphor* (Routledge & Kegan Paul, London, 1980), especially chapter I.
40 For Hamann's references to Warburton, see J. G. Hamann, *Samtliche Werke*, ed. Nadler (Herder Vienna, 1949), vol. 3, p. 217; vol. 4, p. 373; vol. 5, pp. 149, 309. For references to Lowth, see vol. 2, pp. 175, 198, 214–15. On the mediation of Lowth to Hamann via

Michaelis, Lowth's German translator, see Gwen Griffith Dickson, *Johann Georg Hamann's Relational Metacriticism* (De Gruyter, Berlin/New York, 1995), notes to her translation of *Aesthetica in Nuce*, pp. 432–45.

41 R. G. Smith, *J. G. Hamann* (Collins, London, 1960), p. 197. This has translations of some passages, but is largely superseded by the extensive translations in Griffith Dickson, *Relational Metacriticism*. This latter work is now by far the best account of Hamann in English and an important contribution to our understanding of both Hamann and Herder. For Hamann in general see also Nadler, *Samtliche Werk*.

42 Smith, *Aesthetica in Nuce*, p. 192.

43 Ibid., p. 199.

44 Ibid., p. 197.

45 This point is well made by Oswald Bayer in *Schöpfung als Anrede* (J.C.P. Mohr, Tübingen, 1986), pp. 9–32. However, I agree with Gwen Dickson, *Relational Metacriticism*, concerning the implausibility of Bayer's exclusively Christological construal of 'speech to the creature through the creature'.

46 Nadler, *Samtliche Werke*, vol. 2 'Glosse Philippique', p. 174.

47 Smith, *J. G. Hamman*, 'A Flying Letter, First Version', p. 235.

48 Smith, *J. G. Hamman*, 'Golgotha and scheblimini', p. 228.

49 Smith, *J. G. Hamman*, 'Fragments 8', p. 172.

50 Smith, *J. G. Hamman*, 'Metacritique of the Purism of Reason', p. 219.

51 Smith, *J. G. Hamman*, 'Golgotha and Scheblimini', p. 224.

52 Ibid., 200.

53 Smith, *J. G. Hamman*, 'Metacritique', pp. 213–21.

54 M. V. David, *Les Dieux et le Destin en Babylonie* (P.U.F., Paris, 1949), p. 110.

55 Walter J. Ong, *Ramus: Method and the Decay of Dialogue* (Yale University Press, Cambridge, Mass., 1958).

56 Smith, *J. G. Hamman*, 'Golgotha and Scheblimini', p. 229.

57 See Nadler II, *Aesthetica in Nuce*, p. 201 for personification as a leading characteristic of Hebrew poetry and p. 214 for *paranomasia*. See also Lowth, *Lectures* I, pp. 326–8.

58 Smith, *J. G. Hamman*, 'Metacritique', p. 219.

59 Here the development and alteration in my treatment of writing and orality as compared with the original version of this essay is immensely indebted to Catherine Pickstock's article 'Necrophilia: the Middle of Modernity' in *Modern Theology* (September 1996) and Part One of her book, *Seraphic Voices* (manuscript in preparation).

60 Smith, *J. G. Hamman*, 'Metacritique', p. 216.

61 Nadler, *Samtliche Werke*, vol. 2, p. 294.

62 In book six of *De Musica*, Augustine argues for the possibility of creation *ex nihilo*, by analogy to the *novelty* of emergence in time, both organically from seed, and from human art. Here what precedes the artistic product is the *process* of *ars*, and no mention is made of the traditional replete 'idea' in the artist's mind, which merely requires material embodiment. And this seemingly already 'renaissance' conception (which Cusanus later took up) is matched by Augustine's acknowledgment here and elsewhere of relatively different cultural stresses in time and place which yet make up an overall harmony (again Cusa will follow). See Catherine Pickstock, 'The Musical Imperative', in *Angelaki* (forthcoming).

4

The Linguistic Turn as a Theological Turn

1 Introduction

Has language been conceived in a particular way by Christian theology? That is to say, language as such, not just language in its supposedly 'extended' religious uses. This question has not really been properly addressed by the philosophy of religion, nor even by modern theologies of language. And yet it is important for any consideration of the interactions between theology and the philosophy of language to know whether the peculiar shape of Christian discourse with its themes of 'Creation', 'Trinity', 'Incarnation', 'Christology', 'Sacrament', has itself affected Western reflection on language. In particular, has theology contributed to articulations of notions of 'word' and 'sign', of the relation between sign and reality, and the genesis of language itself?

What follows is an attempt both to pose this question, and to indicate an initial answer. Beginning in the eighteenth century, the first two sections of the article seek to show that, contrary to what is often implied, Christian orthodoxy always encouraged the view that language was of human, rather than divine origin. In fact I will further argue that this was but one element in a generally 'rationalist' approach to language on the part of the Church fathers, which included also an instrumentalist view of the relation of language to thought, a strict distinction between 'sign' and 'thing', and a general denial of any sort of 'essential' relation between sign and thing signified. The third part of the paper, however, traces ways in which linguistic instrumentalism came to be gradually modified during the Middle Ages and the Renaissance, partially under the influence of theological doctrine and exegetical method.

In the fourth and fifth sections I return to the eighteenth century, and argue that during this period (the supposed 'age of reason'), Christian thinkers – Berkeley, Hamann, Herder, Vico – significantly modified all the 'rationalist' traits of previous theological conceptions of language. I show that, without succumbing to a hermetic, magical view of language, they nonetheless variously insisted on the indispensability of language for thought, the more than arbitrary relation between signifier and signified, the impossibility of distinguishing 'sign' from 'thing', and an origin of language that is at once both human and divine. To add to the paradox of this belated appearance of a more 'positive', and even mystical view of language, is the fact that it is these thinkers who first introduced a 'modern' linguistic turn into Western thought.

However, in my interpretation, these writers were further bringing to light the metaphysical clarifications implied by Christian doctrine, and most especially the doctrine of Creation. By contrast, patristic and mediaeval thought was unable entirely to overcome the ontology of substance in the direction of a view which sees reality as constituted by signs and their endless ramifications. Only in the eighteenth century did a thinker like Berkeley (supremely) have the courage to give a Christian gloss to ancient Stoic opinions which tended towards such a conception.

It will then be my argument that the post-modern embracing of a radical linguisticality, far from being a 'problem' for traditional Christianity, has always been secretly promoted by it. In the sixth and final section, I argue that what is at issue between a fully objective faith and secular semiotics is not a residual belief in a 'transcendent signified', but rather the conception of *semiosis* itself. The latter, not the former, is the location for Christian ideas of 'God', which are opposed to secular conceptions of *semiosis* as ultimate 'crowned anarchy'. In my conclusion I contend that traces of antique substantialism still survive in this secular view, which makes signification arbitrary and therefore violent. By contrast, only Christian theology, as the conception of a non-violent *semiosis*, is truly 'without substance'.

2 The Uses of Materialism

In the *Encyclopédie* of the *philosophes*, under the article *langage*, one can read: '[the] origin of language is so natural that a Father of the Church, Gregory of Nyssa, and Richard Simon, a priest of the Oratory, have both striven to confirm it, but revelation should have instructed them that God himself taught language to men'. A recent writer, Paulo Rossi, comments on this passage as a striking instance of the 'slow death of Adam'.[1]

Yet, in a way, it is not precisely that, for we imagine this primal deterioration only with post-Darwinian hindsight. Instead, this passage tells us, accurately, that Gregory of Nyssa regarded Adam, not God, as the inventor of language, and, more questionably, it attributes to Gregory a motive of 'enlightenment'; simply, his eyes were struck by the 'naturalness' of the thing. This was exactly what the eighteenth century tried to see as clear and self-evident – the origins of language, its natural foundation and rational succession, and thus the true character of humanity and culture, and the belonging of both within nature. But the real Enlightenment was more coy, and less rash than the Church father; seeing this naturalness, it still did not quite confirm it, but allowed that, in the blink of an eye, revelation might have speeded things up, as it would not have been seemly for the first man in Eden to be without language, the necessary instrument for the conveniences of reason.

It is all too easy to interpret this reserve as prudential caution, or as the lingering traces of a theological world view. This is because it is also natural, for us, as the heirs of positivism, to assume that anthropological and social theory has gradually emancipated itself from explanations in terms of divine causal intervention, opening itself to genuine science to the extent that it permits only human and natural causes. Hence, one frequently finds, in works concerned with the history of reflection on the origin of language, the implication that prior to the seventeenth century the subject was shrouded in the depths of mythic traditions about divine beginnings. It is rarely asked *why* this subject became so central in the eighteenth century, because the burgeoning interest is taken as simply the natural enthusiasm attendant upon a first scientific curiosity. Likewise, what should be disconcerting references to the Church fathers, of the kind I have just cited, are rarely visible to the eye of the modern reader.

In fact this entire field of speculation about linguistic origins has always been traversed by theological interests, and even its relatively recent fruits can barely be classified in terms of a growing beyond theology.

Despite the blindness already instanced, it is Paulo Rossi, in his work, *The Dark Abyss of Time*, who has already begun to break up the received picture. His important contribution has been to show that certain advocates (in differing speculative degrees) of the human origin of language in the seventeenth and eighteenth centuries, namely the Englishmen John Woodward, Edward Stillingfleet, Samuel Shuckford and William Warburton, together with the Neapolitan, Giambattista Vico, were not straightforwardly motivated by enlightenment considerations. Instead, curious though it may seem, they borrow and adapt from the materialist theses of the 'triumvirate of demons' – Hobbes, Spinoza and Isaac de Lapèyrere – in the interests of a strictly Christian apologetic. Their purpose is precisely to refute enthusiasts for Egyptian, Babylonian and Chinese antiquity – hermeticists, Jesuits and others – who discovered in the symbolic writing of these ancient cultures evidence of a buried primordial wisdom, and traces of an original, universal revelation, which was none other than the first handing-over of language to human beings. This was of a piece with an esotericizing syncretism, perceived by our writers as compromising the unique dignity of the scriptures. As the idea of a divinely revealed language lay at the heart of these claims, counter-esotericists would be attracted by the ideas of someone like John Locke, who presented Adam as learning language slowly, and with great labour. Along with the demythologizing of the hieroglyphs went the possibility of doubting the claims of the ancient civilizations to great antiquity, claims which often exceeded the six thousand years of Biblical chronology recently computed by Archbishop Ussher, and also the opportunity to present the cultic use of hieroglyphs as the result of priestly and political trickery. Paulo Rossi correctly points out that the doubting of great antiquity seemed at the time, for Vico and others, the genuinely *critical path*, because such claims appeared to emerge merely from the inevitable 'pride of nations'.

Nevertheless, the apologetic 'use of materialism' against the Egyptian enthusiasts can only appear like a sailing between Scylla and Charybdis. Materialist and empiricist hypotheses seemed to posit an Adam created very imperfect, a being scarcely human. In addition, the thesis of a human invention of language had to include a genetic account of linguistic development, and this was usually (as for Hobbes and Locke) in terms of the elaboration, by figures of speech, of an originally small stock of root words. As these root words stood for pure sensory perceptions, and as it was noted that more abstract and 'spiritual' words bore the forgotten metaphoric imprint of concrete origins, this could appear (as, for example, even Leibniz fears) to have irreligious consequences. More significant still was the shadow of ferality cast by these notions: the threatened loss of the human soul, and our distinction from the beasts.

Not merely had Hobbes implied that human beings would be semi-bestial without language, Lapeyrère had actually produced a volume called *Preadamitae*, which was inhabited in accordance with the shockingly explicit promise of its title. Yet Vico, in all his later writings, does more than merely fence with this shadow of ferality: he actually embraces it – again, as Rossi shows, for genuinely apologetic purposes. The site of ferality is not for Vico, as Rossi well puts it, our category of 'pre-history', but rather the obscure origins of *pagan* history, running parallel to a completely recorded Biblical history. Pagan humanity was, for Vico, literally 're-commenced' after a fall into animality experienced by the sons of Japhet, whereas the descendants of Shem, the Hebrews, had never quite forgotten the language of Adam. Catholic opponents of Vico in the *ferini* controversy which raged in Naples after his death, did not fail to suggest that this compromised the doctrine of the soul. However, Vico always stressed, following Pico de la Mirandola (but ultimately Philo and Gregory of Nyssa) the unique character of the human soul as indeterminate with respect to every finite goal. This indeterminacy is still recognizable in feral 'man' precisely in his placelessness, his 'sylvan errancies' and his promiscuity, whereas animals are, *by nature*, assigned to their proper place. Moreover, Vico also had his Catholic defender, Emmanuele Duni, who was able to produce quotations from Basil, Chrysostom and Eusebius of Caesarea, which appear to hint at a depth of fall which sinks beneath language and into an unregulated animality.

One can take this as a cue for passing from the eighteenth century, towards asking questions about 'the uses of materialism' in the patristic period itself. And first of all one can find some sort of parallel to the apologetic crisis of the later age. In dealing with the question of the origin of the pagan gods, Eusebius of Caesarea notably takes over from an antique materialist text the view that they are the result of political imposture, and the abuse of signs.[2] The Cappadocian father, Basil, was likewise accused by his opponent Eunomius of materialism and Valentinian gnosticism because of his account of *epinoia* as the human faculty which, working under God, can invent language and the other arts of human culture. But his brother,

Gregory of Nyssa, answered back with the charge that Eunomius, who claims that the term *agennesia* has a special linguistic privilege in denoting the very essence of God, and that it is the first and controlling word of a directly revealed language, has borrowed his teachings from the 'hieroglyphic writings'.[3] This could be construed as anticipating seventeenth and eighteenth century attacks on 'Egyptian' mystification.

However, precisely Gregory's invocation of the 'hieroglyphic' thesis points us towards dimensions that we have not encountered in the later writers. What Gregory identifies as the 'daemonic' in the hieroglyphic enigmas is their mixture of the half-human and the half-animal: this, he suggests, is effectively how Eunomius conceives of the divine *logos* – as an 'intermediate' being who is constantly being 'dragged down into a condition subject to passion'. If, he argues, the Son is thus amphibious, then we have 'no reason to be grateful to him for his sufferings' (for it is no longer a matter of a contingent, personal assumption of the human condition). Revealed language or writing, which stands half-way between humanity and God, is seen by Gregory to be of a piece with Eunomius's heretical subordination of the second person of the Trinity. As orthodoxy depends upon the Son's eternal co-transcendence with the Father, and the unreserved character of his taking on of humanity, it cannot allow that any mere portion of human being – whether the soul, reason or language – belongs in any essential way to the uncreated *logos*. Undoubtedly, it is his Christology which encourages Gregory towards the assertion of a human origin of language, and there is a notable symmetry in the fact that the more subordinationist Origen still engaged in Alexandrian talk about Adam's gift of *onomathesia* (a 'natural' revealed language, expressing essences).[4]

It is important to emphasize this point, because otherwise Gregory's views can look to us like 'common sense', whereas even an antique materialist like Democritus ascribed the first words to the work of the gods. Both Gregory's Christology, and his apophatic insistence that no human word can have any privileged referential denotation with regard to God, lead him to construe language as an essentially finite and instrumental matter, linked with the exigencies of communication, and the halting successivity of human reason. Speech is a thoroughly material affair, and words are a matter of accident, convention and agreement. Gregory's conception of language can be legitimately described as 'rationalist', because it banishes any shadows of linguistic mystique as found, for example, in a text like Plato's *Cratylus*, and insists that words are by institution rather than by nature (*phusei*). This also ensures a firm distinction between *res* and *verbum* and the endorsement of the semantic scheme whereby words signify ideas which in turn represent (infinite or finite) actualities.

3 Signum or Verbum

That patristic orthodoxy tended to promote, in the first place, a certain 'linguistic rationalism', can be confirmed by a reading of Augustine. Here one can notice the influence of another materialist philosophy, namely Stoicism. Like the Stoics, Augustine tries to find a 'natural' connection between verbal expression and meaning-content, but this is envisaged etymologically, as a putative tracing of words back to certain root 'names' that possess some sort of physical resemblance or analogy to the thing named. Other parts of the Stoic theory of language which also had an effect upon Augustine were, however, far more sophisticated.[5] Although they still accepted the 'semantic triangle' (word–idea–referent) alluded to above, the Stoics decisively modified this by interpreting the meaning-content (*semainomenon*) not as eternal 'Idea', nor as psychological 'thought', but rather as a *lekton*, a position within a system of signification. Thus they seem already to have recognized Saussure's category of 'the signified' as something distinct from either conscious thought or extensional referent. Moreover, they also appear to have rejected Aristotle's theory of an isomorphic relationship between meaning and object, in favour of the view that the *lekton*, as an 'incorporeal' sign of something else, always *connotes* other elements in a moving continuum, rather than denotes extra-linguistic *onta*. In accordance with this non-realism, a linguistic utterance, for the Stoics, is fundamentally the manifestation of an operational modification by the human material body, which acts, like all bodies, through the power of *conatus*, in the interest of its own self-preservation. Likewise the *lekton of* human speech belongs in the same class as the *lekta* of natural signs (like smoke/fire) which permit predictive and retrodictive inferences. The 'incorporeal' character of these *lekta* does not indicate any Platonic, eternal status, but rather a 'temporally indefinite' character: they are associated with the permanently unresolved circular tension (*tonos*) between 'slack' and 'taut' in the one cosmic substance, which underlies all relations of cause and effect. Ultimately, for the Stoics, universal reason, (*logos spermatikos*), or the creative fire (*pyr technikon*) both sustains and consumes the matter (*hyle*) from which it is perhaps only formally distinguished. This causes periodic cosmic conflagration (*ekpyrosis*) and regeneration (*palingenesis*). Only this metaphysic provides the full context for the Stoic conception of meaning not as equivalence (of sense and object) but rather as a fated connotative or inferential 'tension'.

Augustine's relationship to the Stoic background is a complex one. In the first place, he takes over something of the modification of the semantic triangle. In the *De Dialectica* he says that when a word is spoken not just for its own sake (for the sound, or where the grammatical unit is the focus of interest) but for signifying something else, it is *dictio*, and not just *verbum*.[6] *Dictio*, then, picks out something like the Saussurean 'signifier', while *dicibile* is Augustine's equivalent for the Stoic *lekton* (signified). Following the Stoics he also speaks of a *verbum cordis* or *verbum mentis*, rather than just 'a thought'. Augustine is so aware of the sign-character of words, and the indispensability of the artificial system of language for thought, that in *De Magistro* he declares that one can give the meaning of a word only by another word, or else by a gesture which is still a sort of sign.[7]

In the second place, Augustine actually goes further than the Stoics in one respect, by becoming the first person in history unequivocally to place the linguistic word *itself* in the category of sign: *verbum est uniuscuiusque rei signum*.[8] For the Stoics the word itself still stood in a relationship of definitional equivalence to the *lekta*, if not to referential *res* (as for Aristotle). As Umberto Eco has pointed out, Augustine's conflation was a potentially momentous innovation, because by bringing words under a category traditionally to do with 'natural' relationships of typical implication (as the sequence fire/smoke, considered generically) Augustine opened the way to seeing that word and 'dictionary definition' are never fully reciprocal.[9] Quite to the contrary, words can only be explicated 'intensionally', through a process of semiotic inference which relates no longer (as for the Stoics) more or less readily to nature, but only to a particular cultural–linguistic 'segmentation' of reality.

But Augustine did not take this path. Instead, in the third place, the overall tendency of Augustine's conflation of 'word' and 'sign' discourses is the opposite one – namely to bring the 'natural' realm of the sign itself under the sway of 'linguistic equivalence'. Hence Augustine finally obliterates the Stoic vision of reality as a chain of implications and adopts a semantics and an ontology founded on denotative unambiguity. In *De Magistro* the teacher can finally break out of *semiosis* by simply 'doing' the reality which the sign indicates, although problematic negotiations may arise if he is already performing the action in question. There are, moreover, techniques for 'reducing' every part of speech to a noun, and as a noun, every word stands in a one-to-one correspondence with reality. But this tends to imply that reality itself must be construed hierarchically and denotatively: thus for many of Augustine's mediaeval successors (if not for Augustine himself) on 'the tree of substance' every *res* can be accorded its proper location in terms of both *genus* and more and more exclusive 'specific difference'.[10]

In all likelihood Augustine assumed that he had little choice but to reject the Stoic theory of signs because of its materialism and its fatalism. Concern for the reality of free-will and for the ultimacy of the soul leads Augustine to endorse the 'linguistic rationalism' posited by the Aristotelian semantic triangle. Just as the Stoic metaphysics was in keeping with a theory which tends to identify thought with language, so Augustine's theology was framed in such a way as to posit a purely instrumental status for language, restoring meaning *ante vocem*. While signs are necessary, just as teaching is necessary, both belong to *usus* rather than *fruitio* and their point is to recall *res*, and finally to recall spiritual *res* in the soul, where Christ speaks, wordlessly. Nonetheless, it should be mentioned that these points regard *only* Augustine's treatment of language as such. By contrast, his doctrine of thought as 'inner word' allows a countervailing tendency which construes thought as 'intentional', or as having a sign-character (the Stoic *lekton*) which, especially in the *De Trinitate*, promotes a non-substantive, relational ontology, together with an account of the 'inner' space of the soul as merely the trace of past externality, or else ecstasis towards an externality still to come.

However, since Augustine fails to incorporate actual, material language into this new, relational ontology, and 'exteriorizing' account of the soul, he views even the signs that constitute the Bible as ultimately no more than teaching instruments, almost dispensable for the mature Christian.[11] And Biblical typology, also, falls for him, under the tyranny of 'equivalence'; more so, perhaps, than for Origen. The possibility of allegorical meanings arises beyond the literal, historical level, because certain *res* can also be used as *signa*.[12] But here, especially, the 'natural' sign is thought of on the model of the human linguistic word, reductively considered, in keeping with tradition. Figurative and allegorical meanings are to be resorted to when the literal meaning appears immoral or unsuitable, and these usages have been 'foreseen' by the Holy Spirit as assisting our instruction[13] – partly because of the delight which the mind takes in metaphor and the moral usefulness of the hard work involved. Augustine's hermeneutic rule that one should interpret 'according to charity' supposes an extratextual charity only really arrived at in the immaterial *mens*, whose pedagogic recourse to the text can therefore be somewhat sportive. The *res* which can be used as *signa* are arbitrary equivalents endorsed by the Holy Spirit, and it is only the minds of holy persons which really 'image' the divine reality, and so (uniquely among finite things) can be both 'used' and 'enjoyed' by us.[14] By conflating word and sign, yet placing sign under *usus* and equivalence, Augustine still tends to instrumentalize all that is 'beneath' the soul, despite countervailing tendencies at other moments in his thought.

As we saw in the last section, patristic orthodoxy was able, in its linguistic opinions, to rebut pagan mythological residues, sometimes adapting materialist insights to stress that language is an artificial creation. But the example of Augustine shows that at the same time it tended to strengthen and substantiate the *grammatical* supports of the Greek metaphysics of substance, a metaphysics which even the materialists had not really left behind. These grammatical supports include the *res/verbum* distinction, the idea of 'dictionary' definition, the view that language is only instrumental and the notion that only categorematic terms (especially nouns) and not syncategorematic ones, have real semantic value. The latter opinion, expressed by Aristotle in the *Poetics*, is reflected in Augustine's programme of reduction to *onomata*:[15] if 'connecting terms' are without essential meaning, this permits one to refer language to a reality of substances – of 'things in themselves' – only interrelated by a metaphysical *reductio* to the hierarchically more substantial, more generic, and more 'nominal'.

Such reflections might lead to a questioning of some aspects of the patristic treatment of language. One notices, with Gregory of Nyssa, how Eunomius is also accused of adopting a 'Jewish' point of view, and how insistently Gregory rebuts any Jewish assessment of language as religiously 'positive' by stressing the Christian 'spirit' that surpasses the letter and the law.[16] Likewise for Augustine, the Jews are subjected to the 'bondage of signs' as to realities not yet fully revealed, in contrast to the 'spiritual freedom' of Christians who *know* to what the ancient observances refer.[17] Given this apologetically slanted attitude to language, not even Christocentric concreteness can prevent a certain 'pneumatic' deviation. And while Gregory and Basil are true to Genesis in their insistence on purely human cultural invention, as against Promethean or demiurgic mediations, it can still be doubted whether 'named according to reason', or 'named according to legitimate authority' really does justice to the Hebrew meaning of the 'correctness' of Adam's nomination.

'Linguistic rationalism' ceases to be adequate at the point where the 'surpassing of the letter' promotes a spiritual 'inwardness' which both upholds an unwarranted metaphysics/semantics, and threatens to displace the theological centrality of the connotative matrix of Biblical and ecclesial tradition.

4 Oceanum Mysteriosum Dei

By contrast with patristic beginnings, it is possible to interpret later Christian developments in terms of tendencies towards a more 'religiously positive' evaluation of language. Five elements in particular stand out. First of all, the growth of humanism, from the twelfth century onwards, and the new attention to the particularity of languages. In *De Vulgari Eloquentia*, Dante considers that language is so close to reason that Adam can never have been without it, but must have spoken by divine *afflatus* from the beginning, in response to God's own word, which God will have caused to sound by using the winds as speaking organs.[18] Adam's first word was 'El', a spontaneous shout of praise, and the natural name of God. By contrast with Gregory (whose views he self-contradictorily echoes in the *Paradiso*)[19] Dante is seemingly less rationalist, and yet he begins to envisage the antinomy that will later be formulated by Rousseau – that it is impossible to think of reason before speech, and equally impossible to think of speech before reason.

In the second place one must mention the increasing influence, especially after the Renaissance, of the hermetic writings and of the Jewish Kabbalah, which with its insistence on the mystical significance of the individual letter and the licitness of readings which recombine even the order of the letters, represents the very antithesis of linguistic rationalism. In Jacob Boehme, especially, the quest for *Ursprache*, for the traces of the Adamic language obscured by the proliferation of tongues since Babel, is regarded as a work parallel to the search for the philosopher's stone, and a key to the eschatalogical extension of human knowledge.[20] It should be noted, *pace* Foucault and others, that this 'arational' tendency to essentialize human language *is* a Renaissance, *rather than* a mediaeval phenomenon.

A third element, by contrast, was internal to the development of Christological reflection. Hans-Georg Gadamer and Karl-Otto Apel have both traced the way in which the Trinitarian model of the *logos*, according to which (unlike neoplatonism) the primal 'expressive' emanation is not a declension in being but always co-predicated with the 'original' source, gradually radicalized the Augustinian notion of the *verbum mentis*.[21] The effect was to reinforce its distinction (as *lekton*) from a simple 'idea' in the mind, approximating it more firmly to the notion of a signified which is inseparable from the material system of signification. Both in Aquinas and Eckhart the successive, excogitative, intentional and expressive character of the inner word is emphasized, such that *forma exemplaris* (the 'idea') is increasingly understood as nothing other than the *imago expressa* (the emanating 'inner word'). It should be noted here that Bernard Lonergan's understanding of the Thomist *Verbum* is in many ways misleading. Lonergan seeks to show that the active element in the mind, for Thomas, arises in so far as the mind is able to 'transcend' the intentional concept, or the inner word. He thereby seems to deny Aquinas's clearly articulated belief in a relational 'emanation' at the highest level of the intellectual act, always returning the mind to an intentional 'encounter' with external *esse* at the precise *point* of its own productiveness. Whereas Lonergan at once *reduces* Aquinas to Aristotle (for whom the intellectual act *was* purely intransitive, though teleologically constrained, rather than 'open') and makes him anticipate post-Kantian transcendentalism, it would be more plausible to see a first inkling of 'pragmatism' in the Thomist *verbum*.[22]

In various humanist writers from the fifteenth to the seventeenth centuries, this process of increasingly viewing thought as sign is taken further, in that outward speech itself – the 'signifier' – becomes part of the human *vestigium trinitatis*. Hence the seventeenth-century Italian, Emmanuele Tesauro, gives theological status to *Homo Rhetor*, in the context of a subversive theory of meaning for which the Aristotelian categories of being are always manifested through rhetorical presentation. This means that both the choice of trope (metaphor or synecdoche, etc.) and the specific invented figure, mediate reality in a culturally specific fashion.[23] In his case, as with Baroque humanism in general, there is a veering between, on the one hand, scepticism and a celebration of a merely 'ornamental' and playful rhetoric, and, on the other, an effort to conserve in the notion of the contingently invented figurative 'conceit' (as in that of the artistic 'image') the full Platonic value of a truthful and illuminating 'idea'. The idea is now 'after' the word for the hearer, and no longer 'before' the word for the speaker. Behind this change, one can trace the Trinitarian redefinition of the idea as 'word' or 'art'.

Yet in this respect it is possible to consider aspects of the thought of the earlier theologians Nicholas of Cusa and Martin Luther as 'already Baroque'. Cusanus, following both Eckhart and the humanists, was able to assess the diversity of human languages non-instrumentally and positively as the different 'points of view' of an 'explicating' and always partial human reason, which yet attains a certain 'maximum' exemplarity in the words and actions of Christ.[24] Not entirely unrelated to this was Luther's contention that the Incarnation into humanity was also an incarnation into language: just as Christ was hidden for the Jews under the form of flesh, so he is hidden, though also present for us, under the form of speech.[25]

In a sense the Eckhartian and humanist currents allowed Trinitarian and Christological considerations to work in an opposite direction from patristic times, encouraging a 'positive' conception of language. The peculiar virtue of Cusa's version of the *via negativa* is to inhibit the temptation of this path (whereby it betrays its own intention) to suggest that there is a spiritual élan that can take us beyond language. By stressing that *explicatio* aims to fulfil the Christological *maxi-*

mum, Nicholas makes the unattainable goal *not* 'that which forever escapes linguistic expression' ('Spirit') but rather a divine *completeness* and 'precision' of linguistic construction. (Something perhaps always in any case implied by the Dionysian tradition of 'divine names'.)[26] There is certainly an analogy here to the Kabbalah and with Boehme, yet what should rather be stressed is the contrast – in the Cusan and Baroque humanist theories there is no interest in a mystical *ursprache*, nor in a 'natural' and universal language. Whereas Boehme's hermeticism feeds into the attempts to construct an unambiguous and exhaustive repertoire of linguistic signs which one finds in later rationalism and idealism, the Cusan and Baroque currents produce quite different heirs in Vico, Hamann and Herder, whom I shall consider below.

The tendencies just described do perhaps go in the direction of establishing the sign-character of word, which, as we saw, was obscured by Augustine. And it can be argued, in the fourth place, that mediaeval Biblical exegesis modified Augustine's reduction of 'the natural sign' to the model of verbal equivalence. This was partly a result of the cross-fertilization between commentaries upon the Bible and commentaries on the writing of Dionysius the Areopagite.[27] For Dionysius the ecclesiastical 'symbols' of the liturgy participated in the emanative transmission of the celestial 'hierarchies' which themselves reflected the perfectly equal 'thearchy' within the Trinitarian Godhead. The vertical and participatory character of the Dionysian 'symbol' came to be crossed with the horizontal and 'arbitrary' character of the Augustinian sign. Hence while mediaeval exegesis fully maintained the dualism of *res* and (human) *signum*, it nevertheless tended to understand the *res* alluded to by the primary 'literal' sense of the scriptural signs as ontologically symbolic and inherently polysemous in so far as nature was the language of the infinite God himself. It was only *via* the reference of the text to a real world that was itself both sign and symbol that scripture became *oceanum mysteriosum Dei, ut sic loquar labyrinthum*.[28] Nevertheless, by this path the Bible became the key to an inexhaustible symbolic encyclopaedia of the world.

Umberto Eco argues that the four-fold 'allegorical' (or 'Spiritual') method of reading was a means to reduce and contain the symbolic polysemy of the scriptures. Allegory permitted only four types of sense (literal, allegorical, tropological, anagogic) for each textual extract, and the voice of authority and tradition determined the precise content for each of the four categories. Yet the very notion that the scriptures are 'the content nebula of all possible archetypes' depends entirely (for Christianity) on the belief in the incarnation of the *logos*, and 'allegory' in its specifically Christian usage (after Origen) is precisely the protocol which decrees that all the *res* referred to in the Old Testament point forward to Christ, and that Christ himself embodies an inexhaustible range of meanings which anticipates every individual and collective future. In fact it is *only* this particular coding which *unleashes* the symbolic polysemy, and it is not here possible to draw a clear line between the 'convention' and 'authority' of allegory, and the 'irreplaceability' and free suggestibility of the symbol. Mediaeval allegorizers developed their own diverse webs of intertextuality, though certainly they situated themselves within the *catena aurea* of the interpretative tradition. Yet 'tradition' fell not simply under the rubric of 'authority', but *itself* under the rule of connotation, for it meant that the direct encounter of the individual with the text was in no sense primary; rather, the accumulated allegory and tropology represented by past exegesis now belonged irrevocably with the Biblical world of meaning. Likewise the only access to Christ as 'fulfilment' of all natural and historical promise could only be the endlessly engaged-upon exploration of ever-proliferating implications, whose infinity did yet not detract from the distinctiveness of the Christic *forma*. In this way mediaeval exegesis abandoned the 'equivalence' of *verbum*, for the 'implication' of *signum*, though at the level of *natural realities*, not of human linguistic signs.

And it is important to realize that (even, still, for Aquinas) the path from the literal to the allegorical, tropological and anagogic meanings is precisely what opened up the possibility of *theology* as distinct from mere history.[29] Only gradually did theology detach itself from traditional *lectio*, and become a more purely positive (i.e. *positivistic*) univocal, discourse. Ultimately this involved the loss of the idea that the *res* was also *signum*, and the confinement of scriptural reading to the literal sense. But later on I shall show that it was precisely the partial survival of the allegorical tradition which permitted the seemingly 'modern' linguistic historicism of Johann Gottfried Herder. It is, by contrast, a simplistic mistake to suppose that the confinement to the literal meaning in Protestantism belongs to some sort of inexorable growth of a 'historical sense'. In fact, as Henri de Lubac brilliantly demonstrated, enthusiasts for allegory, from Origen to Erasmus, had no less sense of the literal and historical than those more suspicious of it, from Theodore of Mopsuestia to Martin Luther.[30] Rather, what distinguishes the latter camp, is so extreme a view of the arbitrariness of the 'natural sign' that allegoric anticipation in the Old Testament is always reduced to literal, specific prophecy which can be 'verified'. The problem, then, about the loss of allegory in Protestantism, was that typological fulfilment by Christ was thinned and narrowed down in a way that threatened Christocentricity itself. Inevitably this betokens a theological shift (already begun in the later Middle Ages) from the centrality of participation in Christ to that of the abstract offer of a hypostasized grace. Not accidentally, Antiochene theologians like Theodore, who reduced allegory to external resemblance without real spiritual significance, also regarded Christ's humanity as somewhat 'external' to his divinity. And symmetrical with the thinning of Christocentricity was the loss of ecclesial mediation. When the individual 'directly' confronted the text, the text's finite and self-sufficient denotation (*sola scriptura*) found its equivalent in the internalization of meaning within the private conscience. The Augustinian tendency to make only the mind refract the divine light (when taken apart from his *countervailing* tendency to 'exteriorize' the mind viewed as intentional 'inner word') was now greatly intensified, whereas, by contrast, tropological 'inwardness' had been merely a 'fold' in an unravelling text, a moment which permitted 'the subject' precisely as the decision to be located within the final, public, anagogic consummation of meaning.

If, in these ways, the later Middle Ages and the Reformation reinforced again 'linguistic rationalism', nonetheless the encouragement given to 'the rule of connotation' by mediaeval exegesis was not quite lost sight of, as will be seen.

The fifth factor leading to a more positive assessment of language was precisely what we encountered in section one – that host of spectres raised by the revival of an antique materialism in the seventeenth century, in relation to the origin of language. It was this that made the late seventeenth- and eighteenth-century apologetic use of materialism so ambiguous, and suggested to many, by contrast, the thesis of a mysterious, divine origin of language as a necessary bulwark of orthodoxy. Yet this is *not at all* to say that such persons were necessarily on the opposite side to enlightenment. On the contrary, Rousseau's antinomy, cited earlier, is virtually an expression of the perplexity of enlightenment. If thought, in the tradition of Port-Royal, is a rational art or 'method', working through the orderly manipulation of signs, then how can one conceive of pre-linguistic reason? The treatise on the origin of language by Johann Peter Sussmilch holds that, precisely because of the totally arbitrary and artificial character of language, and *yet* its indispensability for thought, it must have been divinely revealed.[31] Within the inherited set of grammatical–metaphysical assumptions this could appear a rational solution to the antinomy; in fact *only* reason, and not faith, demands this solution.

But more importantly than this, the fears that really were fears of faith about the consequences of materialism led to a questioning of empiricist accounts of the origin of language in so far as these were founded on a name/correspondence semantic theory ('equivalence'), allied to a metaphysics of substance, and a clear distinction of *res and signum*.

First of all one should specify more precisely these fears. John Locke gives a fascinating account of language learning.[32] He stresses against the hermeticists that when Adam names gold by the word 'zahab', so little are any alchemical or kabbalistic profundities involved, that for Adam 'zahab' merely stands for what glitters, like tinsel, or what is yellow, heavy and so forth. He cannot name the essence, gold. But when it comes to ethical terms, linguistic genesis is quite different: these terms are archetypal, not ectypal. Thus Locke speculates that one day Adam noticed that Lamech was sad, and imagining, wrongly, that he is sad because of his wife's infidelity, he coins the word *kinneah* for jealousy, and *niouph* for adultery, *before* these phenomena were yet known. This is conceivable for Locke, because in ethical and cultural matters the nominal essence of a thing – the result of the mental combination of certain 'primitive sensations and reflections' – *is* the real essence without remainder. But this appeared to open up unlimited perspectives of ethical relativism, and Locke himself provides no sure way of showing how inherently moral impulses, as distinct from the contractual observation of certain linguistic rules, may be distinguished from the 'madness' which he admits may often result from the untrammelled association of ideas.

It is probably to fill up this sort of lacuna that in the eighteenth century it becomes vital to see language development more rationalistically as the unfolding 'representation' of a benevolently ordered natural reality. In Gottfried Wilhelm Leibniz, James Harris and Lord Monboddo, this takes the form of seeing linguistic–cultural expressions as guided by an innate rational logic or *mathesis* (Leibniz), or a mental *energeia* (Harris) which is gradually rising to the contemplation of divine archetypes.[33] Yet these rationalist and Platonic attempts to contain the relativist implications of the sensory and metaphoric origins of language are essentially unconvincing because they always posit a prelinguistic force of reason (Harris) or else a 'true', universal language co-terminous with rational analysis (Leibniz).

The oscillations in eighteenth-century linguistic theory between empiricism and rationalism are not, however, what is really interesting. Both philosophies were confined within the inherited metaphysics of substance. More truly significant was the break-up of this thinking, the steps towards a modern 'linguistic turn', beyond linguistic instrumentalism, foundational reason and a nominalist empiricism. Yet what is almost never attended to is the fact that these moves were not made by an unambiguous 'enlightenment', but rather by profoundly orthodox Christian thinkers – by Robert Lowth, Johann Georg Hamann, George Berkeley, Giambattista Vico and Johann Gottfried Herder.[34] As an experiment, I now choose to interpret this linguistic turn not as a secular phenomenon, but rather as the delayed achievement of the Christian critique of both the *antique form* of materialism, and the antique metaphysics of substance.

5 The Traces of Hyle

George Berkeley makes a radical break with tradition by questioning the *res/signum* distinction.[35] The *res* had been distinguishable from *signum* because it was thought of as a terminus, a thing 'in itself', held together by an underlying sub-stantia (even if this is the Aristotelian form/matter union) which was the shadow of antique *hyle* – unformed, uncreated matter. Or else the self-sufficiency of the *res* derived from the metaphysical first principle of a self-necessitated mind or idea which becomes Descartes' 'mental substance'.

Here one may recall, for a moment, Gregory of Nyssa. Despite his 'rationalizing' of human language, Gregory also approximates nature to language, arguing that creation is the true, mute language of God, although unlike human language it is completely indivisible from his purpose and will. For God there is no 'interval' between thought and action so that, as Gregory's brother Basil puts it, with God 'the order was itself an operation'.[36] As Richard Sorabji has recently pointed out, Gregory thinks of creation in terms of certain restricted combinations of divine *logoi*, ideas which in the immanent *Logos* are also actions, and hence like 'verbal expressions'. This is to think of creation on analogy with the combination of words and letters, and on this analogy the notion of substance drops out – as though one were to imagine a 'perfect' writing in which the words themselves constitute the surface on which they are written. To cite Basil again:

> Do not let us seek for any nature devoid of qualities by the condition of its existence but let us know that all the phenomena with which we see it clothed regard the condition of its existence and complete its essence. Try to take away by reason each of the qualities which it possesses, and you will arrive at nothing. Take away black, white, weight, density, the qualities which concern taste, in one word all that which we see in it, and the substance vanishes.[37]

There is nothing, for Basil 'behind' the appearances, 'a base for the base', and nature is finally incomprehensible because 'all is sustained by the creator's power'. The mystery of nature is particularly contained in the fact that, as Gregory says, there is 'nothing in common' between the different qualities or *logoi*, and yet without each of them 'the whole *logos* of body is removed'.[38] Substance is here denied twice over: first in the sense of a sustaining material 'substratum', second in the sense of a discrete immaterial 'essence'. According to the aporetic treatment of substance in the Aristotelian tradition, it is either the one or the other of these purported realities, or else a combination of both, which sustains the relative 'self-sufficiency' or 'self-grounding' of a thing, on the assumption that such a self-standing is the intimate ground of reality. But if, for the Cappadocians, there exist qualities only in combination, then 'self-sufficiency' ceases to be the ultimate measure of the real.

It is these sorts of consideration which Berkeley was able to work up into a new metaphysics, no longer of substance.[39] If, for Berkeley, 'things' are not founded in any *substantia*, but are composed of unsupported sensory qualities, then it becomes impossible to say that they are anything 'beyond' the implicatory network of signs which encompasses our whole practical inhabitation of the world. This is not, of course, to deny that things (which are just signs, or 'ideas') exist without our thinking them; in fact it is central to Berkeley's philosophy to insist on the 'exteriority' of all ideas even so far as they are thought, because he is the first thinker (before Thomas Reid) to break with the Aristotelian realist and empiricist versions of the idea that 'transmissions' from matter enter the mind like a 'recep-tacle'. In doing this Berkeley denies that knowledge is a process of 'cause and effect' between two apparently incommensurable realities (mind and matter) and affirms instead that knowledge occurs in the single medium of 'ideas' or signs, and can be no further explicated than as the reading of signs according to conventions. Here Berkeley had already closed the chapter of 'epistemology' and substituted a sort of 'hermeneutics of nature'. He considers that the 'ideas' of nature are to be regarded strictly as linguistic components, because we never 'know' anything except accord-ing to signifying implication: 'sight is foresight' as he puts it in *Siris* (p. 252) (compare Lowth and Hamann on prophecy in the preceding chapter). Yet at the same time this hermeneutics opens into a metaphysics, because Berkeley thinks that all language must be grounded in the 'mental substance' of mind; words that are not ours, he argues, are necessarily the voice of God.

The new metaphysics is accompanied by a new semantics. If substance drops out, then so also does subject–predicate logic; to attribute something to a thing is now simply further to explicate its definition, which is no longer 'once and for all', but infinitely revisable according to changing networks of relation. Encyclopaedic explication here replaces dictionary denotation and location on the tree of substance. Likewise the 'primacy of names' is overcome. As is well known, Berkeley denies that names stand for abstract universals, meanings purged of any particular reference (as for Aristotle); what is not always brought out is that he blames this mistake on the assumption that denotation is the basic function of words. For this reason, Berkeley is not a simple nominalist, but rather overcomes the entire realist–nominalist problematic by denying that nouns and nominal functions stand for discrete sensory particulars. Instead, they indicate the natural 'linguistic' elements which like letters or words have in themselves a certain abstract and universal character, yet are never found in isolation, but always in concrete combination. As 'divine speech' nature is composed of *nothing but* universals (ideas), but they are only meaningfully articulated 'together'.

The 'universal' character of the individual qualities is, nevertheless, indicated by a certain indeterminacy which, Berkeley insists, should rightly characterize all nominations if they are to be of practical use. This indeterminacy is precisely congruent with the mysterious possibilities of change and recombination. For Berkeley the most abstract terms of our human language – like 'force', 'sympathy', 'motion' – perform a necessary, hypothetical function, because they allow us to conceive of the energies and economies which organize these permutations.[40] In fact these energies and economies are nothing but the direct speaking of the divine mind, but useful fictions like 'force' (unlike the useless and misleading fiction of substance) allow us to imagine our own limited possibilities of intervention in the realm of nature. Likewise, syncategorematic terms or particles, though they do not stand for 'ideas in the mind', can still have meaning because they indicate 'mental operations'.[41] All our linguistic abstractions, for Berkeley, are possible not through prescinding from the concrete, but through the manipulation of signs by which we can make one thing 'stand for' many others; this only makes sense in terms of pragmatic possibilities of prediction, retrodiction and association, plus speculative possibilities of abductive inference to unknown causes which help us to pattern and articulate reality.[42] Words have become rules organizing action, not correlates of 'things'.

What must appear curious today about Berkeley's thought, is the combination of a kind of pragmatist semiotics with the 'exotic' metaphysics of the divine 'language of vision'. Yet viewed historically, the new semantics belongs to the articulation of a metaphysical picture which is full of echoes of the world-view of the Stoics. It is possible, also, that we are victims of a prejudice which imagines that this sort of pragmatism is necessarily a development from the Kantian turn to the subject and critique of speculative metaphysics. In fact, one can argue that Christian thinkers who sought to conceive of the cognitive primacy of human action in more linguistic terms than Kant, never made 'metaphysics' problematical in quite the same way. (By 'metaphysics' here I mean a theological ontology, not an ontology independent of a divinely illumined access to the divine: see chapter 2, 'Only Theology Overcomes Metaphysics', above.) Thus reflections on Berkeley can be buttressed by the example of the seventeenth-century Portuguese Thomist, John of St Thomas, who also developed the insight that our prime cognitive relationship to reality is interpretative, and mediated by signs.

Building on Aquinas's already somewhat 'pragmatist' view that the *verbum mentis* or abstracted generic universal in the mind is at once necessary for knowledge, and yet always connected with 'intending' the real (although one cannot hold up the mental concept for *comparison* with the extra mental *res*), John of St. Thomas claims that in any act of knowing we always substitute an abstract sign for a particular thing known.[43] Reflectively considered, this substitutive relation is only a 'transcendental' and arbitrary one (*secundum dici*), yet for the primary process of knowledge the relation is necessary, and therefore 'real'. The signifier both transcendentally 'manifests' the signified and ontologically substitutes for it in a relationship of dependence. In this way John of St. Thomas places the sign under the category of 'ontological relation' (*secundum esse*) and is thereby able to see a sort of continuum between real relations in nature which constitute 'natural signs' and merely 'stipulated' cultural signs. (This continuum provides a reality to which the eucharistic host can readily belong as a 'totally transparent' real relation, both objective and meaningful – see note 88 below.) The latter, like the former, can become 'indifferent' to the awareness of any particular mind, and also 'indifferent' to the presence or absence of what is signified (smoke still 'indicates' fire without fire). John of St Thomas's semiotics is here unlike that of Saussure, which focuses on the 'arbitrariness' of the relation between the linguistic signifier and the meaning-content of the signified. For John the signified/referent is only *ever* 'manifest' for us in the conceptual signifier. In this perspective, where our knowledge always depends upon the sign mediation, and yet we never 'survey' the transition involved, it becomes hard to say that the sign relation is 'just arbitrary'.

If signs are real relations, and relatively objective, then this places the realm of cultural mediation not at all on the side of 'the subject' or the *a priori*, but rather within the manipulation of a pre-given 'natural' category in such a way that *only* by supposing a 'real' connection (real relation through signs) with physical realities – this relation having the character of a temporal 'event' – do we grasp the true nature of our own cognitive powers. By contrast, as John N. Deely has pointed out, Kant's 'epistemological' prejudices leave him with the position that all our knowledge may be a subjective 'point of view' only transcendentally related to 'things in themselves', rather than the necessary 'leading to something else' supposed by the sign. And it is partly this subjectivism which induces the metaphysical ban, which is precisely a ban on the intervention of theology in our knowledge of this world, on the assumption that we can draw a discrete circle around the way in which things 'appear to us' as knowing subjects.

In Berkeley also, semiotic reflections actually encourage a realist metaphysic in the deepest sense (but a realism without 'reference' or 'equivalence' – a 'realism' construing knowledge as relational event, rather than mirroring representation). Nevertheless, there remains within most of Berkeley's writings an empiricist residue which will not allow him to grasp the sign as a 'real' rather than a merely 'transcendental' relation. This means, also, that he is unable to grasp the possible 'indifference' to the knower of the sign-relation, but remains mesmerized by the Cartesian subject. Despite his radical questioning of the *res/signum* distinction, Berkeley still subordinates *signum to verbum*, not because he any longer sees words as 'standing for' ideas, but because he imagines the self-referential labyrinth of signs as arbitrarily constructed by God. Like Augustine, he is anxious to refute the fatalism and determinism inherent in the Stoic semiotic. Hence Berkeley stresses the absolute heterogeneity and incommensurability of the various different ideas or qualities, especially those perceived by different sensory faculties like sight and touch. We only connect these things through repeated experience of them; thereby God instils in us his arbitrary messages and we know and connect things together 'in the mind of God'.[44] By seeming to deny any 'horizontal' principles of relation among the various qualities, Berkeley appears to lapse back into an 'alphabetic' nominalism, combined with a Malebranchian occasionalism and ontologism which denies secondary causes, and so (heretically) turns God into a finite agent.

Yet Berkeley does not consistently think like this. Rather, he continuously grapples with three problems whose scope surpasses such a somewhat wooden perspective, naturalizing an instrumentalist *verbum*. In the first place, the principle whereby one only grasps qualities in combination seems to mean that absolute heterogeneity is confined to the diversity of senses; by contrast it is *impossible*, for example, to think 'colour' without 'extension'. In the second place, it is not at all clear that Berkeley wishes to be an out and out theological voluntarist, although there are admittedly elements of this in most of his writings, which belong together with the Lockean residue. Thus in *Alciphron*, and elsewhere, there is a tendency to see the quest for ethical goodness as scarcely transcending our obedience to the regularities of the natural language which provides divine instruction for our self-interest here and hereafter.[45] Shaftesbury's stress on *To Kalon, honestum* or moral beauty as a quality aesthetically rather than interestedly recognized is not dismissed, but reliance on this alone is seen as 'enthusiastic', and the criteria offered for beauty itself are the austere classical ones of adaptation to purpose without 'superfluous' ornament. Third, there is the famous problem of Berkeley's real attitude to 'mental substance', the thinking subject. At times in his private notebooks he appears to deny that the mind is anything more than a 'congeries of perceptions' or that the 'reader' really exists outside of his 'reading'.[46] And it is clear that Berkeley locates the continuity of identity in the chain of 'readings' rather than in consciousness (this permits a 'narrative' overcoming of the Lockean problem of non-responsibility for what we have forgotten). The same private notebooks contain injunctions to caution on this subject in relation to 'the Church party', and some commentators have argued that Berkeley's public position is an attempt to preserve the self as substance in order to accord with Christian orthodoxy. However, the notebooks also make it clear that Berkeley never entertained a sceptical dissolution of personal identity, even if he struggled for ways in which to understand it.[47] I shall argue below that despite the need for caution with his fellow Christians, Berkeley's movements away from mental substance are *also* encouraged by his theology and metaphysics.

It makes sense to read *Siris*, Berkeley's final work, as an attempt to resolve these three problems. However, it can be hypothesized, especially in relation to the first problem, that because Berkeley was unwilling to lapse into a Stoic fatalism which sees the connection of signs as a determinate chain (like Spinoza or even Leibniz) nor willing to embrace a fully fledged nominalism–voluntarism, that he is obliged to adopt an 'aesthetic' solution which entails an entirely new sort of discourse – one that is figurative, allusive, arcane.

Siris becomes then the 'romance' of Berkeley's metaphysics of light. In a sense such a romance was already indicated by Basil's *Hexaemeron*. Here, already, the first word of the divine language was light (Genesis 1:3) and 'the divine word gives everything a more cheerful and a more attractive appearance'.[48] But the romance departs drastically from Berkeley's previous philosophic essays, because light is now identified as the Stoic *pyr technikon*, the 'living omniform seminary of the world', or as an energetic *medium* which carries all the heterogeneous qualitative elements. Twentieth-century empiricists have expressed bewilderment at this introduction of a seemingly superfluous 'essential' force, and assume that this is incompatible with Berkeley's rigorist campaign against material substance. However, *Siris* reaffirms all Berkeley's previous positions and makes it quite clear that the 'aetherial fire' is not an underlying substance, nor yet *even* a single tensional force into which all physical causation can be resolved, on the Stoic model. Instead, Berkeley is interested in envisioning connections that are 'on the surface'; he is attempting to think the ultimate harmony and unity of the world, or the connections that somehow pertain between the irreducibly heterogeneous. Light, for Berkeley, is a medium of difference, the process of natural *semiosis* itself. Because he does not want to reduce the differences to the merely arbitrary, nor to the rationally determined, he can only grasp the process as a unity in aesthetic terms – as a harmony which itself defines, in its particular forms, just what the rationally harmonious is. Hence the poetry, the Baroque superfluity and 'enthusiasm' of this discourse (obviously, the fact that Berkeley has chosen 'light' as the vehicle of this romance, however much he may seriously have 'meant' this, is not ultimately fundamental to the philosophic point he is trying to make about 'the medium of difference'. Light is simply the most natural figure for 'that which appears'.)

It is absolutely vital to grasp that Berkeley does not propose light, in Stoic fashion, as a single connective principle; instead light is the vehicle, not just of different qualities, but also of an incalculable number of different relational and causal principles. Berkeley propagates in *Siris* a 'theological' physics that will rejoice in this contingency and diversity.[49] Yet he takes a Platonic and aesthetic step beyond voluntarism: the 'mutual relation, connexion, motion and sympathy of the parts of this world' is such 'that they seem as it were animated and held together by one soul'.[50]

By introducing 'light' as the beauty which holds in unity the heterogeneous, a beauty which Berkeley connects with divine glory and the light of Christ's transfiguration,[51] he is able to prevent the loss of substance leading to a sceptical dissolution, or else to determinism, or again recourse to an arbitrary will acting behind the heterogeneous signs to hold them all together. This means that *semiosis* now involves real relations, substitutionary transitions which though inscrutable, are more than arbitrary; the signifying relation becomes also symbolic. But obviously this new approach must have a bearing upon the problem of mental substance. In Berkeley's earlier writings there appears to be an oscillation between the idea that there is no power of thought separable from thought in act, and a Platonic–Aristotelian position which says that while the act of thought is identical with the act of the thing thought, there remains a transcendent 'potential' for thought which is like a kind of 'womb' for the ideas, although it is not modified or altered by them like a material substance.

Already, however, despite the affirmation of the identity in act of knower and known, Berkeley affirms a relational 'exteriority' intrinsic to this act which modifies Aristotle even further than the Thomist concept of an intentional relation within the act of understanding[52] (because Berkeley posits a 'direct', unmediated realism). This points the way to a dispensing with 'passively potential', substantial mind 'before' any act of knowing. However, what is striking is that in *Siris* this dispensing is finally achieved with relation to the *divine* mind, leaving the implications for human mind to be mostly inferred.

The earlier Berkeley had created his own dualism which divided the world up between active mind and inert signs (or 'ideas'). Yet confusingly, he talked of a third category of 'notions' which were the vague reflective ideas one could have about the nature of mind itself.[53] However, in *Siris* he makes it clear that 'notions' are not just ideas *about* mind, but rather the energetic manifestation of mind, its indeterminate and 'anticipatory' power. Berkeley says that whereas 'those who have been taught to discourse about substratums' think that one should 'attribute to the Deity a more substantial being than the *notional* entities of wisdom, order, law, virtue or goodness',[54] these notional entities are '*only complex ideas [which being] framed and put together by the understanding are its own creatures and as an idea to govern*' (my italics). The 'notional' is therefore a 'medium of difference' in the same way as light; it is not a power *prior* to the diversity of ideas, rather it emerges only through the complex construction of ideas as their inherent 'order'. But in the complexification of ideas (only *through which* consists the understanding, if no 'mental substance' underlies them) there is somehow present an active element or 'idea' in the Platonic sense which denies their mere inertness and qualifies Berkeley's earlier dualism. He now finally abandons Malebranche, and arrives at a Stoic integration of causality and meaning; yet by construing this integration as aesthetic he seeks to conserve within the activity/meaning of ideas (signs) themselves, a sphere of subjective freedom.

Towards the end of *Siris* it becomes clear that this aesthetic dissolution of divine substance is only sustained in *Trinitarian* terms.[55] The ordering power of the notions is guided by the principle of perfection, the beauty of the Platonic good beyond the true which is also the absolute unity and absolute being of God the Father. Berkeley has here apparently surrendered to the 'enthusiasm' which makes *To Kalon* the ultimate guide; the human soul or person is now said to cohere only in her participation in the divine unity and goodness. However, God the Father is never without God the Son; the divine unity and origin is not 'substantial' but 'notional', because it only *arises* in the articulate 'generation' of truth. The Father, for Berkeley, is the Platonic sun, ultimate goodness, 'the source of light', rather than light or truth itself, but a sun never without its rays which 'effects truth' (*vere efficit*) in an eternal illocutionary act. Likewise God the Son is never without God the Spirit; the rays of light, the *pyr technikon* or *logos spermatikos* never actually exist without the various life which they engender.[56] In this third stage the divine mind achieves a perlocutionary, 'rhetorical' performance; the notions are received as ideas, and this reception constitutes the human subject (the only real goal of creation). This is *not* a sequence of 'cause and effect' (it cannot be, if it applies to God), if one takes as the paradigm of 'cause' the idea that substantial causes 'precontain' their accidental effects. This view is specifically denied by Berkeley in his notebooks.[57] Instead it is a sequence of speaking and interpretation where at each stage the effect 'exceeds' and actually constitutes 'backwards', its own cause. Hence Berkeley adverts to the logic of Trinitarian 'substantive relations' to construct an aesthetic ontology which dispenses with both cause and substance. This does not, of course, mean that Berkeley is in danger of 'pantheism'. The 'romance of light' concerns mainly the created effects of the Trinity, and all finite ideas fall short of infinite perfection. Nonetheless, Berkeley indicates the full consequence of the specifically Judaeo-Christian view that perfection is 'infinity' rather than substance (for the Greeks the 'infinite' still had overtones of the 'chaotic' and confused).[58] The ascent to perfection is no longer a *reductio* to a prior containing cause, but a recovery of the 'lost region of light' which is an infinitely realized communication.

However imperfect are Berkeley's Trinitarian speculations, they do, nonetheless, permit him to articulate a kind of 'divine pragmatics' which is able to affirm, *on a theological basis*, that mind is only present in 'operations about signs'.[59] His entire 'metaphysical semiotics' contrives, through this Trinitarian recourse, to re-exploit elements of the Stoic world-view initially shied away from by the Church Fathers. However, the Stoic construal of meaning as 'tension' still contained the traces of *hyle*, and of the myth of a ceaseless struggle between *logos* and underlying matter. Berkeley's 'romance' effectively re-construes meaning as 'peaceful tension', or as the realization of communication in a dynamic, but harmonious order. The *pyr technikon* is no longer a consuming fire, engendering differences to destroy them, but instead it has been reconciled by Berkeley with Aristotelian teleology and Platonic plenitude. The chain of signification conducts us through ever-renewed difference in the 'divination' of 'natural letters', from tar-water to the *summum bonum* where every difference is preserved.

Thus in *Alciphron*, Berkeley had argued that linguistic signs do not conjure up corresponding ideas in the mind, but rather 'imply relations or proportions of things' and 'direct our actions' by imparting 'something of an active, operative nature', tending to 'a conceived good' which leads us to the ultimate end.[60] In this context the Trinitarian doctrine of 'Creator, Redeemer, Sanctifier' also produces 'no distinct ideas' in us, but acts like an 'algebraic' formula to regulate the entire field of our actions, which are always signifying operations. (Hence Berkeley discovers all at once the 'performative' character of language, and the performative bearing of Christian doctrine.) Accordingly, the doctrine of the Trinity, embodying an aesthetic and communicative ontology, constitutes for Berkeley a kind of metasemiotic principle; a theory about the 'meaning of meaning', and the possibility of the sign-relation.

6 Lingua d'Un Solo Deo

Berkeley's questioning of the *res/signum* distinction, and his theory of a 'natural' language, had an effect upon ideas about the origins of language, and particularly on Hamann and Herder, who attest to his influence.[61] Linguistic genesis need not now seem 'alien' to nature, especially if one digs beneath the levels of alphabeticization and 'algebraic' abbreviation and imagines a more primitive discourse of mimetic sounds and gestures. But the problem of mimesis is really akin to the problem of non-identical similarity encountered in relation to Berkeley's qualities. This is especially the case, if, like Herder, one thinks there is a kind of invisible analogy whereby sound can imitate sight, and image can imitate sound.[62] Walter Benjamin, developing Hamann and Herder's insights, speaks in his 1933 fragment, *On the Mimetic Faculty*, of a 'non-sensuous resemblance'.[63] This idea of an 'inscrutable' resemblance means, for Benjamin, that the symbolic-participatory and the allegoric-conventional cannot really be prised apart in Romantic fashion. For if the sign relation is more than instrumental, then it is only through difference that we know any singular thing, and to that extent the difference is irreducible and 'arbitrary', although it is at the same time necessary and intrinsic to the conception of the thing. All resemblance, as Umberto Eco says, is conventional, defined according a semiotic code;[64] yet at the same time conventions cannot get semiotically established without the 'assumption' of a certain resemblance, or 'appropriateness'.

For Benjamin 'non-sensuous resemblance' is a key to interpreting Herder's category of 'expressivity'. 'Expression' was for Herder ontologically irreducible, because what gets expressed is never just a prior 'content', but always, in addition, something that only appears with the expression itself. Initially, it is only nature that is expressive; Herder, following Gregory of Nyssa and Pico della Mirandola, holds to a thoroughly negative anthropology in which human beings, unlike animals, are characterized by the absence of any dominant faculty or ability.[65] In Herder this is compensated for by the presence of a general faculty of linguistic reflection, but his interlocutor Hamann doubts whether one should think even of this as 'prior' and innate rather than as *the event* of creation rising to full expression under divine grace.[66] For both thinkers, human origins can consist in nothing but the *noting* of the differential expressiveness of nature, and the attempt to bring this to synthetic articulation. More insistently than Berkeley, they stressed the 'always already' of cultural mediation through human language, and Hamann writes, as was discussed in the previous essay, of God's speaking 'through the creature, by the creature'. Within the bounds of 'language as such', given receptivity and non-given creativity cannot ever precede each other. The mystery of the 'beginning' of human language *is* a mystery because even here one cannot elide this responsive element.

Thus human, cultural, expression is always already the expression of difference. Metaphor is placed by Hamann and Herder at the very genesis of language. But it was only possible for them to combine a very 'bodily' and naturalistic account of linguistic origins with primal metaphoricity because they subscribed to an 'expressivist' ontology. This remained inconceivable for nominalists like Locke and Condillac, who by the same token remained confined by the notion that language was to do with the combination of 'prior' ideas and sensations. The real achievement of a non-instrumental and metaphorical conception of language in Lowth, Vico, Hamann and Herder is part of an ultimately theological and antimaterialist strategy. This makes nonsense of Mark C. Taylor's claim that obsession with linguisticality arrives as a 'secondariness' consequent upon the 'death of God'. Instead the death of a merely 'prior', substantial God was already articulated in Trinitarian doctrine, and it was theology itself which initially promoted linguisticality in the eighteenth century.[67]

For, by placing metaphor at the origin, the ultimate resource of a merely materialist critique of culture was thereby precluded: it became impossible to appeal to a basic, universal, natural norm that will still be a human norm. If metaphor is fundamental, then religion ceases to be a mystery *in addition to* the mystery of humanity itself. It no longer appears automatically plausible to understand religion as a later result of the socio-political mystification of signs, nor as a secondary attempt to 'explain' natural phenomena. Instead, original metaphor implies either a primal personification of nature ('paganism') or else a primal response to nature as a personal address ('monotheism'). Thus for Herder 'the oldest dictionary was a sounding pantheon' and the first grammatical *elements* of language were the divine and human heroes of primaeval epic.[68] Likewise, for Vico, the first metaphors were 'narratives in brief', and the first pagan language was disseminated as a theogony which was simultaneously the human 'divination' of the will of the Gods.[69] In these conceptions linguistics is re-located *inside* poetics, and poetic categories *define* the first human *topoi*, the first spaces in which specifically historical recording, and *consequently* (this reversal is entailed) specifically historical action will be possible.

For Vico and Herder language becomes an unsoundable *mythos* which projects not only the divine, but also the human. The apparently mystic, and even 'judaizing' view that the first human words name God, or the gods, returns as a critique beyond critique, as a *metacritique*, to use Hamann and Herder's term. Within the metacritical labyrinth, only intertextual revision is possible: thus Herder re-worked the Christian allegorical principle as a universal theory of historicity in which we constantly revise our existence through re-interpretation of the past which has its whole being in 'prophecy,' or the typological projection of the future.[70] 'Progress' itself is predicated upon this return, and historical advance never transcends the irreducible value of the different perspectives of different places and times.[71] Whereas mediaeval exegesis was only able to found allegorical connotation in nature, Herder locates it also in culture, because even the 'literal level' of language does not now just 'refer' to nature, but rather *expresses* nature, metaphorically.

Herder, however, seems to leave matters at a positive evaluation of difference, whereas Vico had already developed a distinction between desirable and undesirable cultural processes, corresponding to the contrast between the *mythos* of monotheism and the *mythos* of polytheism. As we saw in section one, Rossi has shown how Vico's apparently 'modern' insights are bound within the framework of a strictly Biblical chronology; but one can go further than this to show that Vico's philosophy of history contains a *linguistic* re-working of Augustine's theory of the 'two cities'.[72]

Unlike Hamann and Herder, though somewhat like William Warburton, as has been seen in the previous chapter, Vico was concerned with a *double origin* of language, Hebraic and 'pagan'. No commentator on Vico has yet grasped the real implications of this. It is, first, not at all the case that Vico wished, like Warburton, to safeguard the positively revealed character of Biblical language and culture; on the contrary, despite a probably expedient reference to Adam's *onamathesia* in the *Scienza Nuova Terza*, Vico had made it clear in an earlier version that this 'naming according to nature' is not 'cratylist' in character. Rather, it means only that Adam's language was also 'poetic' – that is to say both material and metaphoric – and that Hebrew language and culture continued to have a primitive 'heroic' and 'poetic' character, while avoiding the illusion that natural 'words' were *substances* or gods. It is usually said, probably correctly, that Vico has relatively little to say about this out of fear of the Inquisition, but (as with Berkeley's 'Church party') the corollary often drawn does not necessarily follow: namely, that Vico *really* thought ancient Hebrew culture was as open to criticism for its superstition and political mystification as that of the 'pagans'.[73] On the contrary, Vico is more plausibly interpreted as offering a kind of counter-Spinozan critical approach to the Old Testament. This is suggested by Vico's claim that the Old Testament narratives (whether or not literally true as to details) offer a more concrete and *realistic* clue to the patriarchal 'time of the families' before the founding of cities, than do the mythical narratives of the 'pagans'.[74]

In the *Diritto Universale* and the *Scienza Nuova Prima*, Vico makes it clear that he connects this difference between a realistic, 'memorizing' narrative and a mystifying, falsifying narrative to two *different* primitive languages, with radically different grammatical principles. Thus when Vico says that 'Hebrew began as, and remained [after the fall] the language of a single God' he means that the Hebrews retained an entire signifying practice which united both their religious observances and their cultural norms.[75] Only, in fact, by superimposing the grammatical and narrative norms of this language upon the pagan myths, does Vico think that he is able to decipher and expose the mystifying procedure of 'the language of the gods'. It is this metacritical procedure and not just chronological norms which Vico has in mind when he says that 'the first principles of the New Science are to be found in Holy Scripture.[76]

By contrast with the 'monotheistic grammar' one is able to perceive that, for the pagans, 'meaning', or the sign-relation, is always construed as 'inhibition of chaos'. *Logos* is a counter-violence that 'stays' an always more primordial violence. Hence, says Vico, the first title of Jove was *stator*, and the significant 'chain of fate' was Jove's 'binding' of the initial human ferality.[77] Although the pagan culture was 'poetic', its mythology was itself characterized by a quest for univocity which reflected a concern for fixation and containment. The 'language of the gods' was therefore not so much metaphoric as dominated by the tropes of metonymy and synecdoche, understood in such a way that the substitutions of effect for cause or part for whole are always regular and predictable. This founds a culture based not on 'prophecy' but on idolatry and divination.[78] Hence the first signified reality, 'Jove', was himself 'bound' by his effects, or the first interpretations of his auguries which also generate his 'offspring', later words which are the 'many gods'. Jove's first words are a fateful 'restriction' and binding of his own anger, and at the same time a command to feral human begins to 'contain' their passions. In the *De Uno* Vico makes it clear that this is a gloss upon Augustine's view that 'pagan virtue' was always limited to the mere 'restriction of anger' through self-control.[79]

But if, then, every act of signification, every sign given, is a kind of 'victory', a binding or 'containment' of the signified, then meaning is fundamentally an obscuring, a suppression. A considerable section of the *Scienza Nuova Terza* is given over to explicating the terrifying consequences of this principle of transmission. According to Vico, for the primaeval pagans the primal signifiers were weapons, and the basic language was war.[80] If the gentile son was to succeed his father, then he must at once suppress his father's memory and appropriate his name, together with all the glory attaching to it. Hence the univocity of the 'poetic universals' which made the 'mythical' Hercules more real than the actual heroes. A lot of ink has been spilt on the question of whether Vico himself 'favours' poetic language or abstract, rational language – in fact Vico makes it clear that he considers the univocity of Aristotelian 'abstract universals' as but *another mutation* of an impulse to univocity built into an evolving 'violent' and anti-historical grammar predicated upon the 'conquest' of underlying substance.[81]

By contrast, Vico suggests that the Hebrew grammar was always dominated by the 'more sublime' and more analogical trope of metaphor. For this grammar, meaning is not a capturing and a containment in the present, but rather a dialectic of presence and absence.

Because signification is not restriction, it is here impossible to carry out predictive 'divinations', or to bind the future. There can only be anticipatory prophecy, which respects the freedom of providence. Vico by no means thinks that the Hebrews, being after all fallen, escaped all culpable violence, but he does identify a series of cultural postures, including greater friendliness to strangers, less possessive concepts of ownership, and, above all, absence of the *patria potestas*, which are all correlates of the principle that meaning is located in gratuitous creation or 'extension', rather than in disciplinary confinement.[82] This is Vico's gloss on Augustine's view that the virtue of the City of God, being able to root out anger and bad passion altogether, is most profoundly the power of charitable donation.

Like Berkeley, Vico had earlier developed a 'pragmatic' account of knowledge which he explicitly connects with the Trinity. Knowledge is constituted in the communicative triad *verum–factum–bonum* (the true/the made/the good) both for humans and for God.[83] In *De Uno* Vico actually gives a socio-historical equivalent for this triad – *tutela–dominium–libertas* (tutelage/language-or-property/liberty) which constitutes a kind of 'political' *vestigium trinitatis*.[84] The triad as a first 'natural law', condenses the rules for peaceful and equitable social transmission and distribution, and in particular it suggests that personhood is only enabled and conserved through natural filiation and cultural affiliation. This principle of sociation surpasses for Vico the pagan and Stoic *conatus* (*or philautia*) where self-preservation is always prior to relation and communication. The Trinitarian superimposition in fact 'decodes' *conatus* as merely reflecting a 'distorted Trinity' where the supposed 'primary self' conceals the constitution of this self through delayed and postponed violence.[85]

What Vico uniquely provides is an argument which connects the suppression of polysemy and the promotion of 'substance' to an entire religious culture which both sacralizes violence, and through its successive self-appropriations violently conceals this source of sacrality. It is thereby doomed both to repeat, and not really to know, its own construal of meaning. The promotion of polysemy, on the other hand, can only be entertained by a culture which assumes the possibility of infinite peace and justice.

7 Theology as Metasemiosis

This 'small encyclopaedia' has sought to trace a seemingly surprising movement whereby Christian thought moves away from a 'rationalist' to a more and more 'mystical' conception of language. And at the same time, it has shown that these 'mystical' tendencies accompany the first 'linguistic turn' in modern thought.

This occasions an impossible reflection: is it somehow the case that polysemy, irreducible semiotic difference, the necessity of language for thought, which carry such 'relativizing' implications, are *themselves* relative to a particular, ultimately religious culture? It is impossible for us really to think about this. We must rather suppose that these principles are themselves 'objective'. Yet it is important, all the same, to realize that they never get concretely *accepted* in a cultural vacuum; rather they are arrived at in specific, often 'strange' ways, and in the contexts of theologies and metaphysics which have the *practical* concern of asking about the kind of ultimate reality in which these principles inhere and therefore about how we are to live them out.

It is then important to realize that 'the suspicion of substance' does *not* arise initially from a 'neutral' rational *critique*, but from a theological *metacritique of* the metaphysical tradition. It may be objected by some that 'substance' is integral to the Christian definition of orthodoxy. Yet it is much more the case that orthodoxy presses against substance; the *homoousion* is really redundant, once the principle of substantive relation is established, and the more the 'personal' union of divinity and humanity in Jesus is reduced to a 'subsistent' one, then the more it is seen as a kind of Nestorian 'aggregation', as Gilbert de la Porrée pointed out in the twelfth century. Gilbert also removed the Greek 'hypostatic' connotations of the Trinitarian *persona* by re-defining the person as 'an incommunicable form', whose positional difference ensures that its individuality cannot be *composed* with other forms, according to its very mode of being, instead of the Boethian 'individual rational substance'.[86] In the next century Aquinas (following Augustine) denied that God can be properly seen as a substance in which anything inheres or an essence to which anything may be joined.[87] Since God is infinite, and beyond the range of applicability of pairs of contrasting notions like 'universal' and 'individual', he cannot be substance in the sense of sustaining something else, not even himself, no more than for Aquinas (in contrast with Descartes, later), God is *causa sui*. Likewise (one may add to Aquinas) he cannot be substance *even* in the sense of 'self-sufficiency', for this notion still suggests an 'outside' by which something remains unaffected. For God's 'simplicity' there is no outside, and therefore it is also beyond the contrast 'self-sufficient' versus affectable-from-without. Aquinas's assertion of the primacy of transcategorical Being and Unity over abstract essence also restricted the role of substance within the created order. For example, he is able to classify the 'intellectual powers of the soul' as 'somewhere between substance and accident' because he is now able to see (following the logic of 'grace') that something can belong to concrete existence and unity and even be the most important thing about it, although it is an 'extra' which does not belong 'essentially' to its 'substance'.[88] This approaches not so remotely to the idea that human beings, in their cultural reality, are only clusters of *differentia*. If one understands these clusters to hold together as grace-given participations in the divine unity and existence of beauty, then this is not an unbearable thought. (It should be noted that while Duns Scotus, rightly, goes further in qualifying hylomorphism by rejecting material individuation, his 'formal individuation' or *haecceitas*, suggests an unlimited number of individual species which are also *substances*. By contrast, Thomist participation in *esse*, prised apart from 'lower level' form/matter dualism, would be commensurate with a reality of shifting identities, composed solely of relative figural differences and affinities.)

A second, more fruitful reflection, arises from the fact that 'the suspicion of substance' leads, in the case of the most 'advanced' eighteenth-century Christian thinkers, in the direction of a kind of primitivism which half-recovers the perspective of pre-alphabtic, hieroglyphic cultures. For these cultures, as Roy Harris puts it, 'reality is still not clearly divisible into language and non-language, any more than it is divisible into the physical and the metaphysical, or into the moral and the practical'.[89] Perhaps this 'totemism' remains the matrix of all 'religious' consciousness, and the kind of intellectual movements I have traced present certain (only approximate) parallels to the 'remythologization' that Gershom Scholem discovers in the Jewish Kabbalah. If the Kabbalist treatment of writing (where even individual letters have semantic value) seems to suggest a kind of nostalgia for the hieroglyphic, 'real', mimetic letters, then it may also be possible to say that alphabetization (invented by the semitic Phoenicians) never had quite the same logocentric implications within the Biblical, as in the Greek tradition. The danger of alphabetic writing is that it may encourage 'fixation' of meaning and the illusion that letters primarily 'stand for' sounds which in turn 'stand for' ideas clearly 'present' to our consciousness.[90] But as against any view that one particular technique is in itself metaphysically fatal, one might rather suggest, (following Vico), that cultures which use hieroglyphs to 'divinate' will continue to 'divinate' with alphabetic letters, reducing truth to determinate manipulation. It is possible that within Hebrew culture the very brevity and fluidity of alphabetic writing assisted the reach and range of a narrative imagination beyond the too-obvious presence of the hieroglyph. Yet at the same time a prophetic and typological culture cannot finally lose touch with these totemic beginnings as it does not seek to obscure its origins, nor the material and metaphoric genesis of its meanings.

It is not then wholly surprising that Christian thought should come to a renewed preoccupation with this genesis. Just as, for structuralists, a novel is ultimately 'about' its self-constitution as a novel, so theology has only ever really been 'about' its own possibility as theology, as 'divine language'.[91] And if it is true that Trinitarian thought has intermittently found it possible to think the truth of polysemy and the original 'totemic' apprehension of being, then this is only because it is also a 'metasemiotic' concerned to think the possibility of polysemy, and the real character of differential substitution. Already, in the tradition, Christian theology has begun to be a metaphysics/metasemiotics of relation, rather than a metaphysics of substance.

As against this reflection, Umberto Eco argues in *Semiotics and the Philosophy of Language* that the only real cultural choice is between a clearly 'coded' and generally understood set of conventions on the one hand, and the control of interpretation by arbitrary authority on the other. The latter is all that the 'hermeneutic circle' really comes to.[92] In his defence of modern, liberal society on the first model, he argues against the opinions of 'nihilist mystics' like Gilles Deleuze or Jacques Derrida, which suggest that symbolic participation and uncontrollable polysemy ('dissemination') threaten every cultural artefact. Instead, Eco claims that there are relatively stable, coded enclaves (firmly distinguishing between *permitted* interpretative laxity and *transgression* of the code itself) and that the 'symbolic' has to be indicated within an otherwise coded text as a 'free' signifier which 'detonates' an infinite realm of possible meanings. The only rational place for the symbolic is within the text of a 'modernist' work of art and not in socially dangerous 'mysticisms' whether atheist or Christian. This view amounts to a clear suspicion of theology's claim, as a metasemiotic, to be at ease with polysemy. Is this claim not just authoritarianism?

But Eco's analyses remain confined (albeit residually) by the Romantic view of the symbol which sets it off against allegory.[93] Symbol, for Eco, is unlike metaphor which *to be understood* must be read non-literally, in a 'transferred' fashion, whereas the symbol has, initially, a sufficient meaning at the literal level. However, if a meaning is over-determined as symbolic, then this cannot merely be indicated (as Eco suggests) by the 'oddness' of its occurrence at a certain point in a narrative – this might only cause us to see an unwarranted intrusion. Instead, certain 'pregnant' associations, already partially coded, are also necessary: a certain metaphoric transference *is* indicated, and this involves certain 'allegoric' conventions also. The 'free association' which the symbol sets off has, in consequence, endlessly ramifying textual and inter-textual implications. 'Coded enclaves' which lay claim to univocity, are not free from subversion, because their relative stability depends upon a suppression of indeterminism, a suppression that must be endlessly repeated and revised, as it cannot be 'fully clear', even within the protocols of its own acts of occlusion.

There is, then, no liberal enclave in which one can shelter from 'mystical nihilism'. The real cultural issue lies between this nihilism and theology. Christian theology has been able, like sceptical postmodernism, to think unlimited semiosis. It is therefore not a mere dialectics concerning the mutual presence of reason, but a 'trialectics' which articulates the deferrals of the sign. The contrast with postmodernism lies at the level of metasemiotics, where the nihilists seem only able to think of signified absence in terms of a necessary suppression, betrayal or subversion. Yet this may still repeat the Stoic theory of meaning as single substantial *process* and self-consumption, a theory which is unprovable, although pure reason cannot outlaw the strange stance of having *faith* in the ultimacy of substance (which means, precisely, continuing to hold to *philosophy*, but fideistically). For theology, and theology alone, difference remains real difference since it is not subordinate to immanent univocal process or the fate of a necessary suppression. Instead, the very possibility of substitutive transference is here held to be a peacful affirmation of the other, consummated in a transcendent infinity. And the seeming arbitrariness of the 'next step' in this process of referral is held to be governed by an aesthetic rule which transcends the polarity of the same-and-determined over against the contingent-and-heterogeneous. Otherwise both chance and determination, or *difference* hypostasized, still present us with the antique aspect of substance, our always 'understood' futility. *O Quanta qualia . . .*

Notes

1 Cited in Paulo Rossi, *The Dark Abyss of Time: The History of the Earth and the History of Nations from Hooke to Vico*, trans. Lydia G. Cochrane (Chicago University Press, Chicago, 1984), p. 265. See also pp. ix–x, 101–7, 168–270.
2 Eusebius, *Praeparatio Evangelium*, 1.1 cap 10; V. cap 5.
3 Gregory of Nyssa, 'Against Eunomius', XII, 4. *Nicene and Post Nicene Fathers*, vol. 5, eds Henry Ware and Philip Schaff (Parker, Oxford, 1893), pp. 266–78. And see III, 7; VIII, 2; also 'Answer to Eunomius's Second Book', pp. 266–78.
4 Origen, *Contra Celsum*, I, 16, 24.
5 See A. A. Long, 'Language and Thought in Stoicism', in *Problems in Stoicism*, ed. A. A. Long (Athlone Press, London, 1971), pp. 73–114, for the relationship between Augustine and Stoicism. For Stoicism and language see also, M. Frede, 'Principles of Stoic Grammar', in *The Stoics*, ed. John M. Rist (California University Press, Berkeley, 1978), pp. 27–75. In the same volume see also Andreas Gralser, 'The Stoic Theory of Meaning', pp. 97–9 and Michael Lapidge, 'Stoic Cosmology', pp. 161–85.
6 Augustine, *De dialectica*, trans. D. Darrell Jackson (D. Reidel, Dordrecht, 1975), chapter V., p. 89.
7 Augustine, 'Concerning the Teacher' chapter 2, in *Basic Writings of St Augustine*, vol. 1, ed. Whitney J. Oates (Random House, New York, 1971), p. 363.
8 *De Dialectica*, chapter V., p. 87.
9 Umberto Eco, *Semiotics and the Philosophy of Language* (Macmillan, London, 1984), p. 33ff. Although I express some disagreements with Eco further on, this essay is deeply indebted to his brilliant historical and philosophic insights.
10 See Eco, *Semiotics*, pp. 46–86. Against the 'tree of substance' one can say that the list of 'essential attributes' of a thing is not finitely fixed or exhaustively determinable.
11 Augustine, 'Christian Instruction', in *Writings of St Augustine*, vol. 4, trans John J. Gavigan (Catholic University of America Press, Washington, 1966), 1.39, 2.2, 2.28, pp. 59, 62, 98–9.
12 Ibid., 1.2, p. 28.
13 Ibid., 2.6, 3.27, pp. 66, 147.

14 Ibid., 1.33, p. 53.

15 Aristotle, *Poetics*, XX. 2–XX. 1.4 (1456. 22–1457. 6). Augustine, 'Concerning the Teacher', p. 363. See also, Jacques Derrida, 'White Mythology: Metaphor in the Text of Philosophy' in *Margins of Philosophy*, trans. Alan Bass (Harvester, Brighton, 1982), p. 223.

16 'Answer to Eunomius's Second Book', p. 270.

17 Augustine, 'Christian Instruction', 3.6, p. 125.

18 Dante, *De Vulgari Eloquentia*, Book One, II–VII.

19 Dante, *Paradiso*, Canto XXVI, 130–1: Opera naturale è ch'uom favella / ma cosi o cosi, natura lascio / poi fare a voi secondo che u'abbella.

20 On this see Hans Aarsleff, 'Leibniz on Locke on Leibniz', in *From Locke to Saussure* (Athlone, London, 1982), pp. 42–84.

21 Umberto Eco, *Art and Beauty in the Middle Ages*, trans. Hugh Bredin (Yale University Press, New Haven, 1986), p. 113. See also Hans-Georg Gadamer, *Truth and Method*, trans. William Glen-Doepel (Sheed and Ward, London, 1975), pp. 378–87; Karl-Otto Apel, *Die Idee der Sprache in der Tradition des Humanismus von Dante bis Vico* (Herbert Grundmann, Bonn, 1980), pp. 79ff., 264–76.

22 See Bernard Lonergan, *Verbum: Word and Idea in Aquinas* (Notre Dame, Indiana, 1967) and S.T.I.Q. 27, 1 ad 2, 3.

23 Emmanuele Tesauro, *Il Cannochiale Aristotelico* (Venice, 1655). See Eco, *Art and Beauty*, pp. 105–7 and F. Hallyn, 'Port-Royal vs. Tesauro: Figure, Signe, Sujet', *Baroque*, 9–10 (1980), pp. 76–85. In the same volume see also Jean-Marie Wagner, 'Theorie de l'Image et Pratique Iconologique', p. 71.

24 Nicholas of Cusa, *De Docta Ignorantia*, II, chapter 9, *Idiota: De Mente*, III., chapter 2.

25 Martin Luther *Gesamt Schriften*, Weimarer Ausgabe, Bd. XV. 37ff. And see Gerhard Ebeling, *Evangelische Evangelienauslegung* (Wissenschaftliche Buchgesellschaft, Darmstadt, 1969), pp. 362–5.

26 In seeing God as the *omninominabile* Nicholas is, of course, in an old Christian neoplatonic tradition – what is innovative is understanding this divine 'inclusion' as embracing also the history of human linguistic performances. This is the reverse side of Nicholas's new concept of the *imago Dei* as residing in human *creative* participation in the emanation of the divine *Logos*. But see p. 83, n. 62 above.

27 See M.-D. Chenu, 'The Symbolist Mentality', in *Nature, Man and Society in the Twelfth Century*, trans. J. Taylor and L. K. Little (Chicago University Press, Chicago, 1983), pp. 124–7. Arguably, however, Origen's exegesis already pointed in the direction of this fusion.

28 This expression of St Jerome is cited by Eco, *Art and Beauty*, p. 149.

29 See Henri de Lubac, *Exégèse Médiévale; Les Quatres Sens de l'Ecriture* (Aubier, Paris, 1964), II, II, pp. 263–302.

30 De Lubac, *Exégèse*, II. II. pp. 198–207, 317–28, 249–352. De Lubac's book is seriously neglected, and other treatments of the topic like those of Beryl Smalley and R. M. Grant appear highly inaccurate in the light of his findings.

31 See Aarsleff, *From Locke to Saussure*, pp. 187–9.

32 John Locke, *An Essay Concerning Human Understanding*, III, VI, 44–7; V, 1–8. And see Aarsleff, 'Leibniz on Locke on Language'.

33 G. W. Leibniz, *New Essays on Human Understanding* (Cambridge University Press, Cambridge, 1980), Book III, 'Of Words', especially pp. 277–82; James Harris, *Hermes, or*

a Philosophical Inquiry concerning Human Grammar (The Scolar Press, Menston, 1968), II. V, pp. 291–303; III. I–V, pp. 306–410; James Burnet, *Of the Origin and Progress of Language* (The Scolar Press, Menston, 1967), vol. I, pp. 52–69, 141–51, 191–209, 246ff.

34 For Lowth and Hamann, see the preceding essay, 'Pleonasm, Speech and Writing'.

35 For the following account of Berkeley I am indebted to Colin Murray Turbayne. See his 'Berkeley's Metaphysical Grammar', in *A Treatise Concerning the Principles of Human Knowledge, with Critical Essays*, ed. Turbayne (Bobbs-Merrill, Indianapolis, 1970), pp. 3–37, and 'Lending a Hand to Philonous: The Berkeley, Plato, Aristotle Connection', in Turbayne, ed., *Berkeley: Critical and Interpretative Essays* (Manchester University Press, Manchester, 1982), pp. 295–310. My account of 'notions' departs, however, from that of Turbayne, as does my reading of *Siris*.

36 Basil, 'The Hexaemeron', in *Nicene and Post-Nicene Fathers*, vol. VIII (Jakes Parker, Oxford, 1895), p. 63.

37 Basil, 'The Hexaemeron', p. 8.

38 Cited in Richard Sorabji, *Time, Creation and the Continuum* (Duckworth, London, 1983), p. 293 and see pp. 290–4.

39 For the account below, see, especially, George Berkeley, *Works*, eds A. A. Luce and T. E. Jessop (Nelson, London, 1964), vol. 2, 'There Dialogues between Hylas and Philonous' pp. 233–5, 245, 249, 253–6; vol. 3, 'Alciphron', pp. 147, 161–2, 166–70, 292–9, 305–29; *Principles of Human Knowledge*, paras 6–14, 18–27, 43–4, 65–6, 98–100, 108–9, 145–9; *A New Theory of Vision*, paras 144, 147; *Siris*, paras 44, 152, 161–4, 206–8, 229, 236–9, 254–53, 281, 304–17, 322–39, 339–43, 368.

40 Berkeley, 'Alciphron', pp. 294–5.

41 *Berkeley's Commonplace Book*, ed. G. A. Johnston (Faber & Faber, London, 1930), 677.

42 I am using C. S. Peirce's category of 'abduction' to explicate the role of 'algebraic' signs or terms like 'force' in Berkeley. Abduction differs from induction because one is not here following a code or a rule of experience which tells one what to infer to from a given sign, but one here has to *posit* the code at the same time as making the inference.

43 John of St Thomas, *Cursus Philosophicus Superlibros Perihermenios* Q. 21. For a modern edition of this work see John Deely, *Tractatus de Signis: The Semiotic of John Poinsot* (University of California Press, Berkeley, 1985); see also Thomas Aquinas, *De Ente et Essentia*, III. 7. Speaking of the human essence, though the point applies to all essences, Aquinas says: 'Although this nature apprehended by the intellect has the character of a universal from its relation to things outside the soul, because it is one likeness of them all, nevertheless as it has being in this or that intellect it is a particular apprehended likeness.' This astonishing passage not only suggests that Aquinas thinks of the genus as operating like a sign, but also that human nature is only discovered in a signifying intersubjectivity. For all universal natures in the intellect are related to the 'outside', (as *esse intentionale*) and earlier Aquinas says 'human nature happens to have the character of a species only through the being it has in the intellect' (III, 6). On this whole area see John N. Deely, 'The Two Approaches to Language: Philosophical and Historical Reflections on the Point of Departure of Jean Poinsot's Semiotic', *The Thomist*, xxxvii (4 October 1974). See also, John N. Deely, 'Editorial Afterword', in *Tractatus de Signis*, pp. 471–512) and Jacques Maritain, *Distinguish to Unite*, trans Gerard Phelan (Bles, London, 1949), chapter 3, 'Critical Realism', pp. 71–136; and *Redeeming the Time* (Bles, London, 1943), chapter 9, 'Sign and Symbol', pp. 191–225. Maritain's rebuttal of Maréchal and the 'transcendental turn' can only be grasped if one understands the use he makes of John

of St Thomas's semiotic. For Maritain this allows a 'modern' grasp of human creativity and historicity to be grafted onto metaphysical realism – though doubtless, he does not take the necessary revisions far enough.

44 Berkeley, *A New Theory of Vision*, 147. It should be noted here that if one accepts the abolition of the *res/signum* distinction, one would have to add to Berkeley (though he may partly imply this) a relativization of the distinction between the relation of signifying implication that pertains between signifier and signified on the one hand, and the merely 'material' relation of contiguity that pertains between thing and thing or different parts of a single thing, on the other. In the latter case, material or figural relations are *also* semiotic in that only by constantly substituting whole for part and effect for cause, do we conceive 'organic wholes' and 'necessary sequences' rather than mere chaotic flux. In the former case, the semiotic relation is also *figural* and bodily rather than mysteriously 'spiritual', such that one should think of it as involving various degrees of spatial or temporal 'stretch', within an ontological continuum (again, this is related to Stoic philosophy. But one needs to overcome any suggestion of a determinate continuum *apart from* its contingent instances). These two aspects – the semiotic and the figural – are seen to come together in the linguistic sentence where the 'syntagmatic', sequential order of meaning, giving the sentence its figurative shape, is only enabled by the 'paradigmatic' associations that already pertain between the linguistic elements. Yet if one reflects on these paradigmatic connections, one can only spell out their logic in terms of 'earlier sentences', earlier figurative sequences, whether temporal or spatial; sequences which *again* assume paradigmatic connections already in place, and so on . . . *ad infinitum*. On the question of sign and figure see J. F. Lyotard, *Discours, Figure* (Klinksieck, Paris, 1985).

45 Berkeley, 'Alciphron', pp. 116–36.

46 Berkeley, *Philosophical Commentaries*, 577, 580; *Berkeley's Commonplace Book*, 659–61, 665, 646, 726–7.

47 Berkeley, *Philosophical Commentaries* 576, *Berkeley's Commonplace Book*, 713, 861.

48 Basil, 'Hexaemeron', p. 63.

49 Berkeley, *Siris*, 243, 252, 281. Berkeley understands this to be Newtonian as opposed to Cartesian physics. He claims to find the principle of the 'heterogeneity of light' in Newton, but he firmly rejects Newton's panentheism which tends to see a vacuous space, or an 'elastic aether' as the direct divine presence: ibid., 238, 249.

50 Ibid., 273 and 252, 281.

51 Ibid., 187.

52 Berkeley, *Principles of Human Knowledge*, p. 99, 'all sensible qualities [ideas] are alike sensations and alike real'. Note that while Berkeley rejects 'underlying' matter, his philosophy is radically corporeal. His statement 'sensual pleasure is the *summum bonum*' is metaphysically grounded within his '*idealism*'(!) and does not just reflect a utilitarianism which he later transcended: *Berkeley's Commonplace Book*, No. 702. See also Berkeley, 'Three Dialogues between Hylas and Philonous', p. 235.

53 Berkeley, 'Three Dialogues between Hylas and Philonous', p. 231.

54 Berkeley, *Siris*, 362.

55 Ibid., 304, 339, 352, 357, 362. Berkeley reads back 'sublime hints' of the Trinity into the Platonic tradition, but he retains, even after Casaubon, the view that this tradition originally sprang from revelation, not reason along: Berkeley, *Siris*, p. 260. A passage in 'Alciphron' (pp. 300–1) suggests that Berkeley believes that the Trinity can stand

without substance. Here he says that the *homoousion* formula intended a *negative* exclusion of polytheism and sabellianism rather than any positive affirmation of a substantial entity.

56 Ibid., 362.

57 *Berkeley's Commonplace Book*, 5. 793: The principle, *Nihil dat quod non habet*, 'I do not understand or believe to be true.'

58 See Sorabji, *Time, Creation*, pp. 186–7.

59 Berkeley, *Siris*, 357; 'Alciphron' pp. 305, 329, 35.

60 Berkeley, 'Alciphron', p. 307. Although, in the Middle Ages, Duns Scotus and William of Ockham had already suggested modifications to the Aristotelian 'semantic triangle', these did not really amount to outright rejection, like Berkeley's position. For the medieval thinkers, spoken and written signs were still the instruments of concepts which were the real, primary signs of things. However, they considered that words primarily signify things rather than concepts, first, because the mind becomes aware of concepts only through a reflective 'second intention', and second, because they both rejected – in very different ways – the Thomist notion that conceptual thought was the primary ontological site of really 'universal' being. For Scotus there was a real universality 'out there', formally distinct from the particulars in which it was instantiated; for Ockham universality had no ontological reality whatsoever, and concepts were merely signs standing for many particulars (see Armand Maurer, 'William of Ockham on Language and Reality', *Miscellanea Mediaevalia*, 13, 2 (1981), pp. 795–802). Berkeley, however, does not see spoken and written words as merely 'assisting' a more fundamental conceptual signification, and he conceives the relationship of word to reality as more active and transformative than representational. If one wished further to position him in relation to the mediaeval debates about universals then one would probably have to say that he is closer to Aquinas than Ockham, because the concept in human language, like the *genus* in Thomist *esse intentionale*, is for Berkeley *at once* 'sign' (as for Ockham) yet *also*, in some sense a 'real' universal. Whereas, for Aquinas, sign is also real universal because it intends concrete particulars which 'participate' in a real (but not formally distinct) essence, for Berkeley this is the case because the natural things on which words operate are themselves 'linguistic', such that the particular constitutive elements of things turn out to have an irreducibly 'universal' character. (The anticipations of both Hegel and Peirce are obvious.)

61 J. G. Hamann, 'Metacritique of the Purism of Reason', in *J. G. Hamann; A Study in Christian Existence*, ed. Ronald Gregor Smith (Collins, London, 1960), p. 213. Hamann cites Berkeley's view that 'general and abstract ideas are nothing but particular ideas, but bound to a certain word, which gives a greater scope or extension to their meaning, and at the same time reminds us of that meaning in individual things'. He then suggests that this semiotic principle makes Kant redundant, and permits a 'metacritique' of the Kantian *a priori*. See also J. G. Herder, 'Ideas for a philosophy of the history of mankind' in F. M. Barnard, *J. G. Herder on Social and Political Culture* (Cambridge University Press, Cambridge, 1969) p. 262: 'as Berkeley observes, light is the language of divinity which our finest sense does but continually spell out in a thousand forms and colours'. For Herder, however, this hermeneutic relation to nature suggests the possibility of a true human development which will be aesthetic; an increase in 'the subtlety of perception'.

62 J. G. Herder, 'Essay on the Origin of Language', in *On the Origin of Language*, eds John H. Moran and Alexander Code (Ungar, New York, 1966), pp. 129–32.

63 Walter Benjamin, 'On the Mimetic Faculty', in *One-Way Street* (New Left Books, London, 1979), pp. 160–3. In the same volume see 'On Language as such and on the Language of Man' (1916), pp. 107–23. This essay perhaps owes more to Hamann and Herder than to the Kabbalah. But Benjamin adds the profound reflection that a surviving perception of *mere* arbitrariness in our linguistic usage, which sets culture 'over against' nature, is precisely the measure of our *fallenness*. Note here that the Saussurean point that e.g. the word 'dark' is in no way like 'the actual dark' is too simple. We only *know* 'the actual dark' through a whole nebula of signifying practices (many of them much more 'iconic' than language) and therefore it is impossible to disprove that even the sound 'dark' does not also colour, for English speakers, our sense of 'darkness'.

64 Umberto Eco, *A Theory of Semiotics* (Indiana University Press, Bloomington, 1979), pp. 66ff.

65 Herder, 'Essay on the Origin of Language', pp. 104ff.

66 Smith, *J. G. Hamann*, p. 81.

67 Mark C. Taylor, *Deconstructing Theology* (Scholar's Press, Chicago, 1982), p. 91. Taylor is following Edward Said here; see note 83 below. When I say 'theology' it is true that I mean here the theologically informed philosophy of lay thinkers. Yet in this period a 'theology proper' which rested on an extrinsicist dualism of grace and nature, a 'foundationalism' of either 'revelation' or 'reason', and a univocal concept of divinity, was often more in keeping with the rationalist temper of the times than a persisting Christian humanism which sought to think more holistically. (This is not to deny that such humanism often suffers the lack of a 'professional' theology.)

68 Herder, 'Essay on the Origin of Language', p. 133.

69 G. B. Vico, *Scienza Nuova Terza* (*The New Science*, in English), paras 403 and 400–519.

70 See Hans Frei, *The Eclipse of Biblical Narrative* (Yale University Press, New Haven, 1986), p. 169ff. (Frei talks of 'typology' where I talk of 'allegory', because, following de Lubac, I see no essential distinction between the two.)

71 J. G. Herder, 'Yet Another Philosophy of History', in F. M. Barnard, *J. G. Herder*, pp. 187–8.

72 Vico, *Scienza Nuova Prima*, Part 3, chapter XIV. Part 3, chapters XXIII–XXIV, 5, IV, in Giambattista Vico, *Opere Filosofiche*, ed. Paolo Cristofolini (Sansoni, Florence, 1971).

73 This would account for Vico's increasing silence about the Hebrews, and the later allusion to *onomathesia*, which appears to exclude the Hebrew culture from the category of human, 'poetic' formation. Yet isolated passages, even in the *Scienza Nuova Terza*, make it clear that no such exclusion is really intended.

74 S.N.T. 165; S.N.P. 1, VII.

75 S.N.P. 3. XXIII.

76 S.N.P. 1. VII; S.N.T. 165.

77 S.N.T. 379.

78 S.N.T. 379: 'They believed that Jove commanded by signs, that such signs were real words, and that nature was the language of Jove. The science of this language the gentiles universally believed to be divination, which by the Greeks was called theology, meaning the science of the language of the *gods*.' See also S.N.T. 374–99.

79 *De Uno* Part 1, chapter XXXVIII, in Giambattista Vico, *Opere Giuridiche* (Sansoni, Florence, 1974). For an elaboration of the critique of virtue as restriction, see chapter 9, 'Can Morality by Christian?' below.

80 S.N.T. 428–35, 529–31.

81 S.N.T. 391, 403. See also *De Antiquissima Italorum sapientia* 2 and 7. V. The 'theoretical' and 'divinatory' chapter of gentile culture explains for Vico why philosophy perpetuates the ahistoricity of mythology. See S.N.P. 1, IX.

82 *De Constantia*, Part 2, chapter X(4), (5), and XI see also IIV(4), (7), (8), (10), (18), X, XI, 2 VIII, in Giambattista Vico, *Opere Giuridiche*. *The Patria Potestas* was the Roman father's right of life and death over his offspring. For the 'sublimity' of Hebrew see S.N.P. 1, IX, 3, LXXXIV.

83 Vico, *De Antiquissima*, 1.1.11. Edward Said and others are facilely modernist and unhistorical in their reading of *verum-factum as* marking out a 'secular' space. *Factum* (the made) is for Vico a new 'transcendental' in the scholastic sense, and thus the necessary 'construction' in human knowledge is *itself* the moment of participation in divine knowing/making. Humans are providentially guided *through* their poetic powers, and Vico is anxious to present this in terms of a Catholic theology of grace steering a 'mid course' between Molinism and Jansenism (see S.N.T. 310 and 130). Rossi's considerations, and my own in this article, show that for Vico the contrast between gentile and Biblical history is not between 'secular' and 'sacred' but between the 'city of this world', distorting both *poesis* and the concept of providence into divination, and the 'city of God' whose true, metaphorical *poesis* is open to providential freedom. See Edward Said, *The World, The Text and the Critic* (Faber, London, 1984), pp. 1–31, 111–26, 290–5.

84 Vico, *De Uno* I, LXXIV, *dominium* is equivalent to *factum* or *verbum* (language) for Vico, because the primitive language concerned the social organization of space. Thus the first signs were *termini* (whence 'terms', says Vico), the boundary-markers of fields which also 'commemorated' the ancestors. Hence to 'own' was to appropriate 'the name', precisely the *grave-stone* of one's father: S.N.T. 529–30.

85 I am only able to state this argument about Vico in abbreviated form here. However, it is clear that the usual presentations of Vico (e.g. that of Northrop Frye), which concentrate on a diachrony of Divine (poetic)–Heroic–Human (prosaic) language are quite wide of the mark. The 'heroic' language of war and sacrifice was for Vico virtually as old as the 'divine' language of divination and even the human language had a primaeval beginning as the grunts of protest of those still-feral humans who were enslaved by 'linguistic man'. This, for Vico, is the *social* origin of a predominantly *vocal* language. Moreover, Vico associates social protest by the plebs in Rome who were still excluded from the full *linguistic* privileges of marriage, burial and divination with reinvigoration, through the first use of *irony*, of figurative (generically 'metaphoric') tension within the metonymic cause/effect relation which 'binds' them to their masters (S.N.T. 403, 414–26, 444). Instead of simply taking 'the effect' (their subordination and exclusion) for 'the cause' (the fully human 'heroes') the plebs come to see that they can also 'take the cause for the effect' and initiate their own exercise *of dominium*. In the early nineteenth century the French Catholic Romantic, Pierre-Simon Ballanche, notably reads into Vico the idea that the Roman plebs were a *figura Christi*, suffering, precisely, 'for humanity'. And in Vico himself the plebeian reintroduction of figurative tension allows a more equitable justice which takes account of particulars and the topical 'scope' of legal issues, but 'perfect' equity only arrives with the merging of Trinitarian faith (culmination of the 'true' monotheistic *poeisis*) and Roman law (*De Uno*, CCXIV, CCXVIII). Thus the synchronic contrast of 'two cities' is secretly predominant in Vico's writings (as regards 'abstract' human language Vico thinks this can aid metaphoric openness and equity if the universal is regarded as a *topos* or aid to discovery, not if seen as a 'closed' essence). See

further, John Milbank, *The Religious Dimension in the thought of Giambattista Vico*, vols I and II (E. Mellen, New York, 1991 and 1992).

86 On Gilbert, see Lauge Olaf Nielsen, *Theology and Philosophy in the Twelfth Century* (Brill, Leiden, 1982), especially pp. 62–5, 149–84.

87 Aquinas also thinks the distinction of divine essence from Trinitarian relations is only *secundum dici*, from our 'point of view' S.T.I.Q. 1 a 28 ad 2.

88 S.T.I.Q. 77 a 6 ad 3. The oxymoronic 'proper accidents' which are the soul's intellectual powers are actually said to *emanate* from the soul like a kind of superaddition. But, as with the *verbum mentis*, Aquinas can *think* the (Trinitarian) oxymoron of 'an essential superfluity' because his entire metaphysics builds up to the paradox of grace: the 'infused *habitus*'. Hence Thomas's 'materialist' (Aristotelian) downgrading of intellect as essence or substance is only allowed by a wholly Christian (and partially neoplatonic) reconception of the 'intellectual light'. John of St Thomas, in the *Cursus Philosophicus*, says that if the grace of the sacrament really proceeds from the sacrament as sign then it must be related to a 'superadded quality', not the essence of the soul. Conversely, the sacrament itself must be a totally transparent 'real relation'.

89 Roy Harris, *The Origin of Writing* (Duckworth, London, 1986), pp. 131–2. See also, Benjamin Lee Whorf, 'Language Mind and Reality' in *Language, Thought and Reality*, (MIT Press, Cambridge, Mass., 1956).

90 See, classically, Jacques Derrida, *Of Grammatology*, trans G. V. Spivak (Johns Hopkins University Press, Baltimore, 1976).

91 One might construe the *Logos* and the *Pneuma* as like Vico's constructive *factum* and receptive *bonum* – 'transcendentals' that are *both* conditions of possibility ('Kantian') *and* participations in the plenitude of the Trinity which is fully true, 'made', good etc. ('scholastic'). Here the convertibility of *esse and verum* is an active conversion realized in the substitutive, expressive relation. However, the formal possibility must be *entirely* taken from a particular history – the Incarnation, the Church. This *contingent* making possible of communication (which means, especially, 'possible through the cross') alone *allows* the double sense of transcendentality (by comparison, Habermas's or Apel's 'bodily *a priori*' is really still a Kantian formalism).

92 Eco, *Semiotics and the Philosophy of Language*, pp. 150–1. But the 'hermeneutic circle' involved in the scheme presented in note 90 is *not* that of Gadamer – that is to say a general, 'transcendental' possibility of a benign to-and-fro as the 'meaning' of being. The Christian hermeneutic circle is only benign *via* the incarnation and the cross. And as 'the word of the Father', it is also the *metaphysical* circle of *exitus* and *reditus*, thinking the 'being of being' along with its meaning.

93 On this, see H.-G. Gadamer, *Truth and Method*, trans. W. Glen-Doepel (Sheed and Ward, London, 1979) pp. 150–1.

Christos

5

A Christological Poetics

The several volumes of Hans Urs von Balthasar's *Herrlichkeit*[1] have presented the argument that revelation needs to be understood in its aesthetic as well as its logical and ethical dimensions if it is to be adequately grasped at all. This thesis is specifically allied to a Christocentric emphasis deriving immediately from Barth, but owing much also to patristic and mediaeval theologians, not to mention the lone figures of Pascal and Hamann. The present chapter attempts to proceed within a kindred ambience, but stress is placed upon the poetic moment in aesthetic experience. By 'poetic' is meant here the realization or manifestation of the Beautiful, in contrast to the being of the beautiful object or the perception of beauty, which is the subject of aesthetics in the Kantian sense. Nevertheless, an ontology of the aesthetic object and a phenomenology of aesthetic experience are implicitly involved in what follows.

The paper will move from a consideration of human poetic existence through a questioning of how Jesus Christ is to be understood in this context, to an attempted presentation of our poetic existence in Christ.

1 The Poetics of Humanity

(a) *Poetic activity*

The poetic existence of humankind can be considered in three ways: first, as a specific activity, second, as a mode of knowledge, and, third, in relation to that integral activity by which we develop as human beings, which is to say, ethical behaviour.

In the first place one may begin with the definition of Aristotle in the *Nichomachean Ethics*, where he contrasts *poesis* with *praxis* by saying that whereas the latter is an act which remains within the subject, the former is an act which passes over into something external.[2] In *praxis* act and end are identical, in *poesis* act and end are distinguished. This definition, as it stands, tells us very little about the precise concern of the activity for the end it has in view. One must explore further. The guidance now offered by Aristotle is primarily negative, in that he is more interested in *praxis* than *poesis* and employs the former notion to restrict what one might call Plato's poetic understanding of ethical behaviour. For Plato human behaviour is to be moulded to the best possible conformity to ideal models. This process can be described as a technical reduction of *poesis* which reduces the act of making to a mere carrying out of preceding theoretical instructions, even if the theoretical grasp is never adequate, and this reserve does *begin* to grant poetic *mimesis* in time a theoretically constitutive role. In the *Poetics* Aristotle clearly shows that he also is familiar with a *poesis* that is not entirely reducible to a speculatively guided technique. Nevertheless, it is arguable that he is wary of *poesis* because a shadow of *techne* hangs over it which Aristotle's categorical equipment is not altogether adequate to banish. For only the 'internal' act of *praxis* was conceivable by him as entirely outside the manipulative anticipations of technique.

This is because in the last analysis Aristotle's metaphysical *schema* seems to demand that all movement is a progression from the privation of potential to the fullness and sufficiency of act.[3] In this context it is hard to conceive of a procession out of an active subject as a positive gain in being, still less as a gain in being for the subject. But this is surely how one wishes to categorize all meaningful human constructs. The human person, who is the producer of significant objects, regards such objects as worthy of maintenance, implying that their absence would mean a loss. Moreover, while he himself bestows meaning on the objects, he locates this meaning within the objects themselves. These circumstances could only be allowed for when Jewish, Islamic and Christian thinkers, above all Thomas Aquinas, in their attempts to do justice to the data of faith, sought to integrate the neoplatonic idea of emanation, shorn of its association with declension of being, with the Aristotelean categories of act and potency.[4] In Thomas we find the idea of *virtus* or active potency: the capacity of an active agent to engender a further gratuitous act, other than the act by which he is in being. Although this emanative act is a mere surplus for living existence, and although in its termination it stands objectively over against the subject, it nonetheless constitutes the subject as a subject. Thomas considered the identity of the subject in terms of the category of *habitus* or habitual character and he explicates *habitus* with reference to the analogical scope of the verb 'to have' as oscillating between predication of 'a state' and predication of relation.[5] It follows that we are habitually related to the products of *virtus* in that we both identify with them as realizing our selfhood in relation to a *telos*, and distinguish ourselves from them in so far as the self is never exhausted by any of its products and so retains *virtus* as its property.

This metaphysics of the person points the way, not followed by Thomas, towards understanding humanity as fundamentally poetic being. On the one hand, humanity exists as humanity in its very expressiveness, the course of its appropriation of its environment as a system of value; humanity constitutes the specificity of its nature within this process. 'Man' is, as Newman put it, 'emphatically self-made'.[6] On the other hand, as the Italian thinker, Emilio Betti, has said, in our relation to our own products there is always a strange tension between familiarity and unfamiliarity.[7] The product itself embodies a certain *virtus* of its own such that it cannot be displaced by the subject who is its author. In consequence, we come to depend upon the world of meanings that we ourselves have constituted to the extent that there is an infinite surplus of meaning in the human symbol and the human text.[8] It is more important to recognize this phenomenon than to explicate it, but one may say that it is linked to three circumstances. First, the fact that our constructions of meaning are also manifestations of life, of energy and desire which we never manage to master consciously in the course of our articulations, such that we have always spoken more than we realize. Second, our own self-awareness arises not in the Cartesian *cogito*, but in our finding ourselves in relation to other beings in whom we both actively recognize and do not recognize our own subjectivity, in an inexhaustible dialectic. In the third place, our products carry not only the charge of our own life and the presence of our human community, but also the ecstatic reach of our intention, although this is simultaneously and equally an intention of our products themselves, which have always already 'dispossessed' us. (Meaning only unfolds through the doings of intending subjects, and *yet* this is never simply 'their' meaning). It is this that ensures the presence of *virtus* in the product. Every act of inventive understanding is like the discovery of something new in the future, which 'occurs' to us, because only the process of completion of the product starts to reveal and define the active potency on which it depends.

The significance of 'poetry' as a human activity is then twofold: in the first place, humanity is the animal who quite gratuitously makes meaningful objects, the 'sign-maker' as the poet David Jones put it.[9] In this activity he becomes human. But in the second place, humanity is always trying to catch up with its own proper destiny. The phenomenon that we are somehow 'overtaken' by our products is seen at the most important historical level as the 'heterogenesis of ends' or the Hegelian 'cunning of reason'. Both these expressions refer to the way in which human historical formations in their development escape their original conscious purposes and yet serve an intelligible function. Hegel detected in this circumstance a process of immanent determinism, others the 'hidden hand' of an interposing providence. The 'heterogenesis of ends', however, was perhaps most comprehensively under-stood by the Neapolitan Giambattista Vico in the early eighteenth century.[10] Vico was reacting against another technical reduction of *poesis*, namely that of Thomas Hobbes's political science according to which man can effectively control his social destiny by obedience to an analytical blueprint. It is important here to note that in Vico the 'heterogenesis of ends' is linked to an account of poetic rather than technical endeavour analogous to the one I have outlined and not to any notions of an inexorable determinism on the one hand or of an *overruling* providence on the other.

For this connection suggests that it is not that later history dispossesses us of an intentional act (*praxis*) once controlled by us and properly our own, but rather that to *act at all* is always to be dispossessed, always continuously to apprehend 'more' in our own deed once it 'occurs' to us, than our first hazy probings towards the formulation of a performance could ever have expected. Thus we are not exactly tragically or comically robbed of 'our own' (Hegel) but rather in every act from its very first inception we are *both* entirely responsible and entirely not responsible. To maintain, nonetheless, in the face of this circumstance, a doctrine of full moral responsibility, requires precisely *faith* that if we attend to God, he will graciously provide us, out of ourselves, with appropriate good performances. The moral actor, since he *is* an artist, is as much at the mercy of 'the muse' (or the Holy Spirit) as the artist.

And yet, as Hegel rightly saw, intersubjectivity here intervenes to make things far more complex: for our receptivity to divine prompting is always preformed by our cultural inheritance (both remote and immediate) such that here again, we always in *every* act take responsibility for what we are also *not* responsible and have not instigated. And in this case, since the co-actor is not God but sinful humanity, that which is both ours and not ours may be something which distorts our 'true' good identity and leads us also to pervert the identities of others. But then in a third way again, the same sundering of 'propriety' intervenes, and this time as the 'heterogenesis of ends' in a radicalized form: to act is to act on others, and so always from the very outset of the act, the act is *as much* that which is received by others as that which is intended by us (just as our act is also that which 'occurs' to us – from God (?) – and again that which is given to us by our predecessors). To be open to the reception of grace in a preparedness to act, is, therefore, to be open to the risk that another may immediately ruin the gracious character of our 'poetic' performance. But even that formulation is inadequate, for without the 'good' reception by the other, or by many others, we should never in the first place receive at all the grace that is our own act: grace is always humanly mediated both before and 'after' its occurrence. And if a process of degeneration of an original 'good' act continues long after its 'original' instance (as, say, Stalinism long after 1917), then the bad later reception *does* inexorably contaminate the series of acts, right back to its origins, for two reasons. First, one can never be sure that the 'original act' could not have been produced in such a fashion as to *better guard against* degeneration (hence the plea, for example, in favour of an originally 'innocent' revolution is *a priori never* tenable), and, second, one can only *conjecture* as to the possibility that the first act could have turned out differently, proved itself to be a different sort of act – since there are no discrete acts – through a better history of reception. Once again it is only faith which can retrieve the first act, or series of acts, in distinction from their consequences, believing that greater openness to grace, from the outset or later (and one can never *exactly* apportion blame here) might have perpetuated or restored the original good impulse.

Hence, once 'heterogenesis of ends' has been radicalized in terms of a 'poetic' account of action, it can be seen that it concerns not a tragic distortion of good intentions which cannot foreknow future circumstances (Hegel), but rather a simultaneous and risky openness both to grace and the possibility of sinful distortion – for which one is both responsible and not responsible – within every action which is always from the first 'other' to itself, and hence always already a series of actions and not a single action alone. But conversely, the later series of actions still forms but a single action, such that all the actors taken collectively in their diachronic series constitute humanity as at last free and responsible. If *they* (through all history) we may believe, are open to receive by grace the work of humanity, then here is only trust, and *no* risk of sinful distortion, since here at last the only other co-partner in responsibility is God. Yet this means: only humans together and through all history are the one *free* human subject, free to receive their own work.

(b) *Poetic understanding*

The poetic operation of humanity is, in the second place, a way of understanding. Here we can find clues in Aristotle's poetics while suggesting that the kind of awareness which it is there said that fictional writings or dramatic performances can bring, is to some extent involved in all human making. Aristotle considers that poetry has in some sense a referential function – that it is *mimesis* – and that it also inaugurates a world – setting up an *ethos* through the employment of a *mythos*. It does not seem to have occurred to him that these characteristics were in any way antagonistic. This is because, as Ricoeur points out in *The Rule of Metaphor*, *mythos* and *mimesis* are really two aspects of a single process.[11] The model of reference involved is not one in which the detached mind can compare, for example, the hero in real life with the hero in the poem, but one in which it is only the *mythos* of the hero in the poem that makes present to us the phenomenon of heroism at all. There is, in consequence, an observed disparity between the poetic heightening of heroic characteristics and their less perfect manifestation in actuality, and this is because heroism is an inherently teleological phenomenon, in which we set before ourselves what we *are* as what we *might be*. It should be noted that teleology here is not necessarily founded on a biological concept, but is implicitly linked to a 'narrative' vision of human life, deriving ultimately from epic and the drama.

Ricoeur, relying on isolated remarks of Aristotle, suggests that this poetic act of understanding through a fiction can be described as a metaphorical act. Nature or *phusis* is an uninterrupted process of generation, but only *mimesis phuseos*, human poetry, has the capacity to interrupt nature by making something reflectively present through something else. As Ricoeur says, the fact that metaphor often appears to be a category mistake, confusing for example a genus with a species, merely points to something deeper: that it is the metaphorical act which in the first place generates the categories of understanding themselves. Primitive humanity, as Vico again was the first to realize, had no abstract concepts at his disposal, and could only arrive at understanding through the creative seizure of similarities and differences.[12] Initially human beings had to substitute one thing for another before they could reflectively isolate the common elements and the differentia. Important though this secondary reflective procedure is – and one should certainly not romantically regard it as symptomatic of human fallenness in the manner of Enrico Castelli[13] – it is easy to forget its essentially *provisional* character because of its immense intellectual and social usefulness.

Because metaphorical *poesis* does not appear to be bound by the principle of non-contradiction – which is not to say that it denies it as a principle of logic for established meanings, but that *poesis* is a logic for the establishment of meanings – it is easy to imagine that it disallows any stability of meaning. It is possible, however, and this is the important point to be insisted upon, to argue, again following a path first opened up by Vico, that there are poetic or concrete universals, just as there are reflective or philosophic universals.[14] It is very difficult for us to grasp this, because we are still to some extent mesmerized by Kant's distinction between pure and empirical reason in the Introduction to *The Critique of Pure Reason*.[15] There he argues that universal synthetic judgements are of two kinds: in the first place, those that are purely *a priori*, of which we are convinced without any external evidence, and in the second place, those that are merely empirical, which we make by collating what is always observed to happen. Some synthetic judgements of which we are universally convinced, however, do not fall distinctly into either category. Many are prescriptive – I would suggest 'Justice must always be seen to be done' in which elements of strong moral imperative and pragmatic worldly wisdom are in almost perfect tension, and in which both contribute to the immediate certainty of the saying. In all cases of this kind there is involved a kind of assent that has to do with the way we commonly behave as human beings, the way we *agree* to behave, implicitly or explicitly. They are *a priori* only in the sense that they invoke the specific ways in which human beings commonly appropriate their experience.

What has this to do with poetry? The answer is that the poetic judgement only creates relatively stable concrete universals through the mediation of this *sensus communis*.[16] It cannot, for example, isolate the *differentia* of the human species as an observed regularity or as an intuited quality, but must instead point to some specific feature such as extraordinary bodily strength and skill as an interpretative key and, through referring other things to this feature, gradually build up a picture. The pure strength of the *figura*, say 'Hercules', is elaborated in the depiction of the uses of this strength. A sense of what is admissible and inadmissible in Hercules slowly develops. A vital stage is, of course, the fixation of these boundaries in memorized and finally written verse (verse *because* memorable) and pictorial representation. As we know, it was through the Homeric poems (in their total history a collective achievement) that the chaotic localization of Greek myth was reformed and redirected. What one must then say is that *poesis*, far from inhibiting clear judgement and discrimination, first allowed it to arrive by providing in the concrete universal a measure and a *telos* for human activity. The poet Paul Claudel said that man is not like the animals predetermined to a particular end but 'obliged to compose for himself reasons'.[17] The first 'reasons' are these poetic ones; while less definable than abstract reasons, they are no less exact according to their own mode. Their exactitude runs more risk of being deceived by phenomenal resemblance, but allows more scope for creative re-application to practical living.

(c) *Poesis and praxis*

Poetic existence can then be described as a fundamental activity and as a fundamental mode of knowledge. But as a third consideration, how does it stand in relation to *praxis* or ethical activity, in which, according to Aristotle, the act is itself the end and we seek to conform ourselves to the Good? *Poesis*, as we have seen, is concerned with discernment of forms that are suitable and fitting, and so with aesthetics and the beautiful. However, since all our discernment proceeds *via* the means of representation, it is not genuinely possible to separate *praxis* from *poesis*. Moreover, it was shown in the last but one sub-section just how there *is* no activity which remains purely with the actor and does not already begin to be an 'alienated' product. It might be protested that a notion of the good which tends to regard it as but the imperative to produce the beautiful risks a dangerous 'aestheticization' in which people are merely reduced to parts of a harmonious whole. But to this one should reply that our sense that self-activating, variable 'parts' of nature – everything tending, in whatever degree, to 'subjectivity' – should somehow 'exceed' the whole, while *still* collaborating to produce an overall harmony, is itself not expressible as anything other than a *richer* more complex vision of what 'the beautiful' might be.

To grasp further the way in which poetics impinges on ethics one may advert directly to Vico, who in the *Sciena Nuova*[18] accounts for the barbarism and savagery of the heroes that goes unreproved in the ancient poetic authors by arguing that we misunderstand their works if we try to measure the heroes against abstract ideas of humanity, when for them 'man' was only *conceived* within the concrete heroic standard. The heroes show god-like power and authority, and this makes them stand out as men who are more than animals. Unheroic men and defeated heroes do not fully enter into the definition of humanity and therefore are properly subject to the arbitrary and god-like whims of the heroes. Something similar has to be said about societies which drown babies born out of wedlock; the certainty of generation guaranteed by marriage so enters into the definition of humanity that these babies fall outside its scope. One may take from these primitive examples offered by Vico a valid generalization: ethical activity always occurs within the bounds afforded by our poetic representations. And that this is something other than relativism should be obvious from the account given of poetic truth. Poetic representations themselves seek to establish a more adequate human *telos*; therefore they belong to a single practical–poetical movement which opens up deeper possibilities of human behaviour. As we have already seen, this truth makes us see just why 'a good intention' is not *yet* the good, and why it is not simply within the control of a good conscience and a good will (as Hegel saw) to perform a good act. At most, we have to be *collectively* open to the receiving of better performed representations which can only 'occur' to us as the arrival of performed 'events'.

From this analysis of the poetics of humanity has been gathered three important notions: those of the 'cunning of poetic reason' in poetic activity; of the 'concrete universal' in poetic understanding; and of the 'poetic boundedness of behaviour' in relation to ethical activity. Before turning to Christology it must be shown how these ideas help us to understand the human confrontation with God, as exemplified in the Old Testament. The Old Testament is chosen not merely because it is presupposed by the person and work of Christ, but also because Christians, Jews and Muslims take it as a standard for the true encounter of God with humanity and because, furthermore, it presents this encounter almost entirely in pre-reflective poetic terms.

2 The Poetic Encounter with God

At first sight the 'cunning of poetic reason' suggests a critical approach to primitive religion. There is something almost fetishistic about our seeking of meaning and value in our own cultural products and it is tempting to see the first gods as the creation of a total fetishism, in which the human power (or *virtus*) of invention is entirely projected upon the things invented. Such a strategy of suspicion is valid and even essential for theology. Nothing, however, except the resources of a *sensus communis* can arbitrate between this and another equally valid strategy in which the way our meaningful products 'occur' to us and so stand over against us, is seen as the human openness to divine revelation. The created natural order shows God to us, to be sure, but there is only a conscious awareness of God if he stands 'ahead of us' in the realm of 'objective spirit' that is human culture. This does *not* mean that God is the immanent process of human understanding, because that conception is ultimately indistinguishable from the idea that God is a pure projection; witness the relation in which Feuerbach stands to Hegel. Rather it means that because our cultural products confront us and are not truly 'in our control' or even 'our gift', this allows that somewhere among them God of his own free will finds the space to confront us also. The transcendental possibility of revelation is the decision of God to create the poetic being, humankind, and with this realization one can, at once, overcome a liberal, merely 'ethical' reading of religion, and also an (equally modern and deviant) positivistic notion of revelation as something in history 'other' to the normal processes of historicity. The event of revelation itself may be defined as the intersection of the divine and human creations. By this is meant that the 'overtaking' by the product of the creative act that brings it forth is now seen as the occasion on which God interposes without in any way violating the range of the natural human intent. At the point where the Divine creation establishes the human creation by overtaking and completing it, thereby exposing a realized intention more primitive than the human intent and fully its master, there is revelation. As Paul Celan puts it in a poem:

EIN DRÖHNEN: es ist
die Wahrheit selbst
unter die Menschen
getreten,
mitten ins
Metapherngestöber.[19]

Such a view of revelation is almost adequate to capture the diverse but analogous senses of the encounter with God as they emerge in the various written genres of the Old Testament. Although it locates revelation primarily in the world opened up by spoken words and even more by human texts, it requires the human inspiration that is their source, and also, because *mythos* is always *mimesis*, some kind of reference to the objective natural order, which includes humanity itself. In the Exodus narratives, for example, natural, God-ordained occurrences (both the cyclical processes of nature, and extraordinary, miraculous events) are brought within the historical order in so far as some attempt is made to give them a meaning. (See section 2, 'Lowth', in chapter 3, above.) Of course, these events may have been historical before the narrators had done their work; but they could not have been historical and so not vehicles for revelation before their appropriation as matter of human significance.

The dialectic of subjective and objective spirit is then doubled in the Old Testament by the dialectic of human and divine Spirit. The quest for the human *telos* is there also a quest for the representation of the unrepresentable, a subjectivity entirely prior to that of humanity. Such a quest can only be valid if it turns into a demand that God himself should establish his own most adequate manifestation within the historical order, a demand that arises within the history of Israel. On the other hand, there is never any question of abstractly isolating the appearance of the divine Beauty from the manifestation of the human *telos*; this is impossible, and, in fact, God's presence or Glory can only be apprehended as something attractive for humanity: something making a valid human demand, which, nonetheless, humanity can never adequately fulfil. This is how one should understand Israel's quest for a mediator who would be both an adequate representation of God to humanity and an adequate representative of humanity to God. Only such a mediator would fulfil God's creative purpose for human beings and so put an end to that contradiction which we find described as a terrible divine anguish in Jeremiah, the anguish of a God whose being *is* his purpose, who is yet despoiled of that purpose. In the prophetic period the prophet himself was the mediator, but already within that period doubts arise about this status, and these are increased with the decline of prophecy. As a mediator, the prophet is a kind of concrete exegesis of God to his people; the doubts concern the ability of man to project such a universal *figura* which would define and delimit the human situation.

It is important that this aesthetic dimension is recognized because it shows that Israel's dilemma is not purely a matter of ethical failure, but neither is it one of a problem of knowledge stemming from the ontological distance between God and man (as Barth in his Hegelian aspect seems at times to imply).[20] Rather, because ethical failure is perceived as increasingly deep-seated, amounting to some permanent impairment of the human will itself, so it is felt in Israel that the ontological distance has become a tragic distance whereby man is unable to form any reliable figurative conception of the order pertaining between God and man and thus lacks a context for acceptable action. The infinity of distance between God and humanity is intrinsically an infinity of promise for endless human advancement; but where the representation of this promise is uncertain, this benign infinite may appear as a Hegelian 'bad infinite' of endless quest for the right sign-post. What Israel stumbled upon was the *aporias* of responsibility I have already detailed. Only *the whole* of historical humanity can be subject to poetic heterogeneity – the 'overtaking' of its own responsibility – without tragedy, since once a sinful *inhibition* of poetic reception has occurred anywhere, *all* reception is distorted, and we all become responsible for acts and representations not entirely our own. Here, the construal of human activity as 'poetic' allows us to see that the *only* sin is original sin, and that Israel alone located sin by discovering itself to be in an impossible quest for the right *figura*, the right 'poetic boundary of representation'.

The above analysis seeks to expound and develop the position of Hans von Balthasar in *Herrlichkeit*. And it is Balthasar who has most persuasively traced the process by which Israel's increasingly anguished vision was fragmented among partly competing figures – of the Priestly-law, of the temple-kingship, of wisdom, and of the apocalyptic visions.[21] In this process which is simultaneously one of disintegration and of fruitful diversification, one thing in particular comes to the fore. That is that as the mediator becomes more and more a purely projected *figure* of the apocalyptic future, so his standing as between man and God becomes less and less clear. This exposes an anxiety concerning human ability to represent God on the one hand and the possibility the God can interpose amongst human works without proper human consent on the other. In the case of the figure of wisdom in the sapiential literature there is a particularly extreme situation; as Gerhard von Rad points out, it sometimes seems to approximate to a divine *Logos* standing in a revelatory fashion over against all human wisdom, while at other times it seems to be a kind of *anima mundi*, or immanent order of the world which man, after his own mode of freedom, must body forth.[22] To the notion of the cunning of poetic reason, therefore, there corresponds in the encounter with God the divine overtaking of human purposes. But in the Old Testament this tends to make both the divine presence and the human *telos* problematic.

The *figura* of the mediator, or the *figura* of God himself, corresponds to the second poetic notion – that of the concrete universal. Here there is a single point to be made. It will be remembered that the idea of the concrete universal was invoked in response to the problem of the stability of poetic meaning. That problem becomes far more acute with reference to God, where to secure a more proper reference one must abstract totally from certain conditions of the image of God: for example, embodiment, duration, real relation to finite entities. How can one achieve this without abstract, reflective concepts such as matter, space, time, relation and so forth? It is genuinely difficult and, to meet this difficulty, the reason of the Greeks became a true witness to the idolatry of the nations. It is possible, however, that reason may commit a greater idolatry by imagining, like Eunomius, the opponent of Gregory of Nyssa, that it has at its disposal proper names for God.[23] It has not, and because this is the case, theology has to seek something other than abstract reflectivity as the basis for critical consciousness. This can be nothing other than the pressure or the infinite power of God upon the finite reality of our representations of his glory, resulting in the constant progress from image to image, each modifying the other in turn. But *this* is possible for a pre-reflective consciousness, and one may now venture to say that the very reason why we recognize Israel as exemplary is that the Jews, uniquely among primitive peoples, possessed a pre-reflective criticality, adequate to theology. Therefore, the Old Testament is not to be considered as inspired because it presents us with some mysteriously infused *static* consistency of meaning, but because it embodies a complex process of internal self-criticism. This is exemplified especially in the injunctions against idolatry and divination; they are extremely difficult to interpret, precisely because they involve variously, in different places, a sense of the ultimate impropriety of all human images, a sense of the relative propriety of Israel's image, and finally the eschatological expectation that God himself will establish his own *proper* image. This critical theology is not the product of an *otherwise* critical poetic consciousness; rather it is only the sense of God that inaugurates a critique of images. All the same it involves a refinement in the presentation of the human *telos*, and consequently a social and cultural critique also. The internal reassessment of ancient law and primitive cultus was simultaneously a new engagement with God and a more accurate definition of the people of God. It has been seen (chapter 4) that Vico in the *Scienza Nuova* exempts Israel from his account of the rise and fall of nations,[24] not out of fideistic piety, but precisely because he considered that the Hebrew injunctions against idolatry entailed a constant critique of the image of man that tended to avoid the kind of poetic category mistake that resulted in the massacre of 'sub-humans' by the heroes and the drowning of illegitimate children. Israel, we can say, possessed what is structurally a construction of herself as the particular children of a divine father and not as a collection of instances of a universally understood species. And yet this construction has become so subtle that all the obvious room for illusion pertaining to such an archaic outlook has been partially blocked out. This achievement serves to stress, not so much that the Hebrews were the recipients of a revelation overriding all human understanding, but that the 'poetic category mistakes' are not part of a process of historical inevitability; rather they are evidence of that general human fallenness, which only Israel adequately understood.

Israel then attained to a poetic problematic of her relations with God and a poetic critique of her images of God. What of the third concept in general poetics – the poetic boundedness of behaviour? Here again at first sight the poetic perspective appears to offer a hostage to critical suspicion: if a human representation such as the Hebrew law is regarded as the necessary paradigmatic standard, then is this not precisely what Paul considers to be the essence of human sinfulness, namely establishing righteousness for ourselves? Yet again there is another way of looking at this. If doing good is not fundamentally a conformity to standards in our possession, nor even the realization of projected understandings of humanity in its active being (ultimately ruled out by Paul), then it can only be our free, gratuitous response to God's free gratuitous gift of more abundant life, including that cultural life that emanates from us, beyond our control, *as* ourselves.

Thus, charity always involves the performance of an unprecedented act of goodness; it establishes new meanings of the Good. In the Judaeo-Christian tradition Good is 'self-diffusing' because it is in this way creative. And this involves a double engagement with *poesis*, both negative and positive. It is true that to act charitably we must break through the existing representation of what is our duty towards our neighbour and towards God, but this does not mean that we arrive at some clearly intuited, universal notion of the Good. That would be to lock ourselves into a deeper illusion, in which the Good was regarded as essentially complete, so that all we had to do was act in obedience to the dictates of our infallible intuition. There could then be no charity. On the contrary, while we have to break through the bounds of duty which 'technically' pre-defines its prescribed performance, we have to discover the true poetic bounds of possibility, allowed for by the *virtus* – the *virtue* – contained in the human product. There is, of course, really a dialectic of duty and possibility, in which duty always has its legitimate moment, and the 'discovery' of the true poetic bounds is in the Old Testament a gradual and never-ending process. But it is our failure to remain in this process that makes wrong-doing assume the ontological seriousness of sin, for it is now an inhibition of God's creative act; an *échec* to the Creation, as Marie-Dominique Chenu has it.[25] In the Old Testament this is most acutely represented by the portrayal in Jeremiah of Jahweh as a bridegroom deserted by his bride, thus incomprehensibly despoiled of the completion of his own being in so far as an act of loving union fails to be such, when it is rejected.

To the problematic Divine overtaking of human purposes and the critique of the images we must now add the idea of sin as a failure of the Creation.

3 Christ as Human and Divine Utterance

The question now is, what difference does Christ make to this picture? In the first place, what light does the figure of Christ in the Gospels throw upon the cunning of poetic reason doubled by the divine command of our intent? It can be said that

Jesus is a very perplexing figure in that his person, words and works seem so inextricably interrelated. Eberhard Jüngel has developed the notion that the Parables are 'performative utterances', involving not so much reference to a state of affairs as the bringing about of a state of meaning appropriate to its context.[26] The words of Jesus are thus 'strongly poetic' in that they establish a new possibility of truth and cannot be abandoned. While Jesus's whole being seems to be directed towards the production of such verbal works as opening up the situation of man in relation to God, it is equally the case that he aims to recover from his more concrete works a plenitude of significance. Here he seems to learn from his own works his own nature, in so far as they are works the Father has given him to do. Yet above and beyond all this, he seems at times to be saying, particularly in St John's Gospel, that he himself is the message. The problematic circle is made finally complete when Jesus insists that the only way to recognize his person is to act in accordance with the meaning of his words and works. One has to say that while the poetic cunning of reason, or the overtaking of our production by our products, is shown even in the case of Christ the maker, that nonetheless the Gospels appear to be invoking a peculiar intensity of presence of the author to his own fictions. It is as if Jesus had a passionate and overwhelming desire to assume his own integrity. Throughout the Gospels it is not so much asserted, as quite remarkably suggested in the structures of the narratives themselves, that this man alone 'caught up with himself', alone performed his destined work, 'the work of the Father who sent me'.

But if this sense of Jesus's peculiar existence is strongest in St John's Gospel, then it must also be noted that it is also that gospel which suggests that Jesus realizes in his own person the Father's work because he is the Father's proper work, the radiance of glory which is not dissociable from the Father's very being. Both witnesses cohere together. Nothing can *prove* or establish the perfection of Jesus's human work, for if it *is* perfect, then the work must itself define the character of perfection. Yet once we are convinced that we are glimpsing such perfection, then are we not also glimpsing the perfection of God? The entire problematic of the divine overtaking of human purpose in the Old Testament points to the coincidence of the divine presence with the human *telos*. In the first place, humanity as poetic being can have no bounds set to his nature; its only adequate, but unimaginable representation, must be identical with the representation that God always makes of himself. The divine reality and the human end which defines human nature do eternally coincide, because God in his being is an infinity of promise for man. In the second place, humanity's fallenness is defined as an inability to inaugurate a response to and realization of this promise, a collapse of the means of representation, together with the loss of the possibility of a non-tragic ecstatically sundered 'responsibility'. Humanity's salvation now demands the fully original divine initiative amongst us; this initiative is adequate because it has established a final representation in the incarnate *Logos*, and because it is adequate, it is ontologically unfailing. Such a divine initiative among men, however, can only be the full manifestation of the divine presence, because God's activity is at one with his being, and the manifestation of the divine presence automatically brings with it the realization, and so representation, of the true human *telos* within human history.

The human perfection that we recognize in Christ cannot then be validated merely from a perusal of the structures of the texts. We recognize the finality of these structures because our sense of their coherence is an acknowledgement of the infinite depths of potential for meaning from which they spring – depths which, nonetheless, are only established in the process of manifestation itself. In our perception of Christ the acknowledgement of a human depth of *virtus* passes over immediately and imperceptibly into an acknowledgement of the divine *virtus* of the Father, in such a way that Jesus is not recognized as the *figura*, Christ, before being recognized as the divine *Logos*, which realizes and establishes, without thereby displacing, the Father's infinite power of origination.

It is as this divine–human person, who has both finitely and infinitely the character of a representation, that we finally recognize in Jesus the divine overtaking and fulfilling of all human purposes. As the divine utterance, Jesus is the absolute origination of all meaning, but as human utterance Jesus is inheritor of all already constituted human meanings. He is a single utterance in his unified fulfilment of these meanings, such that he becomes the adequate metaphoric representation of the total human intent. The foregoing Old Testament and even mythical images of God had their own potential of significance, but this was inhibited to the degree that no picture could be formed in which they all belonged and would become mutually illuminating, in both synchronic and diachronic association. There were only two possibilities: focusing on one figure at the expense of the others – so Judaism emerged, focused round the Law – or an abstract synthesis as carried out by Philo. As Balthasar points out, such a synthesis can only be a betrayal of the plenitude of meaning of the individual figures.[27] By contrast, the poetic synthesis in Christ *returns* us to the figures, because he establishes them for the first time in total interrelation as the true human representation, the true human text.

This leads us naturally to the second consideration, concerning the critique of the images. Here it must be recalled that it was said that reflective understanding, though of inestimable critical service to theology, cannot isolate a *proper* theological sense, a proper word for God. Metaphoric understanding can establish relatively stable universals for the interpretation of finite reality, but no *figura* before the advent of Christ could be uniquely privileged with respect to the representation of the infinite. The Old Testament reaches remarkable heights of monotheistic honesty in suggesting that the simultaneous search for God and for human integrity is threatened by a bad infinite, in which there must be increasing resort to a mere subjective longing. Therefore Cornelius Ernst argued with some justice that only the Incarnation gives us a proper theological sense.[28] But note well that this is a *metaphoric* proper sense (if the paradox may be allowed). In Christ the *figura* of God, as in all concrete poetic universals, stability of meaning is only guaranteed by an appropriate *sensus communis* of its internal textual interactions corresponding to the transcendental subjectivity of the depth of origination which *must* accompany any meaningful artefact.

If this *figura* is privileged with regard to God, then it is, of course, privileged with regard to the whole of human existence. It is not merely the key to all human meaning, but what human meaning is about, the 'meaning of meaning' as Cornelius Ernst put it.[29] This is what one should try to realize concerning our third pair of notions – the 'poetic boundedness of behaviour' and 'sin as failure of the creation' in a Christological context. The Jesus of St John's Gospel says 'If I had not done among them the works which no one else did, they would not have sin; but now they have seen and hated both me and my Father' (John 15:23–4). The sin against the law was not, then, original sin. Original sin can only be defined as hatred of the works and person of Christ. But sin has already been defined as a refusal of the plenitude of creation, the fullness of representation which can only be received by the succession of humanity as a whole. If sin is exposed uniquely through the works of Christ, this must be because there we see that plenitude, that adequate representation, and, in a sense, the 'whole' of humanity, a person who is *more* every one of us than we are ourselves. We now have the true poetic bounds of behaviour and sin is located, so potentially nullified.

If sin is at an end, then charity is engendered. The performance, by us, of new and remarkable acts of charity, is the only demonstration of the true poetic bounds of behaviour, which cannot be proved as such, because Christ is himself the proof of the Good. All the same, an order of priority must be maintained – Christ, then charity – although this is perhaps the most difficult point to grasp. For it is true in one sense that the missing centre in the Old Testament is a constant attention to charity, and this is what St Paul means when he says that the setting up of a final standard of righteousness is the very essence of sin. But the danger here is perhaps to have too abstract a notion of charity which may veer between too purely an 'ethical' idea of an intuited responsibility, and too purely a 'technical' idea of a pre-defined duty. Paul and John elevate charity in the light of Christ, which means that they only glimpse the possibility of charity as a creative goodness which forever presents man with new and appropriate opportunities in particular situations, because they already perceive in Christ's entire activity the plenitude of such a performance: all our work, already made, in advance of us. That is to say, Christ's words and significant deeds open up to all men at every moment *exactly* the right path. This *accuracy* of charity as a creative act (and creation unaffected by sin is intrinsically accurate) cannot be known at first as an abstract possibility, but only as an already realized one.

Nothing so far has been said about the Cross, but even there, perhaps especially there, Christ's ethical work is also a poetic one. One paradoxical reason for our recognition of Christ as the true sign is that all the signs he offers us are broken signs that offer their internal asymmetry as a testimony to their own inadequacy and to the infinite distance between humanity and God.[30] But the fact that this asymmetry is incorporated within, for example, the parables themselves, means that this distance is still to make a demand on man. The body and blood of Christ are supremely such broken signs and moreover, these are signs which Jesus chooses to become in his very being. Here we are presented with death, and this is quite unprecedented. Death is normally a pure negation, but here we have a particular death, death that is literally incorporated into the character of a man, death that is not other to his life. As Ricoeur says, there is a hermeneutic circle of martyrdom and meaning, according to which a martyr's death is only such as a witness to an already established value, but on the other hand values are uniquely established when someone dies for them.[31] Christ's death means that a negation is part of the meaning of his life and work, but because his life and work inform his death, to the point, ultimately, of resurrection, this negation is present in a particular way. The kind of negation involved is not merely analogous to the way in which a picture points to what is unseen, but also to the way in which the omissions in a picture are part of its composition. It may be noted that in some Baroque art a depicted figure itself gestures towards these omissions as a tactic of invoking transcendence by actually calling attention to, without thereby denying the necessity of, its own 'artificiality' and contingency. In its fusing of negative and affective elements the *figura* of Christ may be described as already Baroque (of which style it may indeed be a prime historical source).[32]

The necessary counterpart to the significant and signifying death is the subject which has collapsed into the sign without thereby surrendering, but rather realizing, its subjectivity. It has been recognized, notably by Maurice de la Taille,[33] that on Maundy Thursday Jesus commits himself to death in such a fashion that to withdraw would call his entire mission into question. De la Taille called attention to the formal aspect of the eucharistic dedication with the phrase 'he placed himself in the order of signs'.[34] This placing is not identical with Jesus's death; it requires his death to make sense of it, in such a fashion that, ever since, the eucharist in the Church is seen as a representation of the sacrifice on the Cross. Yet all the same, Jesus's death is the outcome and realization of this deliberate commitment of meaning – 'this is my body, this is my blood'. The words of Maundy Thursday and the acts of Good Friday together compose a poetic act characterized by an 'overtaking', such that the intention of the sign is only realized in the full outcome of its explication. Beneath the superficial contrast of eucharistic sign and actual deed (and passive assent may be, in terms of *praxis*, the most active thing of all)[35] lies a metonymic structure of significant cause realized in significant effect, which is at once an order of events and a sequence of meaning. But the commitment of subjective being to a sign which involves death in the manner outlined in the preceding paragraph is also in its teleological outcome a commitment to death as the reality of sign *qua* sign. For a sign does not have the restricted material potency of an unfinished living being, but the more universally open, active potency of a finished, definable, artefact. And this complete but potent character of the sign is a *function* of its lifelessness. *Only* for God is completeness and total sign-being (in the

Logos which as a complete representation of the paternal subject has a personal, subjective address in its own right) a fact of realization of potential being, and so the sum of total life and not the curtailment that is death. Consequently Christ's death as the termination of his life is necessary to define and give bounds to his subjectivity and so allow his sign-being for man. To be a sign for us at all, he must pass through death, since our signs speak only death; but to signify *absolutely* for us he must also re-define the sign of language as life, as eternal *logos* in the resurrection. Thus the resurrection of Christ, still bearing the marks of his death, exposes this death as in reality the completeness of the divine–human person, the realization (necessarily infinite) of the hidden personal source of *virtus* in the Father, and thereby the *final* sign for human beings.

In the conjuncture of this metonymic death-sign matrix with the fundamentally *metaphoric* character of the sign, we discover the key to the atonement. *Every* sign is a substitution and a representation because it categorically involves the being of one thing – a particular form – only as a relation to other things. In Jesus's metonymic fulfilment of his metaphoric sign character on the Cross, this substitution of himself for all humanity assumes a tragic aspect. The falsities in the meanings engendered by man can only be *transfigured* if their false end of *misrepresentation is* realized and so critically exposed and surpassed. Jesus assumes the burden of these false meanings in a perfectly ordinary human way, in that he is directly and personally abused. But he uniquely takes on the burden of sin because the abuse of Christ defines sin as the ultimate distorted construct, designed to wither all human hope. And this assuming of the burden of sin is an atonement, because Jesus's response is a non-violent one: since he refuses the violence which would actively distort his own work, yet allows to be incorporated into his own person ugly constructions which in their new context assume a different appearance. This is not, of course, the synchronic harmony of the whole as against the disorder of the parts, but the diachronic transignification of the parts in their new formal relationships.[36] The incorporation and transfiguration of the ugly – so must beauty be redefined for a sinful world, that she may maintain the universal character of a transcendental.

4 Human Utterance in Christ

From the above section we may conclude that Christ is the unexpected fulfilment of human intent, the proper word for God, and the true fulfilment of Creation in the realm of human works. Employing these three categories one must now attempt to determine what difference this has made to the poetic existence of humanity. Perhaps here the most formal answers will best preserve an apophatic caution.

We give a practical recognition to Christ as the fulfilment of human intent by regarding our entire lives as nothing but an interpretation of Christ as presented to us in the Scriptures and in the Sacraments. We are not in this situation with respect to any other signs or texts, but only with respect to natural being, including our own. One may talk about other texts as providing a plenitude of meaning, but at some point they fail; they are subject to criticism and we turn away from the task of interpretation towards the task of creating out own, more adequate text. But what Christians effectively claim to be unique about the Christian text is that it ultimately withstands all criticism to such a degree that our understanding must remain within the confines of interpretation in relation to it. And this not because we discover a priority of the linguistic word over all intentions (there can be no duality of word and intention, since as we have seen *every* intention 'occurs' to us as a word *beyond* our intention), but rather because we encounter one person whose expressive being establishes limits which are none other than those of existence itself. Whereas before we were only in a totally hermeneutic situation with regard to nature, now we are in such a situation also with regard to a particular part of artificial – because humanly produced – being. And this portion illuminates the whole of being, so that where before we had to appropriate through 'apostrophe' given existence as a matter of personal significance, now given existence is from the start a personal address: it apostrophizes *us*.

In the second place, Christ is our proper word for God and for true humanity. This proper word is finally taken up into, included in, the eternal *Logos* of the Father. When we see Christ in the flesh, we already see this invisible centre, because our whole perception is informed by the gift of the Holy Spirit, a *sensus communis* inaugurated in us by Christ as an adequate sense of metaphorical judgement that is – though it is generated *through it* – the necessary transcendental condition *for* the adequate concrete universal. That the concrete universal is ultimately an invisible image is already suggested to us, we may venture to say, in the diversity of reports about Christ and the sheer number of traditions that are invoked to build up this *figura*. Only the person formed by the Holy Spirit will see all this matter in its true, infinitely representational coherence, and the search of the individual and the Church down the ages for the true Christ among the memorial fragments is symbolic of an endless, eternal quest for his true objectivity. But there is something even more than this. Because Christ's person is present only in and through his work, this means that it is present in the relations that he enters into with other people and the things of this world; it even has its origin in the assent of his mother Mary to the adequate human representation. Her assent both grows with the unfolding of this representation from its first divine conception in her womb and is also, with the whole pre-history of Israel, constitutive of that representation itself. We stand within the *locus* of the Holy Spirit as the area already given its horizon by the active assent of Mary. Within this space, but to a more restricted degree, our assents to, and fulfilments of, Christ's intentions, realize his true relation to us and belong among Christ's own proper words. In this way, as that mediaeval tradition summed up in Eckhart has it,[37] Christ the *Logos* is conceived again in us – though this may now be understood in more directly linguistic a fashion. It is in this sense of continuing to form the image of Christ that we genuinely participate in Christ and not as a kind of sub-personal, quasi-material inclusion.

Already we begin to see how Christ, while being the realization of human poetic endeavour, also re-establishes it in its true character. Christ is in the third place the true fulfilment of the divine creation in the realm of human works. Because he is simply *there*, as significant object, because he has established his work in what humankind made of him, namely a crucified body, he now makes to us a totally non-violent, unconstraining appeal. This is the *kenosis* which is paradoxically at the heart of a true showing forth, because any exhibition in another's terms is also an accommodation to those terms, and a consequent risk of misappropriation; Christ as the eternal 'all' of humanity may be ecstatically responsible beyond tragic risk, but still in his historical, eucharistic giving he opens himself out to re-crucifixion. But for *us* this continued embracing of risk and tragic responsibility by the *Logos* represents also a chance for true appropriation, meaning the recovering of the bare possibility of *any* true appropriation, any true receptivity of God and recovery of trust in the mode of sundered, ecstatic responsibility. This recovery alone allows us to fulfil our own self-creation. Here the particularity of Christ cannot displace our own particularity, because it includes true relations to every person through the actual linguistic processes of human history. And this means, to every person as she uniquely is. Again and again the parables speak of Jesus as making his followers fruitful. Although they are fruitful as responding to Christ, this means that they are fruitful also through the line of their own proper being, which is to say, their natural expressiveness. Just as the Atonement is more than a moral act because it is a substitution and a representation, so also, salvation is more than a moral event because it is the realization of particular integrity, whether individual or collective. As Balthasar suggests, the doctrine of justification can only ultimately be taught as the history of the saints, the shapes of their lives as they both made them and were given them.[38] In like vein, Gerard Manley Hopkins declared concerning the 'arch-especial spirit', Henry Purcell, 'it is the forgèd feature finds me'.[39] It is this 'forgèd feature' that we seek in the work of Christ, while he seeks the same in our human labour. 'The history of the saints' (and one should take this as broadly as possible) is here something peculiarly Christian in that the possibility of finding one's true image in Christ means that history is now a treasury of human works that may be grasped in a transcendentally unified coherence of meaning.

But one can best realize that the Christian texts allow a rebirth of the human imagination by remembering that the *mythos is* something which opens up reality. The completed work of art is itself like the process of art in so far as it supplements our faculties and enables us to see and to understand more, and to make more significant structures in the future. Of course, this is supremely true of language itself. All that I have said so far implies that our incorporation into the body of Christ provides us collectively with an artificial faculty that is in the unique situation of being as proper to us as seeing or sensing or hearing. In a Christological light one must accept as an almost literal statement Coleridge's famous saying that the Scriptures are the 'living educts of the Imagination'.[40] But this new faculty or facility, though potential to all human work, is really directed in the very core of *poesis* to the vision of Christ himself in the mysterious depths of his procession from the Father. Here our 'total hermeneutic situation' with regard to Christ *both* regards him aesthetically as he is given (Balthasar) *and* regards him *poetically* as he is still being given, re-born, through our own spirit-inspired constructions. And since it more readily seems that what we can 'look at' is in our grasp, is 'given' as a controllable object, then it is rather – to invert the assumption of most 'realisms' – that which comes out of us through our collective making which is more absolutely *a gift*, more absolutely un-possessable, and more absolutely *only there at all* if we contemplate it with love. Thus in the end (beyond Balthasar) it is only *poesis* – with its stress on 'temporal occurrence through us' – which paradoxically secures the primacy of contemplation.[41] Only as makers may we look simply to the day when 'all flesh shall see him together'.

Notes

1 H. U. von Balthasar, *Herrlichkeit, Eine theologische Aesthetik* (Johannes Verlag, Einsedeln, 1961). But following references are to the French translation of Robert Givord: *La Gloire et la Croix* (Aubier, Paris, 1965).

2 Aristotle, *Ethics*, trans. J. A. K. Thomson (Penguin, London, 1976), p. 208. The importance of this distinction was stressed by Jacques Maritain, Eric Gill and David Jones; see, for example, David Jones, *Epoch and Artist* (Faber, London, 1959), pp. 139, 172, 277.

3 See J.-M. Le Blond, *Logique et Méthode chez Aristote* (P.U.F., Paris, 1970), especially pp. 346–72 and 416–31.

4 See J. Finance, *Être et Agir* (Pontifical University Gregoriana, Rome, 1960), pp. 42–78 and 214–54.

5 S.T.I–II.Q. 49 a 1 resp and ad 3; a. 2 resp and ad 1. For the emanations intrinsic to creatures see S.C.G.IV. 11. And for *virtus* (active potency) and 'proper accident' see S.C.G.III, I. 59; S.T.II.Q. 54 43.

6 J. H. Newman, *A Grammar of Assent*, cd N. Lash (Notre Dame University Press, Notre Dame, 1979), p. 274.

7 E. Betti, 'Hermeneutics as the General Methodology of the *Geisteswissensschaften*', in J. Bleicher, *Contemporary Hermeneutics* (Routledge & Kegan Paul, London, 1980), pp. 51–95.

8 See for example P. Ricoeur, *Freud and Philosophy* (Yale University Press, New Haven, 1970), pp. 6–9. H.-G. Gadamer, *Truth and Method* (Sheed and Ward, London, 1975), especially pp. 431–49.

9 David Jones, *Epoch and Artist*, p. 149.

10 Giambattista Vico, *The New Science*, trans. T. G. Bergin and M. H. Fisch (Cornell University Press, Ithaca, 1970), e.g. paras 1097–112. See also John Milbank, *The Religious Dimension in the Thought of Giambattista Vico 1668–1744*, vol. 2, *Language, Law and History* (E. Mellen, New York, 1992), pp. 253–61.

11 P. Ricoeur, *The Rule of Metaphor* (Routledge & Kegan Paul, London, 1978), pp. 9–4.

12 Vico, *The New Science*, paras 400–501; Milbank, *The Religious Dimension*, vol. 2, pp. 9–119.

13 E. Castelli, *I Paradossi del senso commune* (Padua, 1970), pp. 31–74; *I Presupposti di una teologia delle storie* (Bocca, Milan, 1952), pp. 115–55.

14 Vico, *The New Science*, paras 402, 403, 495; Milbank, *The Religious Dimension*.

15 Kant, *Critique of Pure Reason*, trans. N. K. Smith (Macmillan, London, 1978), Introduction, pp. III, IV, V.

16 For the humanist meaning of *sensus communis* invoked here see Gadamer, *Truth and Method*, pp. 19–29.

17 'Obligée de se composer des raisons', see P. Claudel, *Art Poétique* (Paris, 1907), p. 124.

18 Vico, *The New Science*, paras 502–19.

19 'A Rumbling: truth / itself has appeared / among humankind / in the very thick of their / flurrying metaphors': P. Celan, *Poems*, trans. M. Hamburger (Carcanet, Manchester, 1980), pp. 202–3.

20 See R. D. Williams, 'Barth on the Triune God', in *Karl Barth, Studies of his Theological Method*, ed. S. W. Sykes (Oxford University Press, Oxford, 1979), p. 188.

21 Balthasar, *Herrlichkeit*, vol. I, *Apparition*, pp. 254–86.

22 G. von Rad, *Wisdom in Israel* (SCM, London, 1970), pp. 144–76.

23 'Against Eunomius', in *The Library of the Nicene and Post-Nicene Fathers*, 2nd series, vol. V. *Gregory of Nyssa*, eds Henry Ware and Phillip Schaff (Oxford, 1893), pp. 144–76.

24 Vico, *The New Science*, para. 172; Milbank, *The Religious Dimension*, vol. 2, pp. 66–94.

25 M.-D. Chenu, 'Creation et Histoire' in *St Thomas Aquinas: Commemoration Studies* (Toronto, 1974).

26 E. Jüngel, *Gott als Geheimnis der Welt* 2 Auflage (JCB Mohr, Tübingen, 1977), p. 11.

27 See especially Balthasar, *Herrlichkeit*, vol. III, *Théologie, Nouvelle Alliance*, pp. 91–100.

28 C. Ernst, 'Metaphor and Ontology in *Sacra Doctrina*', in *Multiple Echo*, eds F. Kerr and T. Radcliffe (D.L.T., London, 1979), pp. 57–75.

29 C. Ernst, 'A Theological Critique of Experience', *Multiple Echo*, pp. 52–56.

30 E. Jüngel, *Gott als Geheimnis*, pp. 392ff. Also *Jesus und Paulus* (JCB Mohr, Tübingen, 1964), p. 138.

31 P. Ricoeur, *Essays on Biblical Interpretation* (SCM, London, 1981), p. 129.

32 See W. Benjamin, *The Origin of German Tragic Drama* (New Left Books, London, 1963), the section allegory and *trauerspiel* in general, and pp. 177–82, 226–33, in particular. On p. 232 he writes 'The bleak confusion of Golgotha, which can be recognized as the schema underlying the allegorical figures in hundreds of the engravings and descriptions of the period, is not just a symbol of the desolation of human existence. In it transitoriness is not signified or allegorically represented so much as in its own significance displayed as allegory. As the allegory of resurrection.'

33 M. de la Taille, *The Mystery of Faith* (Sheed and Ward, London, 1941), cited in D. M. Mackinnon, *Explorations in Theology* 5 (SCM, London, 1979), p. 178.

34 Cited in David Jones, *Epoch and Artist*, p. 179.

35 This must be the case for the resolution of the martyr. *Praxis* is, of course, still used here in its Aristotelean sense (the Marxist 'praxis' includes many elements here assigned to *poesis*). *As praxis* Jesus's death on the Cross is most perfectly active in the sense that it is entirely his own act, *as poesis* it is most active in the sense that it is infinitely communicable.

36 It is more useful here to think of music than the visual arts, and, in particular, the music
    of the Baroque, where concentration on the forward moving line allows 'suspensions' of
    harmonic and melodic resolutions. While the resulting fragmentation is normally of a
    formal and temporary kind, this is less true of the even distribution of Bach's music and
    the complexity of Purcell's consorts. The best example is the Bohemian J. D. Zelenka, in
    whose music fragmentation reaches such a pitch that resolution is often replaced by an
    obsessive reworking of constantly encircling motifs, and linear expectations are inter-
    rupted by abrupt discontinuities. The unity of this music is only found in a forward
    development that involves a constant 'return' upon seemingly endless perspectives.
    Dietmar Polaczek considers 'more than conventional' Zelenka's placing above the scores
    of many 'secular works' a chronogram which, when deciphered, reads 'Praise and
    Glory to the Man of Sorrows Jesus Christ'. See brochure enclosed in Zelenka, *Die
    Orchesterwerke* (Archiv recordings, Polydor International, 1978); for the music, this
    recording and, more especially, Zelenka, *Sechs Triosonaten* (Archiv, 1973).
37 See H. Rahner 'Die Gottesgeburt: Die Lehre der Kirchenväter von der Geburt Christ
    im Herzen Glaubigen' in *Zeitschrift far Katholische Theologie*, 59 (1933), pp. 333–418.
38 Balthasar, *Herrlichkeit*, vol. III, pp. 375–421.
39 G. M. Hopkins, *Poems and Prose*, cd W. H. Gardner (Penguin, London, 1972), p. 41.
40 See S. Prickett, *Romanticism and Religion* (Cambridge University Press, Cambridge,
    1976), pp. 1–70.
41 I am indebted to Catherine Pickstock for this point, which makes much clearer some of
    my own earlier formulations of a similar kind.

6

The Name of Jesus

In St Luke's account of the last supper (Luke 22:14–38), Jesus is represented as suddenly putting his teaching into reverse. Hitherto, he has sent his disciples out into the world without bag, purse, sword or sandals. Lacking money, possessions and the means of self-protection, they have yet 'lacked nothing' through their provocation of the mercy of others. Yet now, for some reason, this practice is no longer possible: the time of the kingdom is suspended, and it is the 'hour of darkness'. The disciples are told to take up again their money and their possessions, and if they have no sword, to sell their clothes and buy one.

Why must this reversal occur? The only explanation we are offered is put into the mouth of Jesus: he is the person of whom the scriptures wrote: 'And he was reckoned with the transgressors'. But the implication is obvious: if Jesus is to be arrested and convicted he must appear to the authorities to be identified with a group of armed rebels, as a resister to Roman rule. Yet understandably, the disciples are puzzled: just how far are they to go? When the crowd, led by Judas, come to seize Jesus, they want to know whether they are to actually use the swords? (22:49). One of them (Peter, according to John's gospel) assumes that they are, but his presumptuous action is immediately stayed by Jesus. The two swords which the disciples carry, and the single blow against the slave of the high priest are, indeed, 'enough'. Sufficient, that is to say, to secure Jesus's arrest and inaugurate his passion, which is precisely his being 'reckoned with the transgressors', identified with human sin.[1]

This passage provides us with a particularly acute instance of a complexity which is present throughout the gospel accounts. They provide us, not with a single 'story of Jesus', but with two, fundamentally different kinds of story, whose interconnections are inherently problematic. First of all, there is the most straightforward, apparently 'historical' tale of a remarkable man who announced the arrival of a new sort of kingdom, the direct rule of God upon earth, which was still to come and yet already present in his own actions and those of his followers. These

constituted a new practice characterized by the overcoming of pain, death and sin
through miraculous deeds and a proffered forgiveness of sins.

The second story is not so straightforward. In one respect it is a kind of
commentary upon the first story: a 'metanarrative' which discloses to us, in an
obscure and mysterious fashion, the secret significance of what Jesus says and does.
This disclosure is itself a narration because we are told that Jesus is a foreordained
figure: the 'Messiah', the 'Son of Man', the 'Son of God', or '*Logos*' who has
appeared in the world at the right time to accomplish human salvation. Gradually,
the metanarrative interruptions of the primary narrative make it clear to us that
Jesus is more than a mere prophet, and also prepare us for the event of the rejection
of his message and his violent death. The more a general hostility to Jesus becomes
manifest in the primary, 'historical' story, the more the metanarrative intrudes to
rescue this event of rejection from mere contingency, and to relate it to Jesus's
foreordained destiny. Unlike any prophet or hitherto expected messiah, Jesus is to
accomplish salvation and inaugurate the Kingdom *through* expulsion, through
suffering the death of a renegade.

The most extreme point of this intrusion, as in the passage from Luke that I
began with, occurs when the metanarrative commentary actually merges with the
primary sequence of events, and is put into the mouth of Jesus to provide a
motivation for his most decisive act within this series. In terms of the primary
'historical' narrative, the reversal of his teaching about money, possessions and
violence makes no sense at all; it can only be comprehended through the deter-
minations of the secondary metanarrative, according to which Jesus must die if he
is to fulfil his mission. Of course, Jesus cannot be represented as suicidally courting
death at the hands of his enemies: this is why it is said that he must be betrayed and
handed over by his friends – primarily by Judas, but also by those disciples who
wield the swords. But in this fashion not just the person of Jesus alone, but
apparently the whole history of Jesus with Judas, Peter and the other disciples is
assumed out of normal temporality into a vertical drama about cosmic salvation. A
drastic textual alchemy recodes rejection, failure, betrayal and death as the signs
and efficacious sources of life and victory.

Christianity itself *is* this recoding, the rule of the gospel metanarrative, which is
further elaborated in the New Testament and apostolic epistles. However, revision-
ist Christians in the modern era have in effect asked, cannot this recoding be
undone? Despite its palimpsest-like overlay, we can still, it is thought, trace clearly
the outlines of the simple, 'historical' story, which may be its own best self-
commentary: Jesus offers God's unconditional forgiveness; he teaches a new way of
life founded upon non-rivalry, non-retaliation and mutual sharing. Neither of these
elements seem dependent upon the shedding of yet further blood in an atoning
death. However, the Kingdom suffers an initial rebuff: Jesus's mission fails, he is
crucified, and yet in his steadfastness continues to provide testimony to the possibilities he earlier proclaimed. This, in outline, is the substance of all Christian
'liberalism', although today it often comes in a much more convincing 'political'
guise, which insists that Jesus was not teaching merely an idealised ethic for

individuals, but rather inaugurating a new ('revolutionary', but non-violent) social practice, that called into question the arbitrary, domineering character of most legalities and economies.

Such liberalism, at least in its 'political' form, appears to provide an attractive alternative to the rule of the metanarrative – to retrieve what may be a viable practice from under the dead hand of a mythology. For is not the metanarrative culpable? According to the gospels themselves we are with Jesus if we do the Father's works: feed the hungry, free the prisoners, heal the sick, love our enemies. What, then, are they adding, when they say that power to do these things comes from invoking the name of Jesus, and his 'holy spirit' which is transmitted to and by the Church. This double monopoly ties us, first, to a text, and so to the power-wielding expounders of a text, and, second, to an organization which claims access to a power which can be invoked by name, but never described or made identifiably to appear. One might well ask whether this purely nominal power is not just a subconscious cipher for the worldly power of those priestly and political authorities who claim the right to invoke it. The 'cult of Jesus' seems to add nothing to his universal message but a totally esoteric secret which, one must suspect, exists only in the claims made for its existence by those who thereby wield dominion.

And would not the liberals be right were they to discover an incongruity in the currently fashionable yoking of the gospel message to the theme of 'tradition', where this implies the ineffable authority of a practice whose persistence supposedly demonstrates a certain 'wisdom', or even 'correspondence to reality'? For Jesus appears to contribute, in the long term, to the instigation of the universalist emphases of the Enlightenment. In the new community which he announces, particular cultic traditions, racial and even family attachments, become irrelevant: we can relate to all human beings, despite, or through their differences, as sons and daughters of the heavenly Father. And he does *not* present himself as a new sort of heteronomous authority: on the contrary, he denies that he has come as a judge, and encourages people to deliberate for themselves, and to settle issues privately without appeal to the traditional legal powers (Matthew 18:15–20; Luke 12:13–14; John 8:15–16). The new community, therefore, seems to be characterized by individual and group autonomy, as well as social universality.

The question really put by Christian liberals is this: would not authentic enlightenment, a better version of modernity, be opened out through the scraping away of the mythic and cultic overlay from the primary gospel narrative? And at the heart of the cult, making it operative, has lain the doctrine of the atonement, or the view which appears to claim that Jesus's death is salvific because it somehow stands in an immediate causal relationship to all human beings, in a manner transcending normal historical processes. As Jews insist, Jesus's death quite manifestly did *not* redeem, did not bring in the reign of peace, reconciliation and eternal life. The Church seems to make this death redemptive by claiming for it a secret, hidden efficacy which we must 'believe in', 'relate to' and somehow appropriate in our individual lives.

The doctrine of the atonement, like any ahistorical hypostasization of Jesus's person, does not appear compatible with a 'political' reading of the gospel which stresses Jesus's teachings and new social practice.[2] Yet notwithstanding, I now want to argue that one can retrieve this doctrine, along with a 'high' view of Christ's person, precisely by focusing more upon the Kingdom than upon Jesus, and also by trying to spell out more precisely the 'logic' of Jesus's universalism. I shall try to show that while crudely 'cultic' versions of Christianity are indeed misconstruals of this universalism, that, nevertheless, its logic of itself demands the invocation of the name of Jesus, and the linking of the Holy Spirit to a particular tradition of historical transmission. Christological and atonement doctrines are, I shall suggest, theoretically secondary to definitions of the character of the new universal community or Church. And yet, I shall argue, it is precisely through these definitions that one can legitimate the secondary metanarrative and show that it does not obliterate or distort the primary story of the arrival of the Kingdom.

In a way, by starting with the Kingdom, or the universal community, I am being both 'liberal' and 'political'. Yet at the same time I would want to claim that the priority of ecclesiology is logically assumed by the explicit forms of the New Testament Christological and salvific claims, and that these forms and their logic were sometimes enhanced and by no means abandoned during the first few centuries of formulation of Christian doctrine.[3] I should add that in the present chapter I can only offer a sketch of such a claim, which ideally requires more elaborate explication.

However, before making my 'proper start' with the Kingdom, I intend to offer a negative demonstration that a primarily Christological context for Christology cannot take us very far. I have already indicated why I cannot accept a debasedly 'cultic' approach: it seems to say to people, you must accept as a primary 'datum' a basic proposition that God became incarnate, and in addition that his death by violence made atonement for your sins. These assertions confront us in a somewhat 'extrinsic' fashion, and provoke a double objection. First of all, by what process of thought does one arrive at the conclusion that someone is God incarnate, or that a single death is universally efficacious? Second, what difference does the mere *fact* – however astounding – of God's identifying with us through incarnation make to our lives, or even to our pictures of what God is like, what he wants for us? How can mere belief in the event of atonement be uniquely transformative for the individual? To collapse both objections into a single more positive question: how can incarnation and atonement be communicated to us *not* as mere facts, but as characterizable modes of being which *intrinsically* demand these appellations?

So it is pointless to approach incarnation and atonement primarily as revealed propositions. We have rather to look at the gospel narratives to find out what Christ's person and work was *like*, and for what reasons, if any, it should be characterized in absolute, transcendent terms. Writers like Hans Frei and others of 'the Yale school', who are rightly discontented with the extrinsicism of the propositional starting point, have argued that the doctrine of the incarnation is an instruction to take the story of Christ's life as normative in identifying what God is like. The character of Jesus, as it emerges in this story, is a supreme pointer to the character of God himself.[4] This proposal seeks to call us back from empty dogmatic formalism to a concrete content for belief. However, as soon as one starts to analyse the gospel accounts, one discovers that what is apparently concrete and substantial rapidly dissolves into formal mechanisms which are constitutive devices of the narratives themselves. Let me explain what I mean.

First and foremost, the gospels are *not* 'history-like narratives' (in the sense of a predominance of 'literal reference' over allegory in the identification of event and character), nor do they in any way approximate to the 'realism' which is an element in some eighteenth- and nineteenth-century novels.[5] Jesus is not presented to us as a 'character': we are told nothing about his tastes, quirks and inclinations, nor (*pace* Frei) about his 'intentions' – Jesus speaks only of what he does and must do. During the course of the gospel accounts he undergoes no psychological development; their narrative progress is not that of *bildungsroman*, but more akin to the circular plot of a detective story, in which something is gradually disclosed to both fictional characters and to the reader that has really been the case all along. Here it is the truth about the identity of the central character, Jesus. Moreover, this identity does not actually relate to his 'character', but rather to his universal significance for which his particularity stands, almost, as a mere cipher.

The name 'Jesus' does not indicate an identifiable 'character', but is rather the obscure and mysterious hinge which permits shifts from one kind of discourse to another.[6] At the level of the primary narrative, 'Jesus' is the source of a new eschatological teaching, of miraculous works, and of an egalitarian social practice. It is insisted that Jesus is to be 'known' through his works, yet the features of these works most emphasized are their most generic characteristics: he has power over death, disease and the demonic, he associates himself with the marginal and the outcast. Where Jesus himself as *figura* is focused upon, he appears as a superhuman, shaman-like individual, who can appear suddenly and unpredictably, whose birth-place is uncertain, whose dwelling-place is also unknown, but might equally be the mountains, the middle of the sea of Galilee, or the lake-shore.

At the level of the metanarrative, we are told not only that Jesus is to be identified as virtuous through his works, and as being none other *than* his works, but also that the works are to be taken as signs of his unique significance. The metanarrative therefore shifts the emphasis from the works towards the person. Yet this moves us still further away from any concrete content. To identify Jesus, the gospels abandon mimetic/diegetic narrative, and resort to metaphors: Jesus is the way, the word, the truth, life, water, bread, the seed of a tree and the fully grown tree, the foundation stone of a new temple and at the same time the whole edifice. These metaphors abandon the temporal and horizontal for the spatial and vertical. They suggest that Jesus is the most comprehensive possible context: not just the space within which all transactions between time and eternity transpire, but also the beginning of all this space, the culmination of this space, the growth of this space and all the goings in and out within this space. Supremely, he is both word and food: the communicated meanings which emanate from our mouths and yet in this outgoing simultaneously return to them as spiritual nurture.

It is these metaphors, at the heart of the metanarrative commentary, which contain the germs of speculations about 'incarnation' and 'atonement'. And yet the effect of implying that a person situated within the world is also, in himself (like God) our total situation, or that which is always transcendentally presupposed, is to evacuate that person of any particular, specifiable content. It is to ensure that Jesus who is in all places, because he is all places, never in fact appears. Thus for reasons belonging to the logic of discourse, it is indeed true that incarnation cannot be by the absorbing of divinity into humanity, but only by the assumption of humanity into divinity. All that survives that is particular in this assumption is the proper name 'Jesus'. It is certainly the case that by telling stories about a character on earth called 'Jesus', and by putting words into his mouth, the gospels minimally indicate reference to a 'reality' that is independent of their narration. But the use of the proper name does not *show* us this reality. And nor does the metanarrative, unlike the confiding, diegetic voice of a novel, supplement these spare indicators of 'reality' (of words and actions once performed by bodies which organize themselves through language, and are yet, in their physicality, extra-linguistic) with identifying descriptions of physical traits, characteristic actions, tones of voice and tricks of speech. Instead, it yokes the name 'Jesus' to the total context of human life.

The problem here is obvious: do not the metaphors which point towards an ontological discourse of incarnation effectively disincarnate Jesus? The more he is identified with God, the more he becomes abstract, and the less anything appears to be added to our knowledge of what God is like. My contention is that if we approach the gospels primarily as the story of Jesus and of how he wrought human salvation, we will run into this kind of *impasse*, and will be left asking, what does this empty name 'Jesus' really add to the substance of the gospel message? However, the gospels can be read in another way, which gives to the empty name a logical function in their universal proclamation. Along this path, I make my 'proper start'.

The gospels can be read, not as the story of Jesus, but as the story of the (re)foundation of a new city, a new kind of human community, Israel-become-the-Church. Jesus figures in this story simply as the founder, the beginning, the first of many. There is nothing that Jesus does that he will not enable the disciples to do: they will be able to cast out demons, heal the sick, raise the dead, forgive sins. And just as Jesus's proper source and place is not contained within this world, so also his followers are to be 'born again', and so somehow exceed their temporal origins – for if birth, like death, is not an event within life, but the opening of life, then a second birth in the midst of life must unite us, in our particular living identity, with that which opens out all life. Thus according to the gospel for which Jesus is most obviously the pre-existent Son of God, it is also the case that Jesus will no longer need to pray to the Father for the disciples, for they too, by loving Jesus, will enter into the relationship of sonship (John 16:26).

Similarly, the high Christologies of Colossians, the Epistles to the Corinthians and the Epistle to the Hebrews are strikingly yoked to the notion that Jesus is but the foundation of the building and the first of many sons: the *archegon*, or pioneer of salvation, such that 'he who sanctifies and those who are sanctified have all one origin' (Hebrews 2:10–11; Col. 1:15–29; 2 Cor. 3:9–11; 11:1; 2 Cor. 1:307; 4:10–11; 5:13–14, 21; 11:7). Moreover – and this does appear to conflict with *certain* later versions of 'orthodoxy' – our empowerment by Christ both to forgive and to suffer, seems to stretch as far as a continuing ability to make atonement. St Paul's obsession with his own credentials is linked with an understanding of himself as an *alter Christus* whose sufferings are *efficacious* for his brethren, part of a 'filling up what is lacking in the sufferings of Christ for the sake of his body the Church' (Col. 1:24). Thus: 'If we are beside ourselves it is for you' (2 Cor. 5:13); 'Did I commit a sin in abasing myself, that you might become exalted?' (2 Cor. 11:7); 'Be imitators of me, as I am of Christ' (1 Cor. 11:1); 'Anyone whom you forgive, I also forgive' (2 Cor. 2:10); 'If we are afflicted it is for your comfort and salvation' (2 Cor. 1:6). Christians collectively 'comfort with the comfort by which [they] are [themselves] comforted by God' (2 Cor. 1:4) and they are 'a fragrance from death to death' to the 'perishing', but a 'fragrance from life to life' to 'those who are being saved' (2 Cor. 2:14–16). While Christians live, they are 'always being given up to death for Jesus's sake, so that the life of Jesus may be manifested in [their] mortal flesh'. But this is not merely a personal, imitative appropriation, in which our own death is paradoxically a passage to our own life. On the contrary, the passage also works socially and transitively, like the first death which it imitates in this respect also, and consequently *repeats*: 'So death is at work in us, but life in you' (2 Cor. 4:11–12).

Although the Epistle to the Hebrews, by contrast, seems to emphasize the finality of Christ's sufferings – his bearing of his own blood not into the earthly, but into the heavenly sanctuary – it too speaks of a certain repetition of this sacrifice. We cannot, indeed, repeat the sacrifice of Christ by acting as priests who carry the blood of animals inside the earthly sanctuary of the temple, but we *can* repeat it by taking the role of the sacrificed animals themselves, who are buried 'outside the camp': 'Therefore let us go forth to him outside the camp, bearing abuse for him. For here we have no lasting city, but we seek the city which is to come. Through him then let us continually offer up a sacrifice of praise to God, that is the fruit of lips that acknowledge his name. Do not neglect to do good and to share what you have, for such sacrifices are pleasing to God' (Hebrews 13:13–16). Christ has abolished the sacrifices of the earthly city, which involved expelling something into a no-man's land; but instead he has inaugurated a new kind of efficacious sacrifice of praise, self-sharing and probable attendant suffering which unites us with him in the heavenly city, and at the same time totally obliterates, through this final 'exit', all the contours of inside and outside which constitute human power.

Of course sacrifices of praise and good works did not, for the Hebrews, amount
to atoning sacrifices; however, the above passage conjoins such sacrifices with a
'bearing of abuse' which puts us in the position of animals once sacrificed for
atonement. This continuous 'exit' both repeats the initial exit to Golgotha, and is
the reverse side of the single final transit of Jesus into the heavenly sanctuary.
Without the continuous and unprecedented exit, this transit would not be remembered upon earth, and therefore atonement could not be 'efficacious' in any real
fashion within time. The bearing of blood into the heavenly sanctuary is final *as* the
repetition of Christ's exit by later generations, because this movement, unlike
animal sacrifice, is socially transformative. In the new, efficacious mode of making
atonement, suffering is not asked for by God, but is voluntarily embraced when it
is inflicted upon us in the course of our self-sharing and offering of praise.

Jesus, therefore, figures in the New Testament primarily as a new Moses, the
founder of a new or renewed law and community. It is for this reason that he cannot
be given any particular content: for the founder of a new practice cannot be
described in terms of that practice, unless that practice is already in existence,
which is contradictory. This is why Jesus is presented not simply as the source of
the Church, but as arriving simultaneously with the Church. The waters of baptism, the fire of the Holy Spirit, Mary's consent to the incarnation, all in a historical
sense 'precede' Jesus, although Jesus (through a kind of retroactive causality) makes
them operative. If we want to describe a founder precisely in the moment of
origination of a practice, then all we can do is to identify him with the *general norms*
of that practice, and this procedure is followed by the gospels.

This is also why, in representing Jesus as the beginning of a practice, the New
Testament at the same time represents him as the culmination of that practice: not
just the seed, but also the fully-grown tree, not just the foundation-stone but also
the temple, not just the head, but also the body. Christ's full incarnate appearance
lies always ahead of us – *if* we love the brethren, according to St John, *then* he will
be manifested to us (John 14:18–23; 13:34). And in what is perhaps the original
ending of Mark's gospel, the risen Christ is not recorded in his visibility, but as
'going before you to Galilee', the place of the original gathering and going forth of
the new community (Mark 16:7).[7]

Do not these considerations make the 'name of Jesus' somewhat dispensable,
like the name of Moses in relation to the giving of the law? I would answer no, for
two reasons. First of all, as Kierkegaard best understood, Christianity exceeds
Platonism (or at least as the latter is commonly understood). It is not founded upon
the vision of a transcendent original which we must imitate. Instead it makes its
affirmations about the real, and about 'meaning', through the constant repetition of
a historically emergent practice which has no real point of origination, but only
acquires identity and relative stability *through* this repetition.[8] And what is repeated
is not an insight, not an idea (which is properly imitated), but a formal becoming,
a structured transformation. The narrative and metanarrative forms of the gospel
are therefore indispensable, not because they record and point us to a vision which

is still available in its eternal 'presence', but rather because they enshrine and constitute the event of a transformation which is to be non-identically repeated, and therefore still made to happen.

This transformation concerns the fact that, in Jesus's time as now, we live in a world of violence and suffering in which human words and conventions – 'the law' – are powerless over structures of human egotism and over physical death. Human words have a temporary force working in the interests of selfish power, but are ultimately powerless. The gospels, however, narrate Jesus's utter refusal of selfish power, and relate this to a transformation which combines human words with power over violence and death in the suffering body itself.

Following the lead of Louis Marin one can express this change in terms of Levi-Strauss's formula for all mythical transformations: $Fx(a):Fy(b)::Fx(b):Fa - l(y)$ (where (a) etc. stand for terms, f stands for function, -1 signals the reversal and transformation of a term, and in the final element term and function change place). Thus one would get:

Sign(Humanity):Life(Divinity)::Sign(Divinity):Transforming Power of Divine Humanity(Life).[9]

If the suffering body of Jesus becomes an actively suffering body, suffering for the sake of joy, and a greater joy for all, then it becomes the body that is united with other bodies – although this will only finally be fulfilled eschatologically with the cancelling of physical death. And united bodies are the resurrection – the making of words effective and life-giving, because no longer linked to selfish power, which means always the threat to kill, a power of death which in the long run spells the death of power.

The theme of resurrection, and of the Church as Christ's body, in fact restores concreteness to the notion of incarnation. When he was tempted by the devil, Jesus refused to turn the stones into bread, the food that ultimately cannot save us from death, and offered instead the universal spiritual food that is his 'word' or meaningful discourse. At the same time he refused powers of magical immunity and worldly dominion based upon a death-threatening force. Thereby he collapsed the powers that he bore into the impotent realm of signs. Yet according to John's gospel, these emanating signs are finally given to us to eat in the form of a body that does not die, because it is an endless sharing, an endless self-renewing. In the materiality of the new community, that which is universally presupposed by meaningful communication, what one might call its transcendental metaphors – 'life', 'light', 'seed', 'fruit', 'bread' – becomes bodily solidarity. The name of Jesus is attached to a descriptive content at the point where the word of the gospel ceases to be mere teaching, and is made 'real' and powerful in a new social body which can transgress every human boundary, and adopts no law in addition to that of 'life', or the imperative to the greater strength and beauty which is attendant upon a diverse yet harmonious, mutually reconciled community. Yet even the Church can only enter a defining discourse in abstract, 'impotent' terms, which do no more than seek to establish, negatively, its transcendental possibility (the possibility of one mode of human life, not, as for Kant or Habermas, the possibility, or implicit goal of 'human' social life in general, which by no means has necessarily the aim of mutual recognition of freedom or unconstrained communication – aims included, though also surpassed, in the 'Church' project of reconciliation). What proves, positively, this possibility, is the happening of such a community, however spasmodically. In this happening there appears, diversely and continuously, a 'descriptive content'.

The 'sense of continuity', which is necessary for such a community, since harmony is only heard in the succession of time, arises through 'repetition' – despite the non-coincidence of every different moment – without which there could indeed by no *sensus communis*. To this degree, against my earlier remarks, 'tradition' is inescapable, since a thought only 'persists' through a socially and conventionally recognized 'constancy'. Persistence can still be claimed, even though no single element in an inheritance is either sacred or inviolable: if, indeed, it is *only* the past that can be exemplary, this is not because 'proven practices' possess any 'authority' beyond a demonstration of mere pragmatic viability, but rather to the degree that concrete particulars escape into the dimension of inspiring 'principles', without being able to truly escape the marks of their historical genesis. The quarrel of 'conservative' tradition and 'liberal' reason is transcended – and exposed in its mutual complicity – at the point where one recognizes not only the historicity of reason, but also the 'formality' – the aspiration to provide universal, normative contexts – of all the most particular, most intense, most momentous, most generative and therefore most *abstract* events of history.

This brings me to the second, and more decisive reason why the 'name of Jesus' is not simply dispensable. The universality of the Church transcends the universality of enlightenment in so far as it is not content with mere mutual toleration and non-interference with the liberties of others. It seeks in addition a work of freedom which is none other than perfect social harmony, a perfect consensus in which every natural and cultural difference finds its agreed place within the successions of space and time. In this context it is correct to say that the Church is a 'community of virtue' which desires to train its members towards certain ends, rather than a 'community of rights' founded upon liberal indifference.[10] However, the social goals and 'training' are now much more loosely specified than in the antique *polis*. The Church has far less definite ideas than the *polis* concerning the kinds of individuals it desires to produce, and the kinds of roles it wishes to foster, precisely because its 'aim' is sociality and conviviality itself, a *telos* which subverts teleology, because in the continuous 'music' of community, no aspect of life is merely a stage on the way to a final outcome. Childhood, for example, (which in the Church, as not in the *polis*, has equal access to the 'final concerns' of human life) is not to be primarily considered, as many schoolmasters suppose, as a training for adulthood, but rather as a mode of being as directly and absolutely related to the creative action of God (which being eternal, does not seek a goal or follow a plan, but simply happens as a spontaneous, perfectly existent 'excess') as any other.[11] The results of not apprehending this 'transvaluation' of teleology in Christian ethics and ontology are all too likely to be authoritarian in character.

Alongside the search for conviviality, for a 'perfect peace' as Augustine understood it, is placed a deferral of all that is finite to a 'supernatural end': a stipulation that social celebration, to be genuine and secure, must take the form of worship. Here, however, we do not really have to do with a 'transcendence' of the material, social world – for the Christian understanding of 'creation', there is no 'spiritual' aspect of the world that in any way transcends our created (material, social and linguistic) condition. So acknowledging God is not like diverting our corporeal resources to another goal: instead it means, as Spinoza most cogently intimated, never foreclosing the material, social body which preserves itself (or better, nonidentically repeats itself, to modify Spinoza with Kierkegaard) through time, but instead seeking to gain through and for this social body the widest possible 'perspective' upon things, a ceaselessly renewed vision of nature and history.[12] Again, the 'goal' here is not really beyond the 'way', but rather is a kind of recapitulatory retracing of all our steps, a renarration-becoming-reactivation of all that has occurred, in such a manner that what once happened defectively and privatively as 'evil', is repeated only in its positivity, so that some good is taken from everything in so far as it can be 'referred' to a greater good beyond itself, and thus 'redeemed'.[13] This, one must point out, is not a *via negativa* in the false sense of encountering an accessibly 'other' spiritual space, negatively arrived at. There is negativity here in the sense of non-completion: but every new stage in the vision of God is positively added, positively emergent, where a merely expectant negativity turned away from the world would paradoxically leave us practically and materially locked into our merely present finitude.

So while, on the one hand, Christian universalism surpasses the liberal goals of freedom (and this means surpasses Kant, and *also* Hegel and Marx)[14] in seeking a perfect reconciliation that implies an absolute consensus, on the other hand, it is not as clear as Macintyre and others have supposed, that in this consensus it is preferred roles and virtues that are all important, as for earlier antiquity. In educating future generations of Christians, past 'examples' must be cited, yet what is ultimately exemplary here, what must be 'done again', is nothing specific and definable. While not just any act of autonomous freedom, even if compatible with the formal liberties of others, is tolerated by the Church, the (more than 'liberal') business of defining the objectively 'right' action, or 'duty' in a concrete circumstance, is a work of continuous judgement which relies upon, yet constantly surpasses, the influence of habit and stored-up traits of character.[15]

For the consensus sought by the Church is not a consensus in the abstract, concerning a list of the desirable individual virtues. And if it *has* an abstractly specifiable goal, this is now consensus itself, meaning a society without violence and unjust domination. Such a consensus happens, unpredictably, through the blending of differences, and by means of these differences, not despite them. For this reason every human difference is itself elevated to universality, becoming part of a goal which is no longer a goal because it is simply the true happening of Being, without end.

In this light the gospel instruction to love all, is an instruction to narrate all, attain to the highest possible perspective. This would mean carrying out an impossible act of perfect remembrance in which everything that truly *is* – in other words is not disfigured and denied in its active power by the negative work of violence which defines evil – is shown by the fact of its optimal existence to harmoniously co-exist with everything else in the resurrection body. Our remembrance of the name of the founder is really an instruction to remember every name, including that of the founder, as worthily as possible, and to learn from every 'Christian' example. Whereas 'Moses' is just the name of the mediator of the law, 'Jesus' is the name of the new law itself, because now the word of God is found to be located, not in the dead letter of the law over against the power of bodies, but in true, strong, peaceful, relationships, beginning with the practice of Jesus.

This word and this 'person' – meaning the unifying 'shape' of the various stylized and formalized specifications of Jesus's identity in narrative and metaphor – was 'with God from the beginning', was 'pre-existent' in an eternal relationship with the Father, because the mode of divine transmission of the new law must be consistent with its content (means and end being for God identical), which is not an instruction, but the event of personal relating. And because God – who is simply all that there eternally 'is' – does not change, and is not capricious, this transmission must be God himself. I am implying here that an approach to Christology from the context of ecclesiology actually allows a full retrieval of the Chalcedonian position, at which more narrowly Christological approaches are today likely to baulk.

This follows from two considerations. First of all, as I have just suggested, one should take Jesus's 'personhood', after Aquinas, as meaning simply his *being*, the total shape of his actions and words. Jesus is 'identical' with God, not in terms of an underlying 'essence', or his general human 'nature', but rather at the precise point of his irreplaceable specificity, or all that goes to make up his 'personality', including his historical situation and his own response to it (this correct sense of *persona* as personality, affirmed by Thomas Aquinas, has been admirably reinstated by Bruce Marshall, against the general run of modern misunderstandings).[16]

Second, while it is true that there is a certain specific 'flavour' of personality binding the various incidents and metaphors (and so a minimal sense of 'character', despite what I said earlier), the latter are nonetheless essentially formal statements about, and general instructions for, every human life. In consequence, the 'shape' of Jesus's life, his 'personhood' or 'personality', can only be finally specified as the entire content and process of every human life, in so far as it *is* genuinely human life, according to the formal specifications of the gospel narratives and metaphors. If Christ is the total 'context' for our lives, then he is both already and not yet; and *pace* Lindbeck, a 'world inside the text' implies also an imploded and suspended, albeit repeated text.[17] But as such a total context, which in time is both realized and yet not realized, Jesus's personhood must, as Chalcedon supposed, be divine *rather tha*n human, even though every specifiable element in the phenomenon of Jesus is entirely human and temporal. The 'divine personhood' only works as a propositional 'belief' (an aspect which I am not seeking to deny), if it is also taken as a pragmatic instruction to go on re-narrating and re-realizing 'Christ'.

Notice here also, that a 'post-modern' escape from preoccupation with an 'interior' subject and its 'intentionality', allows us to retrieve a more objective understanding of 'personhood', detached from notions of physical individuality, consciousness, will and so forth – all of which were, of course, fully and purely human in Christ. So that Chalcedonian high Christology need no longer seem so embarrassing as it did for modernist theology.

Nevertheless, I do not wish to disguise the fact that I am transposing Chalcedonian orthodoxy into a new idiom which only perfects it by dissolving 'substantial' notions of subjectivity which it did not always fully overcome. The 'persistent' identity of a person does not proceed from any 'subsistent' dimension within the individual (as Aquinas still supposed, for he did not fully appropriate Gilbert de la Porrée's more 'structural' definition of *persona* as 'incommunicable form').[18] Instead, it resides purely on the 'surface' of a series of events which exhibit a certain pattern and coherence. It is, paradoxically, the unique singularity and incommunicability of this pattern (as opposed to the transferability of an accident from substance to substance) which makes it 'repeatable' and further definable beyond the confines of its possession by a single 'individual'.

This formality, linguistically and fictionality of the person or subject permits us to make new sense of Jesus's divine personhood. Here one cannot start from the idea that a perfect knowledge of Jesus involves the recognition of the divine subject of his actions. For it is not, as Bruce Marshall seems to suppose, 'obvious' that 'genuine knowledge of a human history . . . involves recognition of the subject of that history.'[19] This phrasing still suggests that there is an apperceiving subject 'behind' its own history, and surplus to it, whereas a subject can only be 'recognized' in the dynamic form that a particular history is seen to take. When Marshall declares that a phrase like 'the judge judged', unlike a phrase such as 'Jesus possessed a perfect God-consciousness', picks out the specificities of Jesus's history, he is glossing over the fact that 'judged' belongs to the primary narrative, and 'the judge' figures only in the metanarrative, such that this identification of Jesus is just as 'extrinsic' as the ascription of a 'perfect God-consciousness', and no more *demonstrably* corresponds to the data of the primary narrative. Merely to declare that 'God' is the subject of Jesus's history, and to regard the incarnation, in Marshall's fashion, as 'logically primitive', seems to beg the question about how we come, in the first place, to identify Jesus as God.

By contrast, my own position in this article undercuts Marshall's opposition of Schleiermacher/Rahner to Barth, by showing that a treatment of Jesus as primarily the 'founder' of a practice/state of being which is fully transferable to others, does not necessarily involve subordinating Jesus, in Rahner's fashion, to a general 'human' category. On the contrary, the universal repeatability of Jesus is made possible *by* his specific historic occurrence, and this is never 'dispensable' in specifying the conditions of our salvation – as Marshall might fear – because a genuine 'foundation' is not the first instance of a general phenomenon, but rather is itself the 'general', though specific, definition of that phenomenon. It follows (as Rahner failed to see) that Jesus can be talked of as uniquely a 'substitute' and 'representative', not because these attributes cannot be repeated, but precisely in so far as they can be and are.[20]

This kind of approach to the question of why we identify Jesus as God, which is not content with a 'logically primitive' doctrine of incarnation, is not, of course, a matter of 'Christology from below', nor of supposing that from some empirical features of Jesus's life one could extrapolate to divinity. But it *is* a matter of commencing primarily with our pre-dogmatic, hermeneutic treatment of the gospel texts as themselves the code and context for all our other interpretative acts (this indeed means, as the Yale school claims, against a 'hermeneutic liberalism', that scriptural hermeneutics cannot be contained within any general hermeneutic method). Such a proposal would seem to accord with the view of Marshall and the Yale school by according a primary gnoseological value in theology to the particularities of the story of Jesus. However, we take these texts as a final hermeneutic context, in part because we are obeying the hermeneutic instructions inscribed in the metanarrative dimension of this story itself, which instead of 'identifying' Jesus in a normal fashion, declares of him only that he is the 'place' in which all true identities are located. I say, 'in part' because it is nonetheless not *quite* the case that we are here instructed to copy precisely that model which is left wholly undescribed – however salutary such a rendering might be in correcting an over-enthusiastic 'incarnationalism'. We do not obey the hermeneutic instruction blindly, but only in so far as our senses are arrested by the convincing 'attractiveness' of the form suggested by the narratives and metaphors. We have only a frugal outline, painted in clear, primary colours – somewhat *quattrocentro* – yet this sketch still holds us with a certain 'quality' that persuades us to take seriously its abstract import. Yet according to this import, which is exactly what the sketch 'portrays', Jesus is perfectly identified only as the source, goal and context of all our lives: the *esse* of his personality is, in Thomist terms, *esse ipsum*, or the infinite totality of actualized being which is 'eminently' contained in God. If this is the case, then it cannot be true that we have a metaphysically 'initial', perfect vision of Jesus (even if this is not realized all at once at a temporal starting point) which we later approximate through our imitations. On the contrary, only through such imitations, and through observing the likeness of Jesus in others, will a full sense of Jesus's personality be approximated to. To some extent, the observation of *every* human person follows this pattern, but only in the case of Jesus does an accurate rendering of his personhood involve an ultimate attention to everyone, in so far as their truth lies in Christ.

This ecclesiological construal of Christ's divine personhood, which regards Christ as having arrived only in terms of his final, eschatological arrival which is yet to come, has never been quite spelt out by 'orthodoxy', and is missed by the still somewhat 'Christomonist' perspectives of the Yale school.

In the fashion outlined above, there can be, I want to claim, an ecclesiological deduction of the Incarnation. And likewise of the atonement. The danger of a 'cultic' reading of this doctrine is that it will suggest that Christ's death is something in addition to the human practice of forgiveness, whose repetition makes real for us the divine forgiveness itself. If Christ's death is necessary in addition to the practice of forgiveness, then monstrous consequences ensue. We shall have to read the passage in Luke with which I began as saying that Judas and the disciples wielding swords are really, in their treachery, the necessary agents of redemption, and that the Jew's historical function is that of 'sacred executioner'. The same reading, which has been pursued by J. L. Borges and Louis Marin, logically renders Judas our real saviour. Marin interprets 'Judas' in textual terms as a 'shifter' which is semantically neutral with respect to good and evil, old and new covenant, but is, nonetheless, that point without content which allows a mythical transformation, or transition from one semiotic regime to another. The gospels are thus read as parables of nihilism, or of the 'indifference' which undergirds all cultural transitions. Yet what is most curious here, is that Marin can only sustain this reading by adopting a crudely 'mythological' and 'penal substitutionary' interpretation of the metanarrative level, which imports into it much later doctrinal speculation. He relates the action of Judas to the idea of the necessity of penal substitution (which seems to require the 'sacralization' of betrayal) and not to the working of original sin within him, which would ultimately connect it to the contingencies of human freedom. If the latter course is followed, then the archetypal mythical plot, whose reversal hinges upon betrayal, is relativized, because from the divine point of view this transition is only rendered necessary by sin, which is *identical* with the act of betrayal itself. Betrayal is the problem, not the remedy, but divine order immediately converts it into a remedy. Thus if the gospels are read, as Marin suggests, as parables about the nature of meaning or signification, then they are, in fact, unique *denials* of the ultimacy of the 'mythical paradigm' which makes conflict and betrayal ultimate, and appears to contain, from primordial times, a germ of nihilism. For in the gospels Jesus is taken as belonging to an uninterrupted series of 'perfect' events, in his relation to his Father and to the Holy Spirit, where transformations are not the 'dialectical' upshots of violence. This series is exhibited as coinciding, on the cross, with the mythical series, organized by Judas's 'unmeaning', but it absorbs the latter and continues unaffected by it. Jesus's bodily life persists after this encounter, and from this point onwards there are to be many new transitions, at the prompting of the Holy Spirit, yet this series of events will no longer take the 'dramatic', dialectical form of the mythical paradigm, which was 'assumed' only to be abolished. Thus if the emptiness of 'Judas' as shifter betokens nihilism, the emptiness of 'Jesus' as shifter betokens the 'Kingdom' of a harmonious succession of difference. As René Girard intimates, Marin, in reading the gospels mythically, misses precisely their critique of all pagan *mythos*, and of all transcendentally agonistic construals of meaning (the above remarks should also be read as anti-Hegelian).[21]

In contrast to Marin and Borges (as René Girard and Raymund Schwäger have argued) we should say that Jesus's death was almost 'inevitable', because his rejection of violence and rivalry actually negated the basis of all human political and social mechanisms that had hitherto existed, mechanisms from which Judas and the disciples were not fully liberated. The metanarrative commentary put into Jesus's mouth in Luke is to be interpreted ironically. (This is not to endorse Girard's account of the origin of religion solely in the occlusion of violence, nor his tendency to view all mimetic desire as necessarily engendering a conflictual rivalry.) But why, one might ask, is this negation supposed to be only possible for God incarnate? Neither Girard nor Schwäger are fully satisfactory here. In Schwäger's case, he conceives of original sin as mutual inhibition of freedom, and fomenting of violence through the mechanisms of mimetic desire. This is reasonable, but if there is not also an 'ineffable' aspect to original sin, residing in our blindness to the truly desirable (excluding rivalry), then it becomes unclear why Schwäger should think that only God incarnate can 'expose' the futile and sinful social structure of fallen humanity. Paradoxically, a more 'speculative' understanding of original sin, which concludes that by reason of original sin itself its definition must evade us, more functions to point towards the irreplaceability of Christ's specific, concrete manifestation. 'Jesus' – this set of stories, metaphors etc – is necessary for the redemption, not just because he exposes the old practice and defines the terms of the new, but also because the particular way in which he does this enacts and enshrines the *viability* of the new, forgiving practice, by virtue of its unique and universal 'attractiveness'.[22]

To answer the question of why only God incarnate can end violence, one must allude to the view of atonement doctrine that Jesus's death is not merely one isolated act of refusal of domination, but is supposed somehow to enable, in a more than exemplary fashion, similar refusals in the future. This can only mean two things: first of all, on the cross (in its 'textual' positioning, which at once includes, without exhausting, the physical event of the cross and extends to the cross elevated into a figure of meaning), Jesus is 'substituted' for us, because here (as the accounts of the last supper suggest) he becomes totally a sign, here he is transformed into a perfect metaphor of forgiveness. Only because of Thursday's symbolic act of kenosis into a world of signs without power, is Jesus able on Friday to activate this sign in his body (see the previous chapter). And after his death, it is only in terms of signs that one can make sense of a direct, and as it were 'contemporary' relation of his death to the lives of all human beings. Despite the fact that later human beings may stand in no previous relation to Jesus through a chain of historical causality (the Mayas of Central America, for example, before the Spaniards came) they can still establish a relation by treating the event of Jesus, as one can any historical event, as a figure and sign which possess 'meaning' precisely through its capacity to transcend causal sequence and be 'reapplied' in endlessly alien and remote contexts. This means that metaphors of atonement – 'ransom', 'sacrifice', 'victory' – are *not* to be taken realistically, as approximations to an 'atonement in itself', an invisible eternal transaction between God and humanity.[23] Instead, these metaphors represent the actual *happening* of atonement as a meaning in language.

It should be re-emphasized here, that while these metaphors, like Christ's depicted actions, have a relatively formal, abstract and universal quality, they still retain a certain material density which allows us to make (as von Balthasar has emphasized) an *aesthetic* judgement of their ineffably beautiful and 'manifestatory' qualities. But because of their relative generality, such judgement lies very close to creative inspiration for further, more concrete manifestations in the future – as if, as for Coleridge, the gospels were the very fontal springs of Beauty itself. There remains, nonetheless, a difficult problematic of form and content: *every* apparent content, however much more seemingly 'dense' than that of the gospels, can be reduced to form and abstract generality, and yet no abstraction is perfectly abstract, precisely to the extent that there is no way of knowing when we have 'complete' definition of a formal category. Every category remains contingent, and could be otherwise: supplemented or depleted. Meaning expressed through a clutch of mutually supplementing metaphors, such as found in the gospels, particularly well conveys this general predicament of all meaning, its 'concrete universality': the metaphors are inescapably general, and yet also inescapably specific in their individual contingency and arbitrarily extended or restricted number.[24]

The second consideration, in asking why the rejection of mimetic rivalry required the action of God incarnate, runs as follows. If Jesus's death is efficacious, not just as the offering of an enabling sign, but also as a material reality, then this is because it is the *inauguration* of the 'political' practice of forgiveness; forgiveness as a mode of 'government' and social being. This practice is *itself* continuing atonement. For forgiveness involves not simply the bare will to forgive, nor yet the offering of forgiveness on condition of repentance, but rather the transition across this temporal *impasse* through for-giving, giving-for, doing what the other should have done, and providing her with the conditions under which she can do her duty in the future. If atonement, therefore, is nothing *more than* forgiveness, because forgiveness is itself atonement, it follows that for atonement to be materially efficacious it *cannot* be 'once and for all', like *the sign or metaphor of atonement*, but must be continuously renewed. The fully efficacious character of Christ's death must mean that in his death this continuously renewed mode of life is already present, such that this death occurs already within the context of the Church, which is both the transmission of the signs of atonement, and the repetition of an atoning practice (as spelt out by Paul and the *Epistle to the Hebrews*). One can add that the eucharist is *both these aspects at once*.

From this double consideration one can conclude the following: the idea that only God incarnate can make atonement means that an atoning practice can arise

only once the new community based upon the absolute priority of human relationship, so perfectly imaging God, is already in place. After all, unless the textual and
ecclesial representation of Jesus – and so its relationship to Jesus, which must be a
kind of 'incarnation' of the procession of the Holy Spirit – is in some sense
'perfect', how could Jesus's perfection be at all conveyed to us?

Hence the doctrine of the atonement must be drastically reconceived from an
ecclesiological vantage point. As *sign*, the event of the happening in language of the
Church, the atonement occurred 'once and for all'. As real transformation, the
fulfilling of God's will for the perfection of Creation, it goes on happening. In either
case, it is the radical newness of the practice of the gospel, as over against the
tolerated violence of all other human practices, which suggests the total identification of this practice with God himself in its 'inauguration', which includes, of
course, its final scope.

However, all this will not quite do. The recognition of a perfection in Jesus's
practice, and so of the 'finality' of Jesus (which will certainly involve a sifting from
many human 'imperfections' in the ecclesial transmission process) is not simply
forced on us by the gospel metanarratives. However much they may point in this
direction, 'doctrine' takes speculative decisions that are beyond their reach, and at
a higher level of abstraction. These decisions, about, for example, the non-docetic
character of the incarnation, the equality of the *Logos* with the Father, the sufficiency of Jesus's sacrifice, function as a decision to take to an extreme the finality
implied by the metanarratives. This doctrinal movement is governed in part by the
persuasive 'attractiveness' of the gospel accounts, and yet there is an element that
is (at first sight disturbingly) surplus even to this: for nothing in the conviction that
this is the 'highest revelation so far' proves even to our subjectivity that there is not
one higher still to come or that we may not still, secretly, be bound within the proud
delusions of sin. The doctrines of incarnation and atonement as developed in all
their later details foreclose this possibility by identifying a finite set of events and
metaphors with God's 'final' word. What appears to compel the 'highest' versions
of doctrine is not just 'saving the textual appearances' nor *even* the regulative
safeguarding of an already existing, but threatened interpretation at a 'first-order',
devotional level, but rather a supplementary speculative attractiveness in the
notions of a God once incarnate, and a sinless God alone able perfectly to suffer the
effects of sin in one incarnate divine person. There is an abstract and freewheeling
'propositional' element here which is in excess of a primarily regulative function
(although even 'second order' regulation implies a decision about the correct use of
'first order' language, when this is in dispute, and therefore, indirectly, an ontological import).[25] And the excess arises because even the ideas that God was 'once'
incarnate, and 'once' perfectly atoned allow us – despite my earlier remarks – a
certain concreteness in our picture of God: witness the highly abstract concreteness
of much paradoxical imagery in Christian 'metaphysical' or 'conceptist' poetry of
the seventeenth century. This speculative 'excess' actually serves to conserve the
sense of the divine personhood and body of Christ as 'over against' the Church,

despite the fact that he only arrives, from the outset, through the Church ('incarnating' the substantive relation of Son and Spirit). Such a reciprocity is most manifest in the *constitution* of the Church through the reception of the body of Christ in the eucharist, by which it receives *itself*, even though this reception is only possible through the simultaneous *offering* of Christ's body by the Church.[26]

Nevertheless, the speculative aspect of the doctrine of atonement, while perhaps 'excessively' attaching itself to an event that happened 'once and for all', nonetheless does in essence drive to an absolute conclusion the inherent logic of the metanarrative: given the idea that a 'perfect' divine practice arrives with Christ/the Church, the speculation inevitably develops that in the 'beginning' of this practice, there is a perfect suffering of guilt made by the guiltless Jesus, impossible for those whose sin must distort even their awareness and endurance of their own actions. This is, in essence, R. C. Moberly's classic version of the speculation.[27] However his view can be considered to be in essential continuity with an Anselmian approach: for Anselm there is no question of anything being received as a compensatory offering by God, because God, as the most perfect thing that can be conceived, cannot possibly be deprived of anything. Barthian/Balthasarian talk about 'divine wrath' is here 'grammatically' ruled out. Nor does Anselm think that Jesus suffers the punishment that is properly ours, for this would not conform to *iustitia*. Instead, Jesus is held to have restored the lost harmony and order of the creation which constitutes an infinite wrong by comparison with the absolute perfection willed by God, and therefore cannot be 'compensated for' by any act of a fallen, finite creature. Only a human nature that is individuated by a divine personhood is capable of an act which outweighs in the balance the fault of the world's sin. This act involves not just willing the good, but also 'willing the better', in choosing to suffer and die for others. It perfectly 'compensates' for original sin (which was uniquely without prompting or excuse in the face of perfection, and therefore infinitely culpable) in that Adam's succumbing to the devil when he was strong, is matched by Christ's overcoming of death and the devil when he was weak. This superogatory offering that is made by Christ to God (and in fact by Christ's humanity to his divinity, so that Anselm also rules out any Balthasarian romances about 'ruptures in the Trinity') is *not*, of course, needed by God, and therefore it flows back earthwards to redeem fallen humanity. This transformation can also be expressed in the Levi-Straussian formula for myth. Thus:

Death(strong humanity):Life(God)::Death(God):Human power-to-be-weak(Life)

In this transition it is uniquely the case that *only the victim* (God) can offer compensation, and that the offence is only cancelled out when the compensation is given to the guilty party (humanity). Thus Anselm indicates how *iustitia* towards God, or to 'justice itself', can only be paradoxically conceived. For only the perfectly just one can provide compensation for the non-compensatable, only he has the power perfectly to *accept* that weakness and death which is the result of sin.

This is very akin to Moberly's saying that only the guiltless one can be authentically 'guilty', or suffer sin for what it is, despite the fact that he is *not* in sin but has only 'assumed' it.

However, Anselm's talk of 'compensation', of recapitulating Adam's action (which *remains* essentially within a *Christus Victor* mode), and of 'diversion' of Christ's offering from God to us, is still very mythological in character, and does not fully achieve Anselm's aim of demonstrating the rational 'base' upon which the patristic 'pictures' were painted (to adopt his own formulation). To really achieve this one could suggest that one *combine* the speculative notion of a perfect because innocent suffering with the idea that the practice of forgiveness, as surplus to any system of desert or obligation, is able creatively to break out of the blindness induced both by the wrong act of the offender, and by the corresponding anger of the victim. In Jesus we see the perfect 'shape' of forgiveness, and this inaugurates a new form of association which aims to be based on such a practice. A notion of this kind would translate into more conceptual terms Anselm's talk of 'compensation', and of an offering diverted from God to us. In fact the divine–human power provides this 'compensation' which is forgiveness, only for us and for our restoration (as Julian of Norwich taught, God as such does *not* forgive, since he never ceases to *give*).

Thus we see that Anselmian speculation remains somewhat 'extrinsic', unless Christ's quality of perfection is more than something hermetically sealed within his consciousness, but is to a degree 'conveyed' to us in external effects. Nevertheless, the speculation in itself gives a compelling and paradoxical 'picture' of a God who cannot sin and cannot suffer (as I would wish to insist) somehow perfectly registering the reality of estrangement and privation – a paradox which is most unsentimentally spelled out in terms of the idea that only God, as absolute Being, can initially arrive in time at the vision of evil as privation, whereas to the sinner his sin always seems like 'something'.

It has been argued in this essay that, however much one may start out by protesting against an extrinsicism which presents the incarnation and atonement as mere 'facts' which are to be 'believed in', this extrinsicism proves far harder to overcome than one might at first hope, precisely because the historical concreteness of Jesus is forever buried beneath – although at the same time preserved within – an avalanche of metaphors and typological stories which themselves tend in the direction of spelling out the mere formal grammar of the 'fact' of incarnation. (This is, of course, not a matter for 'regret' as the empiricist wistfulness of English theologians tends to imagine: the 'textual' Christ who has always been the Christ who saves us, *is* the real historical 'person' Jesus, for 'real' human identity resides in its 'force' or the effect upon others made by an individual: see chapter 8, 'The Force of Identity', below.) Where we hoped to discover *in what manner* God became incarnate and atoned for us, we discover instead, complexly coded, the mere fact that he 'once did'. The gospels appear to commence a baseless speculation which doctrine then completes.

By contrast, it has been claimed, the only thing which will really remove us from extrinsicism is the primacy of ecclesiology. The most concrete elements in the gospels are the general injunctions and examples regarding Christian practice. Only here do we 'identify' God incarnate, and this identification should be fleshed out in the later history and contemporary life of the Church. Ched Myers declares that '[Fernando] Belo is essentially correct in arguing that on the one hand the temple as the centre of the Jewish symbolic order is replaced by Christ's body, and that on the other, Jesus's body, which becomes absent at his death, is replaced by discipleship practice. In other words, the old cult is not replaced with a new cult, but by practice alone'.[28] But as I have shown, the 'speculative' elements in the New Testament can themselves be understood in terms of an attempt to fully articulate the 'logic' of the Church and of its historical irruption. Even the more abstract speculations of doctrine should be understood in this light: so, for example, the picture of the divine person Jesus Christ as alone 'perfectly suffering' helps to define the Christian community as one hoping to rise not just in theory, but also in universal historical practice, to the divine perspective for which evil is but the contingency of violence, and violence is precisely that which lacks all power and reality, because it is always 'on its own'. And I have shown how the doctrine of Christ's divine personhood confirms the thrust of the metanarratives towards the view that we must look for the concrete, particular Christ – who alone *mainfests* this divine perspective – in the widest possible recounting of true humanity. In both cases, the 'deduction' of Christological doctrine from ecclesiology is clearly a 'leading out' which also moves forwards, beyond mere logical consequence, the speculative exodus which is the self-definition of the Church. Finally, this exodus points to a practice which is only ethical as also liturgical: the ceaseless re-arrival of a harmonious body by the eucharistic ingestion of the body of Christ, whose universality renders this cult an 'anti-cultic cult'.

Perhaps these reflections can assist us in avoiding a Christology which pretends that the world is restored, when it manifestly is not. At the same time, they can help to show why the Church imagined itself through a story about how the end of the world and divine judgement had already occurred – in the name of one who appropriated divine prerogatives of forgiveness, and so refused the powerlessness of human justice.

Notes

1 Louis Marin, 'The Semiotics of the Traitor', in *The Semiotics of the Passion Narrative: Topics and Figures*, trans. Alfred M. Johnson Jr (Pickwick, Pittsburgh Penn., 1980), pp. 93–155. This article is much indebted to both the essays in this volume.
2 See, for example, Fernando Belo, *A Materialist Reading of the Gospel of Mark* (Orbis, Maryknoll, New York, 1981). For some critical remarks about Belo's failure positively to

assimilate the Cross and non-violence into political exegesis, see Ched Myers, *Binding the Strong Man: A Political Reading of Mark's Story of Jesus* (Orbis, Maryknoll, New York, 1988), pp. 403, 469–72. However, Myers does not go far enough. While he is right to refuse a 'cultic' distortion of the gospel (see the end of this article), he is wrong to suppose that Christological doctrine is fundamentally a set of cultic 'rewrites', or that the creation of 'the Church' meant an unequivocal arrival of 'imperial Christianity'.

On the contrary, culticization was a slower, more complex and more resisted process than he seems to allow, and doctrine continues a 'rewriting' which is, as I shall argue, inextricably interwoven with the gospel narratives themselves (and not just intrusive in later 'apocryphal' texts, like the presumed later ending to Mark, where Myers glimpses, on slender evidence, the beginnings of an 'imperial' Christianity, exaggerating the differences in attitude of the new ending to signs, miracles, belief and an after-life, in comparison with the main text). Furthermore, this rewriting, on my argument, does not betray, but rather confirms and elaborates, the content of the new 'revelation' as a new form of social practice.

3 See Rowan Williams, *Arius* (Darton, Longman & Todd, London, 1988).

4 Hans W. Frei, *The Identity of Jesus Christ* (Fortress, Philadelphia, 1975); Ronald F. Thiemann, *Revelation and Theology: The Gospel as Narrated Promise* (Notre Dame University Press, Notre Dame, Ind., 1985), pp. 71–91.

5 Hans W. Frei, *The Eclipse of Biblical Narrative* (Yale University Press, New Haven, 1974), P. 323. Frei defines 'history-likeness' in terms of 'the direct interaction of character, descriptively communicative words, social context and circumstance, whether miraculous or not'.

6 Marin, 'The Places of the Narrative' in *The Semiotics of the Passion Narrative*, pp. 3–21, 34ff.

7 Myers, *Binding the Strong Man*, pp. 398–9.

8 Søren Kierkegaard, 'Repetition', in *Fear and Trembling/Repetition*, trans. Howard H. Hong and Edna H. Hong (Princeton University Press, Princeton, NJ, 1983), pp. 131–231; Gilles Deleuze, *Différence et Répétition* (P.U.F., Paris, 1974). And see Catherine Pickstock, *Seraphic Voices* (manuscript in preparation), Conclusion, for an important modification of Kierkegaard's comparison of Plato and Christianity.

9 Marin, *The Semiotics*, p. 101.

10 Alasdair Macintyre, *Whose Justice? Which Rationality?* (Duckworth, London, 1988); Stanley Hauerwas, *A Community of Character* (Notre Dame University Press, Notre Dame, Indiana, 1981).

11 See Gilles Deleuze and Felix Guattari, *A Thousand Plateaus*, trans. Brian Massumi (Athlone, London, 1988), pp. 232–310. Also John Milbank, *Theology and Social Theory: Beyond Secular Reason* (Blackwell, Oxford, 1990), chapter 11.

12 Robert Hurley in 'Preface' to Gilles Deleuze, *Spinoza: Practical Philosophy*, trans. Robert Hurley (City Lights, San Francisco, 1988), p. iii.

13 See Milbank, *Theology and Social Theory*, chapter 12. An important project for postmodern theology might be to 'Spinozize' Augustine, so as to make him more materialist, but in a fashion playing upon the Stoic resonances in both thinkers – and at the same time to 'Augustinize' Spinoza by modifying the latter's version of *privatio boni*, so as to refuse any necessity to negativity or the 'sad passions' at the level of human temporal being, a necessity which in Spinoza makes a coercive and sovereignly central state essential, and requires also its sacralization. See Deleuze, *Spinoza*, pp. 30–44 and

Christian Jambet and Guy Lardreau, *Le Monde* (Bernard Grasset, Paris, 1978), pp. 225–75.

14 See Milbank, *Theology and Social Theory*, chapters 6, 7 and 8.

15 Ibid., chapter 11.

16 Thomas Aquinas, S.T.Q.III. 17 a 2. See also Bruce Marshall, *Christology in Conflict* (Blackwell, Oxford, 1987), pp. 176–89.

17 George C. Lindbeck, *The Nature of Doctrine* (Westminster, Philadelphia, 1984), p. 118.

18 Lauge Olaf Nielsen, *Theology and Philosophy in the Twelfth Century* (Brill, Leiden, 1982), pp. 62–5, 149–84.

19 Marshall, *Christology*, p. 169.

20 Ibid., pp. 143–204. While it is true that in a certain way this article seeks a path that is simultaneously 'liberal' and 'neo-orthodox', I am not at ease with these usual designations. For Barth's theology seems to turn upon a kind of negative mirror-image of Fichtean epistemology, and in its preoccupation with the problem of knowledge remains 'individualist' in character, and therefore, in a political sense, somewhat liberal. Schleiermacher, on the other hand, was notably critical of Kantian and Fichtean ethics and politics, advocating instead a Platonic 'ethic of virtue', and gives great prominence to ecclesiology in his dogmatics, as evidenced by the following remark concerning the activity of Christ: 'this activity can be seen in its completeness only in the corporate life he founded' (F. D. E. Schleiermacher, *The Christian Faith*, T. & T. Clark, Edinburgh, 1948, p. 377). While Christ is seen by Schleiermacher as founder in terms of the perfection of his God-consciousness, the latter is not transferable to us *en bloc*, or univocally accessible from any position in space and time, like Rahner's 'supernatural existential'. On the contrary, the emotion stimulated by Christ's preaching is always received in a *modified* fashion as a particular emotion which bears the mark of its historical specificity (Schleiermacher, *Christian Faith*, pp. 85–6).

This element in Schleiermacher's thought is illuminated if one pays regard to the origin of his notion of 'the feeling of absolute dependence' in earlier talk of an 'intuition' of boundless infinitude, which owes much to Spinoza's 'third kind of knowledge', and is spoken of as involving an ecstatically enlarged perspective upon reality (see note 13) which takes us *beyond* the confines of subjectivity (which Schleiermacher takes as circumscribing both metaphysics and morality). Schleiermacher's category of 'feeling' may therefore not denote something quite so 'private', indifferent to external changes, and to sociality as sometimes claimed. Nevertheless, it remains the case that Schleiermacher later conceived the capacity for feeling in Kantian terms as a faculty distinct from, though interacting with, those of knowing and doing, and therefore as something at least relatively independent of constructive action and specific conceptualization (whereas for Spinoza, knowing, acting and feeling are entirely coterminous and together more or less 'clear', 'active' and 'capable of being affected'). Although Jesus's God-consciousness is something interfused with his whole series of concrete circumstances and responses, it is still something 'inward' which is 'communicated' to others, rather than something external which only exists *in* this communication, and so is inherently inter-relational. However, Schleiermacher's 'liberalism' and 'subjectivism' is here an extension of traditional, 'orthodox', misplaced preoccupation with what went on inside Jesus's head. A Spinozistic rendering of Schleiermacher, in keeping with some of his earlier inclinations, might help to overcome this subjectivism, and produce a less individualist and so more ecclesiocentric version of 'Christ as founder', which would no longer conceive of any absolute beginning, locked in an inviolable subjectivity, as the first and most precious 'example' of something specifiable (at least in principle) without reference to Christ or the Church at all. (This might appear to contradict the fact that the later Schleiermacher is more cautiously respectful towards the Church, but his desire to make concessions to an established institution is not fully matched by an ontology of religious awareness that would genuinely give primacy to the Christian community – 'Church' in the most vital sense.) See Friedrich Schleiermacher, *On Religion: Speeches to Its Cultured Despisers*, trans. Richard Crouter (Cambridge University Press, Cambridge, 1988), pp. 102, 107–8, 133. I am indebted to John Clayton for conversations and advice upon this matter.

21 Marin, 'The Semiotics of the Traitor'; J. L. Borges, 'Three Versions of Judas', in *Ficciones* (David Campbell, London, 1993), pp. 151–9.

22 René Girard, *Of Things Hidden Since the Beginning of the World* (Athlone, London, 1988); Raymund Schwäger, *Der Wunderbäre Tausch: Zur Geschichte und Deutung der Erlösungslehre* (Kösel, Munich, 1986), pp. 161–92, 273–313; and see Milbank, *Theology and Social Theory*, chapter 12.

23 Here I diverge from Colin Gunton's epistemological 'realism', as expressed in *The Actuality of Atonement* (T. & T. Clark, Edinburgh, 1988), pp. 27–53, 115–43.

24 Despite the Hegelian allusion I do not mean to imply that there is a dialectical passage from concreteness to abstraction, proceeding by 'negation'. On the contrary, every 'element' of the real is simultaneously both abstract and concrete, according to the 'perspective' in which it is regarded.

25 See Brian Gerrish's review of Lindbeck in *The Journal of Religion*, 68, 1 (January 1988), pp. 87–92.

26 See Henri de Lubac, *Corpus Mysticum: L'Eucharistie et l'Eglise au Moyen-Age* (Aubier-Montaigne, Paris, 1949); Michel de Certeau, *The Mystic Fable*, trans. Michael B. Smith (Chicago University Press, Chicago, 1992) pp. 82–5; Catherine Pickstock, *Seraphic Voices*, chapter 4.

27 See R. C. Moberly, *Atonement and Personality* (John Murray, London, 1909); Anselm, *Cur Deus Homo*; Schwäger, *Der Wunderbäre*, pp. 161–92.

28 Myers, *Binding the Strong Man*, p. 406.

Pneuma

7

The Second Difference

1 Introduction

If theology is properly the elucidation of the Godhead of the Son, then it is not surprising that pneumatology should find expression only as an echo, an after-thought. Yet if we are to believe Origen,[1] it is precisely in the distinguished knowledge of the Pneuma, that the distinction of Christianity most lies. Perhaps theology still awaits its complementation by a 'theopneumatics'.

This may be a matter of expectation of the Kingdom.[2] But at the same time, it may be a matter of inadequate reflection upon the manner in which the Kingdom is already present. There appears to be a gulf between the confident proclamation of the Spirit as a separate hypostasis, and the lack of an adequate *rationale* for this separation. Where the Spirit is understood as 'applying' the benefits of Christ, then she[3] seems in danger of being reduced to the power of Christ's person. And the problem is compounded on the level of the immanent Trinity. We can begin to understand the one God who is also difference, who includes relation, and manifold expression. But a second difference? This till smacks of the arbitrary, and the incantatory. It is not surprising that the Eastern tradition since Photius has talked of an absolutely ineffable mystery, which risks reduction to the status of a purely extrinsic *datum*.

In this article I shall argue that we need to penetrate a little more that reserve by which the Holy Spirit is shrouded. Two recent attempts to do so, which I describe respectively as those of 'Catholic transcendentalism' and of 'Protestant Hegelianism', will be shown to be inadequate. Then I shall argue for a new account of the distinction of the Spirit in terms of both economy and immanence.

2 Defining the Problem

But before considering the recent accounts of the identity of the Spirit, I should like to specify at exactly what level this problem exists. It is certainly not a matter of peeling away layers of Western error to discover that it is, after all, only a pseudo-problem. Historians of theology have now followed Pusey in showing that the *per Filium* was widely affirmed in the patristic East (not least by Cyril of Alexandria in connection with his anti-Nestorianism), and that the *Filioque* in the West was mostly not intended to convey a drastically different content.[4] Cyril in the East and Marius Victorinus in the West illustrate how theologians taking seriously the New Testament texts could emphasize both the agency of the Spirit in the life of Christ and the eschatalogical giving of the Spirit *by* Christ. It is in keeping with an outlook that does not yet separate the immanent and economic Trinities, and which insists strongly on the degree of divine condescension to humanity, that such writers should proclaim an eternal procession 'through the Son'.

Instead, it is now recognized that both West and East are the partial victims of rival scholasticisms. Photianism not only consigned pneumatology to a pure fideism, it also blocked the route by which the East might have come to understand the theory of 'substantial relations'. The same exclusion of the *per Filium* must bear some responsibility for the Palamite theology which substituted 'uncreated energies' as the gift of the Holy Spirit for the indwelling of the Spirit in person.

In the West it is seen that the culprit is not the *Filioque*, nor the relational definition of the hypostases, nor even the so-called psychological analogy. (I have no space to consider this here, but elsewhere I argue that Augustine 'pluralized the soul' – without Platonically fragmenting it – rather than 'psychologized the deity').[5] The latter is indeed essential for grasping the Trinitarian *taxis* as a casual sequence that is throughout intellectual in character (whatever else it may also be), remembering that it does this by redefining knowledge as intentional sign, an ecstatic outgoing whose being is in pure self-displacement, and sees this outgoing as guided necessarily by a will also self-displaced as 'desire'.

The culpable theologian is not Augustine, so much as Anselm. It is he who first inaugurated a tendency to subordinate the persons to the substance, by making the Spirit proceed *a Patre Filioque tanquam ab uno principio*.[6] For the *per Filium* is substituted the notion of a procession from Father and Son in virtue of their substantial identity as God. And this revision is indeed on the road to modalism.

But Anselm's influence was by no means total. Alexander of Hales declared that the Spirit proceeded from the difference between the Father and the Son,[7] and Aquinas affirms the *per Filium* sense of *Filioque* (S.T.I.Q. 36 a 3). Several theologians sought to synthesize Augustinian with Greek patristic approaches and in particular Richard of St Victor tried to think of the Spirit as hypostatic (and not merely 'appropriated') love in a fashion that emphatically did not reduce her to a sub-personal 'bond' uniting the Father and the Son.[8]

One concludes that having cleared away certain misconceptions (Photius, Anselm) that have blocked the way to understanding, it is then necessary to penetrate to points in time at which attempts were made to articulate the ontological 'necessity' of the Holy Spirit. But in the next section I shall argue that the solution propounded by Richard of St. Victor is inadequate (although this conclusion does not apply to Augustine himself). This conclusion leads me now to ponder further on a situation in which it appears that the hypostatic Godhead of the Spirit is there as a sort of positive *datum* 'to be dealt with', while one is unable to give a more than formal account of this *datum*, such that one could see, in due measure, why a mere binity would be insufficient.

This appearance is especially unsatisfactory if one rejects notions of revelation as raw 'Christian experience', later brought to reflection.[9] The absurdity of this idea appears in the present case when one considers that without being *in some way* able to articulate to oneself the *rationale* for the personal subsistence of the Spirit, it would simply be meaningless to say 'I have an experience of the Holy Spirit'. Not only should one argue, with Thomas Aquinas, that without the *Filioque* there is absolutely no way nor reason to think of the Spirit's personhood (S.T.I.Q. 36 a 2), one should also insist that the 'experience' of the Spirit as a person cannot possibly be prior to the 'experience' of her mode of procession.

For the accounts of the logic of the Trinitarian processions as given by the Cappadocians, Augustine and Aquinas, are not, as it were, 'optional extras' for theologians only. Instead, they both reflect upon (uncover the 'grammar' of) but *also* deepen and perpetuate the original 'lived thought' which is the only possible content of early Christianity. For this reason, when one notes how pneumatology is often merely the efflorescence of the contentious distillation of Christology,[10] then one is bound to interrogate again the New Testament, and other early writings, to see if there is something we have overlooked. A latent Trinitarian logic, perhaps, in which the sequence of substantial relations can be stated in such a way that threefoldness becomes inescapable.

My case is, that without such a logic, one has not entirely banished the spectres of arbitrariness and positivity nor the alternative shadow of a non-Trinitarian reading of the New Testament. Preservation of the *per Filium* is merely the minimal condition for comprehending the identity of the Spirit. The further task, of understanding why Father and Son can only be Father and Son in the act of spiration, involves attention to history and the development of suitable analogies. It is a mistake to suppose that the latter can be neglected in favour of the former, for the latter continues a necessary reflection already begun in the New Testament itself. The immanent relation of the Son to the Father can only be imaged, as otherwise it does not 'occur' historically. Likewise, if the eternal procession through the Son also 'occurs' in history, then it does so only as a complex metaphorical transaction.

Comprehending spiration will then be a matter of searching for analogies as compelling as the notion of an eternal Father whose Fatherhood exhaustively defines his subsistence (Athanasius) or of a knowledge only attained and realized in an infinite creative *ars* (Eriugena, Bonaventure, Aquinas.)[11]

These analogies are convincing because, with the uniquely Christian concept of an absolutely original and non-declining emanation in the absolute, the *aporia* which opens between a transcendent but isolated God on the one hand, and an intrinsically related, but panentheistically determined God on the other, can be overcome. God, in himself, relates to the creation in his *Logos*. When, by sin, the creation is alienated from God, then this necessitates, as a unique contingency, the making of the *Logos* himself as part of the Creation.

By comparison, the narratives concerning the Spirit appear thin, and weak. No re-conceiving of the relationship of God to the world is involved, and the reflections on Pentecost arrive at no great Anselmian theories concerning the exigencies of this mode of divine involvement. The Spirit is connected with our divinization, but this is presented as the appropriation of a divine–human transaction already accomplished, and the Athanasian confession of the fully divine power required for this appropriation would not necessarily seem to involve any revision in our conception of the Godhead in itself. Thus time and again the Spirit is falsely seen as more immanent, more economic, than the other two persons: a 'go-between God' whose redundant mediation only obscures the immediacy of the divine presence.

3 The 'Catholic Transcendentalist' Solution

Recent Catholic writers – Bouyer, Congar, and Kasper, in particular – have sought a perspective which would combine the Western insistence on *Filioque* with the supposed Eastern maintenance of the Paternal *Monarchia*, and non-subordination of the three persons to the single essence. The favoured candidate for these writers is Richard of St. Victor's development of Augustine's understanding of the Trinity as eternal love.[12] Richard not only enriched the Christian discovery of the personal by redefining (along with Gilbert de la Porrée) the person as *natura intellectualis incommunicabilis existentia*, [13] he also sought to secure more adequately the personal character of the Spirit. According to Richard, 'love' can be ascribed to the persons of the Trinity in three different proper senses; the Father is a purely giving love, the Son a love both due to the Father and giving in turn to the Spirit, the Spirit a love purely received and due. By this utter receptivity, the Spirit is uniquely a hypostasis whose very essence is love. It should be noted here that Richard's single focus on love tends to elide the Augustinian stress that the Son is first of all 'word' or 'reason', and that my arguments will suggest that this is the real source of error.

Walter Kasper, especially, has sought to elaborate this scheme. More decisively than Bouyer or Congar he places himself in a voluntarist line of descent which seeks to comprehend the Trinity entirely in terms of the categories of 'will', 'love' and 'freedom'.

Three elements can be distinguished in Kasper's understanding of the grounds of spiration. First of all he offers a strong version of the *Monarchia*, following Bonaventure in interpreting the *innascibilitas* of the Father as a positive plenitude of substance which is 'given' to the Son, but which the Son cannot exhaust.[14] Second, again echoing Bonaventure, who thought that the Spirit proceeded more 'through freedom', whereas the Son proceeded 'by nature',[15] Kasper associates the 'gratuity' of the Spirit with the 'gratuity' of creation. The procession of the Spirit is a 'theological transcendental condition' for the possibility of creation, as well as for the free response of the creature of God.[16] Third, there is an attempt, as with Bertrand de Margerie, to argue that three is the minimum number for a truly personal community. A face-to-face encounter risks an *egoisme à deux*, and only if what is given is in turn handed on, can the experience of the 'we' arise alongside that of the 'I–Thou relationship'.[17]

My criticisms of Kasper rest upon the grounds that his Trinitarianism is an uneasy amalgam of personalist and Kantian perspectives, and that personalism as received provides a misleading Trinitarian analogy.

The whole argument of the first half of *The God of Jesus Christ* leads *primarily*, not to the Trinity, but to the establishment of God as a transcendent person who is the Father.[18] Despite the attempts (following Balthasar) to edge away from Rahner, an epistemological and individualist starting point for fundamental theology is still firmly in place. Human thought is allowed a pre-theological autonomy, and a pre-theological, Scotist–Heideggerian apprehension of a sheerly categorical *esse*.[19] Within this space is located the human capacity for free response to God, and the aspiration of the human spirit towards an adequate goal, which is infinite freedom. The dynamism of the *analogia entis* and its distinction from an *analogia fidei*, depends according to Kasper upon this categorical structure of the human subject.[20] Despite his strictures on Rahner for pre-determining the content of faith by a transcendental anthropological framework, the same suspicion may attend his work also. It appears permeated by the Kantian view that freedom can only exist imperfectly within natural finitude, and longs after a 'blessedness' granted by the grace of an infinite freedom, in which alone, nature and freedom are thoroughly in accord.[21] Thus 'the God of Jesus Christ' is epistemologically predestined to receive the shape of a primordial plenitude of free, though loving, will.

This must then be related to the observation that Kasper does not consistently accept the essence of the personalist case that personhood exists only in relation. At times he reduces such an ontological definition to a moral argument – namely that we cannot realize love, the true goal of personhood, if we are not open and self-giving. Notably, he believes that the Kantian 'Kingdom of ends' is not a mere rationalist and formalist structure, but a genuine personalist vision.[22] Yet his own outlook is permeated by a Rousseauian–Kantian formalism: to be free, individuals and groups must respect the freedom of others (their 'ideas and interests'), but nothing is said about the concrete content of this freedom, nor about love as primordially attention and constraining presence (for Kasper a benevolence without *eros* precedes attentive response).

When this deficient personalism is related to the Trinity, then certainly Kasper says that the Father can only be a loving Father if he is related to the Son, but what is stressed is the gratuity of the Father's self-giving. Paternal freedom is for Kasper the divine equivalent of the surplus of each human person over relationhood which gives her freedom, and absolute value. But such a liberal–voluntarist onesidedness cannot grasp the Father as essentially Fatherhood, even though this should be secured by Kasper's more or less reasonable view that there is 'one divine consciousness existing in three different modes'.

I want to argue here that western 'bad conscience' with respect to the Paternal *arche* is quite unnecessary, and obscures the really interesting and rigorous notion of an absolute origin that is 'always already' difference and succession. Against the hankerings after a positive *agennesia* I should like to place Aquinas's argument that the non-reversibility of spiration from the Father through the Son indicates precisely *not* an 'order of power', but only an 'order of *supposita*'. Aquinas says that where one has a hierarchical chain of command there is reversibility only in the sense that one can talk of a servant acting by virtue of his master's authority and so 'through' his master. He then notably denies that the Father's causation through the Son is at all analogous to the operation of foundational first principles in the sciences, which always 'act immediately', like a master, through their subordinate instruments. (S.T.I.Q. 36 a 4 ad 4)

By contrast Kasper (following the feudal–contractualism implicit in Richard of St. Victor's model) tends to posit an 'order of power', and risks a subtle variant of Eunomian subordinationism. He is close to reducing the Son's role to a 'passing on' of the substantial essence of freedom from the Father to the Spirit who is the condition of possibility for an absolutely free, but essentially passive, finite response. There is no dynamic reciprocity in Kasper's Trinity, and so a metaphysics of *actus purus* is firmly opposed to any idea of 'divine becoming'.[23] But if one wishes to insist, like Kasper, on 'relation' as the fundamental ontological category, then without an equal stress on a causality that is 'retroactively causative' (and so, in *some* sense, on a becoming), this will end up as an undialectical notion of original hierarchy. The whole problem with the Victorine 'contractual' model is that it fails to see the Father's 'free' love as already 'bound' by the shape of filial return; to see also the Son's love as equally 'free' with that of the Father; and finally the love of the Spirit as active as well as passive, since the Spirit's desire 'beyond' the pronounced word of the Son as it were 'begins again' the original impulse of the paternal *arche* (I take this view to be compatible with that of Augustine).

Kasper's attempt to give more prominence to the Holy Spirit is reducible to a perspective which polarizes the Trinity between an absolute giving and an absolute reception, and plays down the *Logos* character of the Son.[24] He preserves an effectively essentialist view of the *Monarchia*, and also fails to overcome an essentialization of the third person of the Trinity. More, indeed, than a 'bond', the Spirit nonetheless remains for Kasper 'God's innermost essence' which emerges as a kind of subjective reflection in God upon the possibility of the generation of the Son – namely as an act of the divine freedom.[25] This 'consciousness of freedom' also entails the realization for God that the Son does not exhaust the divine freedom, and so it becomes the condition for the possibility of creation.

The all-important relegation of the *Logos* character of the Son belongs not merely to a personalism confused with transcendentalism, but to a personalism which ignores the role of linguistic mediation in personal relationships. By associating the Spirit alone, and not, in the first place, the generation of the Son–*Logos* with God's creative action *ad extra*, Kasper makes the essence of creaturely existence to consist in an absolutely open, individual subjective capacity for response. Divine presence to the world is represented as this aspiration away from the world, rather than in terms of worldly structures which reflect divine intelligibility and beauty. Equally, in relation to God, the mediaeval vision (Eriugena, Bonaventure, Aquinas, Cusanus) of the Father as essentially creative, as 'compelled' in the shaping of the eternal world of infinite ideas by the very act of generation which grounds the creation *ad extra* (S.T.I.Q. 34 a 3), is lost sight of. Yet it was Duns Scotus's disassociation of the act of creation *ad extra* from the generation *ad intra*, and of the divine ideas from the filial *ars*, which really sealed the displacing of the Trinity from the centre of Christian dogmatics.[26] No theology which defines the divine essence, following Scotus, as infinity and freedom (nor even 'freedom in love') will be able to do justice to the theme of essential relatedness, because this must include the idea of a knowledge-through-this relatedness.[27]

It is undoubtedly Kasper's wish to distance himself from Hegel which leads him to emphasize the Father's 'gracious self-communication' in the Spirit over his expressive and in some sense necessary self-communication in the Son.[28] But I shall argue that this is to mislocate the Hegelian error, and it is also to overlook important features of the orthodox tradition itself. In the Bible, Israel's Sonship is indissociable from the carrying of the Word;[29] a careful reading of St. John's gospel would suggest, not merely that Jesus is the perfectly obedient Son who passes on the words of the Father, but that as creatively struggling human being he assumes an enacted form which in its universal significance is the Word of the Father, and that *thereby* he is the co-equal Son (see chapter 5, 'A Christological Poetics', earlier in the volume). As the Cappadocians explained, the idea of an original *arche* that only is through its imaged presentation is a necessary further spelling out of 'essential Fatherhood'.[30] And it is clear that, through a process reaching its culmination in Nicholas of Cusa, *Logos* as reason becomes again *Logos* as language, so making this characterization of the Son fully consonant with the gospels.[31]

My argument later on in this article will be that if one conceives God as 'interpersonal', then one must also conceive him as 'linguistic'. I shall show how this view alone enables one to understand the place of the Spirit. Kasper's purely personalist perspective cannot do so. When he tries to think of the Spirit as personal, and not simply as 'ground of possibility', then he resorts to the need for a 'we' experience, to indicate why a twofold relation would be insufficient. But this is a weak argument: first it is not clear that the 'we' experience – the basis for mass collectivity and politics – is ultimately desirable; second, while it is true that *given* the reality of a plurality of persons any single human relationship risks an *egoisme à deux*, it is not equally clear that this is an inevitable outcome for the relationship in itself, such that there is something self-evidently deficient about the notion of an eternal binity.

This deficiency, I shall argue, only emerges to view, when one includes a linguistic–historical dimension. It can easily seem, to a superficial view, as if a personalism such as that of Kasper's already does justice to this, because it stresses the presence of the other as embodied, as addressing us in particular, time-bound words. Apparently, an instrumentalist view of language is here left behind. Yet, within personalist rhetoric, one discovers a further specification: a division between language and work, between communicative *praxis* and structuring *poesis* such that, as Emmanuel Levinas puts it, 'speech must always attend its own manifestation'.[32] But as Jacques Derrida has shown against Levinas, this opens up an antinomy: if our intentions are only constituted through language, and if the 'exteriority' of the other is only established through spatial relations, then the person *cannot* perfectly 'attend' and preserve from alien definition the linguistic works which nevertheless establish his being; if, on the other hand, there is some realm of absolutely inviolable personal 'otherness', then this must be after all the world of the disembodied Cartesian ego.[33] Personalism still too often suggests an impossible, ahistorical encounter of absolute wills unmediated by a common spatial 'identity', or by signs which through their indeterminacy must always 'defer' not only an absolute meeting with the other, but also our own self-possession. These are uncomfortable thoughts for a contemporary liberal humanism, but are they not rather congenial for trinitarianism which maintains the metaphors of 'word' and 'image' alongside those of sonship?

Many theologians will probably protest that my treatment of Kasper exhibits little interest in his attempt to elaborate a doctrine of the Trinity which remains closer to the New Testament texts. It is this, it might be argued, and not a 'transcendentalist personalism' which governs his stress on the 'Father' who is 'God' for Jesus in the gospels, and on the Spirit which they represent as enabling Jesus's mission.

My contention here would be that Kasper tends to confuse 'levels of discourse', by trying to work certain elements of relatively 'undigested' mythical discourse into the doctrine of the Trinity, which already presupposes a reflective distance from this material. This can be seen in relation to his attempt to formulate a 'Spirit Christology'. Once the notion of the hypostatic union has been established, then the discourse about Jesus's active and passive relationship to the Spirit must, on the secondary reflective level, be related to his single divine personhood.

Kasper's attempt to understand the Spirit as giving the condition for the hypostatic union by first acting on Jesus's humanity to make it perfectly 'open', expresses a view which he cannot really reconcile with the Chalcedonian formula, and which, whatever he says, is hard to distinguish from a *homo assumptus* model.[34] The danger of such a model is that it starts to suggest a universal ontological lack in finite subjectivity, only satisfied by the Incarnation which at last realizes an infinite freedom.

Likewise, to give primacy to 'the God of Jesus Christ' may involve one in an impossible attempt to graft the language of the narrative which *constituted* the Trinitarian experience back onto the Trinitarian language itself – a language which, in a definitive way, registers the consciousness of this constitution. Certainly, we are also to be sons, and to cry 'Abba! Father!', but the acceptance of Jesus's definition of God as Father is inseparable, according to the Trinitarian 'grammar', from our validation of the absolute character of Jesus's mission, in acknowledging his *Logos*-character and eternal sonship.[35] For Kasper what matters is that the one Spirit perfectly operative in Jesus Christ is also operative in the Church; this tends to shift the focus of 'difference' from the Son to the Spirit. But if one rather stresses that the God of the Church is the God perfectly manifested for a fallen world in Jesus Christ as the figural form or 'shape' of revelation in time, then there much more clearly opens to view a 'second difference', namely between the moment of the experience of Jesus, and the moment of the experience of the Church – even though these are not *successive* moments in time, but rather formally distinguished moments (see chapter 6, above, 'The Name of Jesus').

In fact to have a 'bad conscience' about the fact that when the New Testament says 'God' it usually means the Father, is altogether to misunderstand the status of secondary discourse in theology. Although, as Kasper puts it, the Trinity is the 'grammar of doxology',[36] and regulative of Christian prayer and practice, this by no means ought to suggest that it is a merely mnemonic or instrumental device, or even that it is less properly the object of primary *belief*, once formulated. The latter view is tied up with a sort of 'reverse Platonism' which wishes to turn primary discourse and practice into a *foundational* point of reference.[37] Instead, one should note that it is precisely the conceptualisation of the Trinity (co-incident with many iconic and emblematic representations) which appears to invoke the depths of divine mystery. Once one has arrived at this reflective phase, one cannot really 'go back to the original data', because already, and irrevocably, they are hermeneutically transformed.

It was George Berkeley, in *Alciphron*, who expressed this in the most profound manner (see chapter 4, 'The Linguistic Turn as a Theological Turn', above). The Trinity, he declared, is a *sign* which we take to regulate our action towards a conceived end, because it both 'organizes' the other data, and stands for an altogether unknown mode of active being, rather than for Lockean 'clear ideas' in our minds. Berkeley was far ahead of many contemporary thinkers (for example, Ricoeur),[38] in already dismissing the notion that more secondary and 'universal' concepts really transcend the level of the figurative semiotic, by assuming a more 'spiritual' form, and a more univocal content. Universals, for Berkeley, like 'force', 'grace', 'the Trinity' were not abstractions, but concrete signs shaped by their characteristic operations, without which the knowledge and activity which they invoke could not be present to us.[39]

If one realizes that universal concepts do not escape from *semiosis*, and even from iconicity (think of the figure 'I' in arithmetic, and of the diagrams of the Trinity; they do not 'copy', yet they represent in an indispensable way) then one will be able to see how secondary theological reflections are themselves a continuing response to mystery, and not somehow operating at one degree of remove from it (this would finitize the mystery). Neither theological concepts, *nor* 'original' narratives and images are foundational, but a constant movement between the two ensures a mutual enrichment.

By contrast Kasper is guilty of elevating the metaphor of Fatherhood into an over-positive function within his second-level discourse. The same thing applies to the metaphor of the 'power' of the Spirit. Mythic foundationalism then reinforces epistemological foundationalism. Translated into transcendentalist terms 'Father-hood' becomes, after all, the self-positing subject, now, ironically, harnessed to the 'eastern' *Monarchia* rather than 'western psychologism' (which long postdates Augustine's elaboration). Concomitantly, the energetic medium of the Spirit becomes the categorical possibility of freedom which allows the first paternal instantiation of freedom to evoke a commensurate response.

4 The 'Protestant Hegelian' Solution

In recent Protestant writings on the Trinity, a Hegelian solution to the problem of the Spirit's identity is much in evidence: the Trinity itself is seen in terms of God's involvement in historical becoming, and the Spirit as God's eschatological arrival in the Kingdom (or *as* the Kingdom), already anticipated in the Church.

Moltmann, Pannenberg and Jüngel all present different versions of this account. Although Moltmann wishes to repudiate the Hegelian reduction of the three persons to the absolute subject as substance, and goes so far as to deny the *taxis* in favour of a Trinity that can be taken 'in any order', he nevertheless relates it to our progressive ordering towards a free, creative, relationship of 'friendship' to God in the Holy Spirit.[40] His effectively tritheistic perspective permits him to take in a full, 'mythological' sense, the separation of Father from Son in the dereliction of the Cross, and this is integrated with his developmentalism in so far as Moltmann presents the creation as a necessary, primordial suffering which must be passed through by both God and humanity. Thus the Hegelian theme of a necessary alienation is still incorporated by Moltmann.

For Pannenberg also, the Spirit represents the moment of 'resolution' after the 'ambiguous' appearance of God under the form of sin, suffering and death.[41] With more consistency and insight than Moltmann, he retains the logic of substantial relations with respect to historical becoming, such that the Son and the Spirit are 'always already' present as an anticipation of the future which alone finally defines their subsistent content (for the Son, the resurrection, for the Spirit, the Kingdom). This, however, tends to entail a weakening of Moltmann's tragic, staurological perspective, in favour of a developmental immanence of the final, peaceful outcome.

But of the three authors Pannenberg develops easily the most sophisticated account of the personal relations, by insisting (via a critique of Fichte and Hegel), both that God can only be personal if he is personally related, *and* (contrast Kasper) that personhood can only acquire a substantial content in the course of relational *development*.[42] Thus 'becoming' rather than *Monarchia* here gives a Trinitarian account of divine substance. But on the other hand, Pannenberg's *Bildungstheorie* asserts, against Hegel, that substance is not reducible to subject, nor becoming to the formal necessity of subjective realization.

By comparison, Jüngel's Trinitarian model is still Hegelian and modalist, though with voluntarist tinges. For Jüngel, the transcendent paternal subject freely identifies himself with the man Jesus Christ in his death on the Cross. The 'polar tension' of identity-in-difference within the relationship of the man Jesus Christ to the Father replaces the union of two natures under one divine hypostasis as the locus of Jesus's divinity. But this again, is to promote 'mythic' themes – a direct personal relation to God in dialectical tension with a hint of Sabellian patripassianism – onto the level of ontological discourse.[43]

Where, for Moltmann, an eternal priority of persons over relation grounds divine self-separation on the Cross, for Jüngel it is the Cross which occasions the distinction between God and God. The difference between Father and Son is the dialectic of law and gospel, the indissociability of wrath and grace, established through subjective becoming. In consequence the Spirit is the divine love which arises amongst human beings as the revelation of the divine mystery which is also 'the mystery of the world' – a mystery only constituted by the reconciliation which proceeds from the depths of divine self-estrangement.[44]

The common reaction of 'orthodox' theologians to this identification of the Spirit with the eschatological arrival of the Kingdom is to criticize the Hegelian perspective (even in Pannenberg's version) for its concentration upon gnoseological manifestation, divine necessity, and divine becoming. Yet I have already hinted that one might rather understand such emphases as attempts to re-state, in terms of modern historical consciousness, perfectly orthodox aspects of Trinitarian theology which are obscured from view (not surprisingly), by a latent Kantianism.

In the next section I shall consider what validity there is in the identification of the Spirit with the Kingdom. But one's perspective here is necessarily conditioned by one's attitude to the 'strong' Protestant version of Rahner's axiom which declares the identity of the economic with the immanent Trinity. What matters here is to isolate the *real* reason why this might be objectionable.

The real reason is not, as Kasper imagines, that divine freedom is at stake. For against Kasper one should insist that God is the God who is related, who creates, and that from, and within, the 'compulsion' of this immanent goal, freedom (as the Spirit) arises. As a matter of fact the Protestants tend, in essential agreement with Kasper, to give a more voluntarist view than that enshrined in the above statement. What is much more significant is the tendency of these theologians to do without a doctrine of the fall, or to elide fall with creation.

If one claims, in the 'strong' sense, that the economic Trinity is the immanent Trinity, then this *can* open the way to a tragic theology in which one sees that the fall takes away from God's own proper glory, and makes apparently unattainable the divine goal of absolute goodness. At the same time, one might affirm an Anselmian contradiction between how the fallen creation is 'in itself' and how it 'must be' for God – a contradiction taken to its most extreme form by Julian of Norwich, who declared that God never in himself needs to forgive, 'forgiveness' indicating only the re-appearance of the divine gift from a finite, redeemed perspective. In this sense the fall imposes an 'impossible interval' between the economic and immanent Trinities. Or, indeed one might go further to say that the fall alone occasions the *existence* of an economic Trinity. For since the persons act inseparably *ad extra*, they are only distinguishable within the created world via imagings of their substantive relationality in the *ontology* of that world. This is what Augustine searched for in his 'psychological' analogy which is more accurately described as uncovering the ontological structure of historicity. Thereby he rightly refused an economic Trinity conceived of as a kind of divine activity hovering impossibly between the creator and the creation. Properly speaking there is *only* an immanent Trinity, participated in by the creation. However, since the fall 'entraps' the divine glory which is Trinitarian, an 'economic' presence of the Trinity as such in creation (Incarnation, Spirit, Church) becomes tragically necessary.

But *this* tragic theology is not the theology of Moltmann and Jüngel. Instead they embrace a Hegelian theodicy in which necessary estrangement is justified by the final outcome. (Pannenberg provides a more benign, developmental version of this.) This is clearest in the case of Jüngel, for whom creation involves a mythological 'struggle with the *nihil*' and the cross is the deepest reach of the divine 'identification with perishing', through which alone God finally 'occurs'.[45] But *this* 'justification of God through the cross' simply re-writes traditional theodicy. (Compare Mackinnon: see chapter 1, 'A Critique of the Theology of Right' above). Jüngel's governing premise is that of Leibniz – namely that death belongs to the condition of created finitude, rather than being the contingent outcome of the fall.

For Jüngel, in consequence, the Spirit is the final, peaceful consequence of a necessary 'interruption' of life by death and estrangement. This is the really culpable mark of the 'strong' version of Rahner's axiom, just as the really culpable aspect of Hegelianism is the promotion of a gnostic ontology of 'pre-ethical' conflict and contradiction in the substantial order. It is *this* ontology which ensures, in both

Barth and Jüngel, that an otherwise proper gnoseological stress on divine manifestation in Christ will obscure the place of the atonement. Connecting knowledge and salvation is not in itself reprehensible, for a prime effect of the fall is to turn the positive ontological distance between God and humanity into a tragic distance of distortion and confusion, such that one aspect of atonement is indeed a return to a proper awareness of this distance. However, atonement is reduced to a gnoseological event where it is believed that worldly autonomy and human freedom are first properly established by the fall, such that redemption does not re-establish true freedom along with genuine knowledge, but rather reveals 'the truth' or the compatibility of human with divine freedom via a sublated (though not abolished) contradiction.

In so far as 'becoming' implies a gnostic theodicy it is, then, to be rejected, even if the projection of the dynamic (in some sense) into the absolute is still required if one is to establish a 'Trinitarian metaphysics' that is more fundamental than the metaphysics of *actus purus* (though without negating the latter). Jüngel's version of this is inadequate because he claims priority for possibility over actuality in a way which must be interpreted either as the ultimacy of an absolute and undifferentiated subjective freedom, or else as an impersonal, logical structure dictating the attainment of unity through self-differentiation and return to identity (this is close to Fichte's *aporia*, discussed by Pannenberg).[46]

5 The Spirit and the Bride

Yet having rejected the Hegelian *pharmakos* (poison/cure) or 'the knowledge that heals the wound which it itself is',[47] it remains the case that Hegel (*helas!*) is the most profound modern meditator upon the identity of the Holy Spirit. In this section I shall consider the Hegelian themes of the pathos of Christ's absence, of the Spirit's atoning work, and of the connection between Spirit and community. In the following section – turning from economy to immanence, and from phenomenology to logic – I shall consider the Hegelian themes of the Spirit as 'divestment of all immediacy' and as ultimate subjective wisdom.

If, asked Hölderlin, in *Patmos*, 'even the god of gods turns / his face away, so that nowhere one / Immortal more is to be seen in heaven or / On the green earth, then what does this mean?'[48] For Hegel the Christianity which characteristically went on a military quest after the earthly vestiges of Jesus was caught in a profound and ultimate pathos. And even if we (unlike Hegel) accept the bodily resurrection, then the Ascension is likely to appear an anticlimax after this event which overcomes the pathos of nature – its meaninglessness – *and* the pathos of culture – the powerlessness of meaning in the face of death. This overcoming is only available for us in memory, and yet so overwhelming is this memory that human community (because of the Christian-induced collapse of the antique political order) is now founded on this mystery of Christ's absence which makes us, as Hölderlin says, 'an eternal puzzle for one another'. Of course one may say here (with J.-L. Marion) that it is precisely in his ascended distance that Christ gives himself to us in the yet more intimate form of assimilable eucharistic food; yet the presence in the New Testament of a hope for Christ's return, for a renewal of personal intercourse with Christ in his 'present' personal otherness, suggests that the note of pathos is not thereby removed.

But Hölderlin, like Hegel, seeks to move beyond pathos. The point is that 'God's work is not like our own / He does not require everything at once'. The memory of Jesus is a space in which he can 'Shape an image of myself / Like Christ as he was'.

For Hegel this space is a moment beyond that of objective 'representation' in the image of Christ; a moment of the purely subjective appropriation of the significance of Christ's death. Here one should certainly reject the idea that a fully rational presence can finally grasp all aesthetic content, but at the same time one should not ignore what can be salvaged from Hegel's attempt to conceive of a work of the Holy Spirit that is more than a mere application of the work of Christ. What is vital is his pneumatological reformulation of the problematic of atonement.

For Hegel the moment of concrete representation is indispensable because it shows to us (but also is) the objective foundation of reconciliation in God, the absolute. But at the same time this event of reconciliation must be not merely believed in, but actively realized as the existence of a community in which mere 'self-immediacy' is infinitely surpassed.[49]

Here Hegel shows himself to be perhaps a still profounder reader of the Pauline epistles than Martin Luther. For if there is a 'centre' to Paul's theology, then it is surely not 'justification by faith', but rather, 'participation in atonement', the 'filling up what is lacking in the sufferings of Christ for the sake of his body, the Church' (Col. 1:24). This is especially enunciated in the first chapter of the second epistle to the Corinthians (2 Cor. 1:3–12). Not only does this passage make clear that every Christian must personally pass through, and not merely acknowledge, the cross, it also indicates that these sufferings are of 'consolatory' or atoning value to the community (see chapter 6, 'The Name of Jesus', above). When the Spirit herself is referred to by St John as 'another comforter', 'another Paraclete' (St John 14:16) then it is legitimate to understand this as 'another atoner',[50] and to connect this both with the Spirit 'intervening for us with sighs too deep for words', (Romans 8:26) and with the establishment of a community on the unique basis of a free sharing of 'spiritual gifts'.

Vladimir Lossky already approached something like this when he spoke of the Spirit as one who 'effaces himself as a person in our favour'.[51] But this notion is bound to raise the question (already considered in the wake of Hegel by the Catholic Mathias Scheeben and several Russian Orthodox thinkers)[52] of whether the Church is in some way an 'incarnation' of the Holy Spirit. I would rather approach this matter by suggesting that there is a question *Cur Sanctus Spiritus in Ecclesia?* analogous to the question *Cur Deus Homo?*

Through Christ, God is already able to offer to himself an undistorted image of his glory in humanity; at the same time it is not a matter of indifference to the divine being that this glory is not yet restored in its concrete entirety. For this reason, one may tentatively suggest that Christ's outpouring of the Spirit is not simply equivalent to the restoration of our capacity for deification lost since the fall (as for Cyril of Alexandria).[53] Instead, because of the continuing contradiction of the loss of divine glory, the infinite response of the Spirit to the Son is now *eschatalogically identical* with the setting of all human beings on the path of deification, itself a work of inter-human participation and exchange.

In this conception, there is no strict analogy to the Incarnation. Within the Church, there remain many human persons, echoing the supreme response of Mary, and this multiple 'Bride' is not hypostatically united to the Godhead. Instead, there is something like a *communicatio idiomatum* between Church and Spirit, without an identifiable point of union in either nature or personhood.

There is no space to spell out in detail how this version of the Spirit's economy is a valid interpretation of early Christian writings. However, it must rest especially on St John's understanding of the Spirit as imparting to the disciples a knowledge of the Father's dwelling in the Son, and of this knowledge as a beholding of, and sharing in, the glory which the Son had 'before the foundation of the world' (St John 14:10–27; 17:1–26). The second epistle of Clement which speaks of the Church as 'spiritual', like 'our Jesus', as a type of the Spirit, and (perhaps) as 'saving' (2 Clement 14:1–4) preserves, like the Apocalypse of John (where to write to the seven Churches is to write to the seven angels who compose the Holy Spirit: Rev. 1:4, 2) and later Augustine, the early Christian belief in the Church as God's primordial creation, equivalent to personified wisdom in the Old Testament.[54] What should be brought out here, is not so much the hypostatic aspect of this protology, as rather the idea that the Church perpetuates or renews a Creation prior to all coercion and conflict – a city, as Origen so repeatedly emphasises, ruled only be the persuasive power of the *Logos*.[55] Against the Hegelian *pharmakos*, this ecclesiology suggests the dwelling of the Spirit in the Church as an 'always more original' counter-history of peace regained through atoning suffering.

The same ecclesiological perspective will in fact give a more subtle account of the operation of the Spirit in the life of Christ. The statements about Jesus's active and passive relationship to the power of the Spirit mostly refer in their context to the work rather than the person of Christ. This can lead to an interpretation which would connect these statements not to the relation between Christ's humanity and his divinity, but rather to the inherent dependence of the divine Son upon the reception by the Spirit, although this reception is concretely nothing but the *Logos* himself. This dependence is exhibited here below in Christ's reliance (even, ultimately, as regards his person?) upon human testimony and interpretation. Thus for a non-Scotist understanding,[56] insemination by the Spirit and enabling perfection of response coincide in the permissive *fiat* of Mary (S.T.3.Q. 27 a 3); at the baptism and the transfiguration – where to be under the sheltering cloud of the *shekinah*, is to be *with* the attesting prophet and patriarch – human and divine testimony coincide; for St John, human sacramental water, and the unsacred spilling of human blood, stand in an ecclesiastical Trinity alongside the witness of the Spirit (1 John 5:8).

This insertion of Christ into a community of human redemptive action is expressed especially well by the Anglican Baroque poet George Herbert in his poem 'Marie Magdalene': 'her sins did dash / Ev'n God himself; wherefore she was not loath / As she had brought wherewith to stain / So to bring in wherewith to wash: / And yet in washing one she washèd both'.[57]

The relationship of the Spirit and the Bride has, then, a double aspect: first, the one atonement by Christ makes possible a human atoning process; second, because Christ yet *depends* upon this process (that is to say, cannot be sinless himself without the sinless *reception* of himself by Mary/*ecclesia*) and because only the sinless God can make the true, suffering response to Christ (Christ, as God, *cannot* depend on anything created) the Spirit has her own form of *kenosis* in the Church.

Yet this 'theopneumatics' only adds Ecclesiocentrism to Christocentrism. In so far as the Church (the entire, true, historical response to Christ) is a linguistic and eucharistic performance, then this perpetuates the narrative of Christ, belongs on the side of the objective, given, fact of Christ, which precisely as a linguistic representation is able to attain a 'universal' reconciliation. This narrative is indeed perpetuation of the Incarnation, a perpetual transubstantiation of word and matter into Jesus's divinized humanity. It is thereby incorporated back into the divine 'inverbation'.[58]

Vladimir Lossky expressed especially well how the Church is poised between this Christological pole which is 'given', objectifying and organic, and a pneumatological pole which is subjective, interpersonal and always leading us to complete the work of shaping ourselves in the image of Christ.[59]

But this situation is precisely our participation in the intradivine union-through-separation of *Logos* and *Pneuma*. Comprehending this 'second difference' will finally give us an adequate Trinitarian logic.

6 Logos and Pneuma

Hegel's most profound description of the experience of the Holy Spirit is as 'the divestment of all immediacy'.[60] This depends upon the idea that, in Christ, universal humanity – 'humanity as such' – has appeared, but in an indispensably concrete form. All our immediate human identifications and relationships with nature and the politico-religious state are now displaced, because reference to Christ shows their imperfection and less-than-ultimacy. But on the other hand, because in Christ we see the failure of these things, and the mystery of 'an infinite grief', his universal character is in some sense also 'abstract' and 'inward', and thereby remains *purely* a mediation which demands that we propound this mystery and fulfil this reconciliation in the community.

But in dispensing with the Hegelian move beyond aesthetics, one should dispense also with the idea that there is an abstract, alien moment in Christ as concrete universal, a moment which for Hegel is his 'beautiful' rejection of state-coercion. Instead, the concrete community is already *begun* in Christ as the persuasive Church without the state – and this may also be a Church of 'failure'.

The need for mediation then becomes more purely the interpretative exigency which belongs together with the reality of historical 'absence' – an absence which, as indeterminacy of meaning, was already an aspect even of Christ's presence on earth. A 'trinitarianism without reserve' will project this exigency back into God himself. This is only possible if the Son is considered also as *Logos*, meaning an infinite aesthetic plenitude of expression, which yet does not pre-determine, in 'totalizing' fashion, a freedom of interpretation.

Without the *Logos* dimension, there is no ground for the Spirit's hypostatic separation. Thus, even Athanasius is reduced to speaking of the Spirit as 'the image of an image' (which contradicts the Son's plenitude) whereas Basil, emphasizing the *Logos*, identifies the Spirit as the light by which the image is seen, the Platonic 'sun of the intellect', and 'form of the good'.[61] Already, in Plato's Republic, there is the suggestion that nature is especially profligate in respect of the sense of sight, providing not only the seer and the object, but also the medium of illumination, which comes and goes.[62] Basil fulfils this Platonic metaphor in terms of an original separation-in-relation of image and power, of intelligible object and intelligent subject: *Logos* and *Pneuma*.

Still more emphatically than Basil, Marius Victorinus with his *esse–vivere–intellegere* model for the Trinity, proposed a connection of the Spirit with the perfect emergence of understanding. For Victorinus the Father is 'more lack and repose' and appears to 'gain' intelligence and continued life through the response of the Spirit.[63] Victorinus posits a single substantial manifestation of active life which becomes 'form' in the Son but is not thereby exhausted. Understanding *presupposes* form, yet form is only completed through understanding.[64]

Thus Victorinus secures a dynamism in the Trinity which is not based on the 'fontal plenitude' of the Father. Precisely *because* the Spirit is adequately established as a separate *hypostasis* it is also *regressio* in the sense that it renews the fundamental being which characterizes the Father. Somehow, because the divine *actus* is *infinite*, and therefore 'interminably terminated' it comprises a non-temporal dynamic or mutual 'play' between an infinite 'conclusion' of expression in the Son, and an endless 're-opening' of that conclusion by the desire of the Spirit which re-inspires the paternal *arche*.

What may be recovered from both Basil and Victorinus is the idea of a receptive comprehension or judgement constituted through the comprehended image, yet 'retroactively causal' for the form of that image itself. A contemplation or judgement that is 'after' creative action, in a certain sense 'surplus' to it and yet equiprimordial with that action. The so-called 'psychological' analogy developed by Augustine for the Trinity also profoundly concurs with this view, since for

Augustine judgement is realized in 'the understanding' (equivalent to the second person) yet only under the aegis or 'right desire' or 'will' (the third person) which is thereby 'surplus' to judgement and *yet* precisely co-terminous with and only expressed in, its full expression. In other words, the *Logos* pronounces 'the last word', yet its finality is only *subjectively* recognizable. I have developed elsewhere this analysis of Augustine's *De Trinitate*: see note 5 below.

In contemporary terms this suggests a Pneumatology in terms of an 'aesthetics of reception'.[65] Judgement concerning significant form, and the guidance of formal structuration, can never be exhaustively specified by analysis of the structures in themselves. There is a dynamic surplus that surpasses the formal object and constitutes 'subjectivity'. But at the same time, the logic of the Trinitarian relations would resist too 'spiritual' and transcendentalist a version of such an aesthetics. Instead, the categories of reception, and so the constitution of the receiving subject, are entirely derived from 'privileged', selected dimensions of nonetheless objectively recognizable patterns of structuration. As the Spirit *is* only its relation to the origin through the Son, so subjective, aesthetic dynamics are entirely 'inside' textual, poetic dynamics, and it is the non-prescribable character of these dynamics which allows the possibility of the subjective 'reader'.

In this aesthetic model, the place of the Holy Spirit is secured as the irreducibility of the interpretative moment *either* to formal structure, *or* to *a priori* aesthetic categories of subjectivity. In this way a reduction of Trinitarian logic to dialectics, in which (on the Anselmian model) Father and Son as it were 'hand over' the univocal outcome of their intercourse, is overcome. Instead, the Spirit which proceeds from paternal–filial difference is genuinely a 'second difference' whose situation is that of a listener to a rhetorical plea of one upon behalf of the other. As the Father is not immediately available, the Spirit must listen to, judge and interpret the testimony of the Son – a testimony in which 'personal integrity' *is* the content of witness to reality.[66]

The final move is to see that only the 'second difference' establishes difference in an adequate way within the Godhead. The very perfection of relation between Father and Son is in danger of obliterating the usual significance of personal relatedness in which the 'reflective interval' in which I am withdrawn from the other establishes my difference from the other. One can remedy this in terms of a positive *arche* – but this is to unsay original and essential Fatherhood. *Or* one can remedy it in terms of the Spirit, which being constituted by the paternal–filial difference stands at a real reflective distance (reflection in and from the *Logos*) from the Father. The obvious danger here, it might be thought, is to risk losing the personal character of the Son. Is the doctrine of the Trinity a game of intellectual musical chairs in which not all the *hypostases* can be found fully personal stations all at once? A 'textual' view of the person can help here. One needs to think of the Son as word and person inseparably, on the analogy of a human child whose character is formed by the outgoing of parental language and whose reception by the world must interpret the parents back to themselves.

My aesthetic–hermeneutic model for Trinitarian logic is liable to receive two important criticisms. First, there is the Hegelian objection that it posits a 'bad infinite' of never completed understanding. But against this I would place St Paul's statement that the vision 'face to face' is *also* the 'passing from glory to glory' (2 Cor. 3:18). In contrast with the Hegelian identification of infinitude and totality, I would claim that infinity in its positive plenitude (and not just our reaching towards this) is also a constant passage beyond the given. The Hegelian mistake is to imagine that this entails a sheer negative shapelessness, but surely the *in via* can exhibit a consistent, though consistently revised pattern, through all its journeyings. In this way one can claim, against Jüngel, who says that the word of the cross 'corresponds' in its given, 'worldly', autonomous, form to the Trinity, that the developing word of Christ as embodied in the Church and interpreted by the Spirit *can* belong to the *via eminentiae* of the *analogia entis* (which Jüngel dismisses as a bad infinite) without losing itself in purely negative indeterminacy.[67]

My 'solution' is also susceptible to the suspicion that I have fully accepted the terms of post-modernist scepticism. But it is rather offered both with and against postmodernity, in the belief that the latter is confined by a gnostic myth which turns interpretative indeterminacy into an ahistorically determined fate of necessary arbitrariness and despotic concealment. If (against Hegel) one denies that the first logical principle of difference is determinate negation, but rather admits the genuine, positive difference of an aesthetic structure that is freely chosen yet nonetheless 'compelling' and indispensable in its immanent teleology, then there is no reason why mystery and absence should conceal, of necessity, a coercive suppression of possible meaning. And the infinite deferment of self-identity through the mediation of a linguistic work which 'passes away from us' may be originally the mark, not of alienation (which it merely makes *possible*) but of our being rhetorically transported through history by the testimony of 'all of the others'.

As the true validity of post-modernity, trinitarianism exposes (*not* by virtue of an immanent dialectic, but only by subsumption within a more compelling narration) the hermetic myth of the demigod/son/scribe/apprentice who can only purvey by usurping, the verbal power of the god/father/ruler/master (the 'sorcerer's apprentice').[68] The unique Christian separation of *Pneuma* from *Logos* is rather grounded on the idea of a second positive difference which takes absence as the occasion for rhetorical community, and not dialectical unity, nor infinite concealment and betrayal.

7 Conclusion

By arguing for a view of the Holy Spirit which sees the divine glory as 'trapped' in the darkness of human sin and suffering, to such a degree that the 'Christophoric' Church[69] becomes itself an agent of atonement, I am, it may be observed, seeking to mediate between Christian and Jewish mystical visions, and Christian and Jewish versions of the 'People of God'. But Kabbalism is still locked into the *aporia* between the isolated, unified and uncharacterizable God, and the related God of identifiable attributes who is no longer transcendent. For this reason it could only express its insights about the divine pathos in gnostic terms which foreshadow both German idealism and present-day scepticism. The important thing for the future of Trinitarian doctrine is at once to reclaim the themes developed by all kinds of gnosticism in all their profundity, and yet to show that orthodoxy exhibits a wisdom which is beyond even that of the gnostics.

Notes

1 Origen, *De Principiis*, III, 2. In Butterworth's translation, *Origen: on First Principles* (S.P.C.K., London, 1936), p. 29.

2 According to Gregory Nazianzus, the Old Testament announces obscurely the Son, and the New Testament announces obscurely the Spirit: *Theological Orations*, Bk 5, para. 26 (*PG* 36, col. 161 c). Alternative ancient versions of The Lord's Prayer read 'Thy Spirit come' for 'The Kingdom come'.

3 I have chosen to refer to the Spirit by the feminine gender, following certain strands in the Syriac tradition which represented her as a female hypostasis. This does not, of course, mean that I think she is essentially feminine, any more than the Father and Son are essentially masculine. At the same time, if Trinitarian difference is the ground of sexual difference, and manifest in time as the Christ/Bride relation, then the Spirit *is* especially appropriately imaged as that *matrix* in which the Son is engendered, but as an active matrix, and a matrix itself only *possible* 'after' its bearing of the Son (against over-anthropomorphic construals). If sexual difference is taken to be an equal but asymmetric difference, then the above schema radically concurs with my suggestion in this article that the Bride is at least eschatologically equal with Christ, since she finally occupies the place of the Spirit. See Yves Congar, *I Believe in the Holy Spirit*, trans. David Smith (Geoffrey Chapman, London, 1983), vol. 3, pp. 157–60.

4 E. B. Pusey, *On the Clause 'and the Son' in Regard to the Eastern Church and the Bonn Conference; Letter to H. P. Liddon* (Oxford University Press, Oxford, 1876) especially, pp. 99–116 and 127–31; Louis Bouyer, *Le Consolateur* (Paris, Les Editions du Cerf, 1980), especially, pp. 190 and 276; Yves Congar, *I Believe in the Holy Spirit*, especially, vol 3, pp. 31–5. For Cyril, moreover, the Son is no mere passive medium. The Spirit 'derives from' the Son: *Letter to Nestorius* XII (*PG* 77, col. 117).

5 See my article, 'Sacred Triads: Augustine and the Indo-European Soul', in *Modern Theology* (forthcoming, April, 1997). And on the fusing of the Augustinian scheme with Origen's idea of 'the birth of Christ in the Soul', see Bouyer, *Le Consolateur*, pp. 326–7; *Hadewijch, the Complete Works*, trans. Mother Columba Hart O.S.B. (S.P.C.K., London, 1980), pp. 116–20, 350; Thomas Aquinas, S.T.I.Q. 27, a 2, Q. 34; *De Pot.* Q. 10, a 1.

6 Congar, *I Believe*, 3, pp. 98–100.

7 Ibid., 3, pp. 108–9.

8 Ibid., 3, pp. 103–10; Bouyer, *Le Consolateur*, p. 258.

9 I am thinking here of David Brown, *The Divine Trinity* (Duckworth, London, 1985), p. 287, where to 'modern scholarship' is ascribed the remarkable achievement of showing that 'Evidentially, the distinction of the three persons is a more basic datum than their unity'.

10 This does need qualification. In one sense, because Athanasius uses soteriological arguments for the divinity of the Son, he is here *already* thinking pneumatologically. But this still may not give an adequate clue to the distinction between Son and Spirit.

11 John Scotus Eriugena, *Periphyseon; On the Division of Nature*, trans. M. L. Uhlfeder (Bobbs-Merrill, Indianiapolis, 1976), pp. 97, 194–7; Bonaventure, *Itinerarium*, I, 3; Aquinas, *De. Ver.* Q. 3, a 1.

12 Congar, *I Believe*, 3, p. 103; Bouyer, *Le Consolateur*, p. 258; Walter Kasper, *The God of Jesus Christ*, trans. Mathew J. O'Connell (SCM, London, 1984), p. 309.

13 Richard of St Victor, *De Trinitate*, IV, 22, 24.

14 Kasper, *The God of Jesus Christ*, p. 266, p. 134: 'The Father possesses the one divine substance in such a way that he gives it to the Son and the Spirit.'

15 Bonaventure, in I *Sent.* d. 10, a. 2, q. 1; Congar, *I Believe*, 3, p. 111.

16 Kasper, *The God of Jesus Christ*, pp. 226–8, 311; Walter Kasper, *Jesus the Christ*, trans. V. Green (Burns and Oates, London, 1976), p. 250.

17 Kasper, *The God of Jesus Christ*, pp. 289, 308–9; Bertrand de Margerie, *La Trinité Chrétienne dans L'Histoire* (Editions Beauchesne, Paris, 1975) pp. 4–6.

18 Kasper, *The God of Jesus Christ*, pp. 154–6.

19 Ibid., pp. 52–5, 112–13. Heidegger's conception of a non-theological and non-metaphysical 'science of being' proceeds from the Scotist 'univocity of being'. On the significance of this, see Gillian Rose, *The Dialectic of Nihilism; Post-Structuralism and Law* (Basil Blackwell, Oxford, 1984), pp. 104–8. It could be argued that the modern Catholic intellectual acceptance of a 'pluralism' in philosophy based on the epistemological priority of a '*question*' of being is *in itself* a triumph of Scotism over Thomism.

20 Kasper, *The God of Jesus Christ*, pp. 98–9.

21 Kasper, *Jesus the Christ*, pp. 48, 53–5.

22 Kasper, *The God of Jesus Christ*, pp. 18–19, 56–7, 104ff, 290, 306–7; Kasper, *Jesus the Christ*, p. 222: 'Solidarity means giving the individual his own scope.'

23 Kasper, *Jesus the Christ*, p. 250.

24 Kasper, *The God of Jesus Christ*, pp. 184–9.

25 Kasper, *Jesus the Christ*, pp. 53–5; Kasper, *The God of Jesus Christ*, pp. 106, 151.

26 See Etienne Gilson, *Jean Duns Scot* (Vrin, Paris, 1952), pp. 216–306.

27 Kasper, *The God of Jesus Christ*, pp. 151–7.

28 Kasper, *Jesus the Christ*, p. 252.

29 Bouyer, *Le Consolateur*, p. 49.

30 See Aidan Nichols, *The Art of God Incarnate* (Darton, Longman & Todd, London, 1980) pp. 68–72. Bouyer points out that Gregory of Nazianzus actually tends to subordinate the *Monarchia* to consubstantiality: Bouyer, *Le Consolateur*, p. 184.

31 See H.-G. Gadamer, *Truth and Method*, trans. William Glen-Doepel (Sheed and Ward, London, 1975), pp. 366–87.

32 Emmanuel Levinas, *Totality and Infinity; An Essay on Exteriority*, trans. Alphonso Lingis (Martinus Nijhoff, The Hague, 1979), p. 297, and see pp. 226–32.

33 Jacques Derrida, 'Violence and Metaphysics: An Essay on the Thought of Emmanuel Levinas', in *Writing and Difference*, trans. Alan Bass (Routledge & Kegan Paul, London, 1978), pp. 79–154.

34 I.e. a model which compromises the purely divine character of Christ's personhood: Kasper, *Jesus the Christ*, p. 251.

35 Here I would argue that Basil's doxology 'Glory be to the Father and to Son and the Holy Ghost' is valid alongside the older doxology 'Glory be to the Father through the Son in the Holy Spirit'. It need not obscure our entering into the Trinitarian economy if we take this to be a flux and reflux, and our final goal to be the complete 'creative' manifestation of the Son, and the complete 'interpretative' illumination in the Holy Spirit as well as return to the Paternal source.

36 Kasper, *The God of Jesus Christ*, p. 311.

37 See Edward W. Said, 'On Originality', in *The World the Text and the Critic* (Faber & Faber, London, 1984), pp. 126–39.

38 See Paul Ricoeur, *The Rule of Metaphor*, trans. E. Czerny et al. (Toronto University Press, Toronto 1975) pp. 302–3, 313. Here Ricoeur shows his continued allegiance to Husserlian epistemology. This explains why he tends to regard dogmatics as an ideological 'mixed discourse', neither 'originally' metaphorical, nor foundationally speculative.

39 George Berkeley, 'Alciphron, or the Minute Philosopher', Book 7, in *The Works of George Berkeley, Bishop of Cloyne*, eds. A. Luce and N. Jessop (Nelson, London, 1956), vol. VII, pp. 293–308.

40 Jürgen Moltmann, *The Trinity and the Kingdom of God* (SCM, London, 1981) especially, pp. 181–9, 200–17.

41 Wolfhart Pannenberg, 'Der Gott der Geschichte', in *Grundfragen Systematischen Theologie. Gesammelte Aufsätze 2* (Vandenhoek, Gottingen, 1980).

42 Wolfhart Pannenberg, *Grundfragen*: 'Person und Subjekt', pp. 80–95, 'Die Subjektivitat Gottes und die Trinitatslehre', pp. 96–111.

43 Eberhard Jüngel, *God as the Mystery of the World*, trans. Darrell L. Guder (T. & T. Clark, Edinburgh, 1983), pp. 352, p. 367, n. 54.

44 Jüngel, *God as the Mystery of the World*, pp. 343ff, 363, 368–76. Eberhard Jüngel, *God's Being is in Becoming*, trans. H. Harris (Wm. B. Eerdmans, Grand Rapids, 1976), p. 68.

45 Jüngel, *God as the Mystery of the World*, pp. 221–5; Jüngel, *God's Being is in Becoming*, pp. 107–8.

46 For an alternative, if not entirely adequate treatment of act and potency in relation to the Trinity, see Jasper Hopkins, *A Concise Introduction to the Philosophy of Nicholas of Cusa*, (University of Minnesota Press, Minnesota, 1978) 'On Actualised Possibility' (translation of *De Possest*), pp. 93, 121.

47 G. W. F. Hegel, *The Christian Religion* (Part 3 of the 'Lectures on the Philosophy of Religion') trans. Peter C. Hodgson (Scholars Press, Missoula, 1979), p. 55, and see p. 141.

48 Translation of Patmos by E. S. Schaffer, Schaffer, '*Kubla Khan, and The Fall of Jerusalem* (Cambridge University Press, Cambridge, 1975), pp. 296–302.

49 Hegel, *The Christian Religion*, pp. 237–53.

50 Marius Victorinus, *Theological Treatises on the Trinity*, trans. Mary T. Clark (The Catholic University of America Press, Washington DC, 1981), p. 242: 'The Holy Spirit is another Paraclete . . . a co-operator in the mystery of salvation, just as Christ is a co-operator in the true Spirit of sanctification because he is God.'

51 Vladimir Lossky, *The Mystical Theology of the Eastern Church* (James Clarke, Cambridge, 1973), p. 172.

52 See Congar, *I Believe*, 2, p. 88. The Russian speculations are dealt with by Rowan Williams in his unpublished Oxford D. Phil thesis on Vladimir Lossky.

53 Cyril of Alexandria, *Select Letters*, trans. Lionel R. Wickham (Oxford University Press, Oxford, 1983), p. 191.

54 Augustine, *Confessions*, xii, c. 15: 'a certain created wisdom was created before all things, the rational and intellectual mind of that chaste city of thine, our Mother, which is above, and is free'.

55 See, for example, Butterworth, *Origen on Frist Principles*, 1, 2, 10, p. 25.

56 A Scotist stress on the immaculate conception merges naturally with a transcendentalist theology focused ahistorically upon the supernatural potential of each individual.

57 *The Poems of George Herbert*, intro. Arthur Waugh (Oxford University Press, Oxford, 1913), p. 179.

58 On the Lutheran idea of 'incarnation into language', see Gerhard Ebeling, *Evangelische Evangelienauslegung: Eine Untersuchung zu Luthers Hermeneutick*, (Wissenschaftliche Buchgesellschaft, Darmstadt, 1962), pp. 362–5.

59 Lossky, *Mystical Theology*, pp. 174–96. I am also suggesting here, that by associating the 'objective' character of Christ with language one can reconcile the Alexandrian 'physicalist' view of our salvation in Christ with the more spiritual 'new *habitus*' view of Photius and Maximus (see Bouyer, *Le Consolateur*, pp. 289–96). But to develop this idea further one would have to explore the paradox of the single person (Christ) 'dispersed' through his linguistic work and our interpretation of it into 'many words', being united with the many persons (the Church) who again constitute as a historical body, the 'single' united Word.

60 Hegel, *The Christian Religion*, pp. 234–7.

61 'The Book of Saint Basil on the Spirit', trans. Wace and Schaff, *Nicene and Post-Nicene Fathers* VIII (Oxford University Press, Oxford, 1895), p. 15.

62 Plato, *Republic*, Book Six, 5.

63 Victorinus, p. 332.

64 Ibid., pp. 328–32.

65 See Hans-Robert Jauss, *Towards an Aesthetics of Reception*, trans. Timothy Bahti (Harvester Press, London, 1982).

66 See Paul Ricoeur, 'The Hermeneutics of Testimony', in *Essays on Biblical Interpretation*, pp. 119–55.

67 Jüngel, *God as the Mystery of the World*, pp. 226–99.

68 A. J. Festugière, *La Révélation D'Hérmes Trismégiste* (Gabalda, Paris, 1950), vol. 1, p. 347ff.

69 For the phenomenology of 'carrying', and its religious and mythical reverberations, see Michel Tournier's novel, *The Erl-King*, trans. Barbara Bray (Collins, London, 1972).

8

The Force of Identity

My excuse, as a theologian, for addressing below some issues in the history of theology, is threefold. In the first place I am concerned with the way in which much recent treatment by theologians of the Cappadocian position on the Trinity accords ill with the best and especially the most recent scholarship on Gregory of Nyssa. The implication of this scholarship is that many of the contrasts between Gregory and Augustine on the matter of the Trinity have been overdrawn, even as regards the yoking together of Trinitarian with psychological concerns, as I shall later explain. In the second place I am concerned with the relevance of Gregory to contemporary debates concerning the relation of the philosophical category of 'being' on the one hand, to the theological category of 'gift' on the other. Third, and most specifically, I am interested in Gregory's strong advocacy of *apatheia*, both as ontological norm and as ethical goal, which contrasts sharply with a tendency in recent theology either to reject or to qualify *apatheia* in both respects, in the belief that it represents a Hellenic contamination of the Biblical inheritance. In the face of this assumption I shall suggest that *in certain respects* Gregory stresses *apatheia* even more strongly than his pagan predecessors and near-contemporaries, precisely *because* he thinks this is demanded by the deliverancies of revelation and by categories of gift rather than being. This emphasis in his thought may seem, on the face of it, to accord ill with those aspects of his teaching which modern Christians have found congenial, namely his validation (or at least apparent validation) of relationality, communication and growth, distinct personal existence, emotions of certain kinds, generation, and embodiment: in other words all that we might take to characterize the life of persons in material space and temporal duration. We take it that the positive valuation of the latter will be bound to include *also* a validation of the worth of the passions, and in this view we are, indeed, at one with much of ancient philosophy, although it made the correlation for opposite, negative reasons, being somewhat suspicious of the passions along with time, embodiment and spatial relation. From the point of view of both ancient and modern philosophy, it might be thought that Gregory is inconsistent in promoting a positive view of the latter three categories, and yet maintaining, even augmenting, *apatheia*.

However, I shall argue in this paper that Gregory was not necessarily inconsistent, once one has grasped that instead of validating the passions, he attempted the different task of redefining *activity* in such a fashion that it is no longer straightforwardly connected with notions of self-containment, self-sufficiency and autocracy, normally taken to be the reverse of the passion-governed life. Instead, for Gregory, it is possible, at every ontological level, to be in the same instance both receptive *and* donating, *without* being in any sense 'subject' to anything else that is not oneself, or in some way inhibits one's ideal reality. Here to receive is somehow *already* the movement of a counter-donation on the part of the will. I shall describe this conception, which will be further elaborated in due course, as 'active reception'. For now one should note that if it redefines receptivity as action, it equally redefines action as receptivity. In my conclusion I shall suggest why the strategy of embracing 'active reception' might be more radical and more defensible than the modern strategy of abandoning *apatheia*. But first of all I will outline this strategy of Gregory's under four headings: those of reputation, generation, growth and embodiment.

One of the key sites for the tyranny of the passions, according to Gregory, is that of *doxa*, or worldly glory, honour, credit or reputation. As with many of his pagan predecessors, a suspicion of worldly honour goes along with an apparent retreat from the social and political as such.[1] This sphere encourages us to believe in the realities of 'obscurity of birth or illustrious birth, or glory or splendour, or ancient renown, or present elevation, or power over others' as Gregory puts it,[2] whereas such things have no real hold in being. They are all rather a matter of human fictional imputation, and in *Contra Eunomius* Gregory takes a fairly cynical view of human government: it being the case, he argues, that all humans are fundamentally equal as created, no human rule over other humans will ever be tolerated for long, and political history is bound to be a story of rise and fall.[3] In this sphere, prestige is a matter of 'reputation' and reputation is *always* bloated, never adequately warranted. Thus Gregory shares the late-antique tendency somewhat to devalue the political as a sphere of self-realization, in favour of the inner soul, as being more self-sufficient, less prey to the delusions or vagaries of repute and the degradations of time which tears from one every possession, whether of material goods or civic honour. He also augments this shift in so far as he advocates, at least for many, a withdrawal from the institution of marriage. The latter is viewed as peculiarly subject to the dominance of the passions, but not *especially*, and in fact, hardly at all, the sexual passion; much more as tied to the attempt to extend one's worldly glory beyond the present generation, to ensure that sons will preserve one's name along with their inherited possessions.[4] Also with a well-nigh inescapable *melancholia*: to embrace one's wife is always to embrace the one you know you will eventually have to mourn, or else will have to mourn you – therefore it is *already* an embrace of suffering, and a lure which engulfs the present in a perpetual reminiscence.[5] (Gregory of Nyssa would not have liked *Shadowlands*.) Marriage contains no remedy for these things within itself, although it *can* be used for the good, says Gregory, by those with sufficient gifts. For the *weaker* however, virginity is the safer course.[6]

Gregory's critique of marriage shows that he not only distrusts *present* civic glory, but also wishes to escape from all *traces* of human reputation left by time. Hence in *On the Christian Mode of Life* he exhorts us not to follow fashion, or seek truth in inherited opinions, but to turn inwards for the contemplation of abiding truth.[7] This sounds like a thoroughly 'Cartesian' rejection of all inheritance and mere *reception*. However, Gregory builds his entire theology *not* round a defence of the inner citadel against the buffetings of illusory glory, but rather round *a different, and more abiding doxa*, which includes a more positive view of both processes of historical transmission and public visibility.

As to the first, one can mention the prologue to *On the Making of Man*, where Gregory wonders whether he should just praise his brother Basil's uncompleted *Hexamaeron* and not tarnish his reputation by producing an inferior conclusion, concerning Man, since he regards himself as a far lesser thinker.[8] However, he justifies his enterprise by arguing that he will *more* reveal Basil's greatness if he shows that this can engender an equally great work in his disciple. In other words Basil's 'identity' is no longer complete and bound up in his own works, and equally a 'praise' of Basil is no longer just something conferred on him extrinsically, manifesting nothing new of his essential being. On the contrary, Basil's identity resides in the spirit of his writing, in a certain force which can communicate itself, and in praising Basil, Gregory is not just passively recording his greatness, but demonstrating it by *actively* appropriating it, so revealing its fecundity.

As to the second aspect of *doxa*, public visibility, one can mention Gregory's discussion of whether one should reveal one's good deeds in *On the Christian Mode of Life*.[9] Here, following the words of Jesus about not displaying one's piety, Gregory insists that good deeds performed for reputation will *cease to be* good deeds because they are being traded for a perishable, worldly good. However, he also has to confront texts about letting your light shine before men, which suggests that an entirely invisible good could scarcely be a good at all, since it would do no good, and certainly could not encourage in the good. Gregory resolves this *aporia* of virtue and visibility by requiring that we should *give glory* to God alone: that is to say, let shine in our deeds, God's deeds, since all good deeds are given from God.[10] Whereas for the world, virtuous deeds *result* in praise, for Gregory virtuous deeds are *only*, in themselves, the praise of another, attribution to God as their source, which is at the same time an offering of the deeds *back* to God as a return of gratitude. Inversely, in giving us the grace to become virtuous God is glorifying us, that is to say praising us not *for* our virtue, but in order that we can *be* virtuous. Virtue for Gregory is a power, *dynamis*, and a power that we must will, and yet this power, including our will, entirely begins *before us* as the Power of God. And though we receive it, we can *only* receive it actively (else it would not be our virtue) to the limit of our participating capacity. Against Eunomius and his view that the Father's glory is essentially *incommunicable*, Gregory calls attention to the fact that even human creatures, never mind the Son of God, can be glorified by the Father, without finite limit (that means for us, endlessly) with his glory, which is to say his active potential or *dynamis*.[11] The Trinitarian context will offer a yet more radical twist: not only does God's dynamic praise of us precede and produce our virtue, this is even the case (though in an altered sense of 'precede' which involves no temporal priority nor hierarchical supremacy) for the divine *Logos* who is fully and essentially God himself, since the Son *is* the glory and the *dynamis*, besides being the *wisdom* of the Father. And this means that the Father's own virtue *consists* in offering a previously unmerited praise to another, just as he essentially persists also in receiving back this praise.

We are now in a position to contrast Gregory's views of worldly and divine *doxa*. The former is empty, and here praise has a secret priority over what is praised. One would *expect* a contrast to this to be made in terms of an indication of *stable identity*, of what *really belongs* to things and to human beings. In other words, a rejection of the 'rhetorical' world of persuasion in favour of the dialectical realm or vision of abiding realities. Yet Gregory scorns dialectic as much as rhetoric: reality, as the infinite being of God, cannot be grasped under a category, nor can created realities be so grasped either, for they mirror this incomprehensibility and are in a state of constant flux.[12] How, then, can one identify Gregory's discourse, which one notes is marked by the piling up of persuasive arguments after the fashion of the second sophistic, and by the celebration of less ornate but thereby all the more 'sublime' figures of speech which he takes to characterize Biblical writing?[13] I suggest as a kind of *doxologic*, in which persuasion and encomium is not directed towards the 'possession' of glory by oneself or another, but rather to the constant transmission of glory which is all the more one's own insofar as another person can receive it and repeat its force.[14] As with human glory, surprisingly, so *also* in the case of divine *doxa*, praise has priority over what is praised, yet this is no longer secret, but out in the open and with a different intent – not to hoard praise but to exchange it, such that praise is never simply of oneself or of another. Supremely, we *know* in praising God, in offering him glory which is his own, and not in *seeing* God, nor in manipulating men.

This 'doxologic' is followed by Gregory in *The Life of Moses*, where he defines virtue as perfection, as the infinitely active, unlimited, entirely dispassionate life. As such, it cannot be contained, and therefore, unlike Plato and Aristotle, Gregory offers no *logos* of virtue.[15] Nor can he offer his own life, nor could anyone, as an *example* of virtue, since virtue as infinite cannot be 'attained'.[16] All Gregory can do is *exhort* to virtue, and praise a virtue which is *never present*, but which nonetheless arrives through praise, since it is an offering of praise. For this reason Gregory can claim that though we do not know and cannot exemplify virtue, we can still have a part (*mesos*) in it, if we proceed from activity to activity, for activity only *remains* active if it does not seek to lay hold inwardly upon its activity but continuously receives *more* activity from the divine source. In this context a certain reception from the narrated memory of other human beings also is possible: one may praise Moses and offer him as a kind of example, since he was the sublime man who pointed absolutely beyond himself to God, and to the God–Man.[17] In imitating Moses therefore, we are imitating a man who is paradoxically imitating – that is to say following behind the back of – a man who is yet to come: Christ, just as for us also the full body of Christ is yet to be realized, and we 'follow' in its wake. Nonetheless, Moses plays for us a slightly more positive role: his finished life is itself a *mesos*, a part, which has connotations of both 'role' and inheritance (the double sense in English of 'a lot'), just as Gregory insists that Moses played a part in the *politeia*, a political life, but a *polis* now more in time than space.[18] Moses is a more appropriate example than a 'present' contemporary saint, since his life is over and therefore we are less tempted simply to copy it, but see that it is to be taken further, extended differently and yet sustained as the same. In other texts Gregory suggests that properly speaking there is only *one* human being transmitted from person to person[19] – it follows that *epectasis* applies transgenerationally as well as internally, and Gregory does not exhort us 'to leave behind' the Chaldeans and Egyptians in the sense of leave behind history, but in the sense of leave behind our passions, which they allegorically stand for, and pass, *not* from place and body to spirit, but *in every* place and *every* body from passivity to activity.[20]

My second heading is that of *generation*. I have already mentioned how Gregory treats an exchange of glory within the Trinity. The Son is the Father's *doxa*; without the Son the Father is without *doxa* and the glory of both *is* the Holy Spirit.[21] Here the Spirit is 'the bond of glory' in *exactly* the way he is 'bond of love' for Augustine. This giving of glory within God is dealt with by the Bible in terms of metaphors of generation, Father to Son. One of the main questions at issue with Eunomius was how this generation was possible without passion. Eunomius claimed that all generation necessarily involved passion, and therefore that the Son was subordinate to the Father, who is in himself utterly uninvolved in any such transitive activity. To this, Gregory responds that even in the case of human generation, children do not have a different *or* a lesser human essence than their parents. Even though human generation is passionate, it already gives the lie to Eunomius's assumption that cause and effect will diverge essentially, or that a beginning is a kind of pre-containing foundation.[22] (So much for the idea that all the Greek Fathers laid great store on the Father as *arche*, prior to relationality). Furthermore, the *passionate* aspect of human generation is only an aspect of the post-fall emergency economy: humans were originally intended to self-propagate in a purely active mode. Such propagation was restored in the case of the Virgin birth, in which Mary's integrity was not cancelled but rather re-affirmed by her receiving of the *Logos*, when her body was entirely transparent to her active willed assent.[23] This assent involved a speaking of a word from her mind which Gregory presents as a further example of non-passive generation even amongst human beings: it is not that the word receives something from the mind, rather that it *is* the activity outgoing from the mental source. Therefore to defend generation without passivity in God, Gregory makes appeal to certain instances of causality within time to show that such a possibility exists even when generation involves movement and alteration. And, as Michel Barnes has shown, he is involved here in defending a certain account of the diversity of *kinds* of causality.[24] Gregory accuses Eunomius of assimilating all causality to the model of a voluntary, artisanal imposition of form on matter.[25] In so far as Eunomius speaks of *dynamis*, he thinks of it not as a power that is automatically self-communicating, but rather like the power of an emperor which can be exercised or not at will. No action or *energeia* for Eunomius belongs *essentially* to a nature, but arises only for the occasion of producing a particular work (*ergon*) and is precisely adapted to just this *one* work and no other; whereas Gregory points out that many causes produce diverse effects in different receptacles – thus rain always moistens, but quickens myriads of diverse seeds, fire always heats, but heat hardens some things, melts others.[26] Hence in Eunomius's view the Son is an *ergon* caused by an act or *energeia* of the Father precisely adapted to this one work (whereas for Gregory the same causal *dynamis* of the Father both generates the Son and creates the *cosmos* with all its diversity of effects), but the act of the Father is not in itself the Father, who as strictly 'the ungenerate' does not of his essence enter even into causation.[27] Here it is worth noting that while Gregory attacks, on apophatic grounds, Eunomius's *identifying* of God with an essence for which we can give a word – 'ungenerate' – there is another sense in which Eunomius's God is *more* ineffable than Gregory's in so far as it is totally non-participable.[28] Gregory defends not just God as incomprehensible *ousia*, but also God as incomprehensible *dynamis* – as inherently giving and effecting (and affecting).

According to Gregory, to grasp divine causality, one must employ analogically examples of all modes of created causality. The artisanal model applies somewhat to creation, but here it must be supplemented by, and in the case of Trinitarian generation abandoned for, other causal models. Physical generation is one, the generation of mental power in the incorporeal word is another, yet equally crucial is the *much more corporeal* instance of material efflux, or the self-propagation of a material power. Here the supreme example is fire – fire, like mind, is in ceaseless motion, inherently contagious – it exists *to effect*, and it *cannot but* heat. Again and again Gregory says that the Father is like this.[29] Barnes has shown how Gregory is here drawing on a key *motif* within Platonism itself.[30] From the Hippocratic tradition, Plato took over the notion of a 'power physics' according to which the cosmos is composed of fundamental self-propagating elemental qualities usually arranged in pairs of opposites. Unlike the materialist philosophers, the more 'human' scientists, the doctors, refused to treat the *combination* of those elements as merely epiphenomenal in relation to their corporeal components. This, however, suggested that the philosophy of material elements could *not* provide an adequate ontology, and that what arrives *later* cannot be explained as an aggregate of the earlier, but only in teleological terms as an arrival from a transcendent source.

Hence in *Phaedo* (an important text for Gregory) Plato says that the number 2 is not to be explained as 1 plus 1, but as a participation in the form of twoness.[31] However, the spiritual forms *themselves* are conceived *on the model of* power physics. Just as fire heats, so justice makes just and so forth. Despite the continued dominance of the artisanal model in Plato's account of the relation of ideas to matter – i.e. ideas inform a substratum – the transposed power physics gives an idea of participation which the neoplatonists could later develop into the notion of emanation.

Hence Gregory's insistence on *dynamis* represents a very Platonic moment in his thought. And the notion certainly lent itself to thoughts of 'threeness' – for Plato in the *Sophist* there is a *dynamis* to affect *and* a *dynamis to be* affected. The combination of the two is a third reality.[32] However, in that dialogue Plato supposed that real being must be outside affecting and being affected, including being known, and if to the contrary it appears that being *can* somehow be known, then true being must after all embrace *both* the unchanging and the changing.[33] Without truly solving the problem of the self-dissolution in Platonism which this suggests, the neoplatonists insisted that what is truly and absolutely One does, nonetheless, communicate itself, just as the sun must pour forth its rays. Yet Gregory, of course, takes one step further: the source is now in no sense beyond its rays, and there is no way to return to the source by abandoning the rays as merely a mirrored reflection. The Father, Son and Spirit are one equal dynamic display of glory.

While at times Gregory treats the Son as especially 'the power of the Father', at other times he insists that power is common to all three persons in the way that *ousia* is also common. Here his usual mode of argument is from the experience of salvation. The Son saves, the Spirit saves, but only God can save, so all three persons display equally the saving *dynamis* of God.[34] In this case an 'economic' Trinitarian argument is also automatically an immanent one, and one notes that Gregory insists just as strongly as the West on 'one essence' whose nature cannot possibly be in any way defined via personal relation, any more than the fact that I am born declares *what* I am.[35] However, Barnes's remarkable contribution has been to show that Gregory (although in this respect paralleled by Latin treatment of *virtus*) speaks more often of one *dynamis* than one *ousia*.[36] And this term provides something very like a Trinitarian ontology which is in keeping with a doxological discourse, for it mediates between the *ousia* register and the *prosopon* (person) register. What *is* must affect, and for Gregory this affecting is *identical* with the being affected, since there is no 'receptable' *prior* to this being affected, and therefore passivity in the usual sense is denied all ontological purchase. *Yet* generation remains, without suffering and without interval – but thereby, as all the more 'essential'.

Gregory, therefore, charts a specifically Trinitarian path beyond the self-dissolution of Platonism, not available to neoplatonism. Whereas Stoicism construed the equality in Being of both the unaffecting/unaffected and the affecting/affected in terms of a priority of the *cosmos* which rendered Platonic Ideas (the unaffecting/unaffected aspect) mere surface effects ('incorporeals') of a material process in flux,[37] Gregory articulates a paradoxical identity of these two, of unaffecting/unaffected *ousia* and affecting/affected *dynamis* in the transcendent source itself. This paradox is exemplified in Gregory's boldest move against Eunomius when he claims that to deny generation in God actually limits God, precisely because this denial construes God as a beginning (or a foundation). Beginnings, says Gregory, imply also ends and therefore relational circumscription.[38] By declaring that there is some sort of causal transition in God, Gregory negates not only temporal and spatial interval (*diastasis*) but *also* an identification of *adiastasis* with an absolute beginning or absolute presence to self. God's incomprehensibility is not, for Gregory, just an epistemological matter, but is rather ontological, and means that God literally does not comprehend himself. Therefore, although he fully knows himself, this knowing is not on the model of our knowing which is a grasping or manipulative effecting, the Stoic *katalepsis*.[39] And nor is it vision, which also grasps. Instead it is infinite bestowing and bestowing back again. And the same, doxological account of knowing, extends even to human understanding – here also the earlier does not explain, and *katalepsis* is only for purposes of pragmatic technological benefit. There can be no grasp of essences, since the essence of the world is a mirroring of divine incomprehensibility.[40] The world does not comprehend *itself*, cannot be known within itself, but instead, as Gregory repeatedly insists, the *logos* about the world is bigger than the world itself, because it accounts for it only as derived from a transcendent elsewhere and therefore as unfathomable even down to its smallest details. The identity of the world resides in a power from beyond the world that gives the world itself a power to go beyond what is previously given.

The third heading is *growth*. The other site for discussion of passion in Gregory is *the soul*. However, it is linked with the Trinity. In *On the Making of Man* Gregory declares that if the soul is in the image of God and the soul cannot be divided, then this proves that the Trinity cannot be divided.[41] This is Gregory's development of an earlier argument for the unity of God as creator from the unity of the cosmos and the unity of the soul; just as the soul can originate man's diverse activities in the unified body, so God can do many different things in the unified creation.[42] Here, however, it is a question specifically of the three Aristotelian faculties of the soul: intellective, sensitive, nutritive. The difficulty is, can the soul be both threefold and unified, especially as sensitivity and nutrition are involved in *passion*. But here also, as with the Trinity, the solution is provided in terms of a kind of 'active receptivity' even if this is not so immediately apparent.

Commentators have divided concerning Gregory's account of the soul: for some he is essentially a Posidonian – all three faculties belong in some way to the soul, and the passions have a positive educational function. For others, Gregory insists on an absolute unity of the soul in accord with one strand of Platonism. What is quite clear is that Gregory, along with most of his immediate forebears, rejected the account of the soul given in Plato's *Republic*, according to which it has three parts: *nous, thumos, epithumia* – on the usual grounds that this suggested three different people (the 'homunculus problem'). [43] However, Gregory assimilated the Platonic division of the soul to the Aristotelian one, and rejected both in the name of a united and active rational soul. The lower faculties are said to be improperly named 'souls' and more properly called *hormai* (impulses).[44] Nonetheless, he persists in a faculties of soul language and insists that the presence of the rational soul is *necessary* to animate these powers – the mind in order to sense, and a kind of unconscious emanation from the brain to perform all other natural functions, including generation. So how are we to understand how the one, active soul everywhere animates, even when this appears to involve passions?

First of all, one needs to realize that *psyche* for Gregory's inheritance was a fundamental ontological category. In the cosmology which Gregory shared with Basil (see chapter 4, 'The Linguistic Turn as a Theological Turn', above), the universe consisted not of informed matter, but of essentially immaterial qualities: light, heat, motion etc. which have an *abstract* character and so can properly be thought to derive from *mind* (i.e. the mind of God). These elements are held together in harmonic and oppositional arrangements which often counter expectation: for example, light falls. Only our mind grasps these patterns (though it cannot comprehend them) and so knows that they have their origin in mind. The cosmos is therefore *psychically* bound together, just as our souls bind our bodies together. Rather as much later for Spinoza, it seems that for Gregory body and mind never touch, yet are absolutely co-extensive. Now the implication of this cosmology is that Gregory believes he has followed rigorously the logic of creation *ex nihilo: first* there is no passive matter preceding creation and waiting to be informed, but *second* Gregory sees no need to posit created passive matter either (it is true he speaks sometimes of the aeons of time and space as 'containers', but they are not in any sense a substratum).[45] Thus Gregory has redefined bodies as essentially immaterial and active, since their entire being flows from the wholly active God. It is in this manner that Gregory's *Christian* outlook seems to give passion still *less* ontological purchase than for the Stoics or Neoplatonists. In *Contra Eunomius* Gregory says that the break-ups of bodies are not really passions of bodies, but *erga*, works of nature (again, the pre-echo of Spinoza is very strong here).[46] One can interpolate that these break-ups are only passive from the perspective of the individual bodies, and that passivity here contributes nothing (as a substratum would). But only animal bodies would consciously have this illusory perspective, only they would undergo death as a passivity. Death, however, is for Gregory a result of the fall, and therefore the apparent passivity of even individual bodies is essentially unnatural (and here Gregory is able to *transcend* the dualism of perspective consequent upon Spinoza's monistic immanentism).

It is this consideration which helps us to understand how the one rational soul can be linked with apparently passive impulses. Their passionate character is part of the *fallen* economy – punitive, and yet merciful and delaying. For example, the fallen body can still receive being, by eating food, yet this causes it passively to experience repletion and later the passive need to eat again. Our fallen bodies now live for a merciful interval in which we can receive redemptive glory, but still get used up. However, these passionate aspects of the fallen body are not *strictly* to be called passions, according to Gregory in *Contra Eunomius*: real passions involve sin, in other words the state in which the rational soul is *dominated* by such impulses – in which it *identifies*, for example, with our need to possess and appropriate food in order to live, and makes accumulation the goal of life.[47] The fallen *hormai* are neutral, and if we confine suffering to a material level this suffering 'purges' sin by leading it to its result in death. In this way the *hormai* can be put to good use: self-preserving anger becomes anger at sin and so serves genuine self-preservation under grace, and fortitude in pursuing salvation.[48] Desire for things can generate desire for God, and Gregory can use the word *hedones* (feelings) in a perfectly positive active sense.[49] No passion does *not* mean no feeling. Rowan Williams rightly emphasizes the way in which the bodily energies of desiring and self-preservation can in Gregory be used to promote spiritual growth. However, he notes, with some concern, that Moses *does* seem to be presented as having left even such impulses behind.[50] By contrast, I think that this is not inconsistent, because the *hormai* or bodily passions are only a *hinge*; they are not *to remain*, and in this respect Gregory compares them to Paul's faith and hope, which will not remain at the *eschaton*.[51] Suffering, passive desire and self-preservation in the face of the enemy will pass away; since (even if 'neutral') they are merely the outworking of sin, the realization that we have been damaged, impaired in our being, which is to say, precisely, *been rendered passive*. (And again there is an oddly 'Spinozistic' fore-echo). However, an *eros proper to the soul* remains, and is never surpassed, just as the self-directing will, drive, and self-preservation in the Good also remain.[52]

The former, in particular, is fundamentally *receptive* and yet it remains, and has ceased to be regarded by Gregory as a passion. Neither *eros* nor will are for him any longer *subordinate* to reason – like the Platonic baser aspects, or Aristotelian lower faculties – nor are they parts or even faculties of the soul. They are one with reason, but reason is somehow *also* will and *also* eros. This strange mode of unity is presented in *The Life of Moses* and the *Commentary on the Song of Songs* as a temporal oscillation. Frequently we pass from what one might dub a 'neoplatonic' stage when reason 'mirrors' God to either a sublime drive of the will to a God whom we realize we cannot exhaust (but only 'touch') or else a 'wounding' of our tranquil contemplation of beauty by a sublime desire[53] (as it were 'beyond the pleasure principle').

In this oscillation the Spirit leads us to desire the Bridegroom (the Son) and moves us on to the Father as invisible source. However, it then moves us *back* in a circle to Son and to Spirit via the incarnation and the presence of Spirit in the Church.[54] These persons also are equally in the place of darkness and both equally belong to the 'face to face' beyond the Pauline mirror, which direct vision means for Gregory, paradoxically, 'following the back of ' (so that full visibility *realizes* full invisibility). We *follow* Christ with the wings of the dove which is equally the

Spirit's brooding or resting over the Church.[55] Via the flying/resting of the Church in the Spirit we are inducted into the Trinitarian exchange of glory. But this movement of soul into God is also for Gregory a movement *inside* the soul – not from faculty to faculty, but from reason *as* reason into reason as desire and willing, since reasoning is no longer *katalepsis*, but praise and loving and self-exceeding aspiration. So from this we can conclude, after the Mosaic example, that like Augustine Gregory can envisage the soul as modelled on the divine essence, realized through three persons. For he stresses that the same soul can adopt different characters (*prosopeia*) – so the soul is diversified without parts into reason, will and desire, just as earlier we saw many human individuals can be considered manifestations of one collective person. The soul is for Gregory relational and diverse, not in the sense of possessing parts or aspects, but as a *dynamis* moving from relative *stasis* to relative *ecstasis*. Although there is little explicit development of a psychological analogue to the Trinity in Gregory as compared with Augustine, it is still there. And for this reason one must (in the wake of Rowan Williams and Lewis Ayres) oppose the received wisdom which regards the psychological analogy in Augustine as a speculative substitute for a genuine existential experience of the Trinity in the East. This is a false contrast, for four further reasons: (1) it was natural at this time to associate ontological categories for the Trinity with psychological ones; (2) the 'experiential' was by everyone placed in psychological categories; (3) the relation to God *had* to be conceived as a relation repeated within the soul since we do not really relate to God but *participate* in him; (4) to experience the economic is to experience the immanent Trinity, and if God is essentially Triune and we image God, then the soul must be in some sense triune.

These considerations, which tend to justify the 'psychological analogy', thoroughly accord with the notion of 'active reception' whereby in receiving we actively *become* what we receive: the triune God. So, for example, in *The Commentary on the Song of Songs* the Bride first receives from the Spirit, then *becomes* a spirit, first receives food, then provides a banquet *for* the Bridegroom.[56] Gregory stresses that to go on receiving grace we must ourselves give back, and salvation for him means that (in the Spirit) we also, as receiving the life of all three divine persons, can glorify Father, Son and Spirit.

My fourth category is *embodiment*. I have already mentioned that for Gregory the body is by nature active. In *De Anima et Resurrectione* he claims that the Resurrection is possible because the soul is essentially the bond (*sundrome*) between the disparate elements, and that after their dispersal, which constitutes death, the soul preserves memory-traces of them, just as they are in some way marked forever by the bond of that particular soul. Thus reassembly is possible. However, Gregory faces the question, which *period* in a body's life will return? His answer here is no age and no period, since these belong to the revolutions of passion and it is precisely by virtue of the purgation of passion that the body *will* return – as active[57] – but nonetheless *via* passion, the fully adequate passion of Christ. Here 'active reception' takes the form of a clear doctrine of *communicatio idiomatum*.[58] The divine person in Christ is not the 'subject' of sin, for he only enhypostasizes the human nature by way of an unlimited communication of his divine attributes, but he can, nonetheless, be the subject of tiredness and fear etc. which are the 'neutral' outworkings of sin, and assumed as the redemptive 'hinge' of fallen human nature. (This does not necessarily mean that the divine person is 'conscious' of these things. One should note here, also, that it was Arian, subordinationist Christologies which attached imperfect passions to the *Logos* itself.)

A further relevant consideration regards Gregory's general account of the relation of God to the creation. Although, he says, the mind cannot comprehend the incomprehensible, the incomprehensible can incomprehensibly be mirrored in our mind. For were the incomprehensible to be simply *outside* the comprehensible, it would be limited by the comprehensible (or circumscribable) and would therefore *no longer* be incomprehensible. (Here Gregory is alert to what we should today think of as 'set paradox'; this is an aspect of his superseding of philosophical dialectic).[59] In keeping with this transgressive thought, Gregory uses strong 'conjunction of opposites' language with regard to the Incarnation, and also 'boldly conjectures' that our vision of Christ in the body of Christ or the Church *is* the vision of incomprehensible Being realized inside the creaturely domain.[60]

Therefore one may surmise that, for Gregory, although God does not suffer, he nonetheless cannot be outside 'neutral', sinless suffering as it occurs in time, else he *would* suffer it as outside himself, as it occurs in time (of course he does not suffer the real suffering that is sin, since this is sheer non-being). Hence, in Christ's 'passion' one has for Gregory nonetheless the supreme instance of active reception. And just as God as *Logos* is subject of suffering and this, says Gregory, is the greatest of *all* communications of *dynamis*, as it is power manifest in its opposite, weakness,[61] which astonishes the heavenly powers with the force of an ontological revelation, so also the human body of Christ is entirely infused with Godhead, and *in time* transformed into an entirely active body – the passion is only a passage.

Here Gregory stresses the *collectivity* of Christ's body: Christ is *the beginning* and we take him as beginning in order to know what we should desire to be.[62] The World itself, as St John says, will not contain the book of Christ because this *dynamis* in the world which is Christ's body is the world beyond the world – the book that the world exists to become. And the Church as the new creation *is* precisely the world become self-exceeding, looking for itself beyond its seeming totality.[63] One can relate this world turned inside out, exceeding itself, to Gregory's idea in the *Commentary on the 'Song of Songs'* that the psychic life can best be conceived in terms of nature turned against nature.[64] That is to say, instead of simply using the higher senses and especially sight as figures of the psychic life, Gregory follows the neoplatonists and Origen[65] in using all senses as metaphors but *intensifying* them. The soul is now a 'distillation' of sense such that one conceives its life as an inebriation that allows one to get more and more drunk, or as an orgasmic experience in which wanting only comes with fulfilment and fulfilment does not cancel wanting.[66] In other words an entirely active, and in no sense passive or *lacking* desire; but just for that reason all the more erotic. And the resurrected body will itself correspond to this active psychic norm.

Thus Gregory's mystical quest looks to the vision of God as 'mirrored' in the always 'progressing' Christ who is shown in the body of Christ which is the Church.[67] Only by receiving God eucharistically do we see him, and unconstrained activity now means primarily 'receive God inside your soul and body', and not primarily 'enjoy the vision of God'. Here it is notable that the *shape* of our flight, of the Dove, is only given collectively and synchronically in the form of the Church. Hence there is an infinite progress not just temporally forwards – but also spatially outwards, and this tends to provide a *form* for the temporal *élan*. In both cases of *diastasis* one can make an assimilation to, yet also draw a contrast with, the thought of Plotinus. For the latter there is also a kind of *epectasis* and non-lacking *eros*, but one can pass beyond that to a direct communion of the centre of the soul with the centre of the One itself. This is, indeed, no mere monism, but nevertheless it is through our inner contradiction, our termination of relational tension, that we are at last 'alone with the alone'.[68] For Gregory, to the contrary, the distance remains since it persists in God himself.

This same similarity and yet contrast is seen with respect to interpsychic relations in both thinkers. For Plotinus, the souls in the intellectual realm fully penetrate each other, so that greater interiority implies simultaneously a greater spatial *ecstasis*. In this sense Plotinus was not 'anti-political', and he speaks of the final choral dance of the souls 'around' (although he stress there is no real spatial distance) the one centre.[69] In the case of Gregory also, the social and synchronic remains in the eschaton, but because the coordination is here less of a 'pre-established harmony' and more involves a direct distance of relation, it is shown also in the temporal here and now, in an *external* monastic social practice, in which for private possession is substituted an endless handing-on of glory. In this new *polis*, as in Plato's Republic, the superior in wisdom rule (else one has non-rule), but beyond Plato superiority is grasped as something which is only *for time*, and so 'for-a-time': it exists to be communicated to novices, who have the chance to become wise and just in their turn. And this restriction of subordination to a temporal economy is rigorously applied by Gregory also to the internal governance of the soul. Here, again, he outstrips Plotinus in distance from the classical vision: for the neoplatonist the lower part of the soul is still an aspect of real being and 'nothing of real being perishes',[70] whereas for Gregory there is no *ontologically* lower part of the soul, destined to remain even in the final vision. Such things are rather emergency measures, temporary pedagogic devices.

The full significance of this contrast concerns different understandings of 'interiority'. For the earlier antique thought of Plato and Aristotle, the *intra*psychic space was constituted by the gap between the higher and lower aspect (whether conceived as part or faculty): it being the case that the lower soul could not touch the transcendent height above itself without mediation by the higher psychic element, while the higher soul required an inverse mediation to make contact with material reality. This conception renders the 'inwardness' of the soul a mediating phenomenon which is interior to the degree that aspects of the soul are cut off from direct contact with external reality. Inwardness is also constituted by the hierarchic structure which it internalizes: mirroring the government of the cosmos, it must as the governance of a single whole by itself, or 'self-government', take the form of hierarchic rule, since within a whole, constraint of one element by another must be construed as a permanent hierarchy, whereas if something is constrained by an external element ('the other') this may be a temporary and reversible hierarchy (see chapter 9, 'Can Morality be Christian?' below). However, in the case of neoplatonism, 'inwardness' is construed differently, and the usual accounts of this philosophy (and then the Cappadocians and Augustine) as 'deepening' an existing Socratic turn to interiority are somewhat oversimplified.[71] For neoplatonism did not work with a metaphor of form shaping matter, as in the earlier period, which automatically invoked an 'interior' space between two heterogeneous ontological modalities, and negotiated this incommensurability in necessarily hierarchical terms. Instead it adopted a metaphor of falling, reflected, light. What is 'interior', is now the 'mirrored' or 'speculative', and hence internal space is no longer that which is fenced-off against the outside, constituted by the necessary mediation of the low by the high and vice versa, but is rather the direct, unmediated penetration of external light and its ecstatic return back upon itself. There is still hierarchy of course, of source over mirror, but formally speaking there is no limit to the receptiveness of the mirror, and nor does the hierarchy require to be repeated within the space of the mirror; government is now by the external, transcendent other, and is no longer in principle a matter of self-government of the cosmos over itself which is microcosmically reflected in the individual soul composed of hetero-geneous and hierarchically ordered aspects. Now an access to the transcendent is indeed possible by a pure inward turn, precisely because the inner light is *wholly* from outside, and abides entirely *in* its ecstatic return to the external source. So whereas, for earlier antiquity, interiority was at the expense of exteriority, the more drastic interiority of later antiquity (often identified by commentators) was equally a new *externalizing* of the soul (as they usually fail to realize).

However, this new logic of light is more perfectly realized by Gregory of Nyssa than by the neoplatonists, because he fully abandons any notion of an ontologically persisting lower part of the soul, or any receptacle 'other' to what is received, and which is thereby passionate over-against the rays of actuality. Now the mirror truly is nothing but the apparent surface of light itself in its rebound. Thus we can see that, in Gregory, the perfecting of the late-antique notion of an 'ecstatic' and paradoxical interiority is precisely correlated with a more absolute doctrine of *apatheia*.

There are two prime aspects to this. First of all, by linking activity to relation and transmission Gregory has more completely detached the idea of activity from the notion of self-sufficiency. *Precisely for this reason*, pathos thereby loses its ontological space, since this was situated in a relational dependence deemed secondary and deficient compared with self-sufficiency. (It is true that Gregory still speaks of a 'self-determining soul' and a 'sovereign will'; here Augustine's account of will and grace is required to complete the destruction of 'self-government'.)[72] Second, pathos is for Gregory destined to vanish, even in the *cosmos*, as there is no longer even the faintest vestige of underlying 'matter'. Creation, since it is composed entirely of activity, is not a *passive* mirror of the soul caused by the soul's own act of reflection into which it can narcissistically fall, as for Plotinus.[73] In Gregory's writings, reflection involves no such inevitable establishment of a separate and lower reflecting surface apart from those self-rebounding rays of light themselves. Hence as we have seen, for Gregory not only can the soul be a pure mirror, also it is only thus as an aspect of the wider mirror which is the Church, the Body of Christ, eschatologically co-terminous with the redeemed cosmos:

> in her [the Bride] they see more clearly that which is invisible. It is like men who are unable to look upon the sun, yet can see by its reflection in the water. So the friends of the Bridegroom see the *Sun of Justice* by looking upon the face of the Church as though it were a pure mirror, and thus He can be seen by His reflection.[74]

This makes it possible to conclude that whereas earlier antiquity embraced the *civic compromise* of action governing passions, and Plotinus the apolitical retreat into a pure activity of the soul 'without windows', Gregory discovers the body and society as a site of pure activity, or of manifestation of the absolute, and even – in Christological terms – its full and unconcealed presence (the Hegelian echo is deliberate).

Finally, I think that Gregory was right. When we defend pathos we tend to make pity and suffering ontologically ultimate. Endless continued pity is an insult to the pitied, offers them no good gift and pretends to rob them of their own suffering. Likewise the prospect of endlessly continued suffering tends to make us construe virtue reactively, and to imagine a restricting response to a preceding evil as the highest virtue. This dethrones Charity, which presupposes nothing, much less evil, before its gratuitous giving (or at most the recipients of gifts with and as a primordial giving, as in the case of the Trinity).[75] In contrast with aspects of later Christianity, there is little that could be construed as a cult of weakness in Gregory, and he roundly declares that it is no more praiseworthy to be fearful than to be foolhardy, or to suffer than to enjoy merely temporary pleasure.[76] This robustly objective sense of sin is perhaps now more noticeable and appreciable for an intellectual climate informed by Spinoza and Nietzsche than it was for a certain sickly version of Christian Hegelianism, exalting pathos and dialectical negativity, which has persisted from the nineteenth century into the late twentieth.

Notes

1 See Eric Alliez and Michel Feher, 'Reflections of a Soul', in *Fragments for a History of the Human Body*: Part Two (Zone 4), ed. Michel Feher et al. (Zone, New York, 1989), pp. 47–84.

2 Gregory of Nyssa, 'On Virginity', in *Ascetical Works*, trans. V. W. Callahan (Catholic University Press of America, Washington, 1967), pp. 343–71, chapter IV, p. 349.

3 Gregory of Nyssa, 'Against Eunomius', in *The Library of the Nicene and Post-Nicene Fathers*, 2nd Series, vol. V. *Gregory of Nyssa*, eds Philip Schaff and Henry Ware (Eerdmans, Grand Rapids, Michigan, 1979) Book I, section 35: 'And human governments experience such quickly repeated revolutions for this very reason, that it is impracticable that those to whom nature has given equal rights should be excluded from power, but her impulse is instinct in all to make themselves equal with the dominant party, when all are of the same blood.'

4 Gregory, 'On Virginity', chapter IV, p. 349: 'A man must not be thought inferior to his forefathers, he must be deemed a great man by the generation to come by leaving his children historical records of himself.' And see Peter Brown, *The Body and Society* (Faber, London, 1988), pp. 285–305.

5 Gregory, 'On Virginity', chapter III, p. 346: 'whenever he [a husband] is glad with gazing on her beauty, then he shudders most with the presentiment of mourning her loss.'

6 Gregory, 'On Virginity', chapter VIII, p. 352.

7 Gregory, 'On the Christian mode of life', in *Ascetical Works*, pp. 127–58.

8 Gregory, 'On the Making of Man', in *Nicene and Post-Nicene Fathers*, vol. V, pp. 387–427, Foreword, p. 387.

9 Gregory, 'On the Christian mode of life', pp. 134–5.

10 Ibid., p. 134: 'He orders us to refer all glory and to direct all action to the will of that one with whom lies the reward of virtuous deeds.'

11 Gregory, 'Against Eunomius', Book II, 10: 'For the very glory that was bestowed on the lawgiver (Moses) was the glory of none other but of God himself, which glory the Lord in the Gospel bids all to seek, when he blames those who value human glory highly and seek not the glory that cometh from God only . . . For by the fact that he commandeth them to seek the glory that cometh from the only God he declared the possibility of their seeking what they sought. How then is the glory of the Almighty incommunicable . . . ?'

12 Gregory, 'On the Soul and the Resurrection', in *Nicene and Post-Nicene Fathers*, vol. V, p. 439; 'Answer to Eunomius Second Book', in ibid., pp. 257–8, 262; 'Against Eunomius' Book I, 4–6; 'On the Making of Man', X14, 396.

13 See Louis Méridier, *L'Influence de la Seconde Sophistique sur l'Oeuvre de Grégoire de Nysse* (Hachette, Paris, 1906), pp. 69, 195–6.

14 I borrow this term from Jean-Luc Marion's characterization of the discourse of Pseudo-Dionysius. See Jean-Luc Marion, *L'Idole et la Distance*, 'Le discours de Louange', pp. 219–44. However, in Gregory, unlike Dionysius, there is no suggestion of a 'Good beyond Being', and therefore his doxologic remains entirely an ontologic, contrary to that which Marion advocates. For Gregory, God's supreme name is 'to be' as 'is' is included in all other names, and *also* because it is the most apophatic name: we do not know *what* God is ('Against Eunomius', Book VII, 5; VIII, I). Hence, while Gregory's God is as much *dynamis* (and so a 'giving') as *ousia*, *his dynamis* is not 'before' Being. See chapter 2, 'Only Theology overcomes Metaphysics' above.

15 Gregory of Nyssa, *The Life of Moses, or concerning Perfection in Virtue*, trans. Abraham Malherbe and Everett Ferguson (Paulist Press, New York, 1978), Prologue, section 3. It is beyond Gregory's powers 'to encompass perfection in any treatise' (5) as perfection that is measurable is 'marked by certain definite boundaries', yet the perfection of *virtue*

consists in its having no limit, according to St Paul at Phil. 3:13: 'never cease straining towards those things that are to come'. Hence (6): 'Stopping in the race of virtue marks the beginning of the race of evil' and concomitantly one cannot 'grasp perfection with reference to virtue', for 'what is marked off by boundaries is not virtue'. Therefore Gregory concludes 'In effect whether it is a matter of encompassing by the *logos* what is perfection, or showing by one's life that which the *logos* has seen, I say that both the one and the other exceed our powers' (3).

16 Gregory, *Life of Moses*, 8: 'perfection is not marked off by limits . . . it is therefore undoubtedly impossible to attain perfection . . . the one limit of virtue is the absence of a limit (*aoriston*)'.

17 Ibid., 9: Perfection is impossible, yet we are *commanded* to be perfect (Matt. 5:48). Gregory construes this as 'taking part' in perfection or as being 'in proportion' (*pros meros*) to it. This part consists in 'growth in goodness' (10) and cannot be defined except in narrative terms by pointing to a growing, virtuous life, to an *example* of a *whole course of a life*, in this case that of Moses (11). Instead of an unattainable *logos*, 'memory' acts as a 'beacon light' (13).

18 Gregory declares that, in the case of virtue, the epistemic exigency of narrative example may be 'the reason why the civil life (*politeia*) of those graced and elevated [ones] was narrated in such detail (*akribeias historeitai*)'.

19 Gregory, 'On "Not Three Gods"' in *Nicene and Post-Nicene Fathers*, p. 331; 'On the making of Man' XVI. 1., 405. See also, Hans Urs von Balthasar, *Présence et Pensée: Essai sur la Philosophie Religieuse de Grégoire de Nysse* (Gabriel Beauchesne, Paris, 1947), p. 25.

20 Gregory, *Life of Moses*, 15–15. The problem here is, how *can* we repeat the virtue of the patriarchs, since we are not Chaldeans like Abraham, nor were we nourished by the daughter of an Egyptian like Moses. Gregory then proceeds: 'we need some subtlety of understanding and pureness of vision to discern from the history how, by removing ourselves from *what sort of* Chaldeans and Egyptians and escaping from *what kind of* Babylonian captivity, we shall embark on the blessed life'. The phrases in italics translate *poios* and I have substituted them for the translation 'such' ('by removing ourselves from such Chaldeans', etc.) in the English version which seems false, and implies that the allegorical flight is from specific place and time as such (such attachment being construed as the essence of passion), as the solution to the problem of the universal exemplarity of Abraham and Moses. This would imply simply that morality is *indifferent* to space and time, whereas Gregory's allegorical flight is from the Chaldeans and Egyptians taken as passions, and so *his* solution is rather that *in every* place and time we may make a specific escape from the passions which are without true being and therefore unsituated. Since virtue for Gregory means noting definable and universal, but only always specific growth, it must always be in a certain space and time, must always be 'different'. Hence, though he by no means truly attains to this insight, his solution to the problem, how *can* the different be exemplary?, eschews an essentialist resolution (as implied by the English rendering) in favour of a Kierkegaardian 'non-identical repetition'. It is not that the literal movement out of Egypt points to a spiritual *stasis* of essence, but rather that the literal movement figures both spiritual departure from static nothingness *and* a movement for its own sake which will be virtuous and spiritual yet still 'placed' (in space and time) through all its displacements. These considerations are important, for they tend to establish that becoming dispassionate is not, for Gregory, equivalent to becoming without temporo-spatial bodily location.

21 Gregory of Nyssa, 'Commentary on the Song of Songs, in *From Glory to Glory*, ed. H. Musirillo (John Murray, London, 1962) p. 286: 'Now the bond of this unity [Father in Son, Son in Father] is glory'); Gregory, 'On the Holy Spirit', in *Nicene Fathers*, pp. 315–25, 321. Here the Father is King, the Son King likewise, and the Holy Spirit is the Kingship: 'For the son is King and his living, realized and personified Kingship is found in the Holy Spirit.' On the Son as the Father's glory, see Gregory, 'Against Eunomius', Book I, 25: 'we have been taught by wisdom to contemplate the light in, and together with, the very everlastingness of that primal light, joining in one idea the brightness and its cause, and admitting no priority'; Book II, 5: 'He who foretold of himself that he would appear in the glory of the Father, indicated by the identity of glory their community in nature.' Grounding this assertion in the metaphysics of light, Gregory declares at Book II, 9: 'concurrently with the existence of the glory, there assuredly beams forth its brightness'. See also Book VIII, 5: 'he who says that the ray "is not", signifies also the extinction of that which gives light'. Under the figures of 'anointing' and 'sovereignty' (which concern respectively the bestowal or reputation of glory and the effulgence of glory) the Spirit is presented as the resultant and yet pre-enabling 'glorifying' involved in the Father's giving and the Son's receiving of *doxa*, and likewise as 'abstract' wisdom, truth and power at Book II, 2: 'Thus we conceive no gap between the anointed Christ and his anointing, between the King and his sovereignty, between wisdom and the Spirit of wisdom, between Truth and the Spirit of Truth, between Power and the Spirit of Power; but as there is contemplated from all eternity in the Father, the Son, who is Wisdom and Truth, and Counsel and Might and Knowledge and Understanding, and all else that the Spirit is called.'

22 Gregory, 'Against Eunomius', Book I, 52: 'What disadvantage on the score of Being, as compared with Abraham, had David who lived fourteen generations later? . . . For it is not in the power of time to define for each one the measures of nature'; 32: 'Birth is one thing, the thing born is another: they are different ideas altogether.' And see Book II, 11.

23 Gregory, 'Against Eunomius' Book II, 7; IV, 1.

24 Michel Barnes, 'The Power of God: The Significance of Dynamis in the Development of Gregory of Nyssa's Polemic Against Eunomius of Cyzicus' (unpublished Toronto Ph.D. thesis: available on microfilm), pp. 4–18, 259–68.

25 Gregory, 'Against Eunomius', Book II, 9.

26 'On the Soul and the Resurrection', p. 433. See also Barnes, 'The Power of God', p. 363. For Eunomius's view that the same *energeiai* produce the same *erga*, see Gregory, 'Against Eunomius', Book I, 29. Gregory applies the point in a Christological context to argue that God's *dynamis* can touch suffering with its healing power without itself undergoing suffering, for this process involves an alteration of the cause in the effect: 'adapting the exercise of his healing *dynamis* in a manner corresponding to the suffering': 'Against Eunomius', Book VI, 3.

27 Gregory, 'Against Eunomius', Book I, 17.

28 See Barnes, 'The Power of God', pp. 191–268.

29 Gregory, 'Against Eunomius', Book I, 31; II, 9, 15; VIII, 2; 'Answer to Eunomius's second book', in *Nicene Fathers*, pp. 251–300, 273.

30 Barnes, 'The Power of God', pp. 81–191.

31 Plato, *Phaedo*, 960–88.

32 Plato, *Sophist*, 247C.

33 Ibid., 247D–E.

34 Gregory, 'Against Eunomius', Book I, 31: 'Anyone who has gazed on the brightness of fire and experienced its power of warming, when he approaches another such brightness and another such warmth, will assuredly be led on to think of fire . . . Just so when we perceive a similar and equal amount of providential power in the Father and the Son'; II, 5: 'He who shines with the Father's glory and expresses in Himself the Father's person, has all things that the Father Himself has, and is possessor of all his *dynamis*'; II, 15: 'in the Trinity the doctrine of the Church declares one *dynamis* and goodness and essence and glory and the like' for 'if anything should perform the functions of fire, shining and warming in the same way, it is itself fire; so if the Spirit does the works of the Father, he must assuredly be acknowledged to be of the same nature with Him'. Gregory, 'On the Holy Spirit', p. 320: 'we should be justified in calling all that nature which came into existence by creation a movement of will, an impulse of design, a transmission of *energeia*, beginning with the Father, advancing through the Son, completed in the Holy Spirit'. And see Gregory, 'On the Holy Trinity', in *Nicene Fathers*, pp. 326–30.

35 Gregory, 'Against Eunomius', Book I, 31–32; II, 7.

36 Barnes, 'The Power of God', pp. 346–452.

37 See A. A. Long and D. N. Sedley, *The Hellenistic Philosophers*, vol. I (Cambridge University Press, Cambridge, 1987), pp. 162–5, 196–7, 199–202, 240–1.

38 Gregory, 'Against Eunomius', Book I, 42.

39 On divine incomprehensibility see 'Against Eunomius', Book I, 42: 'We find that we are drawn round uninterruptedly and evenly, and that we are always following a circumference where there is nothing to grasp; we find the divine life returning upon itself in an unbroken continuity, where no end and no parts can be recognized.' For Gregory's account of knowledge, see Book XII, 2 and 'Answer to Eunomius' second book' in *Nicene Fathers* plus the preceding editorial note on *epinoia* on p. 249. Also Balthasar, *Présence et Pensée*, p. 63.

40 See Gregory, 'Answer to Eunomius' second Book'.

41 Gregory, 'On the Making of Man', in *Nicene Fathers*, V, I–VI, 3, pp. 391–2.

42 Gregory, 'On the Soul and Resurrection', p. 433: 'The soul is an essence created and living and intellectual, transmitting from itself to an organized and sentient body the *dynamis* of living and of grasping objects of sense'; '[God] penetrating each portion, combines these portions with the whole and completes the whole by the portions, and encompasses the universe with a single all-controlling *dynamis*, self-centred and self-contained, never ceasing from its motion, yet never altering the position which it holds.' There follows (p. 433) an account of man as microcosm and an inference to the soul from the unity yet diversity of the body as parallel to an inference to God from the equally mysterious unity of a diverse creation. The possibility of a *mechanistic* and reductive explanation of this mystery is by Gregory refuted by an appeal to our invention of mechanical artifices themselves: our ability for example to work out the abstract principles of sound emerging from a wind-pipe and then construct a musical instrument, implies 'an invisible thinking nature' (p. 435).

43 Gregory, 'On the Soul and the Resurrection', pp. 439–40. See also, Barnes, 'The Power of God', pp. 308–46.

44 Gregory, 'On the Soul and the Resurrection', p. 442.

45 See David L. Balas 'Eternity and Time in Gregory of Nyssa's *Contra Eunomius*', in Heinrich Dorrie et al., *Gregor von Nysse und die Philosophie* (E. J. Brill, Leiden, 1976), pp. 128–53 and Monique Alexandre, 'L'Exégèse Gen. 1. 1–2a dans L'In Hexaemeron de

Gregoire de Nysse: Deux Approaches du Probléme de la Matière', and comments of
J. C. M. van Winden in *Écriture et Culture Philosophique dans la Pensée de Grégoire de
Nysse*, ed. M. Hart (Louvain, Leiden, 1971).

46 Gregory, 'Against Eunomius', Book VI, 3: 'Nothing is truly "passion" which does not
tend to sin, nor would one call strictly by the name of "passion" the necessary routine of
nature, regarding the composite nature as it goes on its course in a kind of order and
sequence. For the mutual concurrence of heterogeneous elements in the formation of our
body is a kind of combination harmoniously conjoined out of several similar elements,
but when, at due time, the tie is loosed which bound together the concurrence of the
elements, the combined nature is once more dissolved into the elements of which it was
composed. This then is rather a *work* than a *passion* of nature.'

47 Gregory, 'Against Eunomius', Book VI, 3: what is 'truly passion' is 'a diseased condition
of the will'.

48 Gregory, 'On the Soul and the Resurrection', pp. 442–3.

49 Gregory, 'On Virginity' chapter XI, p. 355: where the material elements do not form a
ladder to intellectual beauty, there will be an 'absence, in the soul's faculties of *hedones*,
of that exact training which would allow them to distinguish between true Beauty and the
reverse'. That is to say, feelings are intimately involved in the recognition of God, as
much as in the lapse of such recognition.

50 Rowan Williams, 'Macrina's Deathbed Revisited: Gregory of Nyssa on Mind and Pas-
sion' in *Christian Faith and Greek Philosophy in Late Antiquity*, ed. L. R. Wickham and
C. P. Bammel (E. J. Brill, Leiden, 1993), pp. 227–46; Gregory, 'On the Soul and the
Resurrection', p. 440; *The Life of Moses*, 157.

51 Gregory, 'On the Soul and the Resurrection', p. 444: here Gregory reads Paul as also
saying that every evil spirit will be annihilated along with every passion. Thus Gregory's
universalism is profoundly linked with his doctrine of *apatheia* and refusal to give
anything outside God and his active *dynamis* any ontological purchase.

52 Gregory, *The Life of Moses*, 2231: *eros* is a *pathein* which 'seems to me to belong to the
soul which loves what is beautiful'; 'Commentary on the Song of Songs' in Musirillo,
From Glory to Glory, p. 272: '*agape* that is strained to intensity is called *eros*', section 237.

53 'Song of Songs', in Musirillo, *From Glory to Glory*, pp. 178–9, 191, 200, 206, 263, 270,
272.

54 Ibid., p. 219: 'Perhaps if I may venture a rather bold conjecture, in seeing the beauty of
the Bridegroom in the Bride they are really admiring the invisible and incomprehensible
as it is in all creatures'; p. 272: 'he who sees the Church looks directly at Christ – Christ
building and increasing by the addition of the elect. The Bride then puts the veil from
her eyes and with pure vision sees the ineffable beauty of her Spouse'. There is a linking
here of Christ's indwelling in the Church, his bride, with the beatific vision, which is to
be construed in terms of the coincidence of that vision with the eschatological perfecting
of the Church as an extension of the work of incarnation (p. 288): 'that day when all will
look to the same end, when God will be all in all and all evil will be destroyed, and all men
will be united together by their participation in the Good'. At this point the Church not
only fully manifests Christ, but also fully manifests the Holy Spirit, spoken of in terms
of a flying/resting maternal Dove which infuses the Church with its glory (pp. 286–8).
We are able to contemplate the Spirit, because she was first received by the incarnate
Christ and thence transmitted to the disciples, the beginning of the Church (pp. 187,
287).

55 'Song of Songs', in Musirillo, *From Glory to Glory*, pp. 286–8.

56 Ibid., p. 237: the *bride* calls the *bridegroom* to her feast: 'surpassing all bounds of gener-osity'. Nothing makes clearer the radicalism of deification in Gregory: the relation of Christ to the Church actually manifests the *reciprocity* of Trinitarian gift-exchange. By grace, we return God's gift to God.

57 Musirillo, 'On the Soul and the Resurrection', pp. 462–3. Caroline Walker Bynum points out that Gregory combines the Origenist conception of the body continuing to evolve beyond death under the impulse of a seminal *eidos* with Methodius's anxious insistence on return of the same body. Perhaps, as she thinks, the synthesis is contradic-tory, but it might be possible to read Gregory as stressing the discontinuity between the *diastasis* of time and the somehow remaining *diastasis* (which he *usually* affirms) of eternity. In the latter, *every* active moment of time returns, so that Gregory is more concerned with the resumption of our whole life in time than with the return of the 'same' elements of the body, whose 'marking' by the soul can only be through the course of their *flux*, and not in spite of it: Caroline Walker Bynum, *The Resurrection of the Body in Western Christianity 200–1336* (Columbia University Press, New York, 1995), pp. 81–6.

58 Gregory, 'Against Eunomius', Book VI, 4: 'even those names which are great and divine are properly applied to the humanity, while on the other hand the Godhead is spoken of by human names. For it is the *same Person* who both has the Name which is above every name, and is worshipped by all creation in the human name of Jesus'.

59 On mirrored incomprehensibility, see Gregory, 'On the Making of Man', XI, 4, p. 396; 'Answer to Eunomius' Second Book', p. 264. Regarding 'set paradox', see 'Against Eunomius', Book VI, I.

60 Gregory, 'Against Eunomius', Book VI, 4: 'that unspeakable mixture and conjunction of human littleness commingled with divine greatness.' For Gregory, God also works more generally within the creation by fusion of opposites. See 'On the Soul and the Resurrec-tion', p. 433. The cosmic and Christological aspects of this theme come together in the 'Commentary on the Song of Songs', p. 218: 'that manifold quality of the divine wisdom which arises by the union of opposites, has only now been clearly revealed through the Church: how the word became flesh, life is mingled with death, in his bruises our wound is healed, the infirmity of the Cross brings down the power of the Adversary, the invisible is revealed in the flesh, the captives are ransomed, He Himself is both purchaser and price'.

61 Gregory, 'Against Eunomius', Book VI, 2: 'we do not say, that one who touches a sick man to heal him is himself partaker of the infirmity, but we say that he does give the sick man the boon of a return to health'; 'the Father does these things [the crucifixion and resurrection] by his own *dynamis* by which he works all things'.

62 Ibid., 'Against Eunomius', Book VIII, 2; Gregory, *Life of Moses*, 147, 251. On the transformation of the human body see *Life of Moses*, 30: 'What is impassible by nature did not change into passible, but what is mutable and subject to passivity was trans-formed into impassibility by participation in the immutable. That Gregory regards Christ's life as 'metahistorical' in the sense of showing and making possible again the nature of *every event, every passage*, is shown at *Life of Moses*, 119 in his words regarding the cloudy pillar, a type of Christ: 'What we hear from the history to have happened then, contemplation of the divine word shows always to happen (*eisai ginesthou*).'

63 The Mallarmean echo is deliberate. See Gregory, 'Against Eunomius', Book VI, I: 'For verily the Godhead works the salvation of the world by means of *that body which encompassed it*, in such wise that the suffering was of the body, but the operation was of God' (my italics); 'Answer to Eunomius' Second Book', p. 262: 'Holy Scripture omits all inquiry into substance . . . For this reason John said the world could not contain the books of what Jesus did' and 'the whole creation cannot contain what might be said respecting itself'. In other words the essence of the world lies paradoxically beyond the world, and still more paradoxically, this 'beyond' once entered *into* the world. This idea links also to the Church as 'a re-creation of the world . . . a new firmament': Musirillo, *From Glory to Glory*, p. 273.

64 'Song of Songs', in Musirillo, *From Glory to Glory*, p. 154 (concerning the 'spiritual senses') 'What could be more paradoxical than that nature itself should purify its own passions. For in words that seem to suggest passion it offers us precepts and instruction in purity.'

65 See Emilie zum Brunn, *St Augustine: Being and Nothingness* (Paragon House, New York, 1988), p. 10: zum Brunn stresses that metaphors of food and fullness were already used by the neoplatonists.

66 On spiritual sense as a 'distillation' of the physical senses see Musirillo, 'Song of Songs' in *From Glory to Glory*, p. 224. On non-replete yet replete *eros*, see p. 270: 'The veil of her [the Bride's] grief is removed when she learns that the true satisfaction of her desire consists in constantly going on with her quest . . . seeing that every fulfilment of her desire continually generates a further desire for the transcendent', and p. 176, 'her thirst is not quenched even though a whole cup is brought into her mouth, but she asks to be brought into the very wine cellar, and have her mouth held right beneath the vats, bubbling over with sweet wine'.

67 Musirillo, 'Song of Songs' in *From Glory to Glory*, pp. 219 and 285, 286 for the 'flying/resting *motif*'.

68 Plotinus, *Enneads*, 6. 9. 8 and 20: 6. 9. 10. And see J. M. Rist, *Plotinus: the Road to Reality* (Cambridge University Press, Cambridge, 1967), pp. 225, 230.

69 Plotinus, *Enneads* 6. 9. 8.

70 Ibid., 4. 7. 14; 1. 1. 12; 6. 4. 16.

71 See, for example, Charles Taylor's version in his, nonetheless, exceptionally insightful *Sources of the Self* (Cambridge University Press, Cambridge, 1989), pp. 115–43.

72 Gregory, 'Against Eunomius', Book II, 11: 'our soul is self-determining . . . with sovereignty over itself'; Gregory, 'On the Soul and the Resurrection': 'Now liberty is the coming-up to a state which owns no master and is self-regulating (*autokrates*).'

73 See Alliez and Feher, 'Reflections of a Soul'. Also Julia Kristeva, 'Narcissus: The New Insanity' in *Tales of Love*, trans. Leon S. Rondiez (Columbia University Press, New York, 1987), pp. 103–22. On interiority and mirrors in Gregory see 'Commentary on Ecclesiastes', in Musirillo, *From Glory to Glory*, p. 102: 'in gazing upon his own purity he [a Man] will see the archetype within the image'; 'Commentary on the Song of Songs', 164: 'For all the perfect virtue of God sends forth rays of sinlessness to illumine the lives of those who are pure, and these rays make the invisible visible, and allow us to comprehend the inaccessible by impressing an image of the sun upon the mirror of our souls'; 'On Virginity', chapter XI, p. 356: the 'virgin soul' is 'like a mirror beneath the purity of God.'

74 'Song of Songs', in Musirillo, *From Glory to Glory*, p. 219. The final coinciding of the mystery of the Church with the mystery of all creatures is declared in a preceding passage (p. 218): 'Perhaps, (if I may venture a rather bold conjecture), in seeing the beauty of the Bridegroom in the Bride they are really admiring the invisible and incomprehensible as it is in all creatures.'

75 See chapter 9, 'Can Morality be Christian', below, and John Milbank, 'Can a Gift be Given?', *Modern Theology*, 2, 1 (January 1995), pp. 119–61.

76 See Gregory, 'Of Virginity', chapter XVI, p. 362. Here Gregory enunciates an important critique of melancholia and resentment: whereas, he says, some are slaves to pleasure others 'fall a ready prey to melancholia and irritation, and to brooding over injuries, and to everything that is the direct opposite of pleasurable feelings, from which they are very reluctant to extricate themselves ... But God is not pain any more than he is pleasure . . . but very wisdom and sanctification, truth and joy and peace and everything like that ... It matters not whether we miss virtue in this way or in that.' And see Gregory, 'Against Eunomius', Book VI, 2 for a critique of *sym-pathia* in the passage already cited above in note 58.

Ethos

9

Can Morality Be Christian?

Let me tell you the answer straightaway. It is no. Not 'no' there cannot be a specifically Christian morality. But no, morality cannot be Christian. All those obscure men of Whitechapel and thereabouts, the Muggletonians and members of other forgotten sects and their heir, William Blake,[1] were no doubt muddled, culturally ill-fed and heretical, and yet in their central antinomianism they were essentially right. And had they known it were but struggling to say what Catholic tradition itself implies (but has never perhaps adequately articulated), that is, that Christian morality is a thing *so* strange, that it must be declared immoral or amoral according to all other human norms and codes of morality. I shall try to demonstrate this by taking five marks of morality, and then contrasting them with five notes of Christianity. The five marks are Reaction, Sacrifice, Complicity with Death, Scarcity and Generality. The five notes are Gift, End of Sacrifice, Resurrection, Plenitude and Confidence.

Let us begin by considering the reactive character of virtue. 'I heard a devil curse / On the heath and the furze / Mercy could be no more / If there was nobody poor', sang William Blake.[2] Here the devil's wisdom is that of morality as such. It may seem that only the hypocrite and self-deceiver will justify poverty as a field for the exercise of mercy. But Blake's point is that *every* act of mercy, in so far as it rejoices in itself, rejoices also in its occasion. Quite often, also, as when one gives alms to beggars, one is *perpetuating* that occasion, not merely meeting a need, but by meeting it reproducing it; therefore not as it might appear, simply cancelling an ill, but cancelling it in such a manner as to ensure its re-occurrence, *unless* what we give enables an end to beggary as such. The occasion for the exercise of mercy is here itself an evil – a condition of physical misery, which moreover can only be lived out in a somewhat evil manner: as another poet, Charles Baudelaire, noted, the beggar's supplication is automatically an accusation, a curse of the potential benefactor should he fail to be such.[3] But every occasion for every 'good' act is always like this – there is always some initial evil, some deficiency, some threat, some terror, something to be warded off. This condition moreover is never simply passive, never just evil *in itself*, but also always evil towards us, even if what it threatens or disturbs is simply our peace of mind, even if what it assaults is merely our conscience. Hence virtue is paradigmatically heroism, the essence of manhood in action, *virtus*, the male force which sustains the bounds of self, or the bounds of the city. It is that which wards off external danger, so always sustaining both a *here* and an *elsewhere*. To be virtuous is to be brave, to show fortitude, constancy, to stand firm. Even the seemingly opposite action, which magnanimously gives, and does not withstand, *nonetheless* withstands the threat of the supplicant, and through a slight concession holds back an utter loss. To sustain this concession *also* requires nobility, strength and self-control, especially control in a measured giving in order not to get carried away in the counter-luxury of self-abandonment. But what, you might ask, of simple respect for another person's life, liberty and goods, which will include the honouring of one's words? For here neither resistance to encroachment, nor outgoing generosity are implied, but rather mutual co-existence, the crucial non-trespassing upon which modern freedom is founded.

In response I would ask why it is that respect for life, liberty and truth are the subject matter of a law, a moral commandment? Why do they not simply *occur* as manifestations of life, if they are the circumstances of mutual co-existence as they claim to be? If they *are* material for law, then that means they are *threatened* circumstances, threatened by each and every one of us all the time. The law assumes that each is a threat to all, that we are *tempted* to murder, to rob, to lie, that we will conceive these things to be to our advantage. Thus the law and all of us collectively *hold back* a threat to all of us, and *concede*, all of us to all of us, the meagre gift of survival, ownership and literal truth. This logic of policed concessions has been continually extended, through history, by the processes (identified by Rousseau and Marx) of disappropriation, usually in the name of collective security in the face of an external threat. For the more the means are taken away from individuals or groups of individuals to survive 'naturally' or self-sufficiently, the more forged chains of mutual dependency can be appealed to in order to undergird appeals to self-limitation or one's (sacrificial) duty to society. Primary accumulation provides the capital stocks that morality draws upon; this process alone defines the bounds of self as one of ownership and mutual delimitation in the face of an always preceding real or phantom danger.

Hence we only acknowledge an *observance* of laws in the face of a threat to them, the threat of our own inner temptations or else outward violations by others.

For in this case, as in all cases of virtue, the greatest virtue is seen in the face of the greatest iniquity. Mother Teresa needs Calcutta: it is not just her literal burden, but also her burden of ambiguity. And it is not merely a question of the greatest virtue: as Milton put it, there is no 'cloistered virtue', because an untested virtue cannot be known to be present, even in potential. The monks may not receive the accolade of martyrdom by marauding Danes, but at least, to be seen in their sanctity, they must endure with patience the stresses which creep into even the most sequestered shade.

Hence virtue is always reactive: it always secretly celebrates as its occasion a *prior* evil, lives out of what it opposes. In this circumstance, Friedrich Nietzsche saw a ground for still further suspicions: for if these prior evils have not yet recognized themselves as such, but are only named evil by the supposed good which resists them, then are they not simply, even in the case of the presence of human agency, spontaneous natural manifestations of energy, knowing no vindictiveness? Whereas, to the contrary, if virtue takes its starting point in a *threatened* position, and one must concede that to be threatened is something bad, generating fear, insecurity, self-enclosure and so forth – something *morally* bad, not just a non-moral evil – then virtue is bound to begin with envy, spite, pettiness, priggishness and self-righteousness, *however* seemingly good its cause. Here, at the beginning of *every* virtue, lies a failure to turn the other cheek. Worse still, no external encroachment, no seeming violence, is obviously violent in an objective and unquestionable sense. No, violence has always to be judged, since every encroachment, every invasion, including an imperial one, may be a gift, an alien strengthening; we have to decide as to whether it strengthens or weakens us. Is it rape or is it consummation? The difference is never simply visible. And this applies not just to external encroachments, but to the various forces which rise up within ourselves: one can ask *are* all our passions, which bear ourselves out of ourselves, inherently threatening to ourselves, as Greek antiquity tended to consider? Is there a violent tearing apart of our true self at work here? Or to the contrary, does our true self only emerge on this journey out of itself? Of alien visitations and internal irruptions we must always *interpret*: is this violence, or is it gift and giving? Too often, virtue does not pause for thought here, but something seemingly other is demonized. Especially that which is strong, overwhelming and indefinable, the creative energies of ourselves and of others.

So far, so Nietzschean. Yet Nietzsche mostly dwelt on the case where virtue makes a virtue out of necessity: the weak celebrate their weakness, the herd celebrates its herdness. This, however, is only one *instance* of reaction. One can argue that, in many cases of strong, heroic action celebrated by Nietzsche, one is not dealing with something 'spontaneous', but in this case *also* with something reactive, with a defence of the tribe, or at least of the tribe's record or honour, with a subduing of those who *are* weaker and must be commanded as well as with an *overcoming* of one's own stasis, one's own lusts and passive desires. And of course Nietzsche is himself *explicit* about this ascetic self-overcoming as the character of heroism, and of the positive transvalued values which he recommends.[4] At this point therefore, it would seem that Nietzsche fails to see a common *genus* containing both morality hitherto, which he takes to be the morality of the weak (but I would take to be equally the morality of the strong) and his own mode of trans-valued virtue, which is creatively self-legislating and extrinsically normative for the weaker who cannot be self-governed. For *both* old and new moralities are occasioned by something than can be overcome, therefore *both* are reactive. The question, can there be a *non*-reactive mode of morality, is one which Nietzsche after all did not ask. Here, as we shall see, it seems to me that such a question *was* already asked by Plato, by St Paul, by Augustine, Luther and Kierkegaard, not to mention the disreputable men of Whitechapel and thereabouts. Paradoxically, it is Nietzsche's prime targets who had already carried out a transvaluation which Nietzsche but half carries through.

My second mark (of the Beast, as may by now be surmised) is Sacrifice. If virtue is reactive and responds to a danger, then it must make an effort. If such an effort is considered praiseworthy, then this is because it is not easy to make, for to the external danger is added its wicked little inner secret agents: our lazy, cowardly and destructive passions. On their account there must be an inward overcoming to match the outward one. Therefore an inner sacrifice is required, a cruel foregoing of something which at least a part of us would like to enjoy. But also an outer sacrifice, since in resisting the external threat the hero runs a risk and must be prepared to lose his life. This is not, usually, in order to save himself, unless he faces a fate worse than death; since most fates are preferable to death, it will usually be to save others or a whole which *counts higher than himself* – just as, within himself, his own integrity, his own honour, his own rationality, counts higher than his momentary passions. So with sacrifice a distinct new element has been added to that of reaction. Yet there may be a complex link between the two. Why should there be any danger, any initial evil? There would be none if the hero or the city was inviolable. And why is this not the case? Because they have a *weak link*, a vulnerable point of entry. This point must be guarded, or governed. One can even go further: Without this weak point to be governed there would *be* no discrete self and no walled city. For both these things have an interior. Something is taken to have an interior, to be enclosed, even though everything can be unravelled and every part of every substantial thing *is* in principle just as superficial as every other part, because some parts are defined as lower, or lesser, than other parts. Thus there are both governed and governors in soul, body-and-soul or city. If the higher parts, the governors, *represent* the whole more than the lower parts, then they alone touch the external surface, and one can only reach the lower parts – the people or the passions – by passing through the gate of ruling authority which grants permission to enter – the sovereign power in the city, or reason in the soul. The space between high and low now becomes – by convention alone – an *interiority*, an absolute 'inside' because it is not as near the outside as the governing powers above it (which are nearer the sky, gods, or whatever), *nor* as close to the outside as the governed powers below, since the passions are closer to the earth. Here 'below' is the most vulnerable point of entrance, guarding an interiority which can *only* be constituted by the convention of a hierarchy. Thus one can conclude that to sustain a *reaction* there must be a vulnerable point which paradoxically allows there to be an integral whole to react to a threat in the first place. There is a whole *because* it is a threatened whole, because the external threat has already wormed its way within. Hence to resist or to react, the whole must overcome itself, must *sacrifice* that part, those parts of itself which are alien or else not essential, but superfluous (although dead heroes are *not* lost, but sustained in the most eternal and essential aspect of themselves, their reputation). Just as sacrifice alone sustains a totality, so, also, we can see that sacrifice is never of one for another, but always a matter of self-sacrifice for one's higher self and of part for whole, for even the individual who dies for his friend dies rather for the idea of his being contained within the greater whole which is the circle of friendship: he is consumed by what must henceforth, without him, be an abstraction.

We can see from the foregoing two things, primarily. First of all every ethical command of duty requires a violent renunciation, a subordination of the part to the whole. Therefore in the command to be good, there is no entire good, but always the loss of some good, always a maiming, and how, one might ask, can we usually be confident that the good of the whole is truly more than the good of the parts? Yet more seriously, if to be good is an absolute, if the good is precisely that which cannot be negated or lessened, else one has its opposite, evil, how can there be good at all without an entire good? We have seen that the second mark of virtue is sacrifice, that this is its only proof, but the proof proves also its futility, its final *lack* of complete virtue, and therefore of *any* virtue whatsoever. The second point is that since sacrifice is self-sacrifice of self to self, the ethical imperative has no regard for the other any more than to one's own self-integrity. To respect the other in his non-objective subjectivity, which is the rule in Levinas as much as in Kant, means only to place first the general community, which is bound together by such respect for generalized otherness (a generality which Levinas only *purports* to overcome). For no *other* ever demands my self-loss, my giving myself up – *no neighbour*, but only a threat to the neighbour which is at the same time a threat to a community principle of mutual self-sacrifice to maintain solidarity in order to preserve the *fiction* of community on into the future. In morality there is no love for the other nor opening to the other, but always and everywhere a principle of *self-government*, whether of the soul or of the city. In order that the totality may be, and be the site of a principle, it must rule itself, divide itself from itself, sacrifice itself to itself. Thereby it repels the intruder pre-defined as evil.

The third mark of morality is Complicity with Death. If Reaction requires Sacrifice, then both concern death: in fact a threat of death repelled by a willingness to die. Death for death to *secure* life against death: this is 'morality', this is 'ethics'. Without death, there would be no need to be good, violence would be but sado-masochistic fun, and not even that, since death alone gives such play its spice, so apparent violence would be reduced to no more than nursery give-and-take, a virtual utopia without consequences. So ethics must covertly celebrate death, for only our fragility elicits our virtue. The New Testament is for this reason right to

view sin and death as an inseparable pair: because we are dying we can be threatened, because we are dying it is possible for us to do harm. What would human evil
amount to, without its natural accomplices, death, pain, disease, and so forth?
Of course there is social ostracism, exclusion from the human conversation, but
the one ostracized is a danger, and danger finally threatens death. Moreover,
ostracization is itself a threat of death, and verbal insults and exclusions can only
operate with metaphors of death, pain and disease. For the New Testament, death
has arrived in the world as a result of sin, but equally sin itself *is* sin because it
negates being, because it deals death, because it *invents* death; therefore it is sin
because it invents the possibility of sin and the need for morality, not at all because
it offends a moral law. As Bonhoeffer stressed, 'Christian ethics' *opposes* the knowledge of good and evil, which all morality seeks, because this is *itself* the evil that
institutes evil along with the good.[5]

Thus it is not merely that in the face of death the moral law is impotent, but also
that it assumes and requires death's existence, since it always views death as an
enemy to life rather than as the passage of life to further life; for this reason it seeks
to shore life up against death, and to erect an illusory spatial enclave against the
ravages of time.[6] Virtue is what holds death back, inhibits death, protects people
from death, even though, from a Christian point of view, death is also remedy and
mercy. For by sinning one has cut oneself off from the source of life which is God;
out of a weak fear and need for security founded in self one has established the
kingdom of weakness which is death and dying, and precisely the best thing for the
weak (as Nietzsche rightly says) is that they should die as soon as possible. Thus,
given death, given *this* fact which is fact itself, for death alone establishes demar-
cated spatial boundaries, death alone stops the flux (so that every merely empiricist
philosophy points to death alone, its one delight), given the death-fact, the best we
can do is to be virtuous, not kill and not cause to suffer, become doctors and firemen
and so forth. Yet all these triumphs are enabled by the continuation of death which
is the only factual form that sin can take, its one mode of actuality, although it is
always in reality the termination of the actual, since every isolatable being is already
at an end, already is not, is 'known as dead'. And to hold death back, to perpetuate
life for a while, is also to perpetuate a life which must in the end die all the more,
as the Greek fathers perceived in relation to the married vocation viewed as a desire
for posthumous eternity in the memory of offspring (see the previous chapter, 'The
Force of Identity'). Virtue perpetuates dying and the possible exploitation of dying
by the murderous, greedy and slandering. Whereas the only remedy for death is its
hastening, a speedy death as soon as possible, virtue postpones this only possible
cure for death, death itself. Here, in hastened death lies for us the only absolute
good, a kind of negative image of paradisal goodness in the fallen world.

Death makes life scarce; it causes it to be in short supply, despite the fact that life
is a mysteriously self-renewing force, absolutely without cause, unless we take the
heuristic fables of science for truth. Thus the fourth mark of the moral beast is
scarcity: because life is in short supply, because it might run out on us, sooner or

later, we must invest, we must insure.[7] Ethics is not written philosophy, it is banks, it is sexual jealousy, it is the sacrifice of self-realization for the sake of others, it is insurance companies, mortgages and the stock exchange. For in fearing that there will not be world enough or time, we insist on our identity, our truth, our space, denying that of others – thereby rendering their coyness *always* a crime. This, according to Luther, is why *stealing* is a temptation; *not at all* because there is a limited supply and we should allow others their share, as legalism presumes, but on the contrary because we fear there will not be enough for us. Thus, in the *Treatise of Good Works* Luther declares, regarding the commandment not to steal – which he takes to be God's word and eternal (not reactive) law as a commandment of faith and not of law without faith – 'A man is generous because he trusts God and never doubts but that he will always have enough. In contrast a man is covetous and anxious because he does not trust God'.[18] Do not steal means, for the gospel, positively 'be generous', and as Luther further says, 'faith is the master workman and the motivating force behind the good work of generosity'.[19] Generosity or true not stealing acts out of the assumption of plenitude, our confidence in God's power.

That remote and bastard descendant of Luther, Friedrich Nietzsche, repeats the same thing in his own fashion. For in *Thus Spake Zarathustra* to possess noble virtue is to be *creatively* generous, or to act out of a plenitude, and to act thus is to pass beyond oneself, to die and not to avoid or seek to limit death.[10] However, for all that Nietzsche specifically opposes sacrifices of the individual to the state, or to the spatial, political present, he still nonetheless speaks of a sacrifice of the present for the sake of the future superman; he still sees an *acceptance* of the given fact of death, along with the given facts of human disease and weakness, as occasions for the exercise of heroic strength and sacrificial offering.[11] There is in all this still a mode of scarcity in operation, allowing no eternal room for me and my body, since the plenitude of the eternal flux at some point cancels *me* out. Likewise the heroic creator must ultimately *sacrifice* a joy in receiving; Zarathustra longs to receive but is doomed to be a lonely sun, alone guaranteeing his own light, his law.[12] And as one source, he is inevitably in *conflict* with other sources; thus while Nietzsche admits a plenitude of sources, they must struggle for the *ground* of unity, and of absolute sovereignty. This quality 'rule' is therefore *in short supply*, whereas a fuller conception of a *plenitude* of laws and virtues would have to contain a faith in the possibility of their analogical blending, or the chance that my specific law might be a mode of *receiving* your specific law and so forth. A vision, indeed, of ontological peaceableness, as a condition we do not instigate, but even in our creative giving receive as a prior gift from an eternal source. This would abolish Zarathustra's isolation, it would end his sacrifice of a delight in receiving if to give at all one *must* receive, from a divine source of plenitude which legislates, diversely but harmoniously. And of course, in the Christian vision of a triune God, even the giving God is simultaneously a receptive God, rejoicing in his own alterity. So Nietzsche's vision of joyful agonism, far from being a glimpse beyond ethics, sustains – *precisely* – morality as a heroic operation in conditions of scarcity. Nonetheless Nietzsche himself was perhaps close to perceiving this, and to supplementing his will to power with a doctrine of faith in bodily resurrection. However, the eternal return, unlike faith in bodily resurrection, sustains a dualism: by identifying with eternal, impersonal joy, we joyfully embrace the *necessity* of sacrifices, weaknesses and losses in the present, including the political present. Here plenitude is but an attitude and cannot be made eucharistically manifest; nor does one look to any eschatological future which will expose death and scarcity to have been enacted illusions.

However, Nietzshe's transvalued value, which is gift, once it is understood in a more Christian and therefore yet *more* radically anti-moral way (as I have just sketched out) ceases to be in any way reactive: it is rather entirely gift which acts out of the plenitude of always more to come. A genuine gift is excessive since it is not required, and it occasions not a loss but a gain in subjectivity for the giver which is reinforced by the counter-gift of gratitude from the recipient. In *this* virtue is to be found no sacrifice. Moreover, the genuine gift can in no way be anything commanded, anything pre-defined or required, as for example alms to beggars. The latter is not, as we might suppose, supremely charity. Charity is supremely free-giving to our *friend*, not the stranger or enemy (although a giving may *make* a stranger a friend), for as Blake declares 'Who loves his enemy hates his friend / this is surely not what Jesus intends' – without knowing it echoing Aquinas's explanation that love for enemies (for those who hurt or threaten us) is only higher because made possible as an expression for our love for God, in other words as a manifestation of the *supreme* friendly love (ST.II.II.Q. 27 a 7). Hence if supernatural, complete virtue is charity, gifts which are merely requirements or duties are not ethical or virtuous at all, and the command to give or to love is supremely paradoxical. For the virtuous resides in the unnecessary exception, it is always singular, and therefore impresentable.

Thereby Christian virtue stands in absolute contrast to my fifth mark of ordinary morality which is *Generality*. This criterion deems that a moral act is one which falls under a category (as Kant said) of what should *always* be done, and despite the Kantian reference this is *as true* (for example) of the imperative 'cultivate the virtue of truthfulness' (which might not imply strict truthfulness on this or that occasion) as the deontological injunction 'always tell the truth'. (Aristotelian ethics, despite its focus upon teleological flourishing as defining true 'natures' or the good, remains in the case of the human ethical good, throughout reactive because it is entirely concerned with limiting excessive passion and securing a relatively secure and autonomous happiness. Purely invulnerable virtue exercised for its own sake is for Aristotle intellectual, contemplative and non-relational: outside the sphere of friendship and outside the sphere of *ethical* activity.) It is this generality which ensures that the moral command is a law or general prescription, including a prescription of virtue. But we have already seen that such generality is only required because of the prior assumption of external threat, internal weakness, death and scarcity. The eternal demand for uniformity is paradoxically an emergency measure to sustain a unity of a thoroughly abstract kind. And it is precisely because of this abstract character of the law that, as Paul realized, the law is a letter that can never be fulfilled. Not in the sense that love can never be fulfilled, since this follows from the *inherently* excessive, self-exceeding character of love, but in a sense which follows from law's presumption that something is *lacking*, and that something will resist it. The abstractness of law ensures that we will never have sufficiently accorded to its demand which can always be more perfectly embodied. We are here to *give up* to a degree our concrete desires for possessions, other people, self-expression and so forth, and this giving up being defined as running against the grain, and as for the sake of an abstract principle, not a concrete benefit, can never, in the nature of things, be complete. In this game of struggle with self in the name of written principle we are not to win: these 'letters', as Paul declared, remain over against us, alien to our life and to our willing, if willing be regarded as primarily a self-willing. The letters always threaten us, they require the death of ourselves, and they counterpose to death-dealing sin a threat of judicial death as a sanction. This abstract impersonal justice must always have its real truth in concrete revenge carried out by threatened, established interests. In consequence, as Paul puts it in *Galatians* (Gal. 3:10–13), to be under the law is to be under a curse; to remain in the place of cursed impurity, and to have the threat of further slander hanging always over our heads. Whereas if we fail to receive divine *grace* and to be simultaneously gracious to others, still no judgement, no punishment from God follows: simply we do not receive anything any more, we are self-judged, alone, in hell.

To the abstract generality of law, Paul opposes the *specificity* of divine gift which always takes the form of particular gifts in the sense of specific talents or charismata: these are 'different gifts according to the gift given to us' (Rom. 12:6). Again, in *Galatians*, he says that if we realize that we each have an absolutely *specific* work to do, we will stop supposing we can compare ourselves in virtue to our brethren. Each has his own load to bear, yet as Paul has just said that we must bear each other's burdens (Gal. 6:2–4) or in other words that the gifts which are talents or roles must be given, passed on, exchanged for the furtherance and education of others, it is clear that there is no denying here of analogical resemblance between 'gifts' (in the sense of both presents and talents), since this is the very condition of peace within the body of Christ. Each gift, each talent ('virtue') is absolutely unique, yet each repeats non-identically and so *exactly* the grace of God which is transcendentally, inaccessibly One. And because we are talking about unique talents (roles, virtues) which are received, not achieved by self-conquest, it is better to speak of a 'charismatic ethic' or an 'ethic of gift' than a Christian 'ethic of virtue' – although one might also define this gift-ethic as an *anarchic* virtue-ethic.[13]

In contrast to this *transcendental* unity of the gift, according to Paul, the generality of the law is expressed in its compulsive (and non-analogical) multiplicity, that is, its attempt to secure a finite, spatial catalogue of virtue, an exhaustive list. Hence laws are many and (Gal. 4:9) derive, not from God but from the diverse (and *weak*) powers of the air, although their operation is permitted by God (Gal. 3:19). Legality therefore, even Jewish, is *polytheist* and not monotheist, because *not diverse enough* – not absolutely divine and so absolutely many-in-one. It is for this reason that the will of one man – Abraham – for a specific future heir who will receive the full gift, the full promise of God, outweighs the entire generality of law (Gal. 3:5–18). The legal principle of absolute respect for the will of the dead, whereby law seeks to use the finitude and finality of death to gain authority for itself, in fact, as Paul realizes, altogether subverts the law, because will is absolutely singular and specific and can in principle therefore will *against* the law's command. Hence the sovereignty of law can never *enlist* the sovereignty of will. It is this singularity and resistlessness of the will of the father for an heir, which the gospel reinvokes as a new *concrete* university of love, over against the alien artifice of legal generality. Thus, as the young Hegel realized, the gospel does indeed resurrect 'life' and 'nature' against culture in its inimical aspect. For beyond the legal state, the Patriarch in his Rousseauian 'self-sufficiency' is recovered, although this is only an autonomy from the point of view of the state, in the sense of freedom from abstract obligation. In reality, the Patriarch is within a preceding faith-covenant of paradoxically 'obligated gift', supremely exemplified in the *excessive* 'tie' to future generations.

Gradually, the five notes of the gospel have been heard by contrast, and they can now be more exactly sounded altogether, in harmony. They are Gift, End of Sacrifice, Resurrection, Plenitude and Confidence. In the beginning there was only gift: no demon of chaos to be defeated, but a divine creative act; this virtue of giving was not required, was not necessary, and so was a more absolute good, complicit with no threat, which in relation to gift is an entirely secondary will to self-possession, to non-receiving of life and so to death. Under the original will of God, no sacrifice of self is required, and while it is true that under the dispensation of death, this *will* (when the occasion arrives) be necessary, we should never fall into the trap of an absolute celebration of self-sacrifice, especially our own. Luther's view of why stealing is wrong seems almost closer to the idea that stealing is not truly in our self-interest than many more moralizing accounts. Nevertheless it really accords with neither, but is grounded in a refusal of the contrast between my interest and that of the other. I exist in receiving; because I receive I joyfully give, and one can add to Luther a more Catholic stress that one can only receive God who is charity, by sharing *in* the giving of this charity – faith *is* (against Luther) from the outset a *habitus* and from the outset the work of charity, our work only in so far as it is God's.[14] So I exist and persist also in giving, which is prior to any sacrificial loss. But all the same, our worldly logic wonders, why should we trust the giver for whom giving is easy? Thus so much Victorian theology falls into the pseudo-profundity of seeing God's love as taking its *origin* from the sacrifice on the cross, or else as only guaranteed by the cross. Under the dispensation of death indeed, we only see gift via sacrifice, but the genuine sacrifice, supremely that of the cross, is only recognized as such in so far as it is the *sustaining* of joyful, non-reactive giving, by a hastening of death as the only way of continuing to give despite the cancellation of gift by death. We assume that the trained man, the man of uncloistered virtue, the man of Sparta or Gordonstoun who has played at danger, will face danger well. But this man, as Rousseau suggested, will be accustomed to the imagination of danger, which always threatens to outreach any bravery.[15] Moreover, his assumptions of ever-present danger will have accustomed him to *compromise* with danger, to negotiation with the enemy. By contrast the innocent man, the man who has known nothing but love, will see in even the smallest danger, the slightest hint of death, an absolute harm, a mere nihil, a nonsense, and because he has known something absolutely prior to all fear, he will not now cease from loving, but go on loving by fearlessly embracing death. (This is why Tolkien's insertion of 'hobbits' into a heroic world is profound, and is profoundly Christian).[16] Hence only God, who experiences nothing of evil, who does not in any way suffer, acts without fear in the world, does good for the first time in the world. His yoke is easy, his burden is light; so he bears it, and we bear it.

It follows that to act morally is to act out of God's original intention of plenitude, and this is why the torah of the Old Testament (the least legal of all law codes) condemns not just human but animal shedding of blood – the shedding of the blood *of* animals and *by* animals – and treats death as an alien impurity.[17] Despite scarcity, despite our submission to the law which it imposes, we must act as *if* there were plenitude, and no death, since to believe is to believe that this is what really pertains, despite the fall. It is, of course, quite simply impossible to be a Christian and to suppose that death and suffering belong to God's original plan, or that the struggle of natural selection (which one doubts is even proven as a full account of evolution) is how creation *as creation* rather than thwarted creation genuinely comes about. To do so is to embrace a sickly masochistic faith, against the explicit words of scripture (and one notes here the co-belonging of 'kenotic' and evolutionary Christologies).

To believe in plenitude is to believe in the already commenced and yet-to-come restoration of Creation as Creation. Within this belief alone, as Nietzsche failed to perceive, one can cease to be 'moral'. This belief is belief in resurrection. As resurrection cancels death, and appears to render murder non-serious, it restores no moral order, but absolutely ruins the possibility of *any* moral order whatsoever. That is to say, any reactive moral order, which presupposes the absoluteness of death. For the Christian, murder is wrong, not because it removes something irreplaceable, but because it repeats the Satanic founding act of *instituting* death, or the very *possibility* of irreplaceability, and absolute loss. But in the resurrected order there need be no law even against such Satanism, because it is so manifestly senseless, because this possibility occurs to no one, because here the only law is that of *nature*, that of *life*, but specifically human life which consciously partakes of the creativity of God. Here, at last, in the Resurrection, there is only natural law (and in *this* sense I concur with Oliver O'Donovan).[18] For in the resurrected order, in the life of our vision of God in his final Christic manifestation, the occasion for the exercise of death-presupposing virtue (as Paul says) drops away, and only charity – gift and counter-gift – remain.

So far we have heard the notes of gift, plenitude and Resurrection. The latter sounds also the End of Sacrifice, since now at last it is fully moral to give ourselves sacrificially – as the only mode in the fallen order by which we can continue to give

– because we now have confidence that this does *not* cancel out our own existence. Christ goes to his death blindly, but *yet* in absolute trust of the father; we can give ourselves non-suicidally unto death, since we know that in this dying we also live. Resurrection in fact does not simply negate fallen death, but reinstates a fully human and natural death, namely the offering of ourselves back to God in recognition of our own absolute nullity and entire derivation from him. Whereas, in moral sacrifice, the parts are given up for the whole, passions for the intellect, and heroes for the city, in Christian sacrifice, as Kierkegaard says, the whole itself – the person and the city together – are *absurdly* given up, *not* for any higher gain, but for or *as* the receiving back of themselves as a gift from God which is same-yet-different,[19] since we only receive God as non-graspable, as always already in every moment different and so precisely *temporal*. Moral sacrifice is ended in the total sacrifice of the cross which is non-identical repetition, or absolute singularity of virtue (virtue as the performing of a unique role, a unique *consistency*, as anticipated by Cicero in *De Officiis*[20]).

Finally, and through all these other notes, there sounds the note of *confidence*. Whereas Augustine had discovered original sin to be pride and desire, Luther and then Kierkegaard claimed that the desire to command, desire to possess and prideful delight in domination of others all originate in a still more original *fear* that the unknown is not to be trusted, so requiring legal security in ourselves.[21] (However, it should be noted here that if one wishes to maintain, against Luther, the Catholic supremacy of charity, one should rather see fear as co-original with pride and concupiscence – for the priority of fear over the latter in Kierkegaard precisely correlates with a priority of faith over charity in the order of redemption). Hence for Luther, the first *virtue* is that of faith, just as Plato in the *Phaedo* suggested that the only way to cast out fear was not to resist it and be brave like heroic warriors but to know and contemplate the Good as something invulnerable to fear.[22] For all that Luther fails to see that faith is from the outset received and enacted charity or a *habitus*, he nonetheless and in a remarkable fashion shows how every good work is itself nothing but faith or confidence. The confident man, believing in plenitude, does not steal, and does not need to tell lies to protect himself. The confident man, trusting in God, is like the good husband who never needs to impress his wife with an exceptional work nor needs a manual of instruction[23] for marriage, but out of his confidence *improvises* exactly good and always non-identical good works all the time, *each* of these good works being of *equal* value – as every good is absolute, and to be good must belong to an entire, an infinite good without exception.[24] The Christian good man is simply for Luther an artist in being, trusting the perfect maker of all things. Essentially his message is that of Augustine: without the virtue of worship there can be no other virtue,[25] for worship gives everything back up to God, hangs onto nothing and so *disallows* any finite accumulation which will always engender conflict. Confident worship also knows that in offering it receives back, so here the temporal world is not denied, but its temporality is restored as gift and thereby rendered eternal. Only the vision and hope of heaven makes us socially and politically just on earth – and how is it, one wonders, that we have ever come to think otherwise?

So no, the Christian man is not a moral man, not a man of good *conscience*, who acts *with* what he *knows* of death, scarcity and duty to totalities. He has a bad conscience, but a good *confidence*: for he acts with what he does not know but has faith in. In absolute trust he gives up trying to be good, to sustain a right order of government within himself. The Romans that Paul wrote to did this already, but they still needed a letter from Paul – to hear what? Simply to hear the other, receive the other, and through the other receive the gratuitous God. Cease to be self-sufficient in the face of scarcity. Instead to be good as first receiving from the all-sufficiency of God, and acting excessively out of this excess.

These three virtues alone abide: faith, hope and charity, but the greatest of these is charity.

Notes

1 See E. P. Thompson, *Witness Against the Beast: William Blake and the Moral Law* (Cambridge University Press, Cambridge, 1993). Not to mention the fictions of Peter Ackroyd and Iain Sinclair. Thompson stresses that the English antinomians usually radicalized Lutheran justification by faith and did not, like Hogg's 'justified sinner', press Calvinist predestination to amoral conclusions.

2 Notebook poem not finally used for the *Songs of Experience*, cited in Thompson, p. 206.

3 See Charles Baudelaire 'Counterfeit money' and 'Beat up the Poor!' in *Paris Spleen*, trans. Louis Varèse (New Directions, New York, 1970), pp. 58–9 and 102–3.

4 See Friedrich Nietzsche, *Thus Spake Zarathustra*, trans. R. J. Hollingdale (Penguin, London, 1969), esp. pp. 95, also 97, 101, 136–8, 299.

5 Dietrich Bonhoeffer, *Ethics*, trans. Neville Horton Smith (SCM, London, 1963), p. 3. I am grateful to Linda Woodhead for reminding me of this.

6 On these twin themes, see Catherine Pickstock, 'Asyndeton: Syntax and Insanity', *Modern Theology*, 10, 4 (October 1994), pp. 321–41.

7 I owe this notion to Regina Schwartz, who develops it in her forthcoming book, *The Curse of Cain: The Violent Legacy of Monotheism* (Chicago University Press, Chicago, 1997).

8 Martin Luther, 'Treatise on Good Works' in *Luther's Works*, vol. 44, ed. James Atkinson, pp. 109, 3.

9 Ibid. See also 'Lectures on Galatians' in vol. 26, ed. Jaroslav Pelikan, pp. 158–63.

10 *Thus Spake Zarathustra* 44–45, 77, 94, 99–101.

11 Nietzsche, *Zarathustra*, 44, 60, 87, 97–9.

12 Ibid., 129–30.

13 See Jean-Michel Rabaté and Michael Wetzel, eds, *L'Ethique du Don: Jacques Derrida et la Pensée du Don* (Métailié-Transition, Paris, 1992); Jacques Derrida, *Given Time: 1. Counterfeit Money*, trans. Peggy Kamuf (Chicago University Press, Chicago, 1994). However, my 'gift ethic' is not Derrida's, which is first (admittedly) unrealizable and second (in my view) still reducible to a reactive 'ethic of duty'. For my construal of the debate on the gift see John Milbank, 'Can a Gift be Given', *Modern Theology*, 2, 1 (January 1995), pp. 119–61.

14 Luther, 'Galatians', p. 167; 'Treatise on Good Works', p. 26.

15 Jean-Jacques Rousseau, *Émile*, trans. Barbara Foxley (Dent, London, 1974), p. 22.

16 See, especially, the dying Thorin's eulogy of Bilbo: J. R. R. Tolkien, *The Hobbit* (G. Allen & Unwin, London, 1990), p. 258: Hobbits, he finally realizes, are both brave and cunning *because* they prize naive festivity above the dwarfish interest in accumulation and preservation.

17 See Robert Murray, *The Cosmic Covenant* (Sheed and Ward, London, 1992).

18 See Oliver O'Donovan, *Resurrection and the Moral Order* (IVF Press, London, 1989).

19 Søren Kierkegaard, *Fear and Trembling*, trans. H. and E. Hong (Princeton University Press, Princeton, 1988).

20 Cicero, *On Duties*, I, 107, 110–11, 114–17.

21 Søren Kierkegaard, *The Concept of Anxiety*, trans. H. and E. Hong (Princeton University Press, Princeton, 1992).

22 *Phaedo*, 68D–69C: Socrates: 'all except philosophers are brave through fear . . . My dear Simmias, I suspect that this is not the right way to purchase virtue, by exchanging pleasures for pleasures, and pains for pains and fear for fear . . . as if they were coins'. Notice that Plato already links 'morality' with *capitalization* (and that Derrida's reading of Plato can take no account of this).

23 This is not to say that there cannot be 'exemplary' treatments of the complexity of non-reactive charity. As the Lutheran examples show, (and Augustine and Aquinas also stressed) under faith and charity one can speak again of diverse virtues – truthfulness, fidelity, steadfastness and so forth – yet their character is transformed. For example in charity there is an *essential* patience which respects our ontological distance from God, a distance we rejoice in as it alone gives God to us. Hence the patience of faith is *not* in a sulk, is not putting up with anything. However, it is precisely *this* patience which, in the fallen world, can put up with *everything*. (I am grateful to Oliver O'Donovan for asking me to clarify this point.)

24 Luther, 'Treatise on Good Works', pp. 26–7.

25 Augustine *Civitas Dei*, XIX 4, 21.

10
The Poverty of Niebuhrianism

In this chapter I shall be attempting to criticize the influential notion of 'Christian realism' as derived from the writings of the American theologian, Reinhold Niebuhr. I shall suggest that the 'realities' to which it appeals are not the realities of history, nor the realities of which Christian theology speaks, but simply things generated by its own assumptions, its own language and rhetoric. It will emerge that 'Christian realism' has a tendency to become the opposite of what it claims to be – that its pessimism turns into over-optimism, its pragmatism into idealism, its anti-liberalism into liberalism, its confidence in God into confidence in humanity. At the end of the paper I shall consider, by contrast, the nature of a genuine Christian realism.

By 'realism', 'Niebuhrians' seem usually to have three things in mind. First of all, there is the notion that there are non-negotiable 'limits to human ethical possibilities', second, an invocation of the doctrine of original sin, and third there is the insistence that any Christian consideration of ethics, and in particular social and political ethics, must be 'practical' in character. I shall now deal with these three aspects in turn.

1 Limits to Ethical Possibilities

For many years the insistence that there are bounds to human moral improvement has been a popular theme on the political right, although this emphasis is not necessarily allied to conservatism. It is important to be reminded that the Niebuhr of *Moral Man and Immoral Society* castigated the American middle class, recommended a programme of civil disobedience by American blacks, expressed admiration for Gandhi, defended the notion of class struggle, and gave a qualified approval

to socialist revolution in certain circumstances.[1] Whereas today's Niebuhrian conservative thinks primarily of the intrinsic tendency to evil in individuals, and the
consequent need for 'law and order', the original Niebuhr was much more worried
(in the spirit of Lord Acton) by the corruption that always goes with the exercise of
power. 'Realism' for Niebuhr in this context was to realize that tyrannies and
injustices upheld by force could only be resisted in the same kind. Politically,
'realism' cuts both ways.

The substantive analyses of political and social processes in *Moral Man and
Immoral Society* are impressive. This is for two reasons. First, Niebuhr adduced a
great wealth of empirical examples, which give the lie to Christian liberal fallacies
about achieving political change solely through an exercise of personal goodwill and
increase in rational education. Second, beyond this merely empirical level, Niebuhr
borrowed some elements of a Marxist analysis which permitted him to show,
against the liberals, that the American constitution is not a neutral norm guaranteeing liberty and justice for all, but is itself ultimately an instrument of the dominant
powers in American society. At this stage of his career, Niebuhr's pessimism had
a basis not just in empirical analysis, nor solely in metaphysics, but in the view
that there is at work in history certain long-term cultural tendencies which are
at present causing social conditions to deteriorate. This impulse produces the
structural causes of decline and fragmentation – increased technologization, and
increased division and appropriation of labour. So one could say that in the thought
of the early Niebuhr there was present a genuine realism in the philosophic sense:
he claimed that certain *objective* and *regular* causal processes were at work in the
human world, even if these were ultimately the contingent upshot of certain human
historical choices. I am not here concerned with the question of whether these
claims were true or verifiable, simply with the fact that they were claims of a clearly
'realist' kind.

When Niebuhr abandoned the Marxist element in his thought he abandoned
also this sort of realism. He did not adopt an alternative explanatory scheme which
would make equally strong claims about socio-economic processes. Thus his later
social analyses appear vaguer and less cogent. He tended to refer in a loose way,
based on sketchy empirical observation, to various sorts of powerful interest groups
and the need to maintain a balance between them, without any attempt to give a
systematic account of the nature and types of these groups. Nor did he note the
relative cultural domination exerted by some groups as against others.

But throughout his writings Niebuhr also makes claims about 'reality' that are of
a fundamentally different sort. Here I wish to dispute the notion that these claims
truly deserve the label 'realist'. Even the early Niebuhr was not content with
pointing out the way in which our given historical circumstances limit the chances
we have of behaving ethically. If this were all he meant by 'Christian realism', I
would have no quarrel with him. Nor is the issue to do with the 'inescapability of
the tragic'. I fully accept the view that the nature of our present historical condition

is such that we are faced with tragic dilemmas in which it is impossible to avoid some complicity in evil (see chapter 1, 'A Critique of the Theology of Right', above). What I do quarrel with is the attempt to ground these claims, first, in certain notions about 'human nature', and second in a particular version of the theology of original sin.

In Moral Man and Immoral Society Niebuhr added to his empirical and historical observation, theories about the limits to ethical behaviour which are built into human nature, as part of a created condition which is thought of as setting the bounds for all possible history. These restrictions consist in the limitations of human intelligence and human imagination, and also in the nature of group identity.

The first thing to be said about the notion that human finitude is an impassable barrier to the actualizing of the good life in the human world, is that it is Stoic in character. The later Niebuhr attempts a much more theological analysis of the limits of morality in terms of original sin, but does not abandon this Stoic dimension. In chapter 5 of *An Interpretation of Christian Ethics*,[2] Niebuhr attributes to he Stoics the discovery of natural law as the view that life in its 'essence' ideally involves much more than is possible in our concrete historical existence; our actual lives must be conformed to this essence as far as possible. It is this understanding of natural law to which Niebuhr *himself* adheres.

This point appears to be fatally overlooked by many of Niebuhr's readers. The reason for this, I think, is that in the chapter referred to, Niebuhr is offering a critique of the political stance of 'Christian orthodoxy', which he considers to be based, precisely, on the Stoic natural law. However, Niebuhr's criticisms are quite restricted and precise. There has, he thinks, been too much concentration in Christian tradition on the *Ius Gentium*, (the 'law of nations'), that part of the natural law which dealt with the restricted embodiment of absolute ideals in particular traditions and circumstances, rather than the *Ius Naturale* (natural law) proper, which actually defines those ideals.

This has resulted, says Niebuhr in the debasement of the *Ius Gentium* to *mere* custom and expediency. Christianity is seen to have tended to set impossible *personal* perfectionism over against a dangerously exaggerated *political* pessimism. Occasionally, as in Luther's exhortation to the peasants, the perfectionism is hypocritically intruded into the political sphere. The essence of the latter is seen to consist in a necessity for violent coercion that results from the fall; yet often this imperfect power has been wrongly treated as sacred, as the direct presence of a divine created order.

Readers are often so encouraged by this apparent repudiation of a 'two-kingdoms' political theology, that they fail to notice that the basic Stoic pattern is still affirmed by Niebuhr himself. The fundamental assumption here is that the gospel, which teaches 'an ideal of love' only, is thereby unable to generate a political, or *even* a social ethic. 'For this reason', says Niebuhr, 'Christianity really

had no social ethic until it appropriated the Stoic ethic'.[3] Christian love – a vision
of ideal aspirations – is then assimilated by Niebuhr to the absolute principles of
Stoic natural law, although it is supposed to attain to a higher grasp of such
principles. What the gospel lacked, and what Stoicism supplied, was a grasp of *Ius
Gentium*, or 'the most logical modification and application of the ideal in a world in
which life is in conflict with life'.[4] However, according to Niebuhr, the perfectionist
character of Christianity has tended to prevent a rational commerce between the
ideal and the real, a commerce which, if now restored, would allow the higher ideal
essence of Christianity to 'come through' to the social and political realm.

Admirers of Niebuhr are consequently able to affirm that he does, after all,
permit a Christian influence in the political sphere for the exercise of *agape*. But he
does so only in the crassest possible manner. Love is inherently to do with the ideal
rather than the actual, and with individual aspiration rather than social cohesion.[5]
Liberty, and the autonomy of the individual, belong to the absolute demand of love,
but social equality does not. Love has to be mediated to the social realm by the
intervention of a purely instrumental reasoning which is able to deduce that freedom can only become real in society as a result of our adopting an *abstract* principle
of equality. It is here that Niebuhr reveals his essential liberalism: in the first place
he endorses the rationalism of the Enlightenment as the only thing that can make
Christian principles at all politically effective; in the second place equality or equity
is not seen as a goal of general human fulfilment, but merely as an intellectual
device needed to regulate a sphere of permanent and insoluble conflict. Niebuhr
says 'there is no final principle of arbitration between conflicting human interests
except that which equates the worth of competing individuals'.[6] This sounds like
the mere 'equality before the law' which liberalism upholds – a stance of neutrality
in the face of rival claims which cannot be settled in terms of genuine equity.

The basic focus of Stoic ethics is on the encounter between an absolute spiritual
ideal and a 'chaotic' finite world which it does its best to regulate. This morally
negative rating of nature and finitude is fully taken over by Niebuhr: 'the forces of
nature are in conflict with the necessities of man as spirit';[7] 'in every human
situation and relationship there is an ideal possibility, and there are given facts of
human nature, historic and fortuitous inequalities, geographic and other natural
divisive forces, contingent and accidental circumstances:[8] '[inequalities] may be,
and usually are, caused by forces of nature and history which an intelligent control
of social life can greatly restrict and sometimes completely overcome'.[9] Again the
liberalism emerges: there is an original natural imperfection which can be gradually, instrumentally, remedied. This is just the same as Kant's hope that politics
might be so pragmatically arranged as to harmonize 'automatically' with the moral
demands of the individual conscience, which in themselves belong purely to a
realm of disembodied rational spirits.

Niebuhr, as we have seen, is surprisingly candid in his opinion that Christianity
to be socially effective required to be supplemented by Stoic natural law. But is not
this concession, one may ask, precisely an admission of paganism? St Augustine in

the *Civitas Dei* would seem to confirm this when he contrasts pagan virtue, which is simply (like Niebuhr's social ethic) an exercise in 'damage limitation' that takes for granted an *original conflict* which has to be contained, and Christian virtue, which is able to root out the very source of evil because it takes for granted *original created goodness*.[10] Niebuhr contrasts love with law by saying that the latter necessarily involves a response to already existing disorder; but he compromises himself with paganism by suggesting that this somehow makes love ineffective at the level of *being*, at least within any finite order.

In his contribution to *The Cross and the Bomb* (a collection of essays published during the cold-war era), the Anglican Bishop Richard Harries effectively took over Niebuhr's Stoicism and correctly perceived that it goes very nicely with a response to the problem of evil like that of John Hick, a response stressing the element of immaturity or ignorance in our 'fallen' state, rather than tragedy or betrayal. So Niebuhr declares: 'That we have only a limited capacity to take into account the interests of others is not the sign of some dramatic fall from grace, but an indication of our immaturity'[11] and again, 'we are infants struggling through to maturity rather than perfect beings thrown out of paradise'.[12]

It is extremely curious that such statements should be envisaged as part of an outlook which 'takes sin seriously'. In fact, if we have decided that failures of the intelligence and failures of the imagination with respect to moral behaviour are to be ascribed to 'natural limitations', much of the sting can be taken out of human culpability, and even the most horrendous sins can plausibly be seen as part of an educative process. Once we have adopted Niebuhr's Stoic assumption that there are 'natural barriers', there are very few errors which they may not be used to explain. It is, I think, the subtle tendency of this sort of thinking which caused Harries to underestimate the seriousness and danger of the *sin* of possessing nuclear weapons. If we secretly imagine that 'immaturity' is the original and dominant element in human sinfulness (an idea almost ludicrously far removed from the gospels), then we may well come to imagine that the nuclear threat is just this immaturity writ technologically large, and that it can be *contained* by a series of threatened parental punishments in the shape of deterrence systems which are there to remind us of the consequences of our own actions.

This is in fact how Harries interpreted the nuclear reality. Not only is deterrence implausibly assimilated to the rule of international law; this human 'parenting' is then underwritten by a *divine* parental surveillance. Harries appeared to subscribe to an eighteenth-century political theology in which God's moral government of the universe is partially administered through human laws, and was rigorously consistent in his conclusion that even nuclear weapons are part of God's providential government, that even here, to quote his words, 'there must be divine mercy as well as divine severity'.[13]

The notion that the finitude of our understandings and imaginations constitute inherent limits on the possibility of ethical behaviour, a notion which secretly encourages *optimism* in both Niebuhr and Harries, is not as plausible as might appear. One can imagine a perfect community in which limited understandings and imaginations keep pace with an equally limited and particular life of virtue. This tends to show that the hypothesis of 'natural limits' to ethics outside ethics is dubious, because while we can think of many empirical instances where failure of intelligence or imagination has inhibited a person's moral vision, it is equally true that in any given instance it is always possible to connect this failure with moral inadequacy either in the particular life of the person herself, or in the lives of others. To say, 'but the intention was good, its implications were simply not seen or foreseen' is inadequate, since moral insight *is* a matter of expanded understanding, even of prophetic foresight (where time reveals 'unintended' consequences which *implicitly* follow from a certain decision, rather than from its perverse 'mistaking' by others, then one has to say, these consequences were *after all* logically intended by an intention of inadequate scope of projection. And even the distinction between 'implicit tendency' and 'perversion by others' is by no means absolute, and is rather a matter of always difficult discrimination: see chapter 5, 'A Christological Poetics' above).

Let me clarify these points a little. There are two sets of confusions here. The first has to do with the fact that Niebuhr accords the imagination a relatively humble and instrumental role. It is seen as essentially to do with a capacity for empathy with other persons and situations; it extends our range of awareness, but it is not, in itself, a power to evaluate or judge. For Niebuhr, imagination is outside the realm of ethical intuition, and the same goes for the exercise of 'understanding'.[14] He has, therefore, no idea of a discursive 'practical reason' in the Aristotelian sense, and no idea of ethical action as linked to 'expanding vision', a process in which one's apprehension of the world is inherently evaluative, and rational assessments are inseparable from the ordering of one's desires. But if we do see the relevance of 'imagination' to ethics in this way, then it is clear that limited vision cannot be finally divorced from culpability. The extreme and decisive examples here are at the socio-cultural level. Some cultures fail to accord infants, or social inferiors, or strangers, a full status of humanity. The individual in such societies is the prisoner of these classifications; he can only decide and act ethically within the way of 'arranging', picturing and speaking of the world that his society provides him with in its language and other symbolic systems. As an individual therefore, his moral capacity is extra-ethically constrained (see again, chapter 5, 'A Christological Poetics'). Yet this does not exclude the possibility that one may condemn an entire culture as lacking in vision; certainly individuals are bound within the scripts their culture writes for them, but these scripts themselves are ways of organizing and channelling human desire – they are corporate self-limitations of the will to the good. Presumably, the heart of 'original sin' is the reality of living inside such a distorted and limited 'script' at all levels of our existence.

The second set of confusions has to do with the conception of growth. Both Niebuhr and Harries are trapped by a primitive, evolutionary picture of how things are. In analogy with the Stoic notion of natural law as the restraining of original chaos, this equates development with the gradual overcoming of evil. Just as Augustine exposed the Stoic fallacy, so this evolutionary fallacy was partly exposed by Irenaeus, and more decisively by Gregory of Nyssa. These Greek fathers made the revolutionary discovery that growth might itself belong to the realm of perfection in that it arises not from a progress out of disorder, but from a permanent tension between the uncreated infinity of God and our created finitude. Gregory's notion of *epectasis*, 'straining forward' to God, reveals that perfection for finite beings is development; but it breaks with the pagan Greek assumption that development is just a smooth path away from imperfection towards an optional condition of balanced virtue.

It is for this reason that Christian ethics does not confuse a limited life of virtue with the restrictions of sin, and thereby does not despise the primitive or immature. The limitation of vision that results from finding yourself inside the distortion of a perverse cultural 'script' is not at all the same (or not *necessarily* the same) as the limited vision of childhood, or of the primitive tribe. Here there is a limited range for the exercise of virtue, yet this range may be perfectly defined and be absolutely 'in the direction' of the final truth. Christianity *does* acknowledge 'a cloistered virtue', because Christian virtue is primarily the spontaneous life of creative charity, not the heroic defence of the city walls, nor the gradual sorting out of the mysterious ambiguities of our early years (see the previous chapter, 'Can Morality be Christian?'). Presumably the reason Christians are to 'become like children' is that the childish sense of dependence contains a more telling clue to the way things ultimately are than the adult fantasy of having 'achieved' maturity by the 'conquest' of infantile aberrations.

It is clear then, that Niebuhr's belief that limited imagination and understanding constitute permanent barriers to ethical realization is unwarranted, and in fact ignores the specifically Christian exploration of reality. The belief is clearly traceable to the assumptions of his Stoic idealism,[15] and especially the view that the word 'moral' is not primarily spoken of acts, but of ideals which are apprehended first and foremost by the individual conscience. Of course, if one identifies moral perfection with an infinite realization that would correspond to the infinite character of the intuited ideal, then moral perfection is not possible for finite persons. Similarly, if one supposes that morality is first and foremost a matter of immediate individual intuition, then it follows that a supposedly less perfect grasp of external reality (seen always as 'remote' from us) will necessarily inhibit the practical realizing of prior ideals.

The same individualist assumptions govern Niebuhr's ideas about groups – the third 'natural' factor which is supposed to put a limitation upon ethical realization. He fails to see that *human relatedness* is the primary context of morality. It is especially in the social domain that we realize the inadequacy of restricting understanding and imagination to the role of purveying information about other people, or empathizing with their concerns. Rather, as we reflect on what it is to be historically and culturally situated, we find that imagination and understanding work more fundamentally in the shaping of language to construct social bonds and the proposing of a vision for human beings to share. In so far as rationally and imaginatively established linguistic 'plots' can be said to circumscribe a particular human *ethos*, it makes little sense to think of ethics as somehow 'limited' by the conditions of human social life. In Niebuhr's social narrative, love can only be present as heroic individual self-sacrifice. It is a *secondary* intrusion upon a pattern fundamentally governed by pure power relations. Thus the more original drama of love as mutuality is here relegated to the domain of purely 'natural' (familial) and therefore ambiguous, relationships.

Some commentators have understood Niebuhr's stress on the place of group solidarity in social life to be a mitigation of his basic individualism. This is not really the case. It is true that Niebuhr finds a place for 'the organic unities of family, race and nation'.[16] However, this originally communal aspect of culture is seen as precisely to do with what is natural, given and instinctive, not with what is rational and imaginative. It is an aspect that 'cannot be eliminated' because it belongs to our finitude, and the attempt to do so would be 'demonic';[17] however it has no *positive* value as regards morality. So, for example: 'From the standpoint of certain rational and spiritual aspirations of the human spirit the differences between the sexes are irrational and illogical', yet the social exercise of reason must reckon with 'Biological facts' which 'have determined motherhood to be a more absorbing vocation than the avocation of fatherhood'.[18]

Moreover, Niebuhr's idea of organic unities is a *pluralist* one in the sense that it envisages different, *competing* natural units. This is simply liberalism 'to a higher power' in which groups are thought to multiply and concentrate individual egotism. There is no route, (as say in a more 'mediaevalist' model of pluralism like that of the pre-war Maritain) from particular to universal loyalty, because the latter descends, like a *deus ex machina*, from the heaven of reason:

> Nature, history and traditions create communities and establish loyalties and senti-
> ments which are *bound* (my italics) to be in conflict with the moral, rational and
> inclusive communities and loyalties which human reason can project. Since these
> narrower loyalties result in conflict and anarchy, they must be constantly subject to
> criticism.[19]

All Niebuhr is doing here is giving an ideological picture based on the constant American story in which successive waves of immigrant groups, organized 'organically' within, meet in competition with each other, and also confront the 'enlightenment' authority of the state with its 'neutral' commitment to a regulation of individual and group competition. Niebuhr increasingly interprets this incoherent *mélange* as (at least potentially) an ideal synthesis of the irrationally organic with the rationally individualist.

Thus Niebuhr's finding of a place for organic groups does not alter the fact that he grounds political collectivities on the contract model, which imagines social life as a coming together of individuals who already in isolation possess intelligence, imagination and morality. To acquire these, they must have started to struggle free of their original organic context. It is this model, plus the Stoic ethics, which permits the classic antithesis of 'moral man' and 'immoral society'. Of course Niebuhr is right to point to the collective selfishness of the political nation. But Niebuhr fails to note that this arises not just from atavism, but also from the moral character of the political entity – namely that it is a whole which purports to serve the benefit of its human parts. Jacques Maritain, Niebuhr's French contemporary, exhibits a much more genuine spirit of realism when he says that politics is not a sphere set over against ethics, but a *special sphere of ethics*, with its own specific and particular virtues and goals.[20]

Moreover, it is not enough to relate the especially dangerous selfishness of modern nation-states simply to the inherent nature of groups. It is clear that it has to do rather with the contingent, historical growth of absolute sovereignty. Likewise the selfishness of corporations and trade unions is to be related to the market economy. In older societies where there was an organic hierarchy of inter-locking groupings, 'group selfishness' simply could not have made the *same* kind of sense.

If Niebuhr's claim that the ontology of groups presents an insuperable barrier to ethical perfection is simply the expression of liberal individualism, then it is equally another encouragement to liberal optimism. Whereas the political theorists of antiquity correctly realized that politics was to do with power exercised (and, we can now add, constructed) through language, or with rhetoric, Niebuhr sets up a facile dualism of power over against persuasion. The concept of political power is thereby reduced, as for Hobbes, to mere mechanical cause and effect on the model of Cartesian physics. So Niebuhr thinks of an original 'naked' political power ensuring political compliance, which is gradually commuted and concealed in the course of historical development. But the original political power is *not* a 'naked' power. Political power is always already a power mediated in a language which ruler and ruled have in common; and for this reason it always takes the form of a claim to legitimacy, even where this claim is mostly a coercive concealing of its real arbitrary character. Most political control occurs in an area that falls between Niebuhr's poles of 'pure force' and 'pure persuasion', because it involves a kind of persuasion in which spokespersons for particular interests are able to delude people into imagining that these are identical with the common good. Yet the necessity of this appeal to the common good marks the inescapably ethical character of politics.

If, however, like Niebuhr, one imagines that politics is basically technology, a matter of the manipulation of physical forces, then this, of course, engenders an unwarranted optimism. In *Moral Man and Immoral Society* Niebuhr claims that this more scientific attitude to society as supposedly exemplified by Marx, holds out the best hope for human improvement. It is simply a matter of ensuring that well-disposed, altruistic, individuals get more involved with the dirty and technical business of government. Because Niebuhr thinks of moral government not as 'habit' or disposition, but as the acknowledgement of a transcendent ideal, there is for him (and increasingly so in the later works) no real danger that this can be interfered with by involvement with the existential demands of power and compromise (the moral dangers are all back in the forsaken cloister). With the right people in charge there is a good chance that the worst effects of group selfishness can be substantially mitigated by better manipulation of the power structure.[21] As we have seen, this is an essentially Kantian or Stoic political vision.

It is true that in the later Niebuhr the optimism may be more muted. But this is only a change in attitude, not in basic ideas. Thus he still places his main confidence in the balancing of different interest groups within the Western democratic system. The same faith in technological and organizational control leads him to advocate a nuclear balance based on a limited number of weapons and a 'no first use' agreement.[22] This was a position favoured by many Christian multilateralists during the cold-war era. Yet this notion that there could ever be any stability in the deterrence systems depended upon the totally non-realist ignoring of the fact that one can never guarantee the working of such technical devices as 'no first use' in a situation of basic enmity, the only situation that sustains nuclear weapons in being. It was because there was already, in a certain sense, a war between America and Russia, that one could never produce any purely promissory arrangement, however organizationally safeguarded, that would have cancelled out the possibility of one or other side acting on the basis of unwarranted suspicion, or taking a calculated risk in order to impair the global position of the adversary.

The trouble about questions like 'Could Christians find deterrence morally acceptable if allied to a no first use agreement?' is that they are not really questions about the actual world at all, and therefore do not deal with *genuine* possibilities. Thus the question as falsely posed in the abstract is already imbued with the assumption that such a peculiar conjuncture is truly imaginable; and this in itself tends to shape our judgement in advance. It is as if one was suddenly not talking about a United States which had systematically built up a nuclear arsenal as part of its programme of imperial expansion, nor about a Soviet Union which had done the same in the interests of defending its existing empire. But it is these political *realities* that were the *real* ethical problems. Hence the cold war only finally came to an end (at least in its ideological form) when one of these potential realities – as it happened the Soviet Union – was subject to internal critique and internal collapse. But so long as these two political realities remained in existence, there was not the slightest reason to suppose that multilateralism was the more 'realistic' option.

To the contrary, devices for limiting deterrence like 'no first use' are unrealistic and inconceivable because the nuclear situation is subject to a double tension: the 'rational' political ambitions of the protagonists persist to the brink of war, still attempting to manipulate all the irrationalities of the nuclear threat, and inversely, the devising of nuclear strategies already marks an entry into the game of war, which, as Clausewitz so decisively demonstrated, can only be successfully played as the acceptance of risk and chance.[23] Niebuhrian 'realism' is unable to envisage the long-term tendency in human affairs not to the gradual containment of conflict, but to its final and catastrophic extension.

2 The Nature of Original Sin

In his work *The Nature and Destiny of Man*, Niebuhr gives a different, more theological account of the limits to ethical behaviour in terms of the concept of original sin.[24] Here he goes some way towards correcting the defects I have described.

This is because, once Niebuhr starts to think more theologically, the limits are located not in a pre-human nature but in human will, not in our finite being as such, but in a faulty response to it, as when we make our wants the measure of reality. Moreover, by asserting that the defect lies in the *will*, which is to do with open possibility, Niebuhr no longer seeks to ground the historical *fact* of human imperfection on speculations about an ahistorical human nature. He recognizes that the notion of an imperfection of the will is inherently paradoxical, because while we recognize it as true that we are never going to will all that we ought, nonetheless we are always able to say in retrospect, with reference to any particular act or omission, 'well, I could have done better'. Niebuhr further sees that the delusion inherent in the latter claim is not to do with some quasi-biological inherited taint, but with the fact that we do not 'begin again' every time we are faced with a moral choice, but rather act as the person we have become as the result of past actions. It is interesting to note that sometimes when Niebuhr is thinking in more theological terms he implicitly moves from a Stoic model to this perspective which owes more to Aristotle. Nothing could be more in keeping with an 'ethics of virtue' than the following statement: 'There is, in other words, less freedom in the actual sin, and more responsibility for the bias towards sin (original sin) than moralistic interpretations can understand.'[25]

However, Niebuhr betrays his own best intuitions. Having grasped original sin as a historical vicious circle of character and action, he confines this to the biographies of individuals. Stoic assumptions take over once again. When Niebuhr asks how the taint in the individual will first arose, he alludes to some sort of pre-human fall which directly affects the life of every human being. The biblically validated notion that our characters are formed and inhibited by our cultural ancestry plays no serious role in Niebuhr's thought. Thus despite his excellent analysis of how the will works, Niebuhr ends up offering original sin as an *alternative* to historical explanations of the deep-rootedness of human evil. This amounts to trying to avoid recognizing at the cultural level, the paradox grasped at the individual level. Here also, all sins have to be referred to past sins, but the paradox appears in its full and ultimate form as the apparent impossibility of positing a 'first sin'. The book of Genesis preserves this paradox by imagining a mythical realm before, yet also at the beginning of human history. It conveys both that human fallenness consists in a succession of historical actions (which include the later sin prior to the flood, and the building of the tower of Babel), and that the initiation of this process involved exclusion from a created realm which we can never return to, nor even locate, in apprehensible space and time. Niebuhr is at fault in wanting to see lost paradise in an immediate relation to every time and place, thereby underrating the role of historical legacy. Harries is even more at fault (though he errs rather in the opposite direction) in denying the once-and-for-all fall from grace which is the absolute *sine qua non of* Christian ethics and which alone permits a recognition of how history seems driven in the direction of catastrophe. As regards the fall, we cannot possibly *substitute* Darwin's narrative for our mythology; only the unwise would search for paradise among the primaeval swamps, whose weirdly monstrous inhabitants betray to faith their non-belonging to the primarily intended created order.

I pose this issue because it raises most acutely the question of Christian realism. For the Christian, a realistic apprehension of the world does not consist in factual survey and surmise, but in an evaluative reading of its signs as *clues to ultimate meanings and causes.* Thus the world is construed as gift and promise, and we construct the narrative picture of a Creator God. But also the world is construed as in some way already, before any traceable historical action, involved in a refusal or wrong apprehension of this gift; it is a world of death as well as life (only masochism can imagine that death is part of the primordial Creation).[26] So we construct the narrative of the fall. In either case, we know the narrative form to be woefully inadequate, but in either case also this form is seen to be indispensable to our doctrine and ontology and, in either case again, to mean what we want to mean, we must uphold its reference to reality – a real Creation, a real loss.

Thus the Christian grasp of reality *right from the start* is utterly at variance with anything the world supposes to be 'realistic'. This is why it is so absurd deliberately to import the world's realism into the sphere of Christian ethics as if, when it came to the practical crunch, we could set our entire religious vision to one side. In Christian terms, it is the world that will never understand the world aright.

One further point must be made about the dire seriousness of Harries's error. The view of the world which tells us that morality is a rational struggle out of immaturity may be relatively benign, when not conjoined with any view of existence overall. But when this is incorporated into the theological struggle with the problem of evil, then we get those monstrous pictures of God, and the absolute relativizations of finite evils (including death) which are so entirely destructive of human morality. Darwinian Anglicanism can only assume an essentially sinister form.

Yet the recourse to evolution, and the evils of finitude and immaturity, often strangely and inconsistently co-exists, within 'Christian realism', with an appeal to original sin which is vague as to its origins, but like Niebuhr, appears to think of it as standing in some immediate, but non-historical relation to every individual. The tendency to call in 'original sin' as an explanatory *diabolus* actually reduces the significance of particular, empirical sins. So we find that conservative politicians appeal to original sin as an alibi for their actions. The idea of original sin as individual and ahistorical here merges with the notion of government as a technical manipulation of chaotic human forces. Thus organized political power is strangely seen as itself *immune* from this taint, and it is absurdly imagined that it can keep the effects of this taint 'under control'. This is precisely *not* to have a doctrine of original sin. One of the clearest messages of the New Testament is that this mere legal 'containment' is ultimately futile because the sinful legacy can resurface, with more powerful aids, exactly at the point where the good will considers that it is in command.

It is a failure to grasp this understanding which leads to an over-estimation of the ultimate historical importance of existing political systems in the western world. This seems to be especially the case when we consider that the liberal ideologies which they represent in effect reduce legal rule to precisely those merely negative, containing capacities, of which the New Testament is so suspicious.

3 The Workings of Practical Reason

I want now to consider the third claim of 'Christian realism', namely that it is concerned with what is practicable. From the foregoing it will already be seen that Niebuhr does not simply appeal to considerations of an objective, unproblematically 'practical' nature. Rather he constructs a certain notion of the practical through a series of dualisms between individual and public, fact and value, ideal and consequence, which are baseless except as transcriptions of the working values of modern Western society. Because Niebuhr thinks of ethics in terms of private assent to the intrinsic goodness of certain ideals of action – the realm of the spirit – he thinks of the external, historical world as the merely physical sphere of cause and effect. His social ethics is then a mixture of disinterested idealism and pessimistic pragmatism. The private realm of ideal obligation and the public realm of cause and effect only interact at certain points – namely the moments of ethical decision.

In another article in *The Cross and the Bomb* which was written by Gerard Hughes, we can see the extreme results of this fact-value dualism with respect to the nuclear debate.[27] Hughes effectively argued for the position that there are actually no ethical disagreements in cases where the *grounds* for disagreement are truly ethical. He clearly accepted Kant's view that when it comes to ethical understanding we are all on equal terms, and all equally capable of recognizing the moral rightness or wrongness attached to certain 'types of action' described in simplified, idealized fashion. Real disagreements only arise concerning the classification of real concrete actions, and these are to be decided according to a merely empirical assessment of the likely consequences of such actions. Hughes actually used the term 'manifold of human behaviour'[28] as if in looking at human society we were really confronted with the kind of mass of isolated bits of information which Kant believed was the prelude to the work of rational (and private) schematisation.

Thus Hughes blandly assumed that we are all agreed on the one surviving moral issue, namely 'is nuclear war right or wrong?', and calmly announced, as if it were the most uncontroversial thing in the world, that the questions 'has the nuclear deterrent prevented war?', 'would unilateral disarmament reduce tension?', 'would any war between East and West turn into nuclear war?' and, most significantly of all, 'what kind of action is the present possession of a nuclear deterrent?', are all purely *empirical* questions into which moral judgement does not enter.[29] This is, of course, precisely to reject the Aristotelian–Thomist understanding of ethics as the exercise of the practical intelligence – as the exercise of understanding *in* willed action; and so one can only protest when Hughes presents this 'ethic of consequences' as meeting the traditional Catholic demand that ethics should be a 'practical science' (as if this meant, including a 'practical *bit*').[30]

Hughes failed to see that his thought embodies a fundamental collusion between the viewpoints of an ethics of obligation on the one hand, and a consequentialist ethics on the other – a collusion that is characteristic of post-Kantian Christian ethics, and that is very well exemplified in the thought of Reinhold Niebuhr.

Once one realizes this, then the issue becomes no longer, as Hughes thinks, the questionability of the act–consequence distinction, but rather the questionability of the dichotomy between principle and consequence. If we revert to the traditional Augustinian–Thomist, pre-enlightenment ethics and recover a genuine notion of an ethical *end*, a goal and purpose, then this dichotomy is transcended. In the true notion of an 'end', we can recognize that certain actions have a tendency to produce certain results which can only be understood in terms that are simultaneously descriptive and evaluative – as when we say, for example, that someone has satisfactorily performed their task as a teacher. On analogy with this one can say that the deterrence system is wrong, because inherently, *as a matter of intentional conduct*, it tends towards the destruction of human trust and security, and to an encouragement of aggression and indifference in individuals, and ultimately towards the destruction of physical well-being, which is a good in itself and the foundation of all other human good. I suggest that this effectively spells out what ordinary people generally mean when they say that nuclear weapons are 'wrong'.

Once this principle/consequence dualism is overcome, then one can see why the act–consequence distinction must be maintained. For the belief that this distinction is *impossible* to make depends upon the disguising of intentions which is involved in the erecting of dualisms of fact and value, content and structure, in our reflection on our behaviour. To have an intention is at once to make a disposition of the will, *and* to engage with the world in such a way that one's action objectively tends in a certain direction. To prescind from either of these aspects is to lose the specific character of 'intending' itself, as a *moral* thing. Hughes's argument means that he must inevitably so break up the notion of 'intentionality' that, on the one hand, he makes it signify a mere effort of the will, by which we can subjectively and 'internally' re-define the character of any of our actions; and, on the other hand, he uses it for the mere tendency of our actions in terms of amoral and empirical processes of cause and effect. On the first account, the systematic construction of apocalyptic weapons can be interpreted as 'really' part of an intention towards world peace; on the second, we try to assess the outcomes of deterrence and unilateralist options *in abstraction* from the motivations of those involved, and from the possibility of *alteration* in those motivations through shifts in fundamental orientations of hoping or imagining or believing.

If, by contrast, one retains the concept of intentionality, then individual actions stand out with *relative* clarity within the causal process. Of course they must be placed in the context of a long-term pursuit of ethically assessed goals, but one *can* legitimately try to judge (though with no absolute, provable security) whether they are of such a nature as to forward such a pursuit. In addition one can say that while we must take into account the likely responses of others, and that this is part of what is involved in moral action, one cannot ultimately accept entire responsibility for the turning of the results of one's actions towards evil ends through the intervention of the quite different and incompatible intentions of others – what I earlier called their 'mis-takings' – even though such perversion does *in some measure* 'contaminate backwards' one's 'first' intention, since one remains haunted by the thought that if it had been more compellingly, more persuasively formulated, it would have been promoted rather than distorted by others. (See, again, chapter 5, 'A Christological Poetics'.) Nevertheless, the possibility of 'perversion' cannot be held to outweigh the *intrinsic* tendency of a peaceful gesture to encourage a response in kind.

I have argued, then, that Niebuhrian thought represents an unholy alliance of Kantian (idealist and absolutist) and utilitarian (pragmatic and calculating) viewpoints, which actually tends to dissolve ethics altogether. At the same time, by confining 'ethics' to a very narrow domain, it tends to ensure that ethical discussion is never about the real historical world. Thus, as we have seen, Hughes could only deal with the bomb as if it were a sort of providential device for keeping world peace that had suddenly dropped from the sky (so to speak . . .). He did not see the *irrelevance* of asking whether nuclear weapons are morally acceptable as part of a world-governing system when they do not *in fact* exist in that sort of manner, nor for that sort of reason.

4 In Search of True Realism

Too often today we fob off men and women crying out for a word of hope with an academically precise pessimism, which seems to glory less in the cross than in the disintegration of human societies and the coming of despair. We have reached the truly appalling position of pointing to the threat of the atom bomb as evidence of the disorder of our being, and at the same time, like men in a trance, accepting and preparing to follow to the end the way to which such expedients belong, calling it our western way of life.[31]

Those are words of Donald MacKinnon, written in an earlier phase of the cold war, perhaps with Reinhold Niebuhr in mind. They serve to introduce the themes of this final section. First, MacKinnon suggests that one needs to discriminate amongst 'levels of reality' and to remember what it is for the Christian that holds the clue to that level of reality which is deepest of all. Second, these words point us beyond the 'academically precise' tracing of catastrophe (which, however, Niebuhrian realism actually evades) to the possibility of atonement, and an atoning process. Here, because of the fall, virtue must step out of the cloister; because of the cross, death also may be appropriated as the Creator's gift.

With regard to 'levels of reality': so far, in this essay, I have pleaded against Niebuhrian realism for attention both to 'the realities of history', and to the realities spoken of by 'the Christian narrative' (it is precisely these things which MacKinnon accuses Niebuhr of ignoring). But how are these two things really related? Obviously I cannot give an adequate answer here, but I can at least provide a few indicators. History is not a manifold of brute facts; it includes natural events and subjective individual states, but these 'occur' historically, in and through *language*. It is because of this that we can say that history has a logic, a 'plot', and this is a matter of 'realist' apprehension, not abstract idealist speculation.[32] In pointing to the realities of human history we are pointing to a 'way' (albeit an utterly contingent way), to a story that is a moral or an immoral path.

At the same time, we read this plot differently and so act differently. Yet there is no unlimited freedom of interpretation, because cultures and societies are organized systems of signs in which certain dominant patterns of sign-making in language are connected to dominant modes of action. Cultures in one sense allow endlessly variant 'readings'; yet each reading must be answerable to what the basic patterns of what counts in the culture as meaningful speech will permit. The truth of the matter is that we cannot understand the interpretation of cultures so long as we think of it as something undertaken from outside the 'text' or 'script' of cultural life itself by some disembodied spiritual observer. We must realize that the reader is in a position akin to that of the actors *within* the 'text' itself. The interpreter is still inside the fundamental movement of what he or she is trying to interpret, a movement which constantly both affirms and modifies its basic 'themes' by the constant addition of the new things that are said *about* it ('rhemes', to use linguistic parlance). So too, what is being interpreted can be seen as a 'spiritual' reality insofar as it constantly acts on and modifies the intentions and meanings of those who have produced it – the individual author in the case of a written text, and the many 'authors' or actors in the case of human history.

This perspective must govern the way in which we regard a Christian reading of history. To some considerable extent we may see the same historical reality as other people. Christians and non-Christians alike can to some degree point to the same objective causal processes. But this is only possible because we are all actors in the same drama, and still affirm and uphold certain patterns of meaningfulness which alone permit these processes to work. In so far as Christians do not ultimately take these processes as final, determined, absolutely 'given', they assert that they themselves are involved in and shaped by a limited reading or misreading of the total human story so far (just as Marx effectively describes capitalism as a systematic disordering and obscuring of communication).[33] It is historically the case that Christianity has exposed certain features of the secular historical process in such a way that what once appeared absolute and natural was shown to be contingent. The greatest example of this is Augustine's demonstration that in so far as the Roman political model of justice is based on the model of 'restraint of chaos', it turns out to have its *real* basis in the arbitrary coercive power of freemen over slaves, Romans over strangers.[34]

These 'exposures' of the historical plot may be to some extent assimilated within non-Christian language, though this assimilation usually remains incomplete. But we can say that, in this negative sense, Christians see a different historical reality. We must realize this, if we are not to confine Christianity to a realm of 'pure value', or else to cordon off the narratives of the New Testament as a sacred enclave within an otherwise secular process. Moreover, the exposures are only the reverse side of positive *disclosures* which revise the thematic structure of the way we narrate our history. These revisions intrude both in our 'acting out' and in our 're-telling' of the collective story. In the first case, we try to practise a mode of life which reveals 'creative charity' as more fundamental to the way things truly are, although given the fact of catastrophe, this mode of life may now only be finally re-attainable by way of a tragic passage through the drama of sacrifice.

In the second case we make an attempt to extend historical disclosure to the level of a comprehensive view of how things are. All our history remains an *interpretation* of what is given – the natural world – and even in so far as our ideas of 'the good' emerge only in fictional projections, it remains the case that these pictures are constructed out of natural configurations. In so far as such projections are 'inhabited' by concrete characters, we can discover various goods as the *real* qualities of acting human subjects. Our historical and moral existence may belong entirely inside a world of signs which at all points depends on convention, but at the same time it is just this inescapable 'conventional' network of similarities, differences, echoes and allusions which most finally ties us to concrete reality, and to nature itself. Just because the entire world only arrives to us as language, so also language only arrives to us as the world, whose specificities surprise us and remain beyond our grasp or control. Christian 'conventions' of language, it might be said, are just one possible Ariadne's thread through this labyrinth which is also a way of the labyrinth itself. And yet they are uniquely more than this: they are also the threading of event to event in peace, and the trust that the *entire* labyrinth can eventually be so interwoven in harmony.

It is this unique perspective which denies that what constitutes the gulf between nature and culture is some extra element of 'spiritual' life in culture. Rather, in the Christian perspective, this gulf is contingent and related to death.[35] It is death alone that sets up a tension between meaning and reality that is otherwise without foundation; death and all its lesser attendants of disease and natural disorder. Death supplies the 'pathos' of nature, the fact that nature's meaning has now become elusive. Death supplies also the 'pathos' of culture: the fact that cultural patterns of meaning cannot overcome the harsh limit set by human mortality.

This, presumably, is why only *resurrection* reverses the effects of the fall. In the resurrection, our human historical narratives, and attempts to extend this narration to the ultimate 'way things are' – the closing of the gap between nature and history that we call mythology – come together. At this point myth ceases to be just myth, yet the import of this breakthrough is that the myths themselves are to be taken with utter, though cautious, seriousness. In the face of the resurrection it becomes finally impossible to think of our Christian narrative as only 'our point of view', our perspective on a world that really exists in a different, 'secular' way. There is no independently available 'real world' against which we must test our Christian convictions, because these convictions are the most final, and at the same time the most basic, *seeing* of what the world is.

All this has to be said if the ultimate error of 'Niebuhrian realism' is to be thoroughly exposed. This consists in its supposing that there is some neutral 'reality' to which Christians bring their insights. But Christians, like everyone else, are scions of language, bound to structures in which reality is already 'worked over'. Like everyone else we assume that our constant revisions of our language are evidence that it is indeed *reality* we are dealing with, but either the *entire* Christian narrative tells us how things truly are, or it does not. If it does, we have no other access to how things truly are, nor any additional means of determining the question.

In assuming, on the contrary, that 'reality' can be empirically and neutrally assessed, Niebuhrian realists are too often betraying the entire Christian reading of history. Amidst the tragic exigencies of life the cross may be postponed; but finally it is the only way that can undo tragic contradiction, and pass beyond catastrophe. At the same time, we have to take the 'postponement' seriously. There is no 'cheap peace' because our entire conduct is penetrated by violence. As we know so well, even most forms of persuasion (and if we eschew violence, but still want to encourage virtue, only persuasion is left) are thoroughly coercive. We need in consequence to find a language of peace, and this is presumably a reason why we point to *one* drama of sacrifice in particular. Truth and persuasion are circularly related. We should only be convinced by rhetoric where it persuades us of the truth, but on the other hand truth *is* what is persuasive, namely what attracts and does not compel. And Christians only see this *entire* attraction in the figure on the cross, a specific and compelling refusal to return evil for evil, made not in a gesture of despair or resignation, nor even of mere ethical self-offering, but rather in the confidence that a giving unto death is finally to be revealed, as 'a return', as a gain of the true self-expending and yet also self-realizing self. In the attraction of this figure we see atonement and resurrection inseparably, as Donald Mackinnon frequently insisted, fused in one.

This disclosure exposes the way in which violence is embedded in the dramas of the world,[36] both in the endless repetition of vengeance, and in death which sustains this possibility and confines moralists to a reactively violent limiting of violence and self-abandoning altruism; such embedded violence is something not to be mitigated, after the fashion of Christian conservatives, by a reference to 'natural limits', nor to a purely abstract notion of original sin. But at the same time it is not so alien and terrible that it is not in the last resort a matter of human willing, human structures of behaviour, and a human nihilistic reading of death as final destruction. The gospel denies that such evil can be endlessly held in check. But it does affirm that it can be altogether rooted out within the fellowship of those who follow the way of Christ, who has recovered for us the true pattern of perfection, the original *logos* of human existence, which is a power working prior to any taint of evil. Moreover, because the Cross and resurrection reveal to us that this pattern is recovered precisely at the point of suffering and despair, no 'ethical limitations' can ever be ultimate for the Christian. We start reading reality (and remember that this is in itself a blank page before our act of engaging with it and speaking of it) under the sign of the Cross.

Of course this must include political reality. The Cross was a political event and the 'apolitical' character of the New Testament signals the ultimate replacement of the coercive *polis* and *imperium*, the structures of ancient society, by the persuasive Church, rather than any withdrawing from a realm of self-sufficient political life. And from the cross we re-shape our metaphysics. We are no longer dealing with Harries's divine ruler, and God's inability finally to 'force' evil is no more a limitation on his omnipotence than (according to Thomas Aquinas), the divine non-cognizance of evil 'in itself' is a limitation upon his omniscience. Evil takes away from power and takes away from knowledge, by distorting them both. It is true that in this world we are tragically forced to compromise with this ignorance and this impotence. But such compromise becomes finally absurd when we are dealing with a secular process that is increasingly able to concentrate in its service the whole vast range of human vice and weakness such that anarchy is now order, and order the perfected 'power house' of anarchy. When confronting Leviathan, we have to invoke the true power of the cross; otherwise have we not abandoned the reality which we serve?

Notes

1 Reinhold Niebuhr, *Moral Man and Immoral Society* (SCM, London, 1963), pp. 113–200, 241–9.
2 Reinhold Niebuhr, *An Interpretation of Christian Ethics* (SCM, London, 1936), pp. 149–79.
3 Ibid., p. 160.
4 Ibid. On the same page we are informed that 'the ideal of love . . . knows nothing of the recalcitrance of nature in historical existence'.

5 See also Reinhold Niebuhr, *Reflections on the End of an Era* (Scribner's, New York, 1936) p. 209: Niebuhr refers to 'the persistence and inertia of collective egoism against the aspirations and demands of the spirit'.

6 Niebuhr, *An Interpretation of Christian Ethics*, p. 157.

7 Ibid., p. 164.

8 Ibid., p. 157. Note the phrase '*fortuitous* inequalities'.

9 Ibid., p. 159.

10 Augustine, *The City of God*, trans. H. Bettenson (Penguin, London, 1972), Book XIX, pp. 843–94. Niebuhr does indeed develop a doctrine of *Iustitia Originalis* which is rightly conceived as love or 'the sense that there ought not to be a sense of ought'; see Reinhold Niebuhr, *The Nature and Destiny of Man*, vol. I (Nisbet, London, 1944), p. 311. However, because Niebuhr rejects the ontological reality of a lost paradise, 'original justice . . . really represents the requirements of human freedom in its most ultimate sense', ibid., p. 292. In other words 'original justice' is really a transcendental category, and on p. 309 Niebuhr equates the sense of original justice in part with the Stoic trust in the ultimate order of things; again the existential and finite is seen as a constraint upon perfection. Thus Niebuhr does not grasp Augustine's vision of the ontological primacy of perfection for life here on earth. And because he associates the social with finitude and constraint, he is never able, as is Augustine, to see love as the original law of human *social* being.

11 Richard Harries, 'Power, Coercion and Morality', *The Cross and the Bomb*, ed. Francis Bridger (Mowbray, London, 1983).

12 Ibid.

13 Ibid., p. 88.

14 Niebuhr, *Moral Man and Immoral Society*, pp. 23–50.

15 Niebuhr continues to adhere to the Stoic structure of natural law which contrasts the constraints of nature and the freedom of the spirit throughout his writings. See, for example *The Nature and Destiny of Man*, vol. I, pp. 308–9. Here again, Niebuhr modifies, but does not reject, the Stoic scheme. The post-war article 'Christian faith and Natural law' exhibits it as still in full force. Christian love and freedom surpass any conceivable Stoic grasp of ultimate rational freedoms, but they do so in an entirely transcendental direction. Thus 'all human life stands under an ideal possibility purer than the natural law' (meaning here an exact *grasp* of first principles): see Reinhold Niebuhr, *Love and Justice* (World Publishing Company, Cleveland and New York, 1967), p. 51. Niebuhr still advocates a *Ius Gentium* conceived as a mediation between transcending love and finite nature: between these two 'all kinds of *ad hoc* restraints may be elaborated and defined. We may call this natural law', ibid., p. 54. It is true that Niebuhr talks of the finite limits in terms of 'the boundless assertion of the self' (p. 54) but on p. 51 he defines the 'sin of history' as 'the effort to hide finiteness *and to pretend a transcendent* perfection [i.e. love] *which cannot be achieved in history*' (my italics). Niebuhr views negatively the displacing of Stoic by Aristotelian influence in Christian history: see, for example, Reinhold Niebuhr, *The Self and the Dramas of History* (Faber, London, 1976) p. 183. Alasdair Macintyre interprets the Stoic ethical model as the most important conveyor of an ethic based on the supremacy of rule and law, rather than on goal and virtue, whereas Niebuhr's essential legalism is shown in the way love must be edged to the margins of his world. See Alasdair Macintyre, *After Virtue* (Duckworth, London, 1982).

16 Niebuhr, *An Interpretation of Christian Ethics*, p. 162.

17 Ibid., p. 163.

18 Ibid., pp. 163–4.

19 Ibid., p. 163. In some of Niebuhr's later writings we find the view, not altogether remote from the writings of Dooyeweerd and the Dutch Calvinist school, that Calvinist thought, exemplified in England by Hooker, then passing its legacy to Locke, Burke, etc. achieved a synthesis of organicist and democratic–nationalist elements. However, while Niebuhr cites Hooker's argument which regards tradition as 'unfolding reason', and so in pleading for customary law is pleading for 'the votes of the past', this vision does not really penetrate his own argument at any depth. Thus Niebuhr declares: 'the issue solved by Hooker and the later Calvinists is how to relate the freedom and justice of a democratic society to the organic stabilities of a more traditional society. This requires that new and more adequate *equilibria of power* be substituted for the disbalances which created injustice' (my italics): *The Self and the Dramas of History*, p. 197. Here again, organicism, with its collectivities, represents the *necessities* of nature, while freedom and justice come from eternal reason mediated to earth in the form of a liberal control of group conflicts. Loyalty to this rule may be reinforced through association with a traditional 'organic' symbol like constitutional monarchy; ibid., p. 192.

20 See, for example, Jacques Maritain, *Integral Humanism* (Notre Dame University Press, Notre Dame, 1973), p. 134; *Man and the State* (Chicago University Press, Chicago, 1951), p. 56.

21 Niebuhr, *Moral Man and Immoral Society*, pp. 231–57. See esp. p. 256: 'If the mind and spirit of man . . . tries only to make the forces of nature the servants of the human spirit and the instruments of the moral ideal, a progressively higher justice and a more stable peace can be achieved.'

22 Reinhold Niebuhr, *Love and Justice* (The World Publishing Company, Cleveland and New York, 1957), p. 237.

23 See Edward Thompson and others, *Exterminism and the Cold War* (Verso, London, 1982), the essays by Thompson, Davis and Kaldor, and Carl von Clausewitz, *On War* (Penguin, London, 1983), especially the comparison of war to the exchange of trade, pp. 201–3.

24 Reinhold Niebuhr, *The Nature and Destiny of Man* (Nisbet, London, 1944), vol. I, pp. 190–281.

25 Ibid., p. 266. Yet despite this, Niebuhr's account of individual sin is, even at the individual level, affected by his Stoic dualism. The ascription of the *habitus* of sin, on the one hand to 'pride', and on the other to 'sensuality', turns out on analysis to mean that we must give spiritual transcendence its due, but we must give confining nature its due also. The tension involved here constitutes anxiety. Niebuhr, on the page quoted, explicitly rejects an identification of original sin with this existential condition, and yet it seems to me that this is belied by the 'deep structure' of his thought. For all the subtle tracing of sensuality to self-obsession and self-escape, there is no counter-balancing understanding of sexual union as a paradigmatic, sacramental realization of self-transcending, ecstatic love. Niebuhr makes the Protestant mistake of seeing *agape* as beyond and above *eros*, including sexual *eros*.

26 One may (with Leibniz) protest that death is simply the mark of finitude; yet it seems to me that what is involved in the Christian definition of *anthropos* as the creature whose

nature it is to transcend itself in the direction of the supernatural (who lives, precisely in this extra 'givenness' of the divine life) is the recognition that finitude is most *properly* the unended *peregrinatio* towards God.

27 Gerard Hughes, 'The Intention to Deter', in Bridger, *The Cross and the Bomb*.

28 Ibid., p. 27.

29 Ibid., pp. 25–7, 29–30.

30 Ibid., p. 30.

31 Donald MacKinnon, *Borderlands of Theology* (Lutterworth, London, 1968), p. 149.

32 Niebuhr does recognize that history is a 'drama', but this metaphor is used to point up its inter-personal and unpredictable character. He does not realize the transferability of the notion of plot-structure to corporate history. See Niebuhr, *The Self and the Dramas of History*, pp. 53–65. This does not mean that plot *predominates* over character; as Balthasar has said, such a 'gnostic dream' would not be a *drama*, but only an empty structure.

33 See John Milbank, 'The Body by Love Possessed; Christianity and Late Capitalism in Britain', *Modern Theology*, 3, 1 (October 1986), pp. 35–67.

34 See Augustine, *The City of God*. And see also my book *Theology and Social Theory: Beyond Secular* Reason (Blackwell, Oxford, 1990), pp. 380–438. At one point Niebuhr himself recognizes that Augustine's realism is profoundly at variance with his own. See Reinhold Niebuhr, *Reflections on the End of an Era* (Scribner's, New York, 1936), p. 220. Niebuhr records only to reject, Gregory VII and Augustine's tracing of state rule to a lustful will to power of men over their natural equals.

35 I do not mean to deny that humanity is supremely cultural being whose nature is not simply 'given'. What I am trying to locate is our persistent sense that this puts us in *discontinuity* with nature, that it takes us 'outside nature'. If this is a history of reinvocations or resurrection, it is also a history of ceaselessly renewed atonement.

36 See René Girard, *Of Things Hidden Since the Beginning of the World* (Athlone, London, 1988).

Polis

11
Out of the Greenhouse

In the false spring of our times, everything painted green: it has become the appointed liturgical colour for our post-historical sabbath. It seems that it is to everyone's taste, the guarantee of minimum respectability. A 'Green party' exists, but does not get very far, because it appears to appropriate for a particular cause the symbol that belongs to all. The colour has a utopian hint, or rather that of a puritan arcadia, but at the same time it soothes the passages of capitalist economic exchange. More than that: the guarantee of a 'good', 'healthy' relation to nature, as to one's own body, in addition to a diminution of 'risk' *from* nature, increases surplus value. Capitalism has already incorporated, in the interests of profit, the new religiosity of our times, which takes the form of transcending one's humanity in order to celebrate nature or animality as the 'other' with which one nonetheless seeks to become united.

I do not want to be misunderstood, and I have myself 'voted Green' in despair at the decay of any other anti-capitalist politics, and in substantial agreement with much of the Green programme. The planetary structures which support life have been dangerously interfered with; much natural beauty, along with the delicate and long-developed harmonies of people's everyday environments, has been ruined or destroyed. Technology is employed indiscriminately and for the mere sake of size and complexity. However, 'Green consciousness' is not the complete answer to all this: in too many ways it may collude with precisely what it purports to oppose.

I am thinking in particular of its assumption that at the root of our ills lies a distortion or misperception of the relation between human beings and nature: our destruction of the natural environment is attributed to our supposed hubris in relation to the natural order. In response, we are exhorted to affirm nature, and

This chapter is based on a paper given to the environmental philosophy seminar at Lancaster University. I am very grateful to Robin Grove-White, Bronislaw Szerszynski and Paul Morris, without whose stimulus the chapter's argument could not have been developed.

downgrade humanity. If nature has been abused by humanity, runs the (faulty) logic, then nature herself will offer us the corrective: 'obedience to nature' will prove the salve for our planetary ills. Thus ecology offers itself as a new natural law, and even the Vatican shows signs of concurring. Obedience to nature can, of course, despite her supposed percipiency, take radically opposed forms: either, assuming she speaks in scientific tones, we are adjured to submit to a utilitarian calculus of maximum well-being for the planet and its sentient life, or else, assuming her utterances to be more oracular, to rediscover the lost aesthetic and spiritual values, which these deliverances impart.

But there is nothing at all new here. These high-tech and new age remedies for our modern predicament, the over-reachings of science, themselves repeat precisely modernity, and the gnoseological framework within which 'Science' has been able to establish cultural hegemony. After the collapse of the mediaeval consensus, faced with the difficulties of containing the conflicts amongst communities of diverse belief, the early modern age already fled to the arms of nature as support for a new objectivity. Human relations had proved recently problematic; they were now to be mediated by the certain laws governing the inter-relation of physical bodies, and the supposed transparency of 'experiment'.[1] Displacement towards nature was therefore in place from the outset of modernity, although 'nature' was also from the outset a cultural construct: initially a disguised projection of a new mode of human power, operating less according to a consensus (imposed or spontaneous) about goals and values, and more according to the formal manipulation of quanta of power and information. This both encouraged and depended upon their concentration at the sovereign centre, which was increasingly defined *through* this concentration, rather than its position at the apex of a complex hierarchy expressing a value-laden set of mutually positioned priorities.

In the face of the emergency of divided Christendom, knowledge and power were reconfigured together. During the mediaeval era, all social action and understanding was subordinated to salvation, the eventual gaining of the beatific vision; but now the pursuit of power as the mere guarantee of order – *any* order – was allied to the new legitimation of inquiry as mere *curiositas*, finding out for the sake of finding out.[2] Any secreted knowledge could now be deployed on behalf of power, and knowledge defined as prying is none other than the power of vision to survey its objects with impunity (however much, through the dialectics of the gaze, such impunity may prove to be an illusion).

I am indicting the usual villain, then, as 'Green consciousness' would have it? Dualism of body and spirit, the latter representing and mastering the former? Body or nature drained of value and meaning, spirit reduced to the emptiness of subjective autonomy? Yes, but I am also contending that this is only part of the picture. The new configuration of the relation of mind to body, humanity to nature, was an aspect of a new configuration of inter-human and inter-bodily relations. When these had been complex and hierarchical, then environmental space had expressed and constituted such complexity and hierarchy. It was emplotted with auratic signs that constrained trespass on one sanctum by another, and prevented a lone sovereign rule through the reduction of space to a single abstract medium, where all can be made equivalent as different permutations of geometric extension. Such a *self-identical (simple) space* (see the following chapter, 'On Complex Space'), is precisely what permits the project of a comprehensive scientific knowledge of nature, based on a disinterring of its 'fundamental' workings, whose infinitely complex combinations do not outpace the projective reach of combinatorial calculus.[3]

The change in inter-human relations was prior and more basic; but the exigencies of social order which required the rule of spatial equivalence, and the possibility of an objective, totalizing comprehension of space in terms of quanta of extension and energy, involved also an instrumentalization of nature, and a more emphatic version of humanity as its spiritual master. Yet the dialectics of the gaze ensured that the scientific *voyeur* must forever succumb to the fascinations of 'passive' nature, which alone guarantees his authority. The new knowledge which infuses the new power relies for its prestige on its absolute faithfulness to nature, its waiting upon her for the deliverances of truth. This is so much the case that inter-human relations, the relation of subject to subject, are now only legitimated and guaranteed by the humanity–nature relationship, the relation of subject to object. Hence while it remains transcendentally the case that the nature–human (body–spirit) relation is only an aspect of the inter-human relation – an inter-bodily *and* linguistic relation – an apparent inversion of this priority is nonetheless a logical consequence of the modern configuration of social relationships. This is not *merely* because humanity now basks in the democratic identity of 'conqueror of nature', but more crucially because nature herself now yields up scientific and social 'laws' to the theoretic gaze or practical attempt at manipulation. For this reason, to identify the ecological villain as humanism, and to argue that the prime corrective for our ills must be 'submission to nature', may be to overlook the fact that this is to remain firmly within an existing paradigm. I am not, however, trying to present a straightforwardly 'humanist' case, nor arguing that modernity has deserted a 'spiritual', inter-personal realm: on the contrary, the point is more that modernity has tended to refuse subjectivity to nature and concomitantly embodiment to 'value', thereby *constructing* nature as 'objective', over against the personal as unstructured interiority. From either side the reality of 'embodied signs' which structure us as much as we them, which are as much 'natural' as 'cultural', is overlooked.

If, for the reasons just intimated, it may be not so clear that 'humanism' is the villain, it is equally unclear that the villain is secularization. For from the outset, the shifts I have just detailed were usually accorded a religious tinge. After the collapse of the English Republic, natural philosophers posed as the new priests of the universal temple of nature, and favoured experiments which were supposed to verify the presence of 'spirit' working in the interstices of matter – thereby steering a mid-course between materialist atheism on the one hand, and sectarian enthusiasm (whose access to 'spirits' is private and uncheckable) on the other.[4] From the outset, also, a religious immanentism was in vogue: God as embodied in nature, as gravity, mysterious ether, active principle, world-soul, general law; newly limited by the intractabilities of matter, and newly verifiable through the evidence of his operations.

Almost imperceptibly this immanentism can later take on a romantic tinge: nature, it is now felt, should be thought of less mechanistically, God less as spiritual regulator of a machine; instead, we need metaphors of dynamic organism, spontaneous creative self-shaping. The way to get in touch with spirit comes increasingly to be through aesthetic intuition, rather than purely objective verification – yet through this shift nature remains the remedy, and its harmonies the salve for sundered human community. During the Romantic era, existing construals of the nature–humanity relation came to be more critically regarded, and yet the modern idea that this relation holds the key to our social ills still retained its grip. Then and since, nature has sometimes been regarded as an alien objectified sphere which must be fully humanized, or else it has been seen as the repository of modes of being suppressed by the conscious reasonings of humankind. But in either case the solution is always: heal the nature/spirit divide, mend the damaged relation between mind and body.

And what is more curious here is that this is not simply a modern fixation, but has a specifically pre-mediaeval, pre-Christian antecedent in the thought of Plato. If, as Heidegger alleged, the Platonic conception of *theoria* imposing its rule on unruly matter is one source of Western technological fixation, one must nonetheless wonder whether anti-humanist ecologisms really escape this parentage, or do not rather invert its legacy, which thereby persists. The individual soul and his/her body; the soul and its relation to the cosmos: this locus abides in our new/old age. And it results in consequent evasion of the issue of human community, of symbolic orderings, of always coded material practices.

Some old-fashioned, still perhaps valid Marxism, needs repeating here. The nature/spirit divide is not objectively real, even as a phase in a dialectical process: rather it is ephemerally re-produced in capitalist/bureaucratic divisions of law from morality, public from private, male from female, factual from evaluative, inert and manipulable from subjective and decisive.[5] 'Nature', like private life, is turned into the repository of what capitalism denies or relegates: community, mutuality, objective aesthetic value. It becomes the site of our longings, and this location is confirmed by the evidence that loss of community, and of public beauty, is accompanied by exponential destruction of wild and cultivated nature. The remedy for destroying nature, thought many romantics, must surely be – turn to nature. But no: as I have tried to argue, modernity is *already* in part the turn to nature, this is itself part of the problem. 'Green consciousness' inherits the blindness of Romanticism at this point.

For by 'turning to nature', we cannot really find the key to 'value'. Its beauties we always 'complete', and so produce in language, symbol and artefact as much as discover. And alongside beauty, we encounter also in nature the ambiguous terror of sublimity: overwhelming, unpredictable power, continuous destruction. Also ceaseless violence, suffering, indifference to parts, manic sustaining of the whole over long eras . . . then all as if nothing had been. If such a description is pathetically fallacious (although the fallacy is limited by the spread of sentient life), then the fallacy is only the upshot of seeking 'value' outside human cultivation.

However, the turn to nature is now underwritten by 'eco-theology', the Christian manifestation of Green consciousness, ecological new-ageism.[6] Characteristically, it seeks to re-endow nature with sacral value. There may be nothing wrong with such an agenda so far as it goes, but to offer this as a cure-all ignores the fact that, while primordial sanctifications of nature often accidentally imposed limits on the instrumental use of nature, they had no necessary moral, nor ecological intent. On the contrary, such a consciousness often consorted with, celebrated, sought to appease, the terrors of nature through the counter-terror of sacrifice. Mythical consciousness, for example that of the ancient Greeks, recognized that any culture involved the upsetting of a pre-given natural balance, but regarded this as something to be practically coped with through caution and appeasement, rather than as a rank error, or occasion for moralizing.[7] Within the confines of superstitious inhibition, one can even recognize a kind of instrumentalism already here in place.

Sacralizing nature still carries with it the danger of acquiescence in terror. As surplus to a merely moral response, it can too easily be in tension with it. Moral response alone can regret the ravages of time, safeguard the individual animal from death, protect species and preserve sites of natural beauty. None of this seems to require any valuation of nature as such, nature as a whole. Indeed it could easily be given a manichean rationale, and there do appear to be such overtones in, for example, Albert Schweitzer's respect-for-life philosophy.[8] The Old Testament attitude which did not want to muzzle the ox too hard, that sought to embrace a particular symbiosis of humans, animals and plants within its notions of 'cosmic order', was not in love with immanence and process, but rather with eternity and transcendence. For it valued the individual, and attributed to her 'out-standing' a permanence of value. This was not the bloody Dionysian riot of seasonally renewed fruition and decay.

The dangers of pure immanentism seem obvious: resignation to death and redundancy, to the 'natural law' of competition. Exactly what, for such an outlook, inhibits an ecological fatalism of the kind which assumes that humanity's gloriously natural self-vaunting is doomed to an equally natural demise, although the planet will continue, at least for aeons? 'Anti-anthropocentrism' retains its logic at this extreme, but collapses into paradox as a basis for a more ethical response to the environment. For *only* within human linguistic community are individuals, including animals and plants, fully valued, only within human community occurs aesthetic appreciation of nature, which must always include a productive discrimination. Humanity is the event of this sort of valuation, such that to deny anthropocentrism is inconsistently to deny the transcendental condition of possibility for a certain sort of ecological concern; that a 'desirable environment' cannot be dumbly, objectively realized, I shall argue below. A consistent refusal of anthropocentrism would have to argue away human uniqueness, our being made in the image of a God 'who saw that it was good'; but thereby we would be reduced to the status of most powerful creatures in the universe, no longer fit subjects for moral/aesthetic environmentalist appeals. The only remaining imperative would be that of ecological sacrifice. The law of fatality would invite us, as the strong, to gloriously submit ourselves to the yet stronger, the planet as such, the self-maintaining totality.

While we should, of course, respect ecological mechanisms, to expect from these mechanisms the key to all modes of evaluation (so exceeding 'anthropocentric' ethics), is to acquiesce in the notion that there is such a 'readable' fatality, such a manifest possibility of knowing what 'the whole' requires. The danger is that claims to have identified 'optimum' environments, the most 'natural' and 'sustainable' balances, will often mask the ruses of human power and ambition.

Eco-theology may not entirely escape the danger of under-girding this crypto-fascism, because, instead of finding in Biblical tradition ample support for recognition of animal subjectivity, the careful tending of nature, and divine glory and sublimity as disclosed therein, it insists (after little historical reflection), on jettisoning orthodoxy, and constructing a more purely immanent, embodied, developing, limited Godhead. It assumes that re-sacralizing nature, and dethroning a supernatural God, must obviously be the key to our sick condition. But this repeats the facile mis-deduction I have already noted: we have been nasty to nature, so let us have more nature, more science even (after all its *about* nature, and quantum physics is really taoism and so forth). Also more Creation, more animality, more body . . . and less fall and redemption, less doctrine of sin, less history, less humanity, less spirit. Never mind that 'spirit', as the realm of culture, is the only possible *source* of all our eco-problems, such that their solution demands that this realm be set to rights, *not* asked to efface itself before an affronted nature. Such a request can only serve as a device of the powerful, because there *is* no isolatable nature other than that fantasized by culture. Remembering that the worst we can do to the planet is only likely temporarily to discommode it, and perhaps to destroy ourselves, we should realize that environmental problems are entirely our problems, problems of our making, our perception, and our attempts to relate as human beings.

Instead of recognizing this, eco-theology prefers to repeat the specifically modern turn to nature, and to perpetuate specifically modern natural theology. Thus we get – and I will not delay the reader unnecessarily – the world is God's body; he is not omnipotent, but does his best (as a liberal headteacher), to persuade recalcitrant nature (pure More and Cudworth); Creation is not *ex nihilo*, but an evolution from small time beginnings somewhere on the cosmic prairie, to 'ever greater complexity' – evidently a very good thing. Despite ecological–nuclear catastrophe, things are automatically getting better and this is called 'redemption'. The fall is dispensed with, and the myth, not the event, is held to be our 'first disobedience' and 'source of all our woe'.[9]

The common thread here would seem to be the replacement of the 'drama' of fall and redemption with an account of the evolution of spirit from matter and its continual struggles with and against it. The implications of the traditional Christian account of the drama are just not attended to. Far from properly instilling a world-hating pessimism, the fall underwrites a non-fatalistic optimism: in its gloomier aspect, the doctrine only acknowledges what all can already half-see: that evil is always already begun, and unable to reverse itself, because inscribed in death, suffering, and the chain of human error which has no traceable origin and appears doomed to limitless perpetuation because of our scarred psychic inheritance. By contrast, the true novelty of the doctrine is to announce that this 'always already' is, nonetheless, itself an intrusion, a distortion of the Creation as first made and intended. Without the fall, we would be left, not with the benignity of 'original blessing', but instead the terror of evil and suffering regarded as necessary outcomes of evolutionary experimentation.

And it should be noted here – against Robert Murray in his otherwise splendid work, *The Cosmic Covenant* – that a strong Augustinian insistence on 'fallenness' as characterizing both humanity and nature, is but a *counterpart* to a doctrine of the original perfection of creation as being without death, violence or enmity between creatures, whose centrality to Biblical teaching Murray so comprehensively demonstrates. Augustine's account of 'original sin' precisely regards violence and death as ontologically intrusive, as the transcendental conditions for even the *possibility* of sin (though equally, as the *manifestation* of sin). By comparison the Judaic doctrine that there exists from the outset a self-seeking and aggressive *yeser* in our nature, alongside a more peaceable *yeser*, a doctrine favoured by Murray over that of 'original sin', quite manifestly *fails* to give an adequate conceptual translation of the Biblical narrative vision of original perfection, and to the contrary, still shares with all paganism, especially that of the Greeks, a psychic dualism which results in a merely 'reactive' or 'self-governing' view of Virtue.[10] (See chapter 8, 'The Force of Identity' and chapter 9, 'Can Morality be Christian', above.)

As with the fall, so also with redemption: the orthodox view provides hope for overcoming all violence and death and lends meaning to the suffering of the individual who can regard it as expiatory and reclamatory of the fullness of Being. Because redemption has its source in an excessive 'elsewhere', which conserves, inviolate, the original imagining of perfection, no default need be retrospectively justified, no *impasse* need be regarded as an occasion for despair, nor for giving up the struggle against domination. But eco-theology instead places its faith in a process, the chance workings of a 'divine lure', and writes off sufferings as unfortunate necessities. Instead of the divine promise of liberation from sin and suffering, we are offered a suffering God who sympathizes and suffers with us. 'We're all in it together' says this mythical headteacher: a Nobodaddy if ever there was one.

Sallie Anne McFague has given us the most consummate summation of this morass: an American Green leisure theology, enabling the self to communicate with the cosmos in time off from work. According to McFague, God does not in fact sympathize with *us*, so much as with *his own body* – 'God cares about the world as one cares about one's own body, that is with a high degree of sympathetic concern'.[11]

'Sympathy with one's body'; this in an (of course) anti-Cartesian essay which traces a lot of trouble back to spirit/body dualism. An essay which also informs us that the old monarchic God offered 'control through violence and repression', while insisting that within God's body (which evidently will not allow him much sleep), evil and violence have a creative role to play. Recalling what I said at the outset about the displacement of the intersubjective (and inter-bodily) in modernity, by a new version of 'Platonic' spirit/body fixation, it is evident that McFague walks slap-bang into this trap. Supposedly, she makes God less spiritual – and less phallic, *naturellement* – so he's a real guy you can relate to, talk to, negotiate with and, indeed, fondle. However, he's still got this head bit (where he 'reflects' etc) that sticks up above his body, and looks down upon it with *sympathy*. Beheading is not on the cards, since, if God just feels and suffers as/in his own body, his charity is no more. Given that the world is God's body, something approximating to a 'distanced' love can only be conserved by reinstating the dualistic distance of body from spirit. A distance which cannot really substitute for the inter-personal one, because here God does not freely permit creation, which in turn can freely offer him praise, but instead is merely one, 'spiritual' factor within the world, which in turn imposes limiting constraints upon him. (Note that while a divine 'body' has inappropriate connotations of limit, it may be possible to think transcendence yet more radically than the tradition, by denying that 'mind' or 'spirit' is any more 'unlimited' than matter, with the consequence, perhaps anticipated by Tertullian, that a Creator God quite 'independent' of his Creation, can, nonetheless, be thought of as being as much 'material' as 'spiritual';[12] such an option would be far more radical than the proposal to interpret the world as God's body, which turns out to be yet more immured in 'Platonic dualism' than the traditional construal.)

McFague fortunately manages to avoid the line taken by some other process-theology influenced exponents of eco-theology: namely that God as 'lure and process' is somehow required by the factual evidence, which cannot be accounted for in terms of the mere operation of chance in evolution.[13] Of course we can never be in a position to know just what is and is not compatible with the ultimately aleatory, and McFague rather sees acknowledgment of God as a matter of belief related to the support of good human practice. Her test for a theological model is, does it support good practice now? But the assumptions that are made here about the linkage of myth/belief and actual behaviour, are too easy. There are no *obvious* correlations. McFague says:

> The monarchic model encourages attitudes of militarism and dualism, and conduces control through violence and oppression; it has nothing to say about the non-human world. The model of the world as God's body encourages holistic attitudes of respect for and care of the victimized and oppressed. It is non-hierarchical and only acts through persuasion and attraction; it has a great deal to say about the body and nature.[14]

Note once again the great weight accorded to sheer *prominence*: a lot more *said* about body, nature, creation, science etc. will do the trick.

But two further points arise. First, only an absence of specific historical detail allows these correlations their plausibility: exactly which important Christian theologian envisaged God as a Monarch who acted on, and had knowledge of things, outside himself? Answer: none. By contrast, and to compound the error, human kings were often thought of as having extended bodies in the realms they ruled.[15] A God conceived in this sort of image (and we have seen how McFague fails after all to behead the Monarch), a God whose body in the world is a something we stumble up against, is a God who exercises a compulsive constraint *over-against* our freedom, like the King's official eyes and limbs, which are everywhere. Not the God whose power is the creative ground of our freedom.

The second point is this: all models, images, signs, symbols and so forth are indeterminate and ambiguous. They do not self-evidently dictate a practice; rather the practice further defines the model. *How* it conceives God's Kingship and so forth is partially known from a society's social practice. Inversely, practice always involves some theoretical assumptions, whose implications nonetheless leave much scope for argumentative development. McFague makes it sound as if we are quite *clear* about practice and appears priggishly certain about what we ought to do, which attitudes we need to adopt. Theological models are just invoked as functional supports for this. They do not therefore *reconfigure* our practice, although this seems odd if so much practical ill is blamed upon the old dualistic and hierarchical doctrines. Did theory determine practice in the past, though not today? But for now, at least, we are left in no doubt which way round it is. We all, of course, know what to do, and all that is expected of theologians is that they should back this imperative up with a suitably honed model, and get rid of the nasty old one (and its mysterious, lingering, phallic theoretical potency which seemingly allows it to subvert the natural order of 'priority of *praxis*').

But we *don't* know what to do. *This* is the problem, and this is what is being evaded by green consciousness and eco-theology. Their core instruction is 'survive', yet nearly all dilemmas exceed that injunction in the direction of 'survive in what way?' Since we cannot, beyond a mere agreement to survive at present, take decisions that are genuinely in common, we cannot either produce physical environments of convenience and beauty, because these would reflect and embody a common civic life: constitute, materially, a mode of human reciprocity collectively affirmed. It is here that the real 'religious' problem arises. The question of 'what binds us together', a something that nature cannot supply – the 'Spirit' which speaks to us after all, subjectively and enthusiastically (but not before or without our public discourse). If we knew what rule was for, if we could somehow reconcile democracy (and so renew it) with *paideia*; if we knew whom to encourage and whom to restrain; what to produce and why; the just measures in exchange between diverse products ... *then* we could inhibit our economism and technologism and protect our environment. However much more urgent such protection may daily become, this still does not alter the necessarily indirect path to the healing of our environmental woe, which is most fundamentally *perception* (but not *mere* perception) of such woe, as the evidence of subjectivity in what we find 'intolerable' – and when – seems to indicate.[16] Scientific 'fixes' may well be found for those problems that most starkly endanger our current notions of wealth and essential well-being, but this will not necessarily prevent their constantly mutated re-emergence, nor, emphatically, will it deal with our subjective, aesthetic sense of despoliation. That requires a civil knowledge not currently available, but not, by contrast, appeals to a fantasized and sacralized wilderness.

And I have heard that magical musical bears are good to eat.

Notes

1 See Steven Shapin and Simon Schaffer, *Leviathan and the Air-Pump* (Princeton University Press, Princeton, NJ, 1989); Amos Funkenstein, *Theology and the Scientific Imagination* (Princeton University Press, Princeton, NJ, 1986).

2 See Hans Blumenberg, *The Legitimacy of the Modern Age*, trans. Robert M. Wallace (MIT, Cambridge, Mass., 1986), pp. 229–457.

3 On the contrast of mediaeval 'complex space' and modern 'simple space' see chapter 12, 'On Complex Space', below.

4 Shapin and Schaffer, *Leviathan*, pp. 283–332. See also, Michael Buckley *At the Origins of Modern Atheism* (Yale University Press, New Haven, 1987).

5 Gillian Rose, *The Broken Middle* (Blackwell, Oxford, 1992). Also Bronislaw Szerszynski, 'On Knowing What To Do: Environmentalism and the Modern Problematic', in *Risk, Environment and Modernity*, ed. Scott Lash et al. (Sage, London, 1995). This article develops in more detail some of the positions of the present essay.

6 See *Liberating Life: Contemporary Approaches to Ecological Theology*, ed. Charles Birch et al. (Orbis, Maryknoll, Now York, 1990).

7 J.-P. Vernant, 'Rémarques sur les formes et limites de la pensée technique chez les Grecs', in *Mythe et Pensée chez les Grecs*, vol. II (Maspero, Paris, 1978). And Bronislaw Szerszynski, 'Religion, Nature and Ethics', an unpublished essay which is the most comprehensive demolition of the Lynn White thesis (that Christianity is responsible for eco-catastrophe) ever written, and to which the present essay is much indebted.

8 See Lois K. Daly, 'Eco-Feminism, Reverence for Life, and Feminist Ecological Ethics', in Birch et al., *Liberating Life*, pp. 88–108 (on Schweitzer, pp. 96–108).

9 See Birch et al., *Liberating Life*, and especially the essays by McFague, Birch, Berry, Daly.

10 Robert Murray, *The Cosmic Covenant* (Sheed and Ward, London, 1992), especially pp. 124–5

11 Sallie Anne McFague, 'Imaging a Theology of Nature: the World as God's Body', in Birch et al., *Liberating Life*, pp. 201–27, this quotation, p. 215.

12 See Funkenstein, *Theology*, pp. 23–117.

13 Charles Birch, 'Chance, Purpose, and the Order of Nature', in Birch et al., *Liberating Life*, pp. 182–200.

14 McFague, in Birch et al., *Liberating Life*, p. 218.

15 See Ernst H. Kantorowicz, *The King's Two Bodies: A Study in Mediaeval Political Theology* (Princeton University Press, Princeton, NJ, 1957), p. 32; Thomas Hobbes, *Leviathan*.

16 The researches of Robin Grove-White, in particular, based on his long involvement in ecological campaigns, have demonstrated this point.

12

On Complex Space

If one is to believe the Italian Marxist, Antonio Negri, the twentieth century has been abortive, the mere outworking of the ideological projects of the century that preceded it.[1] There have been three such projects, all characterized by a refusal to be 'resigned' to the unrestrained rule of the capitalist market: fascist corporatism, state socialism and social democracy. Only since 1989 has the failure and termination of all these projects become fully apparent; only since that new revolutionary date have the historical entanglements engendered by these three programmes finally come unravelled.

In one respect it would seem that the verdict of Antonio Negri is endorsed by Karol Wojtyla. According to *Centesimus Annus*, the papal encyclical issued to commemorate one hundred years of Catholic social teaching since *Rerum Novarum*, the twentieth century measures the distance of a failure which is the inevitable result of a refusal to attend to the wisdom of papal social doctrine.[2] The failure is that of state socialism, Marxist socialism, or indeed socialism *tout court*, for the Pope allows no such subtle discriminations. However, this failure by no means betokens his simple resignation to a 'post-modern' reign of the market; on the contrary, unrestrained capitalism is still to be characterized, as it has been by Popes for a century, as a surrender of justice to power and of truth to opinion.[3] In place of discredited Marxism, Wojtyla offers to workers' movements the relatively untapped theoretical capital of 'Catholic social doctrine'; this, he proposes, will provide the necessary corrective.

However, the Polish Pope is interested in only one-third of the story: he has little to say, first of all, about the demise of social democracy (in the sense of 'reformed capitalism', or 'welfare capitalism') and the evidence that sufficient state welfare provision and trade union rights are predicated upon capitalist growth, and therefore will succumb to periodic downturns in market cycles, and periodically renewed efforts to maximize profits by reducing the proportion deducted in wages and taxes. Witness Britain since the 1970s, and more especially Norway and

Sweden. Second, the Pope has nothing to say about fascism, not simply a long-ago banished spectre, for its shadow today hovers once more over Eastern Europe. This, one might allege, is a subject that has to be avoided out of embarrassment, because it embraces instances where the capital of Catholic social doctrine has already before been invested in practice, with a yield of terror and tragic chaos no less patent that in the case of East European state socialism.[4] Of course many will here protest that fascism and nazism distorted the themes of Catholic social teaching out of all recognition, substituting pagan cults of collective force for a Christian respect for 'subjectivity' at every level. However, I shall argue that, albeit against its apparent 'intentions', the fascist tendency of all *non-socialist* corporatist thought is inevitable. Moreover, I shall also contend that the same tendencies, albeit more muted, are contained in Wojtyla's own economic philosophy, which appears to lean somewhat towards the notion of the 'social market'.

Do these remarks imply that I wish to join an already existing chorus of protest against John Paul II's revival of the notion of a substantive Catholic social doctrine, a chorus consisting of M.-D. Chenu, liberation theologians and others?[5] Not precisely. Here I want to make certain observations intended to re-orientate our perspectives on the recent fissure in Catholic social and political thought, between 'Church social teaching' on the one hand, and 'liberation theology' on the other.

Most of all it must be stressed that in comparing these two things one is not comparing like with like. In the first case one has an ahistorical, prescriptive social vision: here is the general pattern for the well-ordered human society, time and place will supply unprescribed but legitimate variations. In the second case one finds little concrete prescription (economic, political or social), but instead an attempt to give a positive theological construal to certain *temporal* processes which supposedly characterise modernity – the releasing of humanity's rational and political autonomy from religious tutelage, and the gradual flowering of human freedom and genuine sociality. This process is apprehended as being still under way, and as furthered by revolutionary socialism. Since free human practice and the logic of history will 'of their nature' deliver the liberated future, imaginings of future ideal space are relatively inappropriate. Utopianism and specifically Christian social prescriptions are both ruled out by a single gesture which entrusts emancipation to a negative casting-off of mystifying shackles, and the formalism of a truly self-legislating humanity.

On the one hand: space, and sublimely confident authorization. On the other hand: time, and a modest celebration of the human endeavour to be human. Surely the former approach is manifestly conservative and pernicious, the latter radical and enlightened? I want to suggest that things are nothing like so simple, and in particular that in their obsessively temporal concerns and dislike of any direct association of Christian doctrine with socialist vision, liberation theologians are not, on the whole, in continuity with the main lines of Christian and Jewish 'religious socialism'.[6] If one takes here as an example the case of Simone Weil, one finds someone who articulated a sophisticated suspicion of the more teleological and totalizing aspects of Marxism, and endeavoured to imagine patterns of spatial distribution that would eliminate or drastically reduce, the instance of coercive power and arbitrary domination.[7] Weil was no slower to prescribe than Wojtyla, yet her prescriptions were radical, egalitarian, anarchic. Was she guilty of 'deductivism'? Of extracting social norms from *a priori* religious principles in abstraction from all lived actuality? The answer is surely 'no', and the tendency of liberation theologians to brand as 'deductivist' any account of the derivation of norms other than that contained in their own 'priority of praxis' model, disguises from view the degree to which the latter is a fusion of a teleological historicism with a mystical activism which fetishizes outcomes.[8] By contrast, the attempt to envision, as a sort of 'general *topos*', a universally normative human society, may represent not so much a deduction from metaphysical or theological first principles, as rather an attempt to more exactly articulate or concretely envision *in what those principles consist*, such that one is not here talking about any merely secondary 'entailment'. Moreover this envisioning will always draw upon a chain of historical enactments which are irreplaceably exemplary in their performance – and thereby more *exact* envisioning of – the continuously hovering vision itself.

This co-belonging of deed with vision is somehow missed in *both* Papal deduction from theoretical principles of natural law (although this is really only an intermittently present feature of encyclical exposition), *and* the liberationists equally iusnaturalist verifications of doctrine within the text of practice, which grants to the event as event the unwarranted status of disclosure or revelation.

It is no accident that what I have dubbed the 'temporal' obsession of liberation theology stems not from Christian socialism, nor even in the first place from Marxism, but rather from the somewhat whiggish spirit of John XXIII and the second Vatican council. Not content with a belated recognition of certain positive features within modernity, which would have remained selective and discriminating, John and the council had a tendency to baptize modernity wholesale, as the manifestation of a providentially ordained process of increasing liberation and socialization. The 'general direction' is perceived as upwards and progressive. Within this perspective, capitalism was explicitly or implicitly endorsed,[9] and liberation theology merely added a dialectical twist to this endorsement. That is to say, whereas, on the whole, earlier Christian and Jewish socialists followed the perspectives of anarcho-socialists like Pierre-Joseph Proudhon and Gustav Landauer according to whom capitalism is not a necessary stage in the passage to socialism,[10] liberation theologians appear to endorse the Marxist view that proletarianization and concentration of the means of production are necessary stages on the way to liberation and a 'co-operative' society, and must be enforced under state guidance in the case of a 'premature' revolution. (One can have more Maoist, less industrializing, versions of this.) It is true that one finds a certain commendable distancing from this position in the celebration of *the poor* in general, not just the proletariat, as subjects to be emancipated; nonetheless, this distancing is largely rhetorical and not fully coordinated at a theoretical level with the undergirding Marxist metanarrative.[11]

I have said that earlier Christian socialists were readier to prescribe, to articulate the outlines of redeemed human space. But more strikingly, these articulations frequently contain themes much *more* stressed by papal social teaching than by liberation theology. I am thinking of the notes of personalism, distributism, solidarism, subsidiarity, household independence, free association and balance between the rural and the urban environments. Linking all these is the repeated refrain of 'intermediate associations' which variegate the monotonous harmony of sovereign state and sovereign individual. Together, all these themes belong to what I want to call 'the advocacy of complex space', which seems to me to be the key distinguishing mark of Christian social teaching in the nineteenth and twentieth centuries – whether Catholic, Calvinist or Anglican (the Lutheran case is less certain) – in so far as it in any significant way distances itself from modern social reality. What is more, a somewhat similar advocacy seems to be now once more surfacing to view amongst secular radicals.

The disastrous failure of the Marxist experiment in the East has forced most socialists to realize that Marx was simply too cavalier in entrusting the emergence of a socialist society to the logic of history, and, moreover, to see that his advocacy of a necessary phase of expropriation and centralization, along with a permanent element of central 'scientific' direction of society, itself contained the germs of totalitarianism. (This is not to say that in Marx's writings one finds the entire and single source of Stalinist terror.) Thus contemporary socialists increasingly realize that one must marry checks and balances, and a democratic distribution of power, to the simultaneous socialization of human economic endeavour. Likewise they realize that a workable and authentic socialism cannot replace the operation of the market with exhaustive central planning. Instead it must discover a way of ensuring that market exchanges are also democratically or freely assented-to transactions – the outcomes of processes of free and equal negotiation – which repeatedly seek to preserve or extend a distribution of resources held to be 'just'. (Note this is not the same thing as so-called 'market socialism', since, unlike the latter, it accords no place to *pure* market forces of supply and demand, regarded as essentially indifferent to the pursuit of justice and the presence of collective democratic and individual un-constrained agreement. This rules out the exploitation of scarcity and necessity for profit, and the automatic legitimacy of any expressed 'need', while not at all trying to inhibit the free proliferation of needs that can be judged legitimate and beneficial.)[12]

However, in coming to these new realizations about the need for distribution of power, and the necessity actively to institute a socialist market, contemporary socialists know that they are abandoning pure Marxism and attempting to integrate with the Marxist analysis of capitalist economy the programmatic visions of other nineteenth-century socialists like Buchez, Proudhon and Kropotkin. It is also being noted that the 'late Marx' of the *Critique of the Gotha Programme* made certain concessions to the anarchist and socialist critique of his thought, or at least made clearer the ways in which this applied more to Lassalle than to himself: thus he stresses that peasants and petty producers do not constitute 'one reactionary mass', that land as well as labour is a source of wealth, that collectively held capital reserves for the future and taxes for welfare provision must still be deducted from the product of labour (although this only applies to the 'socialist' interval before the advent of 'communist' superabundance), and that the organs of the liberal sovereign state cannot simply be 'taken over' untransformed.[13] In the case of the new eclectic socialism, or else Marxism modified in a socialist direction, we are not then talking about a watered-down socialism, but rather, perhaps, about the *recovery* of socialism and anarchism after the demise of *communism*. I hope, with these indications, to have convinced the reader that the 'spatial' preoccupations of Catholic social teaching, and in particular its advocacy of 'complex space', are not necessarily the property of the political right. (It is indeed arguable that these themes first emerged most distinctly within a left-orientated Romanticism in France before 1848.)[14] Contrariwise, a certain whiggish historicism, perhaps especially in its dialectical version, can also – as much as any spatial fixation – be a source of totalitarian oppression.

However, in the case of papal social teaching, it is obvious that the 'advocacy of complex space' has become detached from socialism. This reflects a more general tendency of the twentieth century, whereby at least up to as far as the 1960's, the themes of regionalism, ecologism, rural Romanticism and the craft association or corporation were mostly colonized by the political right. By contrast the left has allied itself with science, progress, and positive certainty, failing to realize that claims to possess a universal, manifest truth can be the masks of a domineering authority. (And indeed can be used to legitimate racist, eugenicist, imperialist and genocidal policies which have frequently found 'progressivist' advocates on the left as well as the right.) Here we have the outlines of competing totalitarianisms: on the one hand complex space hierarchized, and recruited to the service of crude mythologies, whose quasi-religious yet essentially *secular* imaginings of untrammelled energy obliquely disclose that corporatist fantasy has not really obliterated the formal emptiness of the modern state and market. On the other hand, simple space articulated between the controlling centre and the controlled individuals, an articulation whose supposedly 'social' character barely disguises the fact that this is *still* the simple space of liberal modernity.

In this migration of the theme of complex space from left to right one has, therefore, arguably one source of the tragedies of the twentieth century. But one can claim something further: this migration was already underway after 1848, and was at least mightily assisted, perhaps even *primarily promoted*, by the increasing stand-off between the Catholic Church on the one hand, and socialism on the other, in France, Germany and Austria. Before 1848 most French socialism had a religious, sometimes even an orthodox Catholic character: the primacy of association was connected with the idea of a mystical, religious bonding that would correct the one-sidedness and secularity of enlightenment individualism. But after the revolution of that year, even most erstwhile sympathetic Catholics took fright at socialism, and meanwhile the all-important German social democratic party developed under the aegis of Lassalle and Marx, who were both more positivist, secularist, statist, amoralist and straightforwardly collectivist than the French socialist tradition.[15] The caricatures of socialism presented by *Rerum Novarum* – that it abolishes all private property and threatens the institution of the family – are indeed caricatures even in the case of German social democracy, yet could be applied to the latter with somewhat more plausibility. (It should be added that much papal suspicion of socialism had the character of dislike of a quasi-religious grouping – which socialism was, as much as a political organization – outside the aegis of the official Church: hence the desire for explicitly *Catholic* trade unions etc. more subject to hierarchical control.)

Because of the stand-off between an increasingly atheist socialism, and an increasingly conservative Church – a stand-off which had, I am suggesting, the most momentous, and disastrous consequences – Catholic criticism of liberalism now had to give a reactionary twist to the advocacy of complex space, which had hitherto just as frequently been given a socialist or else a liberal expression (for example La Mennais and De Tocqueville). The fortunes of the word 'solidarity' illustrate this point dramatically. The term was first used with political import by Mirabeau during the French revolution to designate the idea that 'the faith of each is the faith of all' – meaning, of course, republican faith.[16] This notion was then conceptualized by the *socialist* Pierre Leroux, for whom it denotes a kind of Leibnizian pre-established harmony between individuals, constituted not through the imposition of any universal rule, but rather through the unique but perfect reflection of the – otherwise transcendental and unrepresentable – whole in each singular person.[17] However, what matters here are not the metaphysical details, but the attempt to combine the principle of association with that of free independence, in terms of the idea of self-realization achieved in collective harmony with others. This combination is characteristic of French socialism in general, which was therefore already 'solidarist' in character, although it must be noted that the idea receives its most famous expression in *The Communist Manifesto*, when Marx and Engels declare that 'The free development of each is the pre-condition for the free development of all'.[18] It is arguable that this inherited slogan is nonetheless betrayed by communist proposals for centralized direction of what is deemed economically 'essential', which cancel the earlier Leibnizian insight that the essential and universal is infinitely dispersed amongst the free creative judgement of individuals and the constantly re-emergent event of their collaboration.

The concept of 'solidarity' was taken up again in Germany in the second half of the century by Hermann Pesch: it now evolved into a doctrine of 'solidarism' put forwards as an *alternative* to socialism, since it advocates 'solidarity' between persons, *regardless* of the fact that some may be owners of capital, and others dispossessed workers.[19] The question of how equal 'free development' is possible under conditions of such extreme and violently engendered disparity has now been repressed. And so to Lech Walesa . . .

The rough gist of my thesis should by now be apparent. Unlike others on the Christian left, I do not altogether object to the prescriptive tone of Catholic social teaching, nor its claim (as a project) to be an integral part of evangelization (for if it is not, as for the liberationists, then Christianity is paradoxically desocialized), nor to the 'spatiality' of its content. However, much of this content is territory stolen, long ago, from socialists. If Wojtyla is *really* interested in unravelling the tragedy of the twentieth century, and wishes to prevent farcical and tragical repetitions of earlier acts of the tragedy in the East, then he should think back to 1848, he should reconsider the complex historical relationship of Christianity and Marxism *and* socialism, and should consider entertaining a specifically socialist variant of 'complex space'. Only in this way can one sustain a non-resignation to liberal capitalism without lapsing into the dangerous illusions of state socialism, fascism and social democracy.

But why, it may be asked, do I claim that the right-wing versions are necessarily perverse and pernicious 'displacements'? Why, moreover, do I appear to insist that John Paul II's mixture of social democracy and social market must be classified as right-wing and even incipiently fascistic? Before answering these questions I must say more about just what I entertain by the phrase 'complex space'.

So far, for the sake of simplicity, I have contrasted spatial with temporal emphases. Actually this is only a cipher standing for a more complex contrast of different co-articulations of both space and time. Relatively 'utopian' thinkers do not just dream eternal complex simultaneity; they also envisage history as radically contingent and open-ended. This is not at all to say that they ignore questions of necessary pre-conditions and achievability: for example, while the anarcho-socialists Gustav Landauer and Simone Weil contended that the industrial proletariat were in no absolute sense 'nearer' socialism than rebelling Roman slaves or mediaeval peasants, they *also* claimed that a condition of general proletarianization of both manual and intellectual workers would actually *inhibit* a transition to socialism (the argument being that proletarianization would diminish independence, and make them more open to coercive and propagandistic manipulation).[20] On the other hand, more Marxist thinkers do not just espouse a theory of necessary historical stages, they also and concomitantly envisage the ultimately emergent utopian space as a clearly revealed, transparent and so 'simple' space, where every person is in his proper place as a 'producer' – albeit that 'proper' now means, as it properly should, etymologically speaking – *self*-defined. (The self-definition involved here is both of humanity as a whole, as represented by a 'scientific' central direction of society, and of individuals simply 'realizing' unproblematic productive potentials. In either case the 'complexity' that interrupts autonomous space is denied: the irreplacability of individual vantage-points for the making of judgements is disregarded from the centre, while the formation of our capacities and preferences by evolving cultural standards of judgement is disregarded from the peripheries.)

Such co-articulations of space and time can be dubbed, following Michael Bakhtin, 'chronotopes'.[21] What I want to do now is characterize the chronotope, first, of Enlightenment social thought, and, second, that of those nineteenth century thinkers from left to right of the political spectrum who espoused in reaction a 'complex space', which I am now going to re-name 'gothic space'.

First, the chronotope of enlightenment. Here the temporal figure of human growth from infancy to maturity is coordinated with the spatial figure of organic coherence.[22] The past is represented as a time of illusion and confusion dominated by the power of the imagination. Yet imagination is also seen as a surrogate for reason, even as the necessarily confused beginnings of reason, which is only fully exercised in the clarity of the present. *Now* it becomes apparent, after the decay of complex and exotic mythical hierarchies, that political reality is a 'simple space' suspended between the mass of atomic individuals on the one hand, and an absolutely sovereign centre on the other. Despite the merely contractual origins of the state, its actual functioning demands an organic, bodily coordination of the centre and the individual components. There are two divergent ways of conceiving this body: either it is essentially artificial, the result of a subsumption of the atomistic particulars under the ordered judgement of the sovereign head, or else it is 'natural', the unplanned and providential co-ordination of individual desires and choices in the agonistic harmony of a market economy. In either case, bodies intermediate between the state and the individual – guilds, religious associations, universities – tend to suffer reduced autonomy, or else total extirpation. Their corporateness, in line with the traditions of mediaeval Roman law, and its links with *papal* absolutism, is reduced to the condition of *persona ficta*, which as a mere convention cannot accordingly be authorized by pre-given community, but must be a privilege bestowed by the one self-legitimating community, namely the state – whose own fictive personhood is somewhat glossed over.[23]

This enlightenment chronotope can modulate into a Romantic variant, with two distinguishing features, the first of which may, however, be found without the second. First, the whole is mystically elevated as greater than the parts, in such a fashion that the totality is held to transcend the grasp of reason, and must be regarded as the work of an unfathomable nature or providence. Accordingly 'growth' ceases to be the smooth and predictable realization of reason and becomes instead more arborescent, something whose upshots 'reason' must patiently attend. Such an outlook is present in the work of the 'historical' school of jurists, like Savigny. The latter, however, remained wedded to the Roman, civil law, and accordingly to statism and the most fundamental features of 'simple space': his organicism is accordingly focused primarily upon the political whole. By contrast the 'Germanists' within the historical school, for example Grimm, exhibit also a second feature, which more genuinely marks the transition to 'complex space'. For these jurists, as also for many French Romantic liberals and socialists, there can also be *intermediate* organisms, with their own 'group personality' between the individual and state bodies; these organisms have a 'natural' function independent of the fictive creativity of an absolute sovereign rule. Both these modulations interpose the theme of a complex, revived gothic space.[24]

In its espousal of intermediate associations, this 'gothicism' clearly escapes the confines of a sub-personalist organicism more typical of the Enlightenment, which would deprive the 'parts' – individual or collective – of any independent subjective standing. Moreover, corporatism could sometimes escape Hegelian statist restrictions, in which corporate bodies still 'mediate' within a space that retains its essentially enlightenment character of suspension between sovereign whole and individual subjective parts (One thinks here especially of Otto von Gierke and his often more radical followers, such as the historian and Anglo–Catholic theologian John Neville Figgis, in whose spirit I hope the present essay is written.) In fact, in so far as gothicism remained a mere nostalgia for *Gemeinschaft* – neglecting the 'free' component in its advocacy of 'free associations' – it also paradoxically failed to escape the conditions of a specifically *modern* organicism proper to *Gesellschaft*. The interest in 'complex bodies', wherein parts are in turn wholes, and not simply subordinate to the greater whole (the model for this being, according to Gierke, ultimately the Pauline concept of the Church as 'body of Christ')[25] by contrast exhibits a way in which mediaeval exemplars were thought to manifest a crucial aspect of freedom – the freedom of groups – that modernity tends to obliterate. In many ways this interest transcended the terms of the usual 'sociological' contrasts of ancient organicism and modern contractualism. (It is notable that the perspectives of the historian–jurists, with their strong focus on 'discourse', appears in many ways more congenial in a post-structuralist climate than those of the sociologists, who perhaps distorted their work.)

The less statist gothicism tends in the direction of qualifying the importance of the whole/part ratio (affirmed in pre-modernity, but accentuated by the modern 'rule of reason'), with that of the *unit of relation* (taken as essential to the identity of its components) whether between persons, or different groups of persons regarded as possessing collective identity. In this manner the second Romantic modulation is partially wrenched free from organicism, such that multiple associations cease to 'mediate' between part and whole, but become themselves a new sort of context, a never 'completed' and complexly ramifying 'network', involving 'confused', overlapping jurisdictions, which disperses and dissolves political sovereignty.[26] An analogy can be made here with the gothic cathedral: it is a building which can be endlessly added to, either extensively through new additions, or intensively through the filling in of detail. This condition embodies constant recognition of imperfection, of the fragmentary and therefore always-already 'ruined' character of the gothic structure, which, as John Ruskin argued, expresses the Christian imperative of straining for the ultimate at the risk of thereby more comprehensively exhibiting one's finite and fallen insufficiency.[27]

The first modulation also now escapes the organicist major key: not only does the whole exceed the sum of the parts, also the parts escape the totalizing grasp of the whole. For Gierke, this double excess had been initiated in the Middle Ages and was explicitly the result of a linguistic and symbolic reconstrual of space as Christ's body.[28] The Church as a whole was not an enclosed, defensible terrain like the antique *polis*, but in its unity with the heavenly city and Christ its head, infinitely surpassed the scope of the state, and the grasp of human reason. At the same time, what was fundamentally the same excess could be glimpsed in the single person and the Christian association (monastery or guild) whose activities are legitimized by the quest for salvation, not by human law. Like the English historian F. W. Maitland, whom he influenced, Gierke appears to have recognized, against the sociologists, a certain prevailing *individualism* in pre-mediaeval ancient society – whether manifest in the land-ownership of the Germanic village, or in Roman law, which recognized only the literal person on the one hand, and the unlimited state power on the other, conceived as containing persons as functional parts, as they in turn were thought to contain different faculties in their souls and bodies. By contrast, 'organicism' in Gierke's sense, transcends through 'double excess' this part/whole fixation which undergirds individualism and occludes the primacy of social relation. Although it has for Gierke certain roots in primitive 'Germanic' community, it is fundamentally a *sophisticated* attainment, arriving at its zenith in mediaeval boroughs, not villages, and assisted through the evolution of legal 'realist' notions of 'corporate personality'.[29] The *Gemeinschaft* of Gierke, therefore, unlike that of Tönnies and Weber, in no sense belongs to an inevitably 'prior' phase, nor indeed to any necessary phase whatsoever, but is rather a thoroughly contingent product – to such a degree instigated by the Christian 'interruption' of history that his contrast of the 'mediaeval' with the 'antique-modern' (as he puts it) appears to echo Augustine's metahistorical account of 'two cities'.[30]

In Gierke, the note of 'excess' belies expectations that gothic organicism simply respects foreordained 'position'. This is still more the case with Ruskin's gothic aesthetics. In 'The Nature of Gothic', Ruskin claims that 'redundant' ornamentation is precisely the *essential* characteristic of the gothic building, which veers in the direction of being nothing but the piling up of extraneous detail, although were it to reach this decadent extreme (exemplified for Ruskin in certain aspects of the 'flamboyant') then a balancing sense of unifying form (the whole exceeding the parts) would be lost sight of, such that extreme refinement of decoration would revert to the condition of mere 'heap', mere accidental juxtaposition.[31] Nonetheless, it is only the principle of redundancy which is able to mediate between style and function: thus a practical need for light may dictate the cutting of an extra window, irregularly positioned. In a gothic structure this intrusion can still be rendered unobtrusive.[32] Applying these principles to 'social space' (as Ruskin of course envisaged), one finds that redundancy implies respect for the inviolability of personal assent, whether of individuals or corporations; Wojtyla has recently dubbed this 'the principle of subjectivity'.[33] In a 'complex space', there is always room to adjust to the innovations made by free subjects, without thereby surrendering the quest for harmonic coherence.

To fully grasp this spatial conception however, one needs to transcend the idea of a mere structural homology between aesthetic and social space, in a 'geographic' direction.[34] Since human life is both material and social, human work performed, on cathedrals and other physical constructs, does not just 'reflect' a given social order, but also 'poetically' builds it as the space which directs our respective visions, displays exemplary roles, and distributes our routes and circulations, our goings-out and comings-in. Variegated space has to have *literal* embodiment. Inversely, the diversity of this space is a function of the role given to many subjects, as for example the many craftsmen and many craft-guilds operating with relative autonomy (though this should not be exaggerated, remembering the 'excess of the whole', and the now admitted role of mediaeval architects), in the building of a gothic cathedral, or more importantly in the making of a gothic town.

The spatial-aesthetic and the social do not therefore mirror each other, but are jointly generated through property distribution and productive labour and exchange. Thus in the case of 'gothic' respect for subjectivity, the person is granted his own property, or a sufficient space for use and creative self-development which is the material condition for his free participation in society. The household unit is in itself – as it was not for pagan antiquity – a fully constituted and in principle self-sufficient political society, conjoined to wider society in the first place by association for mutual benefit, *not* by a contractual surrendering of supposed 'natural rights'. Just as in gothic architecture, the basic structural unit – for example the arch – is multi-functional, such that it can be infinitely enlarged or infinitely diminished, itself the total context, or linked with similar features to form a wider context, so also the social unit, which at every level marries 'female' household care with 'male' political excellence, can be very small or very large, self-standing or conjoined with other such entities. (This 'gothic' respect for personality embodied in property, and for the independence of the household, is clearly maintained in papal social teaching right up to the present day.) In the gothic vision, association is paradoxically enabled by the constant reserve of a free-standing space which 'exceeds' its own entanglements; this is a concomitant of the primacy of 'relation', or of the 'horizontal'. As regards the inescapable dimension of the vertical and hierarchical, the upwardly aspiring building is simultaneously 'deconstructed', or subordinated to the function of sheltering the many altars, many depictions, many procedures, enacted within its frame.

This is the principle which Catholic social thought will later dub 'subsidiarity', but I should like to mention here that this principle is abused if it is taken to inhibit the intervention of a higher, or indeed merely *other* authority to protect the individual or institution abused by an intermediate one: for example the child mistreated within the family. On the contrary, the gothic perspective implies also – this is the essence of 'solidarity' – that as the individual exceeds the association (or a smaller association exceeds a larger one) it has the right to appeal to others beyond that association, and others may appeal on his behalf.

The above paragraphs give the 'topic' aspect of the gothic chronotope. What of its 'chronos'? Instead of an Enlightenment teleological vision of gradual necessary evolution, one has a *dramatic* sense of history as ceaseless loss and gain: the Enlightenment has gained for us the formal principles of individual liberty and equality, which sometimes guard against the very *worst* tyrannies, but at the same time we have lost certain practices of free association for common purposes. Socialists and liberals who partook of the gothic fascination in the nineteenth century were clearly not simply subject to Romantic nostalgia: their mediaeval interests were selective, and what mainly concerned them was not hierarchical authority, but rather a pervasive legal constitutionalism orientated to consensus beyond mere mutual expediency or contractual obligation; orientated also to the diversification of sources of power, and to a guild organization permitting a measure of economic democracy and collective preservation of standards of excellence. Obviously these concerns were not always free from the taint of anachronistic whiggery (and in England 'whig gothicism', derived in part from the common law tradition, was already fully articulated in the *eighteenth* century), but it is notable that while, in reaction, twentieth-century mediaeval historiography has tended to stress the alien and vertical characteristics of mediaeval society, more recent writers have again started to point out its horizontal, associative, consensual aspects.[35]

In a sense, however, the question of how far such features were ever a reality in the Middle Ages was not decisive for nineteenth-century gothicism. Ruskin, for example, was far from supposing *either* that the mediaeval cathedral perfectly embodied egalitarian features, such that its particular style of 'redundancy' should be copied today, after the fashion of Pugin, *or* that its genuinely 'utopian' features exactly mirrored the society which built it. On the contrary, his Protestant love for mediaeval Catholic art led him to regard the latter as a kind of 'heterotopic' space, foreshadowing later actual or hoped-for developments in other spheres.[36] Similarly, mediaeval corporatism and 'free association' could be regarded as heterotopic in relation to the more feudal and nakedly hierarchic features of mediaeval society, (and also in relation to certain 'proto-modern' features of burgeoning papal and royal absolutism).[37] As indeed barely escaping these, and yet in this very 'ruined' condition as disclosing certain yet-to-be-attained possibilities.[38]

One last decisive element of contrast between enlightenment simple space, and gothic complex space, must be mentioned. The former is 'secular', the latter 'sacred'. In the first case religious authorization or providential intervention is moved to the margins: God commands the absolute sovereign, who then imposes rule according to an *a priori* rational logic of subsumption of parts under wholes. Or else God/Nature coordinates our desires behind our backs, through the operation of the capitalist market.[39] But in the second, gothic case, every act of association, every act of economic exchange, involves a mutual judgement about what is right, true and beautiful, about the order we are to have in common. It is no longer a matter of 'transparent' principles of reason, nor of mere diversification of desire, regardless of what that desire may be *for*. Instead one must distil order out of an irreducible diversity, one must find a measure between diverse things which are, as Aristotle said, inherently incommensurable. The order so discovered, so assented to, tends to be imbued with a 'sacred' character because it cannot be defined, and is always being repeated with a same yet different character, such that, according to the social Christology indicated above, the excess perpetrated ever-anew by the individual is the only possible 'representation' of an infinite excess always beyond our reach. (We are that body of Christ we can never yet see; a kind of 'sublimed' micro/macrocosmic relation is involved here.) The assent which such an order commands must clearly have the character of an allegiance of faith rather than that of a rational conviction.[40]

The gothic vision therefore acknowledges sublime indeterminacy and the inescapability of an aesthetic judgement – of both unity and distinction – which is an imprescribable 'event', not the subsumption of new instances under a pre-given formula, nor a mere 'accurate' empirical observation. Without this binding by pre-given rules, or by what is 'manifestly' observable, the Kantian sway of a self-sufficient immanence is undone; in complex space every judgement 'exceeds', and if it wishes to anchor itself beyond mere 'preference', must seek again the harbour of transcendence. (Though now transcendence secures, not, as sometimes in the Middle Ages, a hierarchy of 'given' essential identities, but rather, in this 'neo-gothic' space, the possible truthfulness of the human imagination.)[41]

To envisage the possibility of judging objectively, without rules, is to envisage the reality of God, and the inevitably religious character of the just society. This must apply also and even especially to socialism, which seeks to surpass the essentially secular formal justice of capitalism (grounded only in consensus and legalized coercion) and yet cannot escape the predicament of judging without precedent. For even a fully free, democratic and participatory society would still have to judge issues not adjudicable through appeal to the principles of freedom, democracy and participation themselves. For example, collective priorities for achievement and use of resources; patterns of distribution of space, time, goods and skills, which inevitably involve 'equalizing the unequal', given that people can never possess exactly the *same* resources (and this of course would not be just or even 'equal').[42] This space of judgement is the space of morality, aesthetics and 'religion'. It is a space which communism (which was invented in the eighteenth century by atheist priests, whereas socialism was invented in the nineteenth by religious laypersons) thought would be abolished with the emergence of a simplified and now specifically *economic* space, suspended between a 'scientific' organization of industry on the one hand, and a supposedly unproblematic realization of individual human capacities on the other. As Jacques Rancière and others have argued, Marxism preserves the classical idea that 'the worker' (as opposed, for the classical *schema*, to the ruler and the warrior) is properly *confined* to the realm of work and animal desires.[43] In classical antiquity the manual worker simply imposed pre-existing ideal forms upon matter; his work in itself was not subject to considerations of 'virtue', or the attainment of socially recognized excellence. Likewise the household, the site of productive provision, was not an arena of 'politics' and dialectical disputation, but of unquestioned paternal control. The Christian gothic 'merging' of *oikos* and *polis*, which as Ruskin in particular grasped, opened the question of virtue exercised within the material sphere of work,[44] is really occluded by Marx. This is because Marx considers that religion, morality and politics will vanish with the arrival of communism, since communism embodies a purely economic social reality, and he still thinks of this enlarged *oikos* on the model of the little antique household as a 'transparent' realm outside the problematic indeterminacy of political association between free citizens. This economic realm is, indeed, no longer managed by the patrician representation of the laws of the *polis* from above, but is instead 'self-managed' according to immanent criteria, and yet Marx's characterization of this realm still echoes the negative exclusions of Platonic and Aristotelian philosophy: work lies outside the sphere of idealizing reason, virtue and aesthetic judgement. Paradoxically, it is only the Platonic exclusion of work from this sphere which engenders the Marxist suspicion that the sphere itself has only illusory existence. That this suspicion is metaphysically, and not critically materialist, is demonstrated by the evident fact that the material realm is *not* rendered transparent once the veil of idealist mystification is lifted. On the contrary, it is idealism which seeks to impose arbitrary fixations, and our material life which remains constantly open to question: what to produce? Where to live? How to measure exchanges, how to pattern collective space and time?

Contemporary socialists are capable of recognizing that a materialist perspective by no means removes the necessity for ethical judgement, yet they tend to halt at the point of declaring that collective judgements must be made democratically, and that the ultimate aims are better fulfilment of basic needs and the promotion of individual choice and autonomy. This is still to remain with enlightenment simple space, since it does not allow that our life in common might transcend the imperative of self-preservation and self-emancipation. Whereas this life always points beyond these imperatives, because complex space has a certain natural, ontological priority, and simple space remains by comparison merely an abstracting, idealizing project. (In this sense Christological space discovers a certain 'natural' legality; however, the construal of this space as harmonious, and the refusal of the simplifying venture, are existential choices, not recognitions of universal rational exigencies.) This is the case because there is no such thing as absolute non-interference; no action can be perfectly self-contained, but always impinges upon other people, so that spaces will always in some degree 'complexly' overlap, jurisdictions always in some measure be competing, loyalties remain (perhaps benignly) divided. It follows that the decisions of freedom which escape the mere provision of 'necessities' (itself an area difficult to enclose) do not easily remain the decisions of isolated individuals or groups alone: the issue of the common good most pointedly surfaces, not in the more abstract deliberations of governments, where, on the contrary, its reduction to utilitarian calculus or promotion of free choice will seem most seductively plausible, but rather in the ever re-encountered 'boundary disputes' and occasions for collective action in the everyday lives of citizens. These disputes and occasions have somehow to be mediated, and where the reality of 'community'

fades, the attempt is made to more and more do so by the extension of merely
formal regulation of human transactions (with its utilitarian and more predominantly liberal individualist presuppositions). More of life becomes economized and
legalized, as legislation seeks – hopelessly – to catch up with every instance of
'overlap', and institute more detailed rules of absolute ownership, whether by
individuals, or legally incorporated groups: so much and no more *for you*; so far and
no further *for you*. Since it can never catch up, and since also it will be bound to
regard non-formalized mediations as merely arbitrary, this explains exactly why the
most capitalist and litigious society in the world – the United States – is also subject
to endemic lawlessness and civil violence at every level.

Without 'community', without its self-sustaining affirmation of objective justice, 'excellence', and transcendental truth, goodness and beauty, one must remain
resigned to capitalism and bureaucracy. This, I think, has often been a 'socialist'
(less frequently a 'communist') claim,[45] and it is clearly an inherently religious one.
And by that I mean that it is inescapably Platonic, Judaic and Christian.

However, it is absolutely crucial to distinguish this socialist advocacy of 'just
measures' and 'proportionate harmony' from its pre-modern variant. *That* depended upon a Platonic or Aristotelian idealism, on founding justice upon fixed
'natural' positions and social roles. It is for this reason, presumably that Aristotle
can say that 'need' is a measure for comparing the incomparable in exchange.[46]
Needs are natural, because they belong to the various social classes according to
their fixed, hierarchic positions: preservation of these positions is what undergirds
'just prices' and supposedly 'natural' exchange (it might be thought that initially
'equal' positions could also support these things; however, equal positions cannot
be fixed and definitely specifiable in the same manner as hierarchic ones, as I
shall shortly argue). Given prior 'natural' distribution, exchange is relatively
unproblematic, and this is why Aristotelian 'need as the measure of exchange' can
later modulate into the rule of 'demand' for the political economists. Although
demand is now, under capitalism, changing and inexhaustible, in accord with a
newly fluid society, it is still conceived as a 'natural' and empirical reality. By
contrast, for socialism, need cannot be the measure of comparison between the
incomparable, for two reasons. First, there is a recognition of the social production
of need, so that it is deprived of its 'natural right', and the 'meeting of needs' is no
longer superior to the judgement of socially desirable goals. Second, a condition of
equality is only formally specifiable, unless one were to suppose the nonsense of
everyone doing and possessing the 'same' things. Unlike hierarchy it dictates no
fixed distribution of roles, and therefore no normal, proper, desires. As with
capitalism, new and unexpected demands will constantly arise, but to conserve
social equality these demands *themselves* will have to be measured, to see whether or
not their fulfilment, and in what degree, upsets or promotes the social balance.
Hence the Aristotelian distinction between initially distributive and later rectifying
justice is considerably muted, for corrective or economic justice can no longer
appeal to a once-and-for-all given order of distribution, but instead distribution

remains always in question, and is constantly being re-enacted. In fact the just order persistently remains to be recognized within the very productive – and no longer merely rectifying or exchanging – acts of bringing it about. In this way economic transactions now come more under the sway of 'political' *phronesis* than Aristotle perhaps presupposed, and indeed become the site for the exercise of 'aesthetic' judgements of the kind described by Kant in his third critique: judgements where we enact no subsumptions, appeal to no certain rules, and *yet* make a social bid for the assent of others.

In line with the above, one can suggest that in upholding the reality of justice, the possibility of human harmony, socialism need not retreat to a premodern contemplation of eternal positions and pre-given hierarchies, although it cannot remain content with a modernist negative unravelling of illusion and contradiction in order finally to unveil a consensus about the unproblematic, à la Habermas. Instead it should embrace Lyotard's post-modern, defined as the post/modus, the 'future anterior', insofar as socialism has to take a wager on justice, on the possibility that we live in a universe where we can be the vehicles for just acts, whose 'characteristic' shape we will continuously *come* to know.[47]

This distinction of the post- from the pre-modern (with the implication that socialism, as the left-wing advocate of 'gothic space', has *always* had a post-modern character) leads me back, finally, to the issue of papal social teaching. The latter has constantly given a centrist or right-wing version of the themes – often originally socialist – of gothic space. Where this is done, I want to argue, one has incipient fascism. Why? For two overriding reasons. First of all, the legacy of traditionalism (De Maistre and De Bonald), and to a lesser degree of neo-scholastic ahistoricism, has led Catholics again and again to assume that a 'natural' social order must still in some fashion be in place ('surely providence cannot have abandoned us?' seems to be the unspoken thought). Thereby one runs into the contradiction of thinking *both* that liberal capitalism subverts the natural order, and yet that it in some sense still discloses it. Catholic social teaching becomes in consequence a grotesque hybrid: liberal, Lockean understandings of property rights, and Smithian construals of the supposed 'contribution' of capital to production are freely incorporated, and yet upon them is superimposed an organicist, patriarchal vision of society.[48] Capital and labour are here constantly conceived as belonging to a *natural* hierarchy, such that they should ideally be united in corporate harmony: this is of course to disguise the initially rawly coercive and quite unpatriarchal origins of the specifically modern power structure. Once one has combined modern formal emptiness and *de facto* rule of coercive power with paternalist sentiment, then what one has is *kitsch*, and a doctrine that in the end will only give a sentimental colouring to, and also emotionally reinforce, a culture of *violence*.

It is of course clear that John Paul II has not returned to a full-scale endorsement of corporatism, but exactly the same misapprehension and sickly false-consciousness informs also the vaguely social market philosophy he seems to espouse, and is capable of engendering a kind of 'soft fascism'. For where a certain practice and ethos of 'welfare' and supposed promotion of the worker's 'humanity' infuse the capitalist firm (though these elements are really strictly functional for capitalist purposes) the encouragement given by a more 'openly' liberal system to workers' generation of their own autonomous counter-authorities, and wresting certain rights and benefits that are *guaranteed* by political powers, tends to be reduced. One approximates that fearful mixture of constant 'concern' and exhaustive reduction of humanity to economic purposes, characteristic of the capitalist Far East (and admired by Walesa; it seems also significant that the Pope now apparently mistrusts a possible 'culture of dependency' generated by state welfare provision).[49]

Thus Catholic social teaching is engulfed in a kind of tragedy. Its 'advocacy of complex space' desperately needs to be heard in an age when those last surviving corporate bodies, still at times 'religiously' held together by the pursuit of collectively acknowledged excellence – namely the 'universities', bearers still of the Latin name for what is more than a mere contractual *societas* – are being subverted and effectively extirpated. Not to mention especially in a country – Britain – which has recently fulfilled the logic of its 'common law's' non-recognition of political as opposed to voluntary and economic corporations.[50] The tradition also poses topical questions: if Europe is to be once again a *communitas communitarum*, then should the stress be upon direct parliamentary democracy, or upon a 'corporatist' higher representation of many bodies at a lesser level? (Perhaps genuine subsidiarity and solidarity demands that the former should qualify the latter, and help to prevent a fascistic degeneration.) However, where modernist elements, rooted in modern natural law doctrines which ground right in the self-preserving impulse of the individual or political whole – absolute, self-alienable property rights as the norm, the fiction that capital constitutes a real motive force, endorsement of political sovereignty at the centre – are smuggled into the corporatist or quasi-corporatist vision, then a violently welded-together Leviathan is secretly baptized as the *Corpus Christi*, and the path of fascistic terror is opened once more.

That the papacy should repeatedly be in danger of perpetrating this insidious hybrid, is, moreover, by no means historically accidental. On the contrary, ever since the mediaeval Pope Innocent IV, its power has always basked in an ambiguity: on the one hand it flourishes by according *recognition* to already constituted manifestations of supra-political complex space – the manifold varieties of religious and semi-religious association – on the other hand, thanks to the originally *canonical* devices of *persona ficta*, it annihilates the integrity of the association through the very act of recognition, by alienating to its own sovereign power, the right of group creation.[51] Papal advocacy of complex space is therefore always likely to be flawed, since the *ecclesiastical* structure it upholds, itself exhibits troublingly hybrid features. Against mere 'political' power, the Papacy discovers and recognizes his own dispersed corporate troops (the hosts of Israel, whom we may indeed applaud), yet by converting discovery into authorization it perfects its own, and more absolutist *imperium*, devouring lesser bodies, while digesting their substance as the fiction of the Papacy's own single, undying body, which supposedly knows no stunted or abortive growths, but only infallible accretions. No mediaeval relic *this* ontology, perfected only yesterday: on the contrary, here is ideal modernist absolutism, just as the smooth additive 'development' of papal doctrine is sublime whiggery. In this fashion, papal institutions themselves provide a soil for the eugenic nurturing of fascistic hybrids, whereas a truly Catholic critique of modernity, if it is not to be perverted, must include an element of self-critique, especially of the character of current ecclesial (and not just *Roman* Catholic) institutions. One can agree with Pope John Paul II: democracy risks surrender to propaganda, and the forgetting of the primacy of truth,[52] yet the antidote to this cannot be *merely* the entrusting of truth to a sovereign power or clerical/clericist caste (although the need for 'hierarchy in time' in the educative dimension of society, for an elite which nevertheless seeks to 'cancel itself' by passing on wisdom, does *need* to be re-affirmed, just as democracy must be complemented by a concern with objective truth and justice). In the end the only security for excellence resides in a republican but complex dispersal of guardianship and trusteeship. How to replace manipulation with education (the development of genuinely desirable human life) in the space of popular culture? Only in theoretical and practical answers to this question, do we discover again the Church, the 'doubly exceeding' body of Christ, the Other Space of our history.

With Catholic social teaching (and writing as an 'Anglican Catholic'), I refuse to be resigned to the present age. I endorse the Catholic advocacy of a complex, gothic space. But the non-socialist version of this advocacy belongs to the history of attempts to overcome or recast capitalism that have gone tragically wrong (and one must remember how much of initial fascist ideology could look benign and congenial). If we wish, in the few years of a century that remain to us and the new millennium to come, both to face up to the modern predicament and yet not succumb to resignation, then I suggest we must re-think the sources of twentieth-century disaster along the lines I have proposed, and consider again the claims of the 'gothic vision' in its socialist, Christian, variant.

Notes

1 Antonio Negri, 'The End of the Century', in *The Politics of Subversion*, trans. James Newell (Polity, Cambridge, 1989), pp. 61–74.
2 *Centesimus Annus* (Catholic Truth Society, London, 1991), paras 12–21, 26.
3 *Centesimus Annus*, paras 30–43.
4 See Donal Door, *Option for the Poor: A Hundred Years of Vatican Social Teaching* (Gill/ Orbis, Dublin/New York, 1987), pp. 57–76, on Pius XI's 1931 encyclical *Quadragesimo Anno*. For the latter see *Selected Papal Encyclicals and Letters*, vol. I, ed. P. E. Hallett (CTS, London, 1932). See also, Michael Novak, *Catholic Social Thought and Liberal Institutions* (Transaction, New Brunswick/Oxford 1989), pp. 69–110; Edgar Alexander,

'Church and Society in Germany', in *Church and Society* (Arts Inc., New York, 1953), pp. 325–583, on German and Austrian Catholic sources of right-wing corporatism, often including a racist component.

5 See Paul A. Lakeland, 'Does Papal Social Teaching have a Place in our World', *Cross Currents*, 35, 4, pp. 393–407.

6 See my *Theology and Social Theory: Beyond Secular Reason* (Blackwell, Oxford 1990), pp. 177–259. Also my article, 'Were the Christian Socialists Socialist?', in *Papers of the Nineteenth Century Working Group*, eds Jack Forstman and Joseph Pickle, vol. XIV, pp. 86–95.

7 Simone Weil, *Oppression et Liberté* (Gallimard, Paris, 1955), especially pp. 194–204.

8 Milbank, *Theology and Social Theory*, pp. 249–52.

9 See Dorr, *Option for the Poor*, pp. 104–38.

10 Gustav Landauer, *For Socialism*, trans. David J. Parent (Telos, St Louis, 1978), pp. 29–46; P.-J. Proudhon, *Selected Writings* (Macmillan, London, 1969).

11 See Gustavo Gutierrez, *A Theology of liberation*, trans. Sister Carrida Inda and John Eagleson (Orbis/SCM, Maryknoll, New York/London, 1973), pp. 29–30, 236–7; *The Power of the Poor in History*, trans. Robert R. Barr (Orbis/SCM, Maryknoll New York/London, 1983) 125–60; J.-L. Segundo, *Faith and Ideologies*, trans. John Drury (Orbis, Maryknoll New York, 1984), pp. 200–18, 251–3, 255, 259, 262–3. In the latter pages Segundo does indeed begin to express reservations about revolutionary expropriation of land, but provides no sufficiently thoroughgoing critique of what is inevitably sinister in the specifically communist programme.

12 On socialism and the market see Pat Devine, *Democracy and Economic Planning* (Polity, Cambridge, 1988); John Keane, 'What's Left of the Left', *TLS* (21 June 1991), pp. 7–8; Robin Blackburn, 'Fin de Siècle: Socialism after the Crash', *New Left Review*, 185, pp. 5–66.

13 Karl Marx, 'Critique of the Gotha Programme', in *The First International and After*, ed. David Fernbach (Penguin, London, 1981), pp. 339–359. On Marxism and anarcho-socialism see also Robin Blackburn, 'Fin de Siècle', and Christopher Knight, 'Christians and the Politics of Liberty', *Theology*, 93 (1990), pp. 191–7.

14 Milbank, *Theology and Social Theory*, pp. 195–202, 'Were the Christian Socialists Socialist?'; Weil, *Oppression et Liberté*, pp. 194–7; Joseph N. Moody, 'Catholicism and Society in France', in Moody, *Church and Society*, pp. 95–187; Jean Bruhat, 'Le Socialisme Français de 1815 a 1848', in *Historire Générale du Socialisme, Tome I*, ed. Jacques Droz (PUF, Paris, 1972); Armand Cuvillier, *P.J.B. Buchez et les Origines du Socialisme Chrétien* (PUF, Paris, 1948); K. Steven Vincent, *Pierre-Joseph Proudhon and the rise of French Republican Socialism* (Oxford University Press, Oxford, 1984); David Owen Evans, *Le Socialisme Romantique: Pierre Leroux et ses Contemporains* (Marcel Rivière, Paris, 1948); Jean-Baptiste Duroselle, *Débuts du Catholicisme Sociale en France 1822–1870* (PUF, Paris, 1951).

15 Moody notes that the 1848 revolution in France was uniquely *not* anti-clerical; modern French anti-clericalism arguably post-dating that event: Moody, p. 130, while G. D. H. Cole records the continuing shock of French socialists at the atheism of their German comrades: Cole, *Socialist Thought: Marxism and Anarchism 1850–1890* (Macmillan, London, 1964), pp. 11, 261–4; *Socialist Thought: The Forerunners 1789–1850* (Macmillan, London, 1967) 179.

16 Evans, *Le Socialisme Romantique*, p. 69.

17 Ibid., pp. 60–9.
18 Karl Marx and Friedrich Engels, 'The Communist Manifesto', in Marx, *The Revolutions of 1848* (Penguin, London, 1981), p. 87.
19 Novak, *Catholic Social Thought and Liberal Institutions*, pp. 69–81.
20 Landauer, *For Socialism*, pp. 16, 123; Weil, *Oppression et Liberté*, p. 211. Those who assume that 'mediaevalism' is just the preserve of the right should attend to the words of Landauer, the assassinated leader of the Bavarian soviet: '[Marx assumes that] when capitalism has gained complete victory over the remains of the Middle Ages, progress is sealed and socialism is practically here' (p. 160); whereas one needs to awaken the 'spirit of just exchange and joyous work' as known in the 'Christian and pre-Christian era of the Teutonic nations' (p. 17) (though at times Landauer compares Germans unfavourably to Latins and Celts, p. 62). Marxists are said to prefer 'a new machine for the transportation of men' to 'the living Jesus on the cross' (p. 64). And finally: 'something like a mediaeval republic of cities or a village *mark* . . . cannot for him [Marx] bear the least similarity with socialism, but a broad, centralized state already resembles his state of the future quite closely' (p. 61). Landauer critically rebuts the idea that capitalist concentration of industry, trade and credit, along with proletarianization of the masses, in any way provide necessary conditions for socialism; on the contrary, the loss of mediaeval 'dispersal' ensures more *adverse* conditions for socialist revolution.
21 See Ken Hirschkop, 'Introduction: Bakhtin and Cultural Theory', in *Bakhtin and Cultural Theory*, ed. Ken Hirschkop and David Shepherd (Manchester University Press, Manchester, 1989), pp. 4–5, 13, 30.
22 See Otto Gierke, *Natural Law and the Theory of Society: 1500–1800*, trans. Ernest Barker (Cambridge University Press, Cambridge, 1958), pp. 50ff.
23 See Howard Caygill, *Art of Judgement* (Blackwell, Oxford, 1989), pp. 38–189. For a shorter summary, 'Post-Modernism and Judgement', *Economy and Society*, 17, 1, pp. 1–21; Steven Shapin and Simon Schaffer, *Leviathan and the Air-Pump* (Princeton University Press, Princeton NJ, 1985), pp. 80–110, 283–345.
24 See F. W. Maitland, 'Introduction', in Otto Gierke, *Political Theories of the Middle Ages*, trans. F. W. Maitland (Cambridge University Press, Cambridge, 1987), pp. xii–xviii. In another essay Maitland vividly describes the nineteenth century's resuscitation of 'gothic space': 'You know that classical distribution of private law under three grand rubrics – persons, things, actions. Half a century ago the first of these three titles seemed to be almost vanishing from civilized jurisprudence. No longer was there much, if anything, to be said of exceptional classes, of nobles, clerics, monks, serfs, slaves, excommunicates or outlaws. Children there must always be, and lunatics, but women had been freed from tutelage. The march of the progressive society was, as we all know, from status to contract. And now? And now that forlorn old title is wont to introduce to us ever new species and new genera of persons to vivacious controversy, to teeming life, and there are many to tell us that the line of advance is no longer from status to contract, but through contract to something contract cannot explain, and for which our best, if an inadequate name, is the personality of the organised group.' Maitland, 'Moral Personality and Legal Personality' in *Selected Essays* (Cambridge University Press, Cambridge, 1936), p. 233. (Note that the shift Maitland refers to, occurred on the whole rather later in England than on the continent.) This exactly captures the demise of a hierarchical and role-determinate gothic, and the return of a horizontal gothic with 'persons' who are again substantively differentiated, and therefore cannot be treated with justice as formally the

same. At the same time they are not arranged hierarchically, are not readily locatable in specific individuals, and possess a more shifting and self-determined identity than their mediaeval equivalents. The 'return of persons' embraces the rising importance of joint-stock companies, trade unions, universities, leisure and educational associations, clubs, non-established religious bodies, and even revived religious communities. It should be noted that one germ of a right-wing corporatism lay in the legal incorporation of capitalist firms on the one hand, often involving semi-official monopoly, and even a quasi-governmental status, and the non-recognition of trade unions and the immunity of its individual members from personal responsibility for acts of the association, on the other.

Another description of the shift from simple to complex chronotope, including the Romanist and Germanist phases, is provided by Paul Vinogradoff, writing in 1892. Before the French Revolution, he says, scholars were 'not sufficiently aware of the differences between epochs; they were too ready with explanations drawn from conscious plans and arrangements. The shock of revolution and reaction taught people to look deeper for the laws of social and political organism . . . speaking broadly, the field of conscious change was narrowed, the field of organic development and unconscious tradition widened. On this basis Savigny's school demonstrated the influence of Roman civilisation in the Middle Ages, started the inquiry as to national characteristics . . . [then] the Germanist school arose to show the extent to which modern constitutional ideas were connected with mediaeval facts'. Paul Vinogradoff, *Villainage in England* (Oxford University Press, Oxford, 1892), 'Introduction', pp. 35–6.

I am grateful to Professor David Sugarman, of the Department of Law, Lancaster University, for discussions and suggestions concerning the corporations debate.

25 Otto Gierke, *Political Theories of the Middle Ages*, pp. 22ff; *Associations and Law: the Classical and Early Christian Stages*, trans. George Heinrich (Toronto University Press, Toronto/Buffalo, 1977), pp. 143–160.

26 See Gierke, *Political Theories of the Middle Age*, pp. 1–100; *Associations and Law*, 67, 151ff, 155–6.

27 See John Ruskin, 'The Nature of Gothic' in *The Stones of Venice, Works X*, ed. E. T. Cook and Alex Wedderburn (George Allen, London, 1904), p. 191, for the injunction to respect 'shattered majesty', and 'not to set the meaner thing in its narrow accomplishment, above the nobler thing in its mighty progress'. Likewise we are to respect deficiencies, irregularities and 'wild and wayward' work (p. 188), since 'the law of human life may be Effort, and that of human judgement, Mercy' (p. 203). This is not, however, to say that Ruskin simply devalues the spatial and static in favour of temporal striving; on the contrary, the point is that one must take the *risk* of embodiment, and only in the very 'failure' of concrete fixation, can striving be apparent. Thus for Ruskin gothic exhibits an oxymoronic 'active rigidity'; its unbending, unyielding, stiff, prickly spikiness, also permits its energetic flow, which depends upon tension (pp. 239ff). (The possibility of psychoanalytic glosses requires no underlining!) In this way Ruskin discovers in gothic space a property resistant to totalization, and a constant 'confession' of its embodiment of human productivity, which is never fully 'realized'; this tends to prevent any alienation or political fetishization of the edifice.

Considering the fashion in which French mediaeval gothic in particular, sought to (almost) dissolve solidity into decoration, and empty space for the reception of light and colour (likewise three dimensions almost into a flat, readable surface, and the surface in turn almost into the flowing line, as celebrated by Ruskin and discussed by Proust), thereby 'denaturing' architecture, and considering also the direct influence of the writings of Pseudo-Dionysius on the first gothic ventures, it is tempting to regard it as 'negative architecture', akin to 'negative theology'. I am grateful to discussions with Alison Milbank on the subject of Ruskin, and gothicism in general.

28 Gierke, *Political Theories*, pp. 22ff; *Associations and Law*, pp. 155–7; Ernst H. Kantorowicz, *The King's Two Bodies: A Study in Mediaeval Political Theology* (Princeton University Press, Princeton, NJ, 1957), pp. 42–87, 273–314.

29 F. W. Maitland, 'Introduction' to Gierke, *Political Theories*, pp. vii–xlv and xxviii: '[Gierke] has incurred the dissent of some of his fellow Germanists for refusing to carry back to the remotest time the distinction between co-ownership and corporate ownership', whereas (p. xxvii) for Gierke it is in the borough of the later Middle Ages that 'the group is first abstracted by thought and law from the plurality'. More especially, see Maitland, 'The Village Community', in *Domesday Book and Beyond* (Fontana, London, 1960), pp. 398–415, for his account of the 'individualism' inherent in the primitive Germanic system of landholding. In the age of Kripke and Lyotard, we ourselves are scarcely able to read with a grave face Maitland's contention here that 'No one who has paid any attention to the history of law is likely to maintain with a grave face that the ownership of land was attributed to fictitious persons before it was attributed to men' (p. 398). And we are likely to recall Marcel Mauss's famous contention (which only reiterates the view of Vico in the eighteenth century) that the *persona* was originally the transferable mask, not the distinguished individual: Marcel Mauss, 'A Category of the Human Mind: the Notion of Person; the Notion of Self', trans. W. D. Halls, in *The Category of the Person*, ed. Michael Carrithers et al. (Cambridge University Press, Cambridge, 1985), pp. 1–26. However, the mask is *not* the legal or philosophic collective personality without definite location in either individual or political ruler or place. Hence the mask must be definitely appropriated by the single individual, and can be acquired through inheritance, or violent seizure. For this ancient mode of individualism, identity itself as mask can be alienated, though property cannot be (through free transaction), as in modern individualism. Yet 'individualism', it still, arguably, is.

30 Gierke, *Political Theories*, pp. 3ff.

31 Ruskin, 'The Nature of Gothic', pp. 243, 262–3.

32 Ibid., p. 212.

33 *Centesimus Annus*, paras 46, 49.

34 For the new geographical interest see Tony Pinkney, 'Space: the Final Frontier', *News from Nowhere*, 8 (autumn 1990), pp. 10–27; Edward Soja, *Postmodern Geographies: the Reassertion of Space in Critical Social Theory* (Routledge, London, 1988). I am grateful to Tony Pinkney, of the Department of English, Lancaster University, for discussions on this topic.

35 See Susan Reynolds, *Country, Kingdom and Community in Western Europe: 900–1500* (Oxford University Press, Oxford, 1984), pp. 1–11. She notes that one finds many groups 'acting on their own initiative and with a relatively small amount of formal regulation and physical coercion' (p. 2), citing, for example, the proliferation of parishes more on the initiative of the laity than the ecclesiastical hierarchy (pp. 5–7), in addition to the proliferation of guilds modelled on monastic organization, celebrating feast days, and assembled for charitable, economic and religious purposes (pp. 75ff). She thereby implies, and indeed explicitly confirms, Gierke's view of the predominantly Christian

context for this practice of voluntary association (p. 7), and qualifies Maitland's judge-ments that local political–juridical institutions (as opposed to economic ones) derived from the royal centre, and that the frequent instance of freedom with respect to small property ownership and ability to choose overlords, necessarily suggests 'individualism'. Rather, this for Reynolds indicates plurality of allegiance and associative bonds, such that 'community' keeps pace with 'freedom'.

Her stress on the prevalence of consultation and consensus appears to be at variance with Alan MacFarlane's version of a return to the 'horizontal' dimensions of the Middle Ages, which stresses individualism as always characteristic of England: Alan MacFarlane, *The Origins of English Individualism* (Cambridge University Press, Cam-bridge, 1979); see also the review by Barbara J. Harris in the *Journal of Social History*, 14, 1 (fall, 1980). However, his reading of Maitland may be one-sided and insular: unlike the Edwardian historian–jurist he generalizes too easily from formal legality and formally free economic conditions, and appears to ignore the crucial Gierke/Maitland contention (which Reynolds' rectifications do not undermine) that the individualist independence of the small property owner in Germanic Villages is 'primitive' (albeit persisting, with long-term consequences in western Europe), whereas the Middle Ages witnesses an *increase* of complex corporate bonds.

In all these arguments, it is obvious that the very idea of a 'free association' permits a certain latitude as to whether one lays the stress on 'collectivism' (i.e. individualism, to be juristically precise), or (Gierkian) 'organicism'. I am grateful for discussions with Professor Jeffrey Richards, of the Department of History, Lancaster University, on Mediaeval communities.

36 Ruskin, 'The Nature of Gothic', p. 237: 'and every discriminating touch of the chisel, as it rounds the petal or gilds the branch, is a prophecy of the development of the entire body of the national society, beginning with that of medicine, of the recovery of litera-ture, and the establishment of the most necessary processes of domestic wisdom and national peace'. Also: 'We don't want either the life or the decorations of the thirteenth century back again . . . all that gorgeousness of the Middle Ages had for foundation or end, nothing but the pride of life – the pride of the so-called superior classes; a pride which supported itself by violence and robbery, and led in the end to the destruction both of the arts themselves and the states in which they flourished', from 'Modern Manufacture and Design', Lecture III of *Two Paths* (1982) in *Works*, vol. XVI. This despite the fact that he is talking about Pisa, and always primarily celebrated secular mediaeval art in the context of the Italian *free city republics*. For heterotopia see Michel Foucault, 'Of other Spaces', *Diacritics*, 16 (spring 1986), and Tony Pinkney, 'The Gothic as Heterotopia', unpublished paper on Ruskin.

37 Milbank, *Theology and Social Theory*, pp. 432–4.

38 See Maitland, 'The Village Community', p. 412: 'throughout the Middle Ages there were here and there groups of freeholders, and even of customary tenants, who were managing agrarian affairs in a manner which feudalism could not explain, and our English law would not warrant, for they were behaving as members of a landowning corporation'. Fragments of Utopia?

39 Caygill, *Art of Judgement*, pp. 38–189.

40 Slavoj Zizek argues that such 'ineffable' identity can only be the upshot of a non-acknowledgement that we worship an empty site X, which merely stands for the inherent

non-attainability of our desire. But that the 'exceeding' dimension of desire is a factor of its nullity, rather than its transcendent guidance, cannot be *shown*. Without the latter assumption one is left with a choice between an atavistic and mystifying right-wing corporatism on the one hand, which suppresses indeterminacy form our view, and the pure instigation of infinitely proliferating individual desires in pursuit of the unattainable void, on the other. Apparently it is on the latter – capitalism – that Zizek pins his hopes for the future of Slovenia and Eastern Europe. Though he knows this is hope in the end of hope . . . and claims that *this* last necessity discloses just why history and philosophy have arrived at their Hegelian terminus. See Zizek, 'Eastern Europe's Republics of Gilead', *New Left Review*, 183 (1990), pp. 50–62. His essay is also relevant to other parts of my paper.

41 See Caygill, *Art of Judgement*, pp. 367–96.
42 See Cornelius Castoriadis, 'Value, Equality, Justice, Politics: from Marx to Aristotle and from Aristotle to Ourselves', in *Crossroads in the Labyrinth*, trans. Kate Soper and Martin H. Ryle (Harvester, Brighton, 1984), pp. 260–330.
43 Jacques Rancière, *Le Philosophe et Ses Pauvres* (Fayard, Paris, 1983).
44 Ruskin, 'Time and Tide by Wear and Tyne', in *Works*, vol. XVII, pp. 379, 384: 'all political economy, as well as all higher virtue, *depends first on sound work*'. On the antique household, see Xenophon, *Oeconomicus*, IV.24–V.18.
45 One must distinguish between the 'Icarian communists', followers of Cabet, and the atheist successors of Gracchus Babeuf, of whom alone Marx really approved. On mainly socio-political grounds, or because they were grounded in an immanentist, natural rights tradition, focused on unproblematic 'needs'? See Droz, *Histoire Générale du Socialisme*, pp. 383–95, Marx and Engels, 'Manifesto', pp. 86–96 (where they also make clear their preference for 'industrial armies' over 'corporate guilds' and fail to explain why the latter are necessarily 'reactionary'); Marx, 'Critique of the Gotha Programme', pp. 353–4.
46 Aristotle, *Politics*, trans. A. T. Sinclair (Penguin, London, 1970) Book One, chapter 8, section 9.
47 J.-F. Lyotard, 'Defining the Postmodern' and 'Complexity and the Sublime', in *Post-modernism: ICA documents*, ed. Lisa Appignanesi, pp. 7–10, 19–26. Here Lyotard correctly links the eighteenth-century sublime in general with the idea of imprescribable judgement which bids for a collective assent containing in consequence a 'promise' of community. This, however, appears inconsistent with the more agonistic emphasis of his major writings, and in *Kantian* terms seems to make more room for 'the beautiful'. (Before Burke and Kant the sublime and the beautiful were not so clearly distinguished: this being the whole – mistaken? – point of Burke's thesis.) In fact by turning the non-representable into 'event', Lyotard seems to 'incarnate' the sublime while preserving its elusiveness, so making it cover again the whole sphere of the aesthetic. In which case there might be an opening for a more consensual (but not Habermasian formalistic) construal of judgement and community than Lyotard seems (mostly) to allow. See also Lyotard, 'What is Postmodernism' in Lyotard, *The Post-modern Condition* (Manchester University Press, Manchester, 1986), pp. 71–82.

The present essay would also question Lyotard's association of 'complexity' with modernity. (Lyotard does not really *approve* of cultural postmodernism in the sense of eclecticism and pastiche.) *His* complex space is only the filling in of simple space with more and more 'indifferent' – it might as well be this way – detail. Only constant indifference (the 'whole' context) and constant variation (the 'individuals') have onto-logical security, whereas for gothic complexity this 'ultimacy' is accorded to intermediate and contingent formations. They do not just 'fill in' a void, they 'represent', in their flux, infinite transcendence.

48 Regarding entitlement to property there have, however, been many oscillations: see Dorr, *Option for the Poor*, p. 48 and *passim*. Also Novak, *Catholic Social Thought*, pp. 69–81, 62–80, on Pesch and von Ketteler's fusions of corporatism with Smithian economic liberalism. It was their tradition which had the greatest influence on papal teaching up to *Quadragesimo Anno*.

49 *Centesimus Annus*, para. 48.

50 See Maitland, 'Introduction' to Gierke, *Political Theories*, pp. xxxiv–xxxv.

51 Ibid., pp. xiv, xix.

52 *Centesimus Annus*, para. 44.

Index of Names

Aarsleff, Hans, 80, 114, 155
Abraham, 210, 228
Ackroyd, Peter, 231
Alexander, Edgar, 285–6
Alexander of Hales, 172
Alexandre, Monique, 212
Alliez, Eric, 208, 215
Anselm, 163–4, 168, 172–3, 174, 182, 188
Apel, Karl-Otto, 17, 92, 114, 120
Aquinas, Thomas, 7, 8, 9, 11, 13–16, 28, 29, 32, 33, 41, 43–4, 45, 46, 47, 51, 52, 74, 80, 92, 93, 96, 110, 120, 124, 156, 157, 158, 167, 172–3, 174, 176, 177, 190, 191, 226, 232, 246
Aristotle, 20, 21, 22, 25, 28, 40, 41, 46, 89, 90, 91, 97, 98, 99, 103, 105, 109, 114, 123–4, 127, 129, 142, 143, 201–2, 203, 206, 226, 238, 243, 246, 252, 281, 282, 291
Athanasius, 174, 187, 191
Augustine, 2, 22, 42, 44, 45–6, 48, 88–91, 94, 95, 101, 107, 108, 109, 110, 113, 114, 155, 166, 172–3, 174, 176, 180, 182, 185, 187–8, 193, 194, 204, 207, 222, 230, 232, 236–7, 249, 252, 254
Ayres, Lewis, 204

Babeuf, Gracchus, 291
Bakhtin, Mikhail, 275
Ballanche, Pierre-Simon, 119

Balthasar, Hans Urs von, 3, 15, 45, 49, 52, 123, 132–4, 136, 141, 142, 143, 163, 175, 210, 212
Barnes, Michel, 199ff., 211
Barth, Karl, 28–9, 36–7, 123, 132, 163, 167, 183
Basil of Caesarea, 87, 91, 97–8, 102, 115, 187, 192, 193, 196
Baudelaire, Charles, 220, 231
Baudrillard, Jean, 27, 35
Bayer, Oswald, 83
Belo, Fernando, 165–6
Benjamin, Walter, 31, 34, 35, 105–6, 118, 143
Benoist, Jocelyn, 50
Berkeley, George, 2, 3, 84, 85, 97–105, 106, 107, 109, 115, 116, 117, 179–90, 192
Betti, Emilio, 125, 142
Birch, Charles, 266
Blackburn, Robin, 286
Blake, William, 219, 226
Blond, Phillip, 38, 50, 57
Blondel, Maurice, 2
Blumenberg, Hans, 266
Boehme, Jacob, 92, 94
Boethius, 41, 110
Boileau, Nicolas, 31, 81
Bonald, Louis de, 283
Bonaventure, 46, 52, 174, 175, 177, 191